VOLUME I

A Biblical History from the Creation of the Universe to the Time of Christ Jesus

HIS STORY
AS A MATTER OF FACT

JEFFREY L. WALLING

iUniverse®

HIS STORY
AS A MATTER OF FACT

Scripture quotations marked KJV are from the Holy Bible, King James Version (Authorized Version). First published in 1611. Quoted from the Holy Bible, King James Version, Copyright c 1913. John A. Dickson Publishing Co.

iUniverse books may be ordered through booksellers or by contacting:

iUniverse
1663 Liberty Drive
Bloomington, IN 47403
www.iuniverse.com
1-800-Authors (1-800-288-4677)

ISBN: 978-1-5320-3618-7 (sc)
ISBN: 978-1-5320-3617-0 (e)

Print information available on the last page.

iUniverse rev. date: 11/27/2017

CONTENTS

CONTENTS

PREFACE

Over the years I have observed children growing up in the church and have seen them full of joy and confidence derived from their faith in God, along with enthusiastic zeal that was instilled in them by their parents. I would watch with utter delight when they would participate in drama skits, testify at home meetings, read scriptures, and so on. I watched as these young men and women entered high school coming out on the other side all depressed, down trodden, and saying they no longer believed the Bible because of the teachings of science and history (evolution) that are contrary to the basic historical chronologies of the Word of God and the overt implications that the Bible is a book of myths.

I often hear clichés cited by Christian authorities (parents, pastors, and teachers) that conflicts between the Christian faith and science are unimportant, and that we should just be content to encourage our children and students to build their relationship with Christ and that will build their faith and trust in the truths of Bible. I am all for encouraging our children and students to build their relationship with Christ; however, young men and women today are more prone to be influenced by their peers who all stand unified in these matters. I am also keenly aware of the shortcoming of that philosophy… and that is the loss of our children due to *the teachings of science and history (evolution) that are contrary to the basic historical chronologies of the Word of God and the overt implications that the Bible is a book of myths.* I personally want to do all I can to combat these losses and the deceptions of these humanistic teachings.

The scripture says in Hosea 4:6: **My people are destroyed for lack of knowledge**: because thou hast rejected knowledge, I will also reject thee, that thou shalt be no priest to me: **seeing thou hast forgotten the law of thy God, I will also forget thy children**.

This is good example of this scripture. I did some research to find any Christian publication that would address all the historical and scientific evidence that supports the biblical model of the universe. I found many good books that addressed particular areas of interest but nothing that covered the gambit from A to Z that could be used as a textbook for Christian educators.

Unfortunately, there is no avenue or medium for our children to receive this information. Our churches are not teaching this in their Sunday schools. Christian schools and home schoolers are not getting this on chalkboards. Parents don't have the resources or tools to prepare and protect their teenagers heading into secular high schools and colleges from the onslaught of anti-Christ teachings.

The conflict is not between science and the bible but rather between humanistic (atheistic) theology and Christianity. The secular schools, based on humanistic theology, are teaching our children that the Bible is just a fairytale and convincing them that science and history has well established that as a fact. They will take a bit of empirical scientific evidence that actually fits the biblical model "as is" and develop an extraordinary theory to make it fit in their evolutionary model, stick it in the middle of several segments of facts so that it blends in, and not tell the student it is just theory, so that it comes across as fact. The student grows up not knowing the difference, becomes a teacher, and teaches it as fact as well. After several generations, it becomes an ingrained fact. I mentioned to someone the other day how the dynamo engine powering the earth's magnetosphere was just a theory with no supporting evidence, and he asked me if I also believed the world was flat. That is how far removed from reality society has become.

> God's word says in 2 Cor. 6:14: Be you not unequally yoked together with unbelievers: for what fellowship has righteousness with unrighteousness? and what partnership has light with darkness? And in Eph. 5:11: Have no fellowship with the fruitless deeds of darkness, but rather expose them. And then in 1 John 1:6 If we say we have fellowship with Him yet walk in the darkness, we lie and do not practice the truth. And finally, in Col. 2:8: Beware lest any man spoil you through philosophy and vain deceit, after the tradition of men, after the rudiments of the world, and not after Christ.

I look at this publication as my "95 theses" that I am nailing to the secular humanists' church doors. I have had enough of the make-believe world that they have created and the pseudoscience that dominates the halls of education these days.

My hope in publishing this book is to start a fire that will burn down the established scholastic protocols, get back to true science and research, and open the doors to be able to go where the science is leading. I want to see the churches that sponsor schools and home schooler's institute this as a textbook (Vol I & II) that is required reading for all high school students. I want Christian parents to read this and be able to obtain knowledge to relay to their kids as they grow up and to put it into their hands to read (and study) as they enter their high school years. I would like to see this being taught in Christian colleges, Sunday schools, special classes, and as a topic at home meetings in churches around the world.

As an added benefit, students going into high school reading this book that have not decided what field of study they are interested in will get an opportunity to be exposed to several areas of interest. The investigation into the various fields of study that are captured in this writing go to a significant depth and will give the reader a real taste for each of those areas of interest, which may strike a chord with them. For instance, take a field of study such as **geology**. The investigation into geology addresses the formation of diverse types of rocks, the strata formations, the makeup and formation of fossiliferous rocks, including the means of transportation, mass, and matrix of the diverse strata. Other areas of interest include **literary analysis** of epic stories such as *The Epic of Gilgamesh, Beowulf, The Iliad*, and *The Odyssey*, and reviews of *The Origin of the Species*. This book in and of itself is an example of investigative journalism. **Genomics**, including various studies in regard to the DNA makeup and its relation to evolution, **anthropology, archeology, paleontology, zoology, meteorology, genealogy, astronomy, earth sciences, evolution and biblical studies** are all interrogated to a significant depth.

INTRODUCTION

There are many secular history books that one can read to get a general knowledge of past events (e.g., "*A Short History of the World*" by Alex Woolf). However, the authors assume that the world is billions of years old and that humans and cultures are the result of uniformitarian processes which comes from the humanistic (atheistic) theology that dominates the secular world. Since biblical and church history is the telling of His Story, that is God's interrelating within his creation, it is necessary to address the various sciences and secular histories in this publication. Biblical history is about God's pervading sovereign presence in all, about all, and through all time, space and matter. Relaying His Story (History) must be based in truth, fact, and reasonable deductive conclusions based on collaborating evidence, which is often ignored or generalized in secular history books. There is nothing in science or history that contradicts the veracity of the Bible. On the contrary, there is overwhelming collaboration of the word of God if taken as presented in the bare essence of the facts (empirical data) and evidence without the spin of secular humanism. This publication is written to supplement other history books that only maintain humanistic doctrinal themes that ignore much of the collaborating historical resources simply because of the author's humanistic religious beliefs.

Much of the scientific facts in this study come from institutes such as the Institute of Creation Research (ICR), Discovery Institute, Answers in Genesis, and creationist/intelligent design (ID) authors (Morris, Barnes, Humphreys, Meyer, etc.), and believe it or not many secular science labs and resources. Much of the rebuttal and criticism of these Christian authors and institutes are born out of less than objective reasoning. I feel it is necessary to address the matter of the authors' integrity and the derogatory comments from their critics. These humanistic responses to Christian scientists and authors are intended to be used to "spin the facts" and as intimidation fronts and many times leave readers with doubts and fears of the sincerity and intent of the authors. This can at the very least cause many to doubt and avoid these areas of interest allowing those of the humanistic persuasion room to advance their make believe (pseudo) sciences born out of their intolerant secular humanistic theology (disallowing the possibility of any spiritual source to the cause and effect of natural processes) in an effort to discredit the Bible and Christian theology.

The biggest targets of secular humanists are the creationist and Intelligent design institutes and authors on the leading edge of science and discovery such as the Creation Science Institute (CSI), John Morris, Dr. Russell Humphreys, Dr. Thomas Barnes, Dr. Stephen Meyers, David Rhol, and David Berlinsky. Most of these authors are Christians and thus believe that they must answer to God for their lives and every word that proceeds from their mouth (and pen) as the word says in James 3:1, "My brethren, be not many masters, knowing that we shall receive the greater condemnation" and Ephesians 5:6, "Let no man deceive you with vain words: for because of these things cometh the wrath of God upon the children of disobedience." [1]. Secular critics, lacking wisdom and fear of God, have no such belief system and therefore believe they have no higher authority to judge their actions or words. They are quick to defame and spew out derogatory comments in their ignorance. These attacks on the character of their targets are not aligned with the reality or of intimate knowledge of the persons they are criticizing. These off–the–cuff attacks serve to add an element of distrust to the source of the information they are refuting. Truth and facts are not relevant to them but rather obstacles to step over or on as a means to an end if it serves their purposes. At the worst, these men of God and institutes may be mistaken, and at best they are precisely accurate. In either case, I would judge them as sincere and earnest in their general character, their research, publications, and results. There is no deliberate attempt to deceive, lie to, or beguile their audience nor is there any underlying political motivation but rather the defense and witness of the truth of God's Word. They, like myself, want to give God the glory due his name and want the truth to have its day! If you read the bibliography of any of these Christian authors, you will quickly become familiar with their respect and fear of God, the Holy Spirit bearing witness if he lives in you. If you ever listen to any of their audio or video, you will be deeply impressed with their humility and gentle spirit. When you read the critics countering the facts and truths of the writings of these men of God, keep in mind that they are not bound to the truth as the men they are criticizing are. They have an agenda (a make-believe world) they support that allows them to disregard facts and truth as opposed to the men they are criticizing that have a faith that binds them to the truth.

The goal of secular humanists is to free humanity from the "religious bonds" that they feel are the cause of the evils in the world (e.g., The Greek and Roman pantheon of gods, the Catholic Church in the Dark Ages, the wars caused by the Islamic faith since the conception down through history to the present). It is in their theology that anything in science or politics that ties society to any form of "religion" is to be quenched, severed, and denied at all cost; included in this cost is truth, facts, and freedom of thought. Richard Dawkins's "The God Delusion", Sam Harris's essay "Science Must Destroy Religion", and what Wall Street Journal calls "Militant Atheism" all emphasize this mandate. Humanism predicates its theology on an assumption that there is no God or spiritual realm of influence in our physical world, only the material world which can be discerned through science alone. This is a blind assumption. As no one can prove whether there is a spiritual world or not, the humanists proceed based on blind faith. Being that humanism is based on faith in a belief system and not empirical scientific data, it too is a religious belief. The aim of secular humanism is to have a society that is governed by the elite (via the socialist state) that does not have to answer to God or the Bible as an authority [2, 3]. Comments made by scientist Neil deGrasse Tyson reflect this sentiment. A tweet by rapper B.o.B. in regard to the world being flat incited the famed scientist to come out with his thoughts on the matter. First, he countered the idea of the world being flat with true scientific facts and then proceeded to establish some boundaries to what he thought B.o.B. should and should not be allowed to say if it were to influence others (which, in its essence, means everything anyone says because everyone in the world influences someone, be it his children, coworkers, students, etc.). Tyson goes on to say, "This whole thing is a symptom of larger problem. There is a growing anti-intellectual strain in this country that may be the beginning of the end of our informed democracy". He goes on to imply that being wrong equates to being harmful and threatens the security of our citizenry. Bill Nye the science guy, another elitist of the humanist persuasion, says anyone that disagrees with him on climate change should be imprisoned (and I'm sure that extends to anyone who opposes his opinions on evolution as well) [4]. In science, where you have many times competing theories, who sets the boundaries for what is right or wrong from Tyson's and Nye's perspective? They would lay with the arbitrary decisions of the ruling elite (predominantly humanist in today's society). Even though B.o.B.'s theory about the world being flat is nonsense, he should have the right to think so (freedom of thought) and say whatever he wants (freedom of speech) in a free society without anyone setting boundaries or bringing criminal charges on him based on their opposing personal beliefs. Tyson and Nye, believing that they are in the mix of the ruling elite, feel they have the right to dictate these matters (because they believe all other theories other than their collective own are not science...which I'm sure includes creationism as they have expressed their opinion in public on these theories as well)[5]. When the elite have the power to establish and execute these sentiments, they will. History is replete with examples of dictatorial regimes, the Romans and their emperors persecuting the Christians, the Catholic inquisitions, the leaders once in power during the bloody revolution in France, not to mention the more recent: Hitler, Mao Tse-tung, Joseph Stalin, Fidel Castro, and many others. It is in the nature of man to exert his will in any sphere he dominates, right or wrong, where the punishment does not necessarily fit the crime but rather serves to strike fear in the subjects of the realm.

Einstein was subject to the same spirit, the same scientific culture that is still in place today. The scientific community of Einstein's day was not nearly as hostile as today's, and yet his theories were initially rejected by the majority based on ignorance, religious intolerance, and elitist attitudes. This is common knowledge, Wikipedia sums it up pretty accurately:

> **Criticism of the theory of relativity** of Albert Einstein was mainly expressed in the early years after its publication in the early twentieth century, on scientific, pseudoscientific, philosophical, or ideological bases. Though some of these criticisms had the support of reputable scientists, Einstein's theory of relativity is now accepted by the scientific community.
>
> Reasons for criticism of the theory of relativity have included alternative theories, rejection of the abstract-mathematical method, and alleged errors of the theory. According to some authors, antisemitic objections to Einstein's Jewish heritage also occasionally played a role in these objections. There are still some critics of relativity today, but their opinions are not shared by the majority in the scientific community.

This is the same spirit that governed in the Dark Ages under the Catholic Church. Truth, facts, and freedom of thought were suppressed to give way to the supreme ruling elite. They were not men of conversion or integrity, and therefore did not fear God, or adhere to the precepts of the Bible, but rather made up their own doctrines - wolves in sheep's clothing. Just as the word of God was inaccessible in Latin through the Dark Ages and only allowed to be read by the priest to keep the people ignorant (hence the term the Dark Ages) and trusting in them for the truth and knowledge, so today the Secular Humanist keeps their "truths and knowledge" hidden in highly technical scientific journals and publications to keep the people ignorant and trusting in the vanguard of the faith to relay truth and knowledge [6]. Human nature has not changed, the elite of today are cloaked as PhDs, scientists, lawyers, doctors, and media personalities aligning with socialist politicians who espouse utopian promises through secular humanist philosophies. The masses trusting the elite (after all, the scientist doesn't have the same human bias as other human beings, they just deal in facts, right?), go along believing that the majority consensus is proof enough they are in the right. Being that many of the citizens of the western cultures today are easily duped because they are ether illiterate, spending their time playing video games or watching TV (movies, reality shows, game shows, etc.) instead of reading books or indoctrinated wholly into the humanistic teachings. We are essentially back in the Dark Ages without the clerical drab, as man will always find a way to digress. Truth, facts, and freedom of thought are being suppressed to give way to humanistic doctrine.

One thing that the secular humanist fails to realize is that it is not the institutes of religion that are constraining and oppressing society/peoples but rather the nature of man to seize opportunities (by maneuvering, conniving, and plotting) that will advance him to the seat of ultimate power whether it be religious institutions, political offices, social comradery of the rich and elite, or big business moguls. In the beginning, the pagan priest had power and influence with the royalty and so vied for position and advancement to benefit from that relationship. When the church was given that status over the pagan religions in the fourth century AD with the Roman Emperors, those pagan priests, seeing that it was the only way to keep that status, converted to "Christianity" and proceeded to vie for advanced positions within the Church without really being converted, only motivated by greed and power. It was these unregenerate men governing the Catholic Church in the Dark Ages that sought to constrain the people by force and fear and so, ignoring the truths of the Bible, created a religion based on the doctrines of men (Eucharist, purgatory, penance, rosaries, indulgences, etc.) and to keep them uneducated, ignorant, and illiterate in order to secure their means of gain, power and control (just as pagan religions, political powers, and the rich/elites did in past generations and the humanist in this generation). So, in most cases the fears and references to superstitions or ante-scientific dogma in religious practice that the secular humanists point to, to justify their Antichrist attitude (lumping all religions into one massive entity whose sole purpose is to control society), are really not from the doctrines of the Bible or true Christianity. Some trivial cases may be from lack of knowledge that science is bringing to light, clarifying misinterpreted or misunderstood scriptures just like it has for misinterpreted or misunderstood scientific theories (e.g., Newton's theory of gravity as it applies to space and time, Einstein's theory of relativity as it applies to the cosmological constant, and Darwin's theory as it applies to macroevolution). Christ came to set us free from sin and death and in the plan of God to bless us and prosper us as we follow him. Now, there is the fact that the natural man is naturally at odds with the spiritual man and therefore anything Christ like is going to leave a bad taste in the mouth of the unbeliever; however, everything God wants of us is for our wellbeing. It was the true Church, the spirit of Christ in men, which delivered society from the Dark Ages through the Protestant movement and successive moves of God's spirit in time. It was the true church that brought about the American Revolution and the separation of the Church and State to ensure that the Dark Ages would not be repeated. It was the true church that influenced the Constitution which allowed the sciences to flourish and brought about the Industrial Revolution. Most renowned scientist of the past and political figures during this time had Christian beliefs. To lump true Christianity with other religious bodies is not duly justified. Christ allows the tares to grow alongside the wheat and the tares dominate much of the time (Mat13:24-30), the humanist looks and all he sees are the tares. Only when one is truly born again of the spirit of God can he see the difference.

Secular humanism, which is a religious faith, has influenced the tenets of science by interjecting its theology into the dictates of science. Secular humanists believe that there is only the material realm. They reject any possibility of the existence of a coinciding spiritual world or a creator over creation and demand strict adherence to a materialistic approach to all facets of life (science, politics, morality, etc.). As such, they adhere to a negative argument as they cannot prove any of their suppositions and therefore have to "believe by faith" that there is no God or spiritual world. To this end they have established a scientific tenet (a principle referred to as "methodological naturalism" or "methodological materialism") that no scientific argument is permitted to invoke "intelligent design" as the cause of any effect in nature or the physical realm. This tenet has no place in science! Just like we were subject to the religious authorities (the Catholic Church) in the medieval Dark Ages, we are now subject to the religious authorities (secular humanists) in this new, modern day Dark Age. If such a scientific tenet were true, then true scientific interrogation should ultimately prove it so, and therefore it is not required to be set as a boundary marker. If such a scientific tenet were true, then all scientific research would return a physical explanation for all inquiry and hence debunk the fallacy of such rationale. As it stands in today's scientific environment, this tenet demands that scientific interrogation be compromised in order to adhere to its humanistic religious faith, regardless of where the scientific research leads to, overruling true scientific inquiry and accepting the hall mark of hollow (pseudo) science to conform to today's humanist beliefs. It is time to put a stop to operating within this faith-based pseudoscience! It's time to stop letting the religion of humanism dictate the boundaries of science and let the science in its own right take us to the ultimate conclusions [3, 7].

The humanist religion comprises the majority of the people in most western cultures around the world today. Hence, they are the ruling majority who alone establishes the rules and guidelines in areas such as government, scholastics, science, and moral issues. They have built a wall about their world within which their parishioners are allowed to operate or move about but are warned to stay away from certain boundary markers. These boundary markers, which they are not allowed beyond, comes from their religion, which disallows the belief in a spiritual realm or sovereign creator. This belief is translated to the principles of science where they are not allowed to invoke intelligent design or any cause from a spiritual source regardless of how many overt clues and indicators point in that direction. Violators of these rules, those who try to move beyond the boundary, are openly ridiculed and even suffer retribution where the vanguard feels the violation warrants it, just as in the Dark Ages. We shall see that the conscious avoidance of these boundaries is the reason for all the unrelenting new theories, when in time, discovery and experimentation have resulted in failure of the preceding theories. Mainstream scientists are not allowed to go where the science is taking them, so they are forced to continually make up theories. There is an exhaustive accumulation of proposed theories regarding all aspects of evolution, the missing transitional fossil strata, and the genome evolution, to the point that it is outright irrational and embarrassing. At what point do grown intelligent men and women become rational and say enough is enough? At what point do these advocates seriously look at the preponderance of the evidence and yield to the collaborating direction it is pointing in?

After some study and observation, this author believes that the advocates of Darwinism fall within three categories, (1) true believers, (2) those who suspect otherwise but are weak and afraid of the retribution, and (3) the majority not educated in technology or science and unaware of how to properly check facts. They are the ignorant sheep following the shepherd, believing their scientific norms are up to par with the truth and the facts. (Sound familiar? Think the Dark Ages.)

The true believers are predominantly educated specialists who grew up in this pseudoscientific environment and truly believe that theirs and their peer's hollow theories (theories without the consensus of empirical evidence or collaborating lab results) are acceptable scientific norms, are acceptable competing theories on some superior scientific level, even when in almost every case the consensus of empirical evidence or collaborating lab results are contrary to their theories. I believe that is because they live in a make-believe world within a tight-knit group where they collaborate with other secular humanistic scientists who operate on the same principles and accept one another's theories and scholarly publications (even competing theories in debate) that to them seems to be within "true science". When confronted with a competing theory that invokes intelligent design, they are confident that their pseudoscientific responses are adequate as that is their experience amongst their peers and the general public. They are rather blind to the fact that their theories are hollow and in most cases even ignorant. Secular humanists ignore the consensus of empirical evidence, mainstream physics, and collaborating lab results that are contrary to their theories.

Those who suspect otherwise but are weak and afraid of the retribution are predominantly a mix of specialists and the well-educated. They would not initiate a conversation about these subject matters and are normally quiet in the public domain not wanting to be exposed and suffer the consequences (ridicule, loss of status, loss of respect, and in some cases loss of jobs). When engaged in these subject matters, they will respond appropriately with the facade that they are hard-core believers.

The majority of society's secular community naturally falls in line with humanist teachings, which are found in all areas of today's culture. This community includes the well-educated and those not so well educated, such as the general public and the illiterate. They are not specialists in these areas, so they trust in the secular humanist specialist, the vanguard or shepherds, to be their defenders. Any half-truth or inaccurate article issued in the press or philosophy teaching in academia questioning the authenticity of the Bible is taken at face value. These anti-religious factions can say just about anything they want to because they know for the most part it will not be questioned. Any creation or intelligent design based publication, book, or article that comes out in public debate will be quickly addressed and suppressed by the shepherds of the faith, referencing these pseudoscientific backed publications that will be bought by the general public. Most will not follow the volley of rebuttals, feeling euphoric that the responses were adequate, technical, based on true empirical data, and well within scientific fundamentals.

Here are some classical examples of this type of conveying:

An article put out by the UK based *Telegraph Science* in July 2017 by Chris Gram initially read "Study Disproves Bible's Claim Ancient Canaanites Wiped". The narrative of the original article reports that DNA studies reveal that the Lebanese are direct descendants of the Canaanites that the Bible claims were wiped out by Israel during the conquest of Palestine (Deuteronomy 20:17), thus disproving the Bible. Any secular humanist reading this article will huff and think "ha…another nail in the coffin" and go off feeling euphoric that his trust in the secular anti-religious dogma is securely positioned. This is an inaccurate statement from the start, as the Bible really says that God commanded the Israelites to wipe them out completely but goes on to say that the Israelites failed to carry out that command (Judges 1:21-36, 2:20-23) and that God then used them to test Israel's faithfulness. After a slew of retorts about the article's inaccuracies were received, the authors went back and edited it to just faintly admit that the DNA study actually confirms the Bible; however, anyone who read the article in the original text will not likely re-read something he already read, leaving the correction little corrective momentum in the minds of the public. Additionally, this article continues to run in several other news journals without any corrections or retractions (or at the most, vague corrections) such as the UK based *Independent & Daily Mill*, *Strange Sounds*, *Science Magazine*, and many others.

Professors teaching philosophy classes in academia are very much guilty of teaching half-truths or inaccurate lessons. A classic example of this can be found in Josh McDowell's book *"Is the Bible True...Really?"* (which I highly recommend be read by every believer). In his book, many of the classical lessons being taught in higher education academia challenge the authenticity of the Bible, which initially seemed rock solid in debunking the historical accuracy and message of the Bible. The following ambiguous teachings are typical of what to expect from your professor if he is a humanist:

1) The text we have today is not in the slightest form of what it was originally; there are so many translational errors, that the message is unrecognizably distorted from the original. They like to retort that we do not have any of the original letters written by the biblical authors; therefore, it cannot be claimed that it is the inerrant word of God.

2) Expounding on the video "Zeitgeist, The Greatest Story Ever Sold", they teach that the virgin birth, the crucifixion, the resurrection, and other key events in the Bible were all plagiarized from pagan mythology of the gods more ancient than the New Testament such as Attis of Greece, Mithra of Persia, Krishna of India, Dionysus of Greece, Appoloius, Sabbati, and others.

The first teaching is ambiguous because it does not specify what we know today in regard to the "translational errors". First, the majority of errors (99%) are either misspellings (e.g., Jonn instead John, which accounts for 75% of the so-called translation errors) or alternative adjectives or pronouns (e.g., using He or Lord instead of the proper name of Jesus), which does not distort the meaning of the verse. That leaves <1% of the errors that may affect the meaning of the verse. This clearly does not affect the message of the Bible. In most cases, with the more than 5,600 historical copies of the New Testament in Greek (and if you include the Latin and other texts, that number is about 24,000), these errors have been cross referenced, identified, and a consensus has given understanding to the purer translation of those verses. In any case, you don't discount the 99% of meaningful verses for the 1% questionable text unless you're a humanist with an agenda. The main events of Jesus's life and purpose are clearly understandable and with the discovery of the Dead Sea Scrolls being congruent with our modern-day translations of the Old Testament, bridging a gap of greater than 1,000 years, there leaves little doubt about the supposed magnitude of distorted text. In regard to not having any of the original letters written by the biblical authors, neither do we have the originals for any other ancient text, such as those authored by Homer, Herodotus, or Aristotle. What we do have are myriads of copies (5,600 Greek copies alone) closer in time to the original than any other historical document. Take for example, the Bodmer Papyri (200 AD), the Beatty Papyri (155 AD), and John Ryland's "St. John's fragment" manuscript dating to 130 AD. The St. John's fragment contains parts of seven lines from the Gospel of John 18:31–33 in Greek on the front and seven lines from verses 37–38 on the back that reads thusly:

John 18:31–33: 31 Then said Pilate unto them, Take ye him, and judge him according to your law. The Jews therefore said unto him, It is not lawful for us to put any man to death: 32 That the saying of

Jesus might be fulfilled, which he spake, signifying what death he should die. 33 Then Pilate entered into the judgment hall again, and called Jesus, and said unto him, Art thou the King of the Jews?

John 18:37–38: 37 Pilate therefore said unto him, Art thou a king then? Jesus answered, Thou sayest that I am a king. To this end was I born, and for this cause came I into the world, that I should bear witness unto the truth. Every one that is of the truth heareth my voice. 38 Pilate saith unto him, What is truth? And when he had said this, he went out again unto the Jews, and saith unto them, I find in him no fault at all.

An Egyptian mummy mask dating from before 90AD made up of scrap paper was found to have a fragment of the Gospel of Mark. These have evidence of the original writings being written before 80AD due to the multiple copies and internal evidence such as the people, places, and events of the New Testament claims, which are historically verifiable and accurate by extraneous sources such as Josephus' *Antiquities of the Jews*, written around 93–94 AD and Tacitus' *Annals* (written *ca.* AD 116), book 15, chapter 44. Compare that to many of the classics such as the history of Thucydides (400BC) of which we have eight manuscripts dating to about 900AD, 1,300 years from the original writings; Aristotle's 49 copies of his *Poetics* (343BC), with the earliest copies dating to 1100AD; and Caesar's ten copies of *Gallic Wars*, written between 58 and 50 BC dating to about 1,000 years after his death. Yet no one challenges their historicity or accuracy on the scale that they attack the Bible.

The second teaching is an outright fabrication. Historically, it is known (but not taught) that the pagan mythology of the gods that include the virgin birth, the crucifixion, the resurrection, and other key elements can only be traced backed to the second and third century AD. The stories of Attis, Mithra, Krishna, Dionysus, Appoloius, Sabbati, and others found in ancient literature written before the writings of the New Testament do not mention any of these events in their story lines; hence, it was the pagan mythology that plagiarized from the New Testament. A quote by Dr. J. Smith of the *Encyclopedia of Religion* from McDowell's book concludes thusly, "The category of dying and rising gods, once a major topic of scholarly investigation, must now be understood to have been largely a misnomer based on imaginative reconstructions and exceedingly late or highly ambiguous texts".

Groupthink[8]

One of the contributing factors with the secular humanist group has to do with the Groupthink mentality, a subject of study when in college that tries to make you aware of some negative traits that can develop within a group that can lead to error in judgment. Being aware of the signs can help group members to come out of that rut if you will.

Many times groups are asked to make one thing, say a fully operational motor vehicle, but end up making something other than the project target, like a scale size plastic model car instead. As this happens many times with teaming efforts there must be some underlying "decision-making processes" behind what is referred to as the "groupthink" phenomena. Groupthink mentality will proceed on an ill-fated course of action despite the evidence that would lead them elsewhere.

There are four main mind-sets that characterize the Groupthink mentality.

1) They make decisions that favor group acceptance over the supposed goals of the group.

2) They reject opposing opinions or evidence that come from without the group screening out "awkward facts or ideas" (minimizing or ignoring empirical evidence and lab test results) and are baffled when the results of their decision come back negative, but not deterred.

3) They take more risks in their decision making as a group than they would as an individual, referred to as the "risky shift" (e.g., postulating theories defying known scientific principles such as entropy as in the case of evolution, geological formations, and the earth core dynamo theory, etc.).

4) They have an unsettling propensity to view group outsiders as "the enemy". This is demonstrated in treating the enemy with disrespect, prejudice, and retribution. (Note that most all the critics of the creationists attribute ill intent and deception as their motivation, in many circumstances people have lost jobs and position due to their part in a publication referencing "intelligent design").

Signs of Groupthink mentality within a group.

1) The group is tight-knit and collaborative. The group tends to be more agreeable and frowns on conflicting opinions of the individuals. They tend not to dig too deep into the conclusion or decisions of the group.

1) They tend to view themselves as the elite because of their position (e.g., specialized knowledge, authority in the community, accreditations, etc.).

2) These groups tend to be isolated from outside opinions or facts that would otherwise "correct false assumptions and misconceptions".

3) One of the major indicators is that individuals caught in the grasp of the Groupthink mentality experience a great feeling of euphoria, hope, and optimism that comes from being comfortably in the center of the majority opinion and confidence in their leader's competence.

The creationist, as opposed to the evolutionist caught in the groupthink mentality, proposes teaching both the creation model and the evolutionary model with their subsequent theories and then looking at the facts and real-time science to compare which one has the better fit. Most all the creationist science books and papers do that. As it stands right now, the only theory permitted in the classrooms or mainstream documentaries is the evolutionary theory. Truth, facts, and freedom of thought is not the goal with secular culture today; force fitting evidence into their presuppositions is the goal at the expense of truth, facts, and freedom of thought [9, 10].

The greatest advantage of being of the intelligent design (ID) or creationist (Christian) persuasion is that they are free to investigate the sciences and histories from both the secular perspective and the creationist perspective. The Humanist parishioners, on the other hand, are taught that the creationist science is riddled with nonscientific jargon and therefore a waste of time, and that they should ignore their publications and arguments. My experience is that most humanists will accept at face value what their shepherds tell them and will not make the effort to fact check or read any refuting argument, creationist literature, or publications with an open mind or critical attitude. As a rule, creationist's papers/publications are written by well-educated individuals with all the accolades and awards as any other scientist. This makes it easy for the Humanist vanguard to pull the wool over their eyes, as they say. People who do not do their homework, check the facts, and critically consider all the data on any subject are easily duped. The Creationist, on the other hand, has access to the experts in these fields of interest who can point out the errors and omission in their supposed scientific publications. The most common error or omission found in most all secular scientific publications in the arena of historical sciences is the pivotal Vera causa of their theories (the critical magic moment is missing, much of the time ignoring known opposing physics or empirical evidence). This is where the creationist peer review reveals the fault in their theories that the Humanist non-expert would not pick up on because they are dependent on their leaders to understand the technical aspects and trust in them to tell them the truth.

Multiple collaboration of evidence per theme (cave drawings, king lists, ancient ruins) forming a consensus.

Scientific and historical evidence ignored and shunned by secular scientists and scholars is abundant and obvious and needs to be critically reviewed and accepted based on the fact that it is from independent sources and collaborative with virtually no opposing evidence to counter the conclusions or suggest some opposing chronological events.

There are innumerable historical documents from every nation around the world that include genealogies, kings lists, ancient manuscripts, and epic stories featuring the likes of Gilgamesh, Beowulf, Marco Polo, and St. George, which are discarded as myths or mysteries leaving a major void in the historical accounts as nearly all the these accounts parallel each other's and the biblical accounts including the Creation, the Great Flood, Noah and his descendants, the Exodus, and dinosaurs in recent history living contemporary with man and so on[11, 12, 13].

Consider this, all of the nations accepted these histories as based in truth up until the humanist theology and the propagation of the theory of evolution began to dominate the public forums in the nineteenth century, attested by the many references in all disciplines of literature of the times (the scientific journals, drama plays of old, writings of royal scribes, etc.). The fact is that these accounts collaborate the biblical account and the accounts of each other. Nations from all quarters of the globe have the same heritage in their ancient writings tying every one of them to the Antediluvian era, Noah and his sons, and the Great Flood. Whenever you have two or more witnesses to an event from independent sources it is a reasonable legal practice to accept those testimonies as true. Any subject matter collaborated by three or more independent testimonies or supporting evidence can be accepted as a well-established truth. How could all the nations of the world have these testimonies and heritage and not be accepted on an "as is" basis? How could they have these stories to the fine details unless they originated and were recorded at the time and down through time from the same source events [13]?

In this publication, we will see that all the quantifiable processes in the universe show elements of a physics property known as entropy, meaning all things measurable are decaying, going from high energy to low energy, from complex to simple, from order to disorder. All the sciences we have can only give us short scientific measurements due to the short time span of the existence of the technologies that support that science compared to the time in existence of the subject matter. All of the results give us a snapshot in time and space, if you will, of that particular subject matter. In all instances, the snapshot shows the evidence of the entropy of that system or event. In other words, the decaying metrics of that subject matter. This supports the biblical creation model of the universe without further explanation, theorization, or experimentation. God created and energized the universe and set it in motion based on a given time span to accomplish his plans. This leaves the secular humanist or evolutionist outside the known physical principles that govern the universe. For every evolutionary related process, they have to **make believe** an extraordinary elucidation to support their theories, and in almost every case they have to deny or defy pertinent scientific evidence. Cases in point, 1) In the theory of evolution they **make believe** that life evolved from simple to complex species over eons of time but cannot explain how the mega super nova complex genome bio-computer evolved to get things started. After 160 years or so of research in the sciences of archeology, geology, anthropology, zoology, and genetics, they still have no actual scientific evidence to prove it as would be expected from the proposed models. They have no undisputed transitional fossil records, or genomic patterns. The model would predict that there should be an equal amount or more evidence in the fossil records to support those presuppositions due to the significant amount of time and incremental forms involved. To date, no strata between the Precambrian and Cambrian (or between any of the higher strata) has been found with the missing links in the hundreds of examples around the world. Scientists claim <.01% supporting cases, such as the odd species representing a singular transformational step and disputed cases within and without their organizations based on flawed dating methods, that they push to the public to validate their claims, thereby spinning the evidence and ignoring the 99.99% short fall. Because of this glaring fact, they have had to **make believe** numerous failed theories (based on new technologies or after peer reviewed articles from creationist scientists challenging them on the missing link strata) over the last 160 years such as the artifact hypothesis, the Lipalian Interval, and the latest theory of punctuated equilibrium. The theory of punctuated equilibrium proposes that the change happens so quickly after long periods of stasis, perhaps a generation or two, that it has little chance to be captured in the fossil record, a convenient negative argument that is proved by the lack of evidence and still has no documented occurrence in current natural processes or genomic patterns. It is just not believable that the transformations happen to all species all at once through several iterations (transformational steps). Imagine an eye or even a DNA molecule being developed with all the specialized components by chance with no intelligent input in one or two generations. This all flies in the face of the actual proven scientific fact of entropy that concludes that every process in the universe that can be measured is decaying, going from complex systems to simple systems, from a high energy state to a low energy state. 2) Another example is the decaying of the earth's magnetosphere where they have to **make believe** a theory about some dynamo engine sustaining a spinning core in the center of the earth. This theory has no supporting scientific evidence and even some contrary evidence such as Mercury having a magnetic field in spite of its slow rotation and the unexpected residual magnetism of moon rocks and planetesimals. This dynamo is needed to produce a steady state magnetic field about the earth in order for it to fit into the supposed long timespans of earth's existence, over four billion years. This is in spite of the fact that the actual science we have has shown the earth's magnetosphere steadily and consistently decaying 10% in the past 150 years, which fits perfectly within the decay matrix on an exponential curve over a 6,000-year period. 3) The actual scientific facts prove that rock formation and fossilization in strata involves rapid physical dynamics to form, usually within days. They **make believe** theories that each stratum represents millions of years, not to mention the **make believe** Oort Cloud and **make believe** lunar origins theories that have no supporting scientific evidence that are only needed to support the supposed long time spans of earth's existence but fit perfectly well into the young earth creation model "as is". [9, 10, 14].

Dinosaurs depicted in ancient cave drawings, stories of dragons and thunderbirds, art, and drawings on textiles and pottery are numerous and vivid in their details and can be found in almost every ancient writing or artifact, yet the secular critics **make believe** they are not real and have a deleterious explanation for all of them. Of course, they would have to, as that is the objective, to sever any ties with biblical connections and conform all evidence to a secular humanistic theology. Discovering dinosaur bones in the eighteenth century in light of the many drawings of dinosaurs made by man, one would naturally conclude they lived with dinosaurs, which would support the biblical model of the age of the earth. However, this cannot be accepted by the humanists or evolutionists, as that would imply that there is a possibility that the theory of evolution is in error or not quite accurate and that the evidence would be more supportive of creationism. They say a picture is worth a thousand words and yet the critic's explanations in opposition leaves one speechless. Occam's Razor is suited in these cases. What we see from drawings, art, and stories is what they saw. That's the accepted premise in all ancient cave drawings and historical documents with the exception of pictures or references to dinosaurs, why is that? There are too many examples with diverse types of creatures identical in imagery to dinosaurs to deny that what they saw is what they drew or wrote about and what they drew or wrote about is what they saw!!! [11, 12, 15]

Definition of **Occam's razor** (parsimony): a scientific and philosophic rule that entities should not be multiplied unnecessarily which is interpreted as requiring that the simplest of competing theories be preferred to the more complex or that explanations of unknown phenomena be sought first in terms of known quantities.

There is so much corroborating evidence to support the biblical account of history that it is virtually without contest unless you want to live in a **make-believe** world that is free from any hint of biblical inference. If you choose to ignore the truth and facts then you choose to live in a **make-believe** world with no true history and no real future. Reality will not sustain hopes based on idealistic thinking and ad hoc theories that have no basis in truth. Based on Occam's Razor, the following can be reasonably concluded from the face value of the evidence:

1) The major portion of the evidence for advanced civilizations appear in the historical record about the time of creation (4000 BC) as can be determined in the biblical genealogies, considering the margin of error of dating methods in the minor portion of cases; hence, the authors of the bible were accurate in their records of this event [1, 16].

2) Based on the overwhelming number of cave drawings, stories of dragons (dinosaurs) and thunderbirds, art, and drawings on textiles and pottery from every nation and part of the world, it can be concluded that men have lived contemporary with the dinosaurs[11, 12, 13].

3) Earth strata was formed instantaneously as a result of catastrophic events, as evidenced in the science of rock formation. Fossiliferous rock requires quick burial and great pressures to form, which makes up 90% of the earth's strata. If it was laid down in an instance then the mass of each laminar strata (some covering several states and a few from Mexico to Canada) could

have only been moved from an oceanic basin by a force on the scale of a global Flood. These elements are seen in models we have from local catastrophic events such as Mount St Helen [9].

4) Noah's Flood is supported by the evident demarcation in world cultures and character traits of civilization in about 2500 to 2350 BC as evidenced in history, ancient writings, and by the sciences of both genomics and archeology [16, 17, 18].

5) The decaying magnetosphere is congruent to where it should be if it had started at the time of creation, if you extrapolate backwards based on the current decay rate along an expected exponential curve [14].

6) The physical facts and evidence in nature showing the entropy of all things supports creation theory in its basic applications in all scientific arenas [8, 9, 14].

7) Archeological patterns of evidence are being discovered nearly every day, revealing names, places, and chronology as recorded in the Bible, confirming the biblical history that was once said to be a myth [1, 19, 20].

8) The numerous ancient writings with some excerpts of the stories of Creation, the gods, the long lives, the Flood, Noah and his sons, and the Babel event are found in every Kings List, national history, cultural genealogy, and epic tale written before 1800 BC, collaborating the purer biblical account [1, 11, 13].

9) The appearance of the completely novel fossils in the Cambrian and later strata with no previous or post intermediates as found and collaborated in all the multiple discoveries since Darwin's time was the result of intelligent design for the lack of any other competing theory and lab test results that prove conclusively that chance and natural selection could not be the cause of macro evolution [21].

10) The discovery of the super complex genome, the most efficient processing system known to man, found in the simplest and earliest known creatures (according to evolution) in the Pre-Cambrian strata, must be the result of intelligent design due to the lack of any other competing theory and lab test results that prove conclusively that chance and natural selection could not be the cause [21].

The Origins of the Species [22]

The following is a summary and analysis of *The Origins of the Species* written by Charles Darwin, first published in 1859 with the sixth edition in 1872.

At the time Darwin was writing the book that would significantly change Western culture, he commented that "the great majority of naturalists believed that the species were immutable productions, and had been separately created". Darwin was a naturalist that spent his life investigating the relationships that plants and animals (Phylum) have to one another and to the apparent progression and ability of these Phyla to adapt to the different geological and climatic conditions both in diverse locations around the word and changes within their habitats. Between his personal investigations and studies by other renowned naturalists, he was prompted to write *The Origins of the Species*, convinced that he had enough knowledge and experience to author such a work.

He refers to his final production as an abstract, an imperfect writing, because he didn't have the time he wanted at his late age to write the full details concerning the facts, examples, references, and experiments that supported his theory. He also acknowledged that his research and findings were limited due to the lack of observable evidence (millions of years would be needed to verify these theories). He reminds the reader continuously that it is all theory and that there were difficulties to his theory, which he promptly addresses again with more theoretical explanations.

In **Chapter I**, Darwin address "Variations under Domestication". Here he points out the variable differences between the domestic plants and animals compared to their counterparts in the wild, attributing those differences to the intentional and unintentional habits, mating, and changing environments under which domestic stock are subjected to. He concludes that there is more traceable variances in the physical and habitual characteristics of domestic varieties due to the intellectual paring and selection of human intervention. With the recording of breeds of all kinds of plant and animal stock, there are historical records to trace the chronology of variations to thousands of years. The ability to change and adapt to varying circumstances are apparent and measurable in the domestic breeds. He also states that it is very difficult to classify the differences along any chronological record of variations as a "variant of the species" or the "emergence of a new species". Darwin himself raised pigeons for experimental purposes. He not only concluded that the variations within the species were the result of purposeful or natural selection but that all the variant forms could be traced back to an original progenitor, original set of parents (particularly the rock pigeon, which is a variation still alive today). Darwin cross–bred several different varieties of domestic pigeons, far removed from the overt characteristics of the rock pigeon, and then cross–bred several of their mongrel offspring, which in turn produced offspring with "beautiful blue coloring, white loins, double black wing-bar, and barred and white-edged tail feathers, as any wild rock-pigeon". He also concluded that all horses alive today originated from the zebra variety of progenitors based on similar studies wherein zebra–like stripes appeared on some of the different body parts, especially the legs and shoulders of the mongrel offspring. He believed he was discrediting the authors of the immutable productions of species, when in fact, he unknowingly was establishing the fact that all the variations within the species came from an original set of parents relative to the "kinds" that came from Noah's Ark. Creationist naturalists believed that the earth strata represented millions of years and that God subsequently created new species after each extinction period. At the time, the creationist naturalists (and Darwin himself) were ignorant of the encoded DNA's resources to adapt to changes in the environment (microevolution), therefore they wrongly concluded the immutability of the productions of species; however, the discovery and conclusions of Darwin within these testable and observable facts did not discredit the creationist model in any way, it just enlightened us to the variable traits that the creator pre-encoded into the DNA. Such is the nature of progressive science. With the discovery and advancement of the technology of the DNA double helix structure, it has been confirmed that Darwin was accurate in his conclusions regarding the rock pigeon and zebra as the original progenitors [23 & 24]. One question that occurs to me, is why does the cross breeding of various animals seem to bring out the original parent type breed of the species and not go beyond that to the progenitor of that species? If the rock pigeon was the first "well–marked species", surely they had to come from an original progenitor as well of a slightly different species; so, why would the cross breeding stop at the "well–marked" juncture of the closet relative and not go further back to identify the previous "well–marked species" that was the progenitor of the species of interest (i.e. the rock pigeon or zebra)? Genomic science cannot go further back either, confirming the microevolution within the species!

In **Chapters II-V**, Darwin addresses "Variations under Nature", "Struggle for Existence", "Natural Selection: or the Survival of the Fittest", and "Laws of Variation". In these chapters Darwin explains the variations that have been observed in response to changing environmental conditions be it climate, competition for food, or other challenging conflicts to survival. He refers to the changes as being prompted by "natural selection" or "survival of the fittest". He concludes that the changes are minute and almost unobservable to the untrained eye from one generation to the next and that it actually takes thousands to millions of generations to affect these changes to produce a new species. His theory promulgates that a variation among offspring that gives it an advantage will befit it in life to survive a given condition that would kill off the lesser equipped relative. For instance, an animal that can outrun his relative or competition in the pursuit of prey will eat more often than the relative, being more fit to survive a dearth, or to escape a predator, one escapes while the other is eaten. In the case of sheep experiencing a severe cold spell, the thicker woolen sheep survive whilst the less woolen sheep die off, leaving the thicker–coated ones to breed amongst themselves producing like kind. With the lesser equipped relative removed from the chain of life, the offspring of the survivor will likely have the same variation that helped the parent to survive and may have additional variations that will give it even more of an advantage and so on, until thousands of generations later you have a new "well–marked species" that has the pinnacle of necessary traits to stay in an unchanged state for a greater period than the period it took to arrive at that state. Darwin uses the finches of the Galapagos Islands to demonstrate his point, amongst many other examples. In his descriptions, he shows the variations in the species, particularly the beaks and the variations between the size and shape of the beaks, that he believes was an act within natural selection due to challenges to the species during wet and dry climatic changes.

In **Chapters VI-VIII, Darwin** addresses the "Difficulties of the Theory", "Miscellaneous Objections to the Theory of Natural Selection", and "Instinct". Darwin acknowledges that you cannot trace these thousands of generational changes through the fossil record (transitional fossils). In regard to the fossil record, he believes they are incomplete, owing their incompleteness to the cyclical nature affecting geological changes throughout the eons of time. He believes there have been periods of uplifts with some periods of stasis, and subsidence with periods of stasis. During periods of uplifts, millions of years of the fossil records are eroded away; during the period of subsidence, the phyla are eventually buried in the sands and are captured in the rock formations after millions of years in time. He does not go into great detail explaining how the phyla are captured in the fossil record. Because Darwin was keen to give enough explanation to mechanisms of the process of evolution but not so with addressing the formation of fossils, it leads one to believe he was ignorant of fossil formations and the need for the phyla to be buried quickly and put under great pressures, which is most ardently related to cataclysmic events and certainly not to uniformitarian processes which he infers and was a prevailing argument at the time. As paleontology was an emerging science at the time Darwin was writing his book, there would have been a significant lack of knowledge concerning rock formation and fossilization processes as we know it today.

In addressing the sheer difficulties nature alone would have had with developing complex systems such as the eye, the ear, and the many diverse organs of the body, Darwin seems to go into personifying nature to get the job done. Darwin makes this statement concerning the development of the eye:

"Further we must suppose that there is a *power*, represented by natural selection or the survival of the fittest, *always intently watching* each slight alteration in the transparent layers; and *carefully preserving* each which, under varied circumstances, in anyway or in any degree, tends to produce a distinct image. We must suppose each new state of the instrument to be multiplied by the million; each to be preserved until a better one is produced, and then the old one is to be destroyed. In living bodies, variations will cause the slight alterations, generally multiply them almost infinitely, and *natural selection will pick out with on earring skill each improvement*. Let this process go on for millions of years; and during each year on millions of individuals of many kinds; and we may not believe that a living optical instrument might thus be formed as superior to one of glass, as the works of the Creator are to those of man".

This borders on giving nature an intellect to be able to "see" the outcome of a decision and then "choose" a path forward to perfection and refinement.

In the remaining chapters of *The Origins*, Darwin addresses subject matters such as hybridism, the imperfection of the geological record, the geological succession of organic beings (including extinction), means of geographical distribution, and mutual affinities of organic beings (morphology, embryology, and rudimentary organs).

Darwin makes assertions that the embryotic development directly mimics the evolution of each of the species. The common progenitor of mammals is said to be of reptilian origin from the Jurassic period (208 mya) [25]. He points to the earliest stages of embryotic development where all vertebrates are virtually indistinguishable and that appear to proceed from fish–like characteristics (pointing to the "gill slits" that are present in all the embryos), to amphibian/reptilian (the yolk sac and long tails), and then mammalian features that are kin to all vertebrates at these early stages. Science has since shown that there is a distinct difference in the embryos' similarities in this stage just

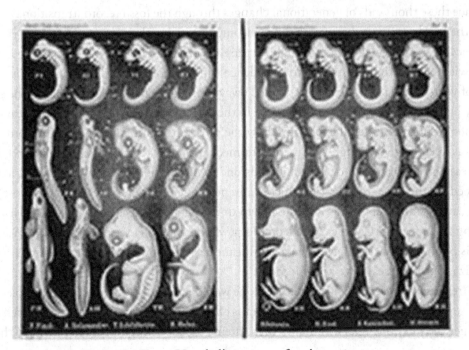

Figure I.1 Ernst Haeckel's images of embryonic stages

before and after these comparable features come into play (referred to as the hourglass model), which does not play well into the presumption that an embryo mimics the stages from emergence to divergence. [26] In 1868 Ernst Haeckel further propagated this notion with his *Biogenic law* (and in 1974 with an illustrated work, *Anthropogenie*) that actually faked the resemblance in these stages (eliminating appendages, copying the same illustration, etc.) that was quickly adopted in textbooks and encyclopedias worldwide [27]. He has since received much criticism from his peers within the scientific community.

"A Professor Arnold Bass charged that Haeckel had made changes in pictures of embryos which he [Bass] *had drawn. Haeckel's reply to these charges was that if he is to be accused of falsifying drawings, many other prominent scientists should also be accused of the same thing ..."* Bolton Davidheiser, *Evolution and Christian Faith* (Phillipsburg, New Jersey: The Presbyterian and Reformed Publishing Co., 1969), pp. 76–77.

"[The German scientist Wilhelm His] *accused Haeckel of shocking dishonesty in repeating the same picture several times to show the similarity among vertebrates at early embryonic stages in several plates of* [Haeckel's book]*."* Stephen Jay Gould, *Ontogeny and Phylogeny* (Cambridge, Massachusetts: The Belknap Press of Harvard University Press, 1977), p. 430.

"It looks like it's turning out to be one of the most famous fakes in biology." Michael K. Richardson, as quoted by Elizabeth Pennisi, "Haeckel's Embryos: Fraud Rediscovered," *Science*, Vol. 277, 5 September 1997, p. 1435.

"When we compare his [Haeckel's] *drawings of a young echidna embryo with the original, we find that he removed the limbs (see Fig. 1). This cut was selective, applying only to the young stage. It was also systematic because he did it to other species in the picture. Its intent is to make the young embryos look more alike than they do in real life."* Michael K. Richardson and Gerhard Keuck, "A Question of Intent: When Is a 'Schematic' Illustration a Fraud?" *Nature*, Vol. 410, 8 March 2001, p. 144.

"Another point to emerge from this study is the considerable inaccuracy of Haeckel's famous figures. These drawings are still widely reproduced in textbooks and review articles, and continue to exert a significant influence on the development of ideas in this field." Michael K. Richardson et al., "There Is No Highly Conserved Embryonic Stage in the Vertebrates," *Anatomy and Embryology*, Vol. 196, August 1997, p. 104.

Modern science has again revealed that the embryonic characteristics that resemble "gill slits" are not related to organs having to do with breathing in the human (or mammalian) embryos. They are neither gills nor slits at this stage, but rather basic tissue folds that eventually develop into parts of the face, bones of the middle ear, and endocrine glands [27]. The tail is actually the initial formation of the backbone on which other bone and body structure assemblies will be attached to as the embryo grows, much like the keel of a boat onto which is the main load bearing and foundational structure on which every other part is built upon. Today, embryologists across the board reject the recapitulation concept [28, 29].

Darwin wrote *The Origins* at a time that indubitably lacked much of the scientific knowledge and technology we have today, especially regarding the genome and geological record. Darwin rightly surmised and concluded those environmental circumstances that cause variations within a species on what we now classify today as microevolution. What he mistakenly presumed due to his ignorance of the genome is that the same mechanisms that allowed for these changes within the species that were quantifiable were the same mechanisms that allowed for changes from species to species (macroevolution) that were not quantifiable, which we know today to be incorrect.

Microevolution: comparatively minor evolutionary change involving the accumulation of variations in populations usually below the species level - Merriam Webster's Dictionary

Macroevolution: evolution that results in relatively large and complex changes (as in species formation) - Merriam Webster's Dictionary.

Microevolution describes adaptive changes or genomic variations that occur within a species in response to changes within its environment (i.e. temperatures, predation, food resources, etc.), genomic influences (diets, parental matches/mismatches, chemical intake, etc.), or other unknown influences. These are not true "mutations" as they are often referred to but rather the redirection or wakening of existing, stored DNA encoded data/information/instructions and disseminated by genetic algorithms that were written by the creator to help the animal to adapt to its changing environment over time.

Macroevolution requires DNA encoding (data/information/instructions/algorithms) that is not preexisting and therefore requires some mutation that has a mechanism to acquire that DNA encoding (data/information/instructions/ algorithms) from some external source. We know today that there are two immutable facts in regard to acquiring DNA encoded data/information/instructions/ algorithms from some external source:

1) there is no known source or mechanism that has been found to reasonably explain where the original DNA data/information/instructions/algorithms came from; and
2) there is no known source or mechanism found to reasonably explain where additional DNA data/information/instructions/algorithms could possibly come from.

Geological Evolutionary Impasse

According to Darwin's principles of evolution, the periodic mass extinctions, the ice ages, and the supposed ongoing geological and climate changes that have affected the natural selection of the species, there should not be one instance where these challenges to life would not invoke either a change or an extinction within any branch of the tree of life according to Darwinian theory. You have two paralleling events that cannot coincide. In regard to the fossil record, Darwin believes they are incomplete, owing their incompleteness to the cyclical nature affecting geological changes throughout the eons of time. He believes there have been periods of uplifts with some periods of stasis, and subsidence with periods of stasis. During periods of uplifts, millions of years of the transitional fossil records were eroded away. With the many geologic events of this nature, (and there must have been many, and they must have been worldwide as all the fossiliferous strata are missing the same segments in every case between every layer of strata in every location around the world), there could not have been many species who would not have been challenged many times along the way. If that is true, then according to the theory, the race begins for the species to evolve and the progenitor to die off or the species to become extinct for lack of ability to evolve. Every time an environment is changed due to periods of uplift or subsidence, new challenges in the form of converging environments, new forms and sources of predation, temperature variances, spatial habitational changes, disruption of the food chain and numerous other environmental effects would be encountered, and you would think they would demand that animals evolve in some manner never to be seen again in the original form except in the fossil record as the theory espouses. Worldwide changes should affect all species everywhere, if not the first time, then surely at some point during these multiple worldwide events and periodic extinctions and ice ages. According to the theory, when a species encounters change within its environment, there is competition between relatives and competing species to survive, which brings out the "survival of the fittest" instinct in the plants and animals. Only the strongest survive, only the fastest survive, only the most cunning survive, and so on. It seems that with these challenges to all species, at one time or another, (actually multiple times), that you should not find any original progenitor alive today; however, that is not the case. There are literally hundreds of what is figuratively called "living fossils" because they are still in existence today in basically the same well–marked forms as found in the fossil records. The fossil records show either extinct fossils or fossils that have survived from the Precambrian, Cambrian, and following periods until today. The one thing the fossil records **do not** show is any strata that reveal the evolutionary changes that would connect any of the supposed different periods of evolution together with sequential stages from one strata to the next, where the species are widely divergent from each other. Not one instance has been discovered to date, no strata with transitional fossils making that grand connection between any of the periods out of at least 11 transitional periods (not including epochs) in literally hundreds of sites around the world. There are about 40 Cambrian fossil locations worldwide. The Burgess Shale in Canada and the Maotianshan Shale in China, for example, were on the opposite ends of the land surface at the time assumed to be in the Pangea supercontinent state (assuming the Americas drifted from the European side of the mainlands) [30] yet holds the same types of fossils and demarcation between the Pre-Cambrian and Cambrian periods; therefore, the subsidence event must have happened at the same time, indicating a worldwide event.

> From Wikipedia: The **Maotianshan Shales** are a series of lower Cambrian deposits in the Chiungchussu formation, famous for their *Konservat Lagerstätten*, deposits known for the exceptional preservation of fossilized organisms or traces. The Maotianshan shales form one of some forty Cambrian fossil locations worldwide exhibiting exquisite preservation of rarely preserved, non-mineralized soft tissue, comparable to the fossils of the Burgess Shale.

So, it would appear that these uplift/subsidence events happened around the world at the same times between each and every stratum, assuming the Darwinian Theory is accurate. If not, then you should have strata from different ages that you could piece together to reveal the evolutionary changes (transitional fossils), which is not the case out of the hundreds of examples. This deduction leads to another impasse. If the transitional fossils were eroded from the record, how did any of the land animals survive during periods of subsidence if it all took place at the same time and numerous times in earth's history? How did any land–bound phyla survive with all the continents under water at the same time for millions of years? This would have also diminished the time it would take to evolve from, say an amphibian, to a small lizard (e.g., *Hylonomus*) in the Pennsylvanian Period (310 ma) to a larger species (Elginia) in the Permian Period (253 ma) [57 my] unless the process started over in every new period at accelerated rates each time.

Figure I.2 *Hylonomus* (Pennsylvanian, 310 mya)   Figure I.3 *Elginia* (Permian, 253 mya)

Evolutionists claim that about 50% of the world Phyla survived the last mass extinction about 65mya. They apparently survived the worldwide subsidence events too (assuming they were washed away by erosion as espoused by Darwin and as evidenced in the oceanic fossils found with the land animals in most all sites of all periods [31]) since we do not have any mammalian transitional links in the strata between epochs since then either [32]. Of course, in modern secular science this is not the case. At no time were all the continents underwater at the same time, and yet 95% of the earth's strata is made up of oceanic sand, cementing agents, and fossils. Even the land animals are found with oceanic fossils in the same beds from every period. Apparently, all the subsidence events happen just before the extinction events as the fossil records are missing the transitional strata but preserved the period's major phylum…repeatedly…for at least 11 geological periods and coinciding extinctions. If none of this makes sense, it is because none of this make sense.

Living Fossils

From the Pre-Cambrian: Most all the **Cyanobacteria** types found in these layers are still in existence in their well-marked stasis condition [33]. The **Placozoa** is another species that has survived, and it too is a surprising evolutionary biologist with DNA as complex as our own. The **Ctenophores** (Comb Jellies) [700 mya] is a phylum of invertebrate animals that live in marine waters worldwide. Their most distinctive feature is the 'combs' – groups of cilia which they use for swimming – they are the largest animals that swim by means of cilia (Wikipedia). These animals are still alive today in basically the same well–marked forms as found in the fossil records. The comb jelly has even a grander surprise. It does not fit in the Pre-Cambrian period with its more complex organization. It has nerves and muscle cells that coexisting creatures do not and on the flip side lacks genes thought essential for animals that low on the evolutionary scale. It was generally thought that sponges were the original progenitor of many a species, but now the comb jelly is throwing conventional evolutionary theology a curve ball [34].

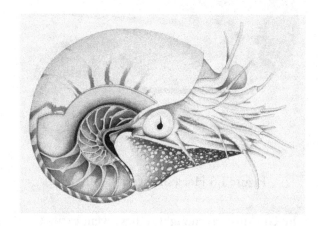

Figure I.4 Comb Jelly (Pre-Cambrian, 700 ma)   Figure I.5 Nautilus (Cambrian, 500 ma)

The Nautilus from the Cambrian Period (500mya) is still alive today in basically the same well–marked form as found in the fossil records [33].

The Horseshoe Crab, found in many places throughout the world, has fossils dating back to 450my in basically the same well–marked form. Today, after having survived all the geological reformations and mass extinctions, their numbers are dwindling due to overharvesting and habitat destruction... how is that possible [33]?

The Elephant Sharks were thought to be extinct for the past 450my but were discovered to be surviving in the waters of Australia and New Zealand [33].

The Glypheoid Lobster, thought to have gone extinct 65mya, have fossils dating back to 300mya in basically the same well–marked form, which were discovered in the Philippines in 1908 [31].

The Cycads have fossils dating back to 230my in basically the same well–marked form. Today, after having survived all the geological reformations and mass extinction, their numbers are dwindling due to extensive collections and habitat destruction...how is that possible [33]?

The P. Palau Cave Eel has fossils dating back to 200my in basically the same well marked form [33].

The Coelacanths were thought to be extinct for the past 65my but were discovered to be surviving off the coast of S. Africa in 1938 [33].

Figure I.6 Horseshoe Crab (450 ma)   Figure I.7 Coelacanths (65 ma)

The Ginkgo was thought to have went extinct 270my but was discovered surviving in China [32].

Figure I.8 Ginkgo (270 ma)

The Dawn Redwood was thought to have went extinct for millions of years but was discovered surviving in remote parts of China [32].

Figure I.9 Dawn Redwood (250 mya)

Additionally, after all the dozens of sites with Cambrian fossils that have since been discovered, Darwin would likely have also concluded that the pattern of evidence is just not there to support his broader conclusions. I believe if Darwin had been privy to the state of the art sciences that we have today, he would not have written *Origins*, understanding that the mechanism for the observable micro evolutionary changes could not be attributed to be the mechanism for his pan–evolutionary theory, which does not distinguish between micro and macro evolution and the consistent findings in the geological record. I conclude this review using Darwin's own thoughts about his work *in light of today's scientific knowledge.*

Several eminent naturalists have of late published their beliefs that a multitude of reputed species in each genus are not really species; but that other species are real, that is, have been independently created. ***This has now been confirmed by the genomic sciences.*** They admit that a multitude of forms — which lately they themselves thought were special creations, and which are still thus looked at by the majority of naturalists, and which consequently have all the external characteristic features of true species —they admit that these have been produced by variation, but they refused to extend the same view to other and slightly different forms. ***They now have a better understanding of which are the created forms of life and which are those produced by secondary genomic laws.*** They admit variation as a *Vera causa* in one case, they arbitrarily rejected it in another, ***assigning micro/macro distinction in the two cases. The day has come*** when what was thought of as a curious illustration of the blindness of preconceived opinion ***was confirmed by science as two distinct mechanisms.*** These authors seem no more startled at the miraculous act of creation then at an ordinary birth. But do they really believe that at innumerable periods in the earth's history certain elemental atoms have been commanded suddenly to flash into living tissues? ***No, they do not, they believe in one act of creation 6,000 years ago and that the geological record is the aftermath of the WW Flood in or about 2500 BC and not millions of years of uniform accumulation.*** Do they believe that at each supposed act of creation one individual or many were produced? ***Today we believe that the basic "kinds" of animals that survived the Flood on Noah's Ark were the progenitors of the variations within the species we have today.*** Were all the infinitely numerous kinds of animals and plants created as eggs or seeds, or were they full-grown? ***Full grown according to the word of God.*** And in the case of mammals, were they created bearing the false marks of nourishment from the mother's womb? ***Now that is a good question, but irrelevant, what difference does make if Adam and Eve had a naval?*** Undoubtedly some of the same questions cannot be answered by those who believe in the appearance or creation of only a few forms of life, or of some one form alone. It has been maintained by several authors that it is as easy to believe in the creation of one million beings as of one; but Maupertuis' philosophical axiom "of least action" leads the mind more willingly to admit the smaller number; and certainly we ought not to believe that innumerable beings within each grade class have been created with playing, but deceptive, marks of dissent from a single parent. ***The creation of many kinds from which many variations have sprung.***

References

1 Biblical References from: The Holy Bible (1913). King James Version. Chicago, Ill. John A. Dickson Publishing Co.

2 Schaeffer, F. (2005). *A christian manifesto*. Wheaton, IL: Crossway Books.

3 American Humanist Association. What is humanism? Retrieved from http://americanhumanist.org/Humanism

4 The Blaze. Watch: Tucker Carlson battles Bill Nye the science guy on global warming. Retrieved from http://www.theblaze.com/news/2017/02/28/watch-tucker-carlson-battles-bill-nye-the-science-guy-on-global-warming/

5 Comedy Central, The Nightly Show. Neil deGrasse Tyson slams flat-earth theorist B.o.B. Retrieved from https://www.youtube.com/watch?v=XHBZkek8OSU

6 Schaefer, F. (1983). *How shall we then live?: The rise and decline of western thought and culture*. Wheaton, IL: Crossway Books.

7 Conservapedia. Methodological naturalism. Retrieved from http://www.conservapedia.com/Methodological_naturalism

8 Groups and teamwork - Jorum. file:///C:/Users/Jeffrey/Downloads/Items-T205_2_section9.html.

9 Morris, H. D. (1985). *Scientific creationism*. Green Forrest, AR: Master Books.

10 Morris, H. D. (2008). *The biblical basis for modern science: Revised and updated classic*. Green Forrest, AR: Master Books.

11 Breeden, D. Ph.D, (2011). *The adventures of Beowulf*. Seattle, WA: CreateSpace Independent Publishing Platform.

12 History's Evidence of Dinosaurs and Men. Retrieved from http://historysevidenceofdinosaursandmen.weebly.com/

13 Cooper, Bill. The table of nations. Retrieved from http://www.biblebelievers.org.au/natindx.htm#Index - The Table of Nations

14 Barnes, T. G. Ph.D, (1983). *Origin and destiny of the earth's magnetic field* (2nd Ed.). El Cajon, CA: Institute For Creation Research.

15 Brett-Surman, M.K. (2000). *Dinosaurs: Revised & Updated*. San Francisco, CA: Fog City Press.

16 Wolf, A. (2008). *A short history of the world: The story of mankind from prehistory to the modern day*. New York, NY: Metro Books by arrangement with Arcturus Publishing Limited.

17 American Renaissance. Why did European DNA suddenly change 4,000 years ago? Retrieved from http://www.amren.com/news/2013/04/why-did-european-dna-suddenly-change-4000-years-ago/

18 Renfrew, C & Cooke, K. (1979). *Transformations: Mathematic approaches to cultural change*. New York, NY: Academic Press Inc.

19 Evans, C.A. (2010). *Holman QuickSource™ guide to the Dead Sea scrolls*. North Nashville, TN: B&H Publishing Group.

20 Mahoney, T. P. Pattern of evidence: The exodus. Retrieved from http://patternsofevidence.com/

21 Meyers, S.C. (2013). *Darwin's doubt*. New York, NY: HarperCollins Publishers.

22 Darwin, Charles (1959). *Origins of the species*.

23 ICR, Pigeon Study Confirms Creation. Retrieved from http://www.icr.org/article/pigeon-study-confirms-creation/

24 The Telegraph. Horses had stripes like zebras until humans broke them in, scientists say. Retrieved from http://www.telegraph.co.uk/news/science/science-news/12076331/Horses-had-stripes-like-zebras-until-humans-broke-them-in-scientists-say.html

25 Sciworthy. Early mammals diverged from reptiles much earlier than thought in the late Triassic. Retrieved from http://sciworthy.com/early-mammals-diverged-from-reptiles-much-earlier-than-thought-in-the-late-triassic/

26 Seeker. Discovery News (2013). Embryos Show All Animals Share Ancient Genes. Retrieved from https://www.seeker.com/embryos-show-all-animals-share-ancient-genes-discovery-news-1766482931.html

27 Center of Scientific Creation. 20 Embryology. Retrieved from http://www.creationscience.com/onlinebook/LifeSciences24.html

28 Denis Mareschal, Paul C. Quinn, and Stephen E.G. Lea (2010). The making of human concepts. Published to Oxford Scholarship Online: May-10. Retrieved from http://faculty.som.yale.edu/georgenewman/documents/13Darwin_and_development_Why_ontogeny_does_not_recapitulate_phylogeny_for_human_concepts_000.pdf

29 Blechschmidt, Erich (1977). *The Beginnings of Human Life*. Springer, NY. Springer-Verlag Inc., pg. 32:

30 Encyclopedia Britannica. Pangea. Retrieved from https://www.britannica.com/place/Pangea

31 ICR. Dinosaurs in marine sediments: A worldwide phenomena. Retrieved from http://www.icr.org/article/8769.

32 National Geographic. Science. Mass Extinctions. Retrieved from http://www.nationalgeographic.com/science/prehistoric-world/mass-extinction/

33 Gizmodo. 12 of the most astounding living fossils known to science. Retrieved from http://io9.gizmodo.com/12-of-the-most-astounding-living-fossils-known-to-sci-1506539384

34 Answers in Genesis. Comb jelly genome mystery generates confusion. Retrieved from https://answersingenesis.org/theory-of-evolution/evolution-timeline/comb-jelly-genome-mystery-generates-confusion/

PART 1

Creation and Antediluvian Era

Record of Creation

The account of the creation of the universe and the world has been recorded in many ancient texts of many cultures throughout the world. The biblical account is by far the most accurate account of them all, as the details are much more specific in describing the processes involved in the creation of the world that match known physics, describing the environment, and the giving of names and times of the genealogies from the Antediluvian period and continuing onto the birth of Jesus Christ. Additionally, these accounts were recorded by men of the times who had a genuine fear of God and were indeed in a relationship with the God who created it all. If it were indeed from God, they would be the more careful to guard the truth and record these events in the most accurate detail as opposed to other ancient writings of pagan authors living in an idolatrous environment influenced by demons (the gods of old) whose perspectives would have been skewed, much like the secular humanist perspective of today. According to the biblical record, God created the earth and everything that was ever physically created about 4000BC. Genesis tells us that God created all things in six days and rested on seventh day. God provided a habitat for the object of his creation, man (Adam and Eve), in the Garden of Eden, where He would meet with them and talk with them regularly [1]. From the description given in Genesis, most scholars believe the location of the Garden of Eden was somewhere in Eastern Turkey where four rivers (Pison, Euphrates, Hiddekel (Tigris), and Gihon) flowed from a riverhead out of the garden. No one can know for sure, as the geology and contours of the land must have been greatly affected by the great Flood of Noah's time.

Figure 1.1 Cosmic Gases and Galaxies

John 1:1,3: In the beginning was the Word, and the Word was with God, and the Word was God... All things were made by him; and without him was not anything made that was made.

Gen 1:2: And the earth was without form, and void; and darkness was upon the face of the deep. And the Spirit of God moved upon the face of the waters.

Gen 1:6: And God said, Let there be a firmament in the midst of the waters, and let it divide the waters from the waters.

Gen 1:7: And God made the firmament, and divided the waters which were under the firmament from the waters which were above the firmament: and it was so.

Gen 1:9: And God said, Let the waters under the heaven be gathered together unto one place, and let the dry land appear: and it was so.

Gen 1:10: And God called the dry land Earth; and the gathering together of the waters called he Seas: and God saw that it was good.

2 Peter 3:5: For this they willingly are ignorant of, that by the word of God the heavens were of old, and the earth standing out of the water and in the water:

These scriptures describe a process by which God first made all astrological objects as bodies of water (the earth, sun, moon, stars, et al) with all the physical properties of water and mass (e.g., molecular structure [H_2O], gravity, orbits, magnetospheres, etc.), then he created the solid matters and associated elements (dry land). So God in six days, the first week in time, created the earth within a solar system, within a galaxy, within a universe.

Gen 1:26: And God said, Let us make man in our image, after our likeness: and let them have dominion over the fish of the sea, and over the fowl of the air, and over the cattle, and over all the earth, and over every creeping thing that creepeth upon the earth., ("Let Us" infers that before creation and time was the Father, the Son & the Holy Spirit)[1].

The Genomic Design

On the act of creation, one of the most significant findings of modern science is the discovery of the genome, best described as "the Mega Super Nova Genome Bio-computer". These basic cells are a combination of complex molecules with interrelated functions (protein/ DNA/RNA/carbohydrates) with a sophisticated relationship that cannot exist independently, the hardware and software of a computer being a suitable but weak analogy in comparison to the algorithms displayed in the genome. The supposed oldest creature ever discovered some 3.5 billion years ago and the basic simplest fauna (microbes) are so complex with such sophisticated programming, including pre-coded algorithms and commands that are time released to give the organism its physical appearance and nature through its life cycle, that the basic "life started one stormy night in a primordial soup" is like believing that a hurricane can sweep through a forest and leave behind a storehouse of dictionaries and encyclopedias complete with deer skin covers and pages full of definitions and subject matter in alpha numeric sequence, which any rational or critical thinker could deduct that giving all the time and chance in the universe this could not be possible [2]. This is definitely an act of intelligent design. There is no mechanism or vehicle in the natural realm known in physics or chemistry that could spontaneously, by chance, *by magic*, generate such intricate molecular structure programmed with such complicated encoding. No mix of enzymes, sugars, protein, and RNA could possibly produce a double helix strand of DNA with all the blue prints and algorithms readymade to build an animal with all the necessary interdependent systems (heart, brains, nerves, blood corpuscles, eyes, etc.). The grand design of the genome demands the existence of a grand designer! Because this issue is such an impossible event in science with the known physics on earth, some secular scientists now **make believe** that life could have started on some other planet (where known physics must not apply) and came to earth on a meteor. This is known as the Panspermia theory [3]. That planet would have to be pretty close by, as meteors travel at a velocity of about 30,000 – 45,000 mph on average and therefore could not be much farther than the next solar system, which is about 4 light years away (Alfa Centauri at 4.37ly). This would be quite a stretch, as an asteroid traveling at 30,000mph would take 100,000 years to reach earth from Alfa Centauri. Other theories include times when our galaxy passes through remnants of other degraded solar systems that could come closer to the earth, except that between the time that planet exploded (creating meteors) and the time the earth would get that close would be about 62 million years (1/4 n1), not to mention surviving after an explosion of that magnitude. That would be some microbe to make it that far for so long in the isolation of space with no habitable environment only to find our little planet in the vastness of space with its billions of symbiotic and conditional perfections such as the placement/relationship in the solar system, the moon, rotation, revolutions, axis tilt°, size/gravity, magnetosphere, potential for atmosphere, water, etc.!

Geneticists have concluded that all people alive today come from a specific individual male and female[4], which confirms both the biblical model and the Darwinian Theory in regard to original progenitors. They also concluded that from generation to generation there is a mutation factor in the genetic make-up of living organisms (copying errors in the male DNA and female mtDNA). These mutations can be calculated (over 100 mutations per generation) and fit well with the laws of entropy [5, 6]. The purity of the genome in Adam and Eve allowed for the non-harmful effects at the beginning of creation with marrying close relatives, such as the sons and daughters of Adam and Eve, before the build-up of deleterious effects of these mutations.

The Fall of Man

After some time, Adam and Eve were banished from the Garden of Eden for their sin of disobedience. They ate of the fruit of the tree of the knowledge of good and evil, even after God specifically warned them not to and warned them of the consequences of doing so. This act of disobedience was inspired by the devil, Lucifer, a former angel banished from heaven for his pride, who manifested as a snake in the garden. It is apparent that there was more interface between the spiritual realm and the earthly realm at that time than that of the present day. God walked on the earth in those days, appearing to men, and so did other spiritual beings[1].

God's plan for redemption is revealed at this time, the first prophecy of the coming of Christ 4,000 years before His time.

Gen 3:15: And I will put enmity between thee and the woman, and between thy seed and her seed; it shall bruise thy head, and thou shalt bruise his heel.

Gen 3:16: Unto the woman he said, I will greatly multiply thy sorrow and thy conception; in sorrow thou shalt bring forth children; and thy desire shall be to thy husband, and he shall rule over thee.

Gen 3:17: And unto Adam he said, Because thou hast hearkened unto the voice of thy wife, and hast eaten of the tree, of which I commanded thee, saying, Thou shalt not eat of it: cursed is the ground for thy sake; in sorrow shalt thou eat of it all the days of thy life;[1].

Man was put out of the garden (paradise) and began to populate the earth. The first two men born into the world after the fall of man were Cain and Abel. After about 130 years and 4 generations, Adam, Eve, and their children had been populating the region.

Where:
Couple (Cpl) = 1 son and 1 daughter (Est 8 Cpls per Cpl per Gen)
Generation (Gen) = 35 years
Non-Producing Generations (NP) = previous generations before the last (still living) no longer producing offspring
Mortality Rate (MR) (based on max 40% mortality rate), **natural causes (NC)** mortality rate [20%] = 1 gen out of 25 (avg. life span at 900 years during this period), cost of human lives due to **wars (W)** [15%], due to **diseases (D)** (and other: accidents & dragon attacks) [5%].

Creation to Cane/Abel event = 130 years (approx. 4 Gens): MR = D = 5%

Gen1 = 1 Cpl x 8 = 8 x .95(MR) = 8 Cpls,
Gen2 = Gen1 x 8 x .95(MR) = 61 Cpls,
Gen3 = Gen2 x 8 x .95(MR) = 462 Cpls,
Gen4 = Gen3 x 8 x .95(MR) = 3,697 Cpls,

Word Population = Gen4 + NP x 2 = (3,697 Cpls + 531 Cpls) x 2 = **8,456 individuals.**

At this time, Cain rose up against Abel and killed him out of jealousy of his relationship with God. God soon confronted him and asked him where Abel was, to which he replied, "I do not know, am I my brother's keeper". God drove Cain and his wife out of the populace, cursed him, and set a mark on him that burdened him and his descendants for generations to follow. Cain in the course of time built a city in the land of Nod named Enoch, after his first born, and established an antediluvian dynasty. After the loss of Abel, Adam and Eve, being 130 years old, purposed to have another child (Seth) to carry on the mantle of righteousness that they believed was on Abel for the afore mentioned prophecy [1]. After this time the population grew exponentially, as mortality due to natural causes did not figure into the equation for the first 900 years. There came to be **2,296,928 individuals** in the next 100 years, 230 years after expulsion from Eden.

Creation to 230 = 230 years (approx. 7 Gens): MR = W+D = 20%
Gen5 = Gen4 x 8 x .80(MR) = 23,661 Cpls,
Gen6 = Gen5 x 8 x .80(MR) = 151,429 Cpls,
Gen7 = Gen6 x 8 x .80(MR) = 969,146 Cpls,

Word Population = Gen7 + NP x 2 = (969,146 Cpls + 179,318 Cpls) x 2 = **2,296,928 individuals.**

The Generations of Adam (Reference Time Line)

Hebrew	English
Adam	Man
Seth	Appointed
Enosh	Mortal
Kenan	Sorrow;
Mahalalel	The Blessed God
Jared	Shall come down
Enoch	Teaching
Methuselah	His death shall bring
Lamech	The Despairing
Noah	Rest, or comfort.

In the Hebrew translation to English of the names of Adam to Noah, a summary of the New Testament message – **the Gospel of Jesus Christ**!

Put those meanings into a complete sentence and you get: Man (is) appointed mortal sorrow, (but) the blessed God shall come down teaching. His death shall bring (the) despairing comfort and rest [7].

After the fall, man began to populate the earth along with the animals. God set the habitation of man and the wild beasts at that time. It is apparent from the evidence in archeology and geology that there were areas where civilization abounded and areas apart from civilization where predators such as dinosaurs and large mammals (such as lion, tigers and bears) made their abode. Where you find abundance of dinosaur fossils, you do not find evidence of advanced civilizations such as in North America, Mongolia, the outlands of China, and Australia. Comparable to today in the plains of Africa, you don't find advanced civilizations in habitats where dangerous predators live, which can only be true of short time span of history [8, 9].

Life at this time was not like anything we know today. The carnal and spiritual worlds were not separated by borders or chasms at this time. Men and angels were free to do as they willed without God's word for divine guidance and light, a hard-bought lesson. Biblical excerpts and ancient manuscripts, such as the many King lists (Sumerian, Egyptian, Chinese, and others), reveal that Satan and the fallen angels manifested themselves to the world as "gods from the heavens" to be worshipped by man. Many of these writings collaborate the stories of these gods mating with earthly women and having offspring that were "men of renown" (demigods) that did exploits and ruled in the earth. Many were giants in physical appearance. The outcome of these cultures led by these evil beings were a people who were unrestrained to do whatever evil and perversion came to their minds. We are told that the environment was a very hot, humid tropical climate as a result of significantly greater amounts of carbon dioxide gases in the atmosphere, creating a greenhouse effect over the whole earth. Instead of raining, a mist came up from the ground and watered the earth. Man lived to nearly 1,000 years old in those days [1].

These were the beginnings of creation at a time when man and beast were descending from a pure DNA structure and the magnetosphere was at its zenith, protecting the earth from harmful cosmic rays. Additionally, there is strong scientific evidence to suggest that there was a much higher content of carbon dioxide gases in the atmosphere of the pre-Flood environment that would have produced a strong greenhouse effect. This would result in warmer climates, which would stimulate plant growth, which would account for the great amount of plant life and larger creatures we find in the fossil record [10]. Additionally, it would dilute the C^{14} thinning out the C^{14}/C^{12} ratio found in the atmosphere. Hence, the combined physical properties of the strength of the magnetosphere and the greater carbon dioxide gases resulted in little to no C^{14} build up in the plants and animals. The earth was not going through extreme seasonal changes like we know today, which may have been due to the earth's axis being more aligned with the earth's solar rotation than today. All these elements provided an environment less degenerative than at any other time in history, contributing to the longevity of God's creation at that time [11].

The evidence in ancient writings are quite conclusive in regard to the manifestation of spiritual entities. God himself manifested in a pre-incarnate physical person and walked and talked with the righteous descendants of Adam and those who called upon his name. To the same degree, the angels, both good and bad, were allowed to manifest as incarnate physical persons. Men worshipped some of the fallen angels as gods. These "gods" were feared because of the great exploits they were allowed to perform in those days, appearing as extraordinary miracles.

Biblical reference to Pre-Flood Interfacing with God, other spiritual beings and man;

Gen 2:16: And the LORD God commanded the man, saying, of every tree of the garden thou mayest freely eat:

Gen 2:17: But of the tree of the knowledge of good and evil, thou shalt not eat of it: for in the day that thou eatest thereof thou shalt surely die.

Gen 3:1: Now the serpent was more subtil than any beast of the field which the LORD God had made. And he said unto the woman, Yea, hath God said, Ye shall not eat of every tree of the garden?

Gen 4:6: And the LORD said unto Cain, Why art thou wroth? and why is thy countenance fallen?

Gen 4:7: If thou doest well, shalt thou not be accepted? and if thou doest not well, sin lieth at the door. And unto thee shall be his desire, and thou shalt rule over him.

Gen 5:22: And Enoch walked with God after he begat Methuselah three hundred years, and begat sons and daughters:

Gen 5:24: And Enoch walked with God: and he was not; for God took him.

Gen 6:2: That the sons of God saw the daughters of men that they were fair; and they took them wives of all which they chose.

Gen 6:4: There were giants in the earth in those days; and also after that, when the sons of God came in unto the daughters of men, and they bare children to them, the same became mighty men which were of old, men of renown.

Gen 6:13: And God said unto Noah, The end of all flesh is come before me; for the earth is filled with violence through them; and, behold, I will destroy them with the earth [1].

The Gods of the Ancient world

The gods of old, myths or legends forged in the fires that tried the ancient world? It would be doubtful that they were myths for all the cultures in the world to adapt such similar stories for their histories based on what would have originated from the contrived story of one individual. There is no precedent for such phenomena in all of history, to choose to believe they are myths identical in all aspects is a leap of faith in and of itself. The Bible tells us of their origins, which puts it at a genesis before any other account of any other culture (Sumer, Egypt, China, etc.). The king's lists and other extraneous ancient scripts infer that the gods of Sumer and Egypt may have come from outer space, maybe even from planetary dominions. These gods introduced astrological happenstance to events and based much of the cause of natural occurrences to the stars [12]. But the truth behind the deception perpetrated by the so called "gods" is that they were fallen angels who were allowed to have dominion in the earth for a while to deceive and test the nations. This time period in His Story was allowed by God so that man could become acquainted with his base nature and the terrifying side of the spiritual world apart from God's rule, authority, and empowerment. The base nature of man, when he chooses to live apart from God, is without restraint and subject to all the natural and spiritual forces that exist in the world. Powerless alone to do good, man will follow the evil in his heart to his own destruction. The results revealed that the heart of man is basically evil and will choose corruption and vice over virtue to the point to where God, being just and patient, had to eventually put an end to the violence and corruption by means of a cleansing flood.

The Bible tells us in Col 1:16, "For in him all things were created: things in heaven and on earth, visible and invisible, whether thrones or powers or rulers or authorities; all things have been created through him and for him."

Job 38:1-7 1 Then the LORD spoke to Job out of the storm. He said: 2 "Who is this that obscures my plans with words without knowledge? 3 Brace yourself like a man; I will question you, and you shall answer me. 4 "Where were you when I laid the earth's foundation? Tell me, if you understand. 5 Who marked off its dimensions? Surely you know! Who stretched a measuring line across it? 6 On what were its footings set, or who laid its cornerstone— 7 while the morning stars sang together and all the angels shouted for joy?

Jesus confirmed the two realms of co-existence, the earthly and spiritual.

John 3:5-13 5 Jesus answered, Verily, verily, I say unto thee, except a man be born of water and of the Spirit, he cannot enter into the kingdom of God. 6 That which is born of the flesh is flesh; and that which is born of the Spirit is spirit. 7 Marvel not that I said unto thee, ye must be born again. 8 The wind bloweth where it listeth, and thou hearest the sound thereof, but canst not tell whence it cometh, and whither it goeth: so is every one that is born of the Spirit. 9 Nicodemus answered and said unto him, how can these things be? 10 Jesus answered and said unto him, Art thou a master of Israel, and knowest not these things? 11 Verily, verily, I say unto thee, we speak that we do know, and testify that we have seen; and ye receive not our witness. 12 If I have told you earthly things, and ye believe not, how shall ye believe, if I tell you of heavenly things? 13 And no man hath ascended up to heaven, but he that came down from heaven, even the Son of man which is in heaven.

John 3:31: He that cometh from above is above all: he that is of the earth is earthly, and speaketh of the earth: he that cometh from heaven is above all.

The beings (Angels) found in the spiritual realm

Rev 5:11-12 11 Then I looked and heard the voice of many angels, numbering thousands upon thousands, and ten thousand times ten thousand. They encircled the throne and the living creatures and the elders. 12 In a loud voice they were saying: "Worthy is the Lamb, who was slain, to receive power and wealth and wisdom and strength and honor and glory and praise!"

The Origins of the Ancient Gods

Eze 28:13-19 13 Thou hast been in Eden the garden of God; every precious stone was thy covering, the sardius, topaz, and the diamond, the beryl, the onyx, and the jasper, the sapphire, the emerald, and the carbuncle, and gold: the workmanship of thy tabrets and of thy pipes was prepared in thee in the day that thou wast created. 14 Thou art the anointed cherub that covereth;

and I have set thee so: thou wast upon the holy mountain of God; thou hast walked up and down in the midst of the stones of fire. 15 Thou wast perfect in thy ways from the day that thou wast created, till iniquity was found in thee. 16 By the multitude of thy merchandise they have filled the midst of thee with violence, and thou hast sinned: therefore I will cast thee as profane out of the mountain of God: and I will destroy thee, O covering cherub, from the midst of the stones of fire. 17 Thine heart was lifted up because of thy beauty, thou hast corrupted thy wisdom by reason of thy brightness: I will cast thee to the ground, I will lay thee before kings, that they may behold thee. 18 Thou hast defiled thy sanctuaries by the multitude of thine iniquities, by the iniquity of thy traffick; therefore will I bring forth a fire from the midst of thee, it shall devour thee, and I will bring thee to ashes upon the earth in the sight of all them that behold thee. 19 All they that know thee among the people shall be astonished at thee: thou shalt be a terror, and never shalt thou be any more.

Isaiah 14:12-14 12 How you have fallen from heaven, oh Lucifer, morning star, son of the dawn! You have been cast down to the earth, you who once laid low the nations! 13 You said in your heart, "I will ascend to the heavens; I will raise my throne above the stars of God; I will sit enthroned on the mount of assembly, on the utmost heights of Mount Zaphon. 14 I will ascend above the tops of the clouds; I will make myself like the Most High."

Rev 12:3-4: 3 And there appeared another wonder in heaven; and behold a great red dragon, having seven heads and ten horns, and seven crowns upon his heads. 4 And his tail drew the third part of the stars of heaven, and did cast them to the earth: and the dragon stood before the woman which was ready to be delivered, for to devour her child as soon as it was born.

Rev 12:7-9 7 And there was war in heaven: Michael and his angels fought against the dragon; and the dragon fought and his angels, 8 And prevailed not; neither was their place found any more in heaven. 9 And the great dragon was cast out, that old serpent, called the Devil, and Satan, which deceiveth the whole world: he was cast out into the earth, and his angels were cast out with him.

2Thes 2:9-10 9 The coming of the lawless one will be in accordance with the work of Satan displayed in all kinds of counterfeit miracles, signs and wonders, 10 and in every sort of evil that deceives those who are perishing. They perish because they refused to love the truth and so be saved.

Satan first reared his ugly head in the Garden of Eden to deceive Adam and Eve into sinning against God with the ultimate goal of stealing the praise and worship of God for himself.

The Echo of the Truth

When put to the test, the Bible comes up as the first "ping" in an attenuating echo amongst many historical documented stories of the life and times of the antediluvian, post–Flood, and Ice Age world tenants. The Bible has been found to be true, accurate, and congruent with discoveries in science, history, anthropology, archeology, genealogy, and other fields of study. Other genesis stories such as the Sumerian and Egyptian King Lists, the Chinese King List, the Indian Vedas, and so on, are invariably lacking in sound theology outside of the basic undeniable truths, events, and evidence that the scribes were recipients of.

The stories in history that echo the genesis of mankind and birth of the nations from various cultures is a natural and expected result of certain undeniable key events that the first generations experienced when venturing forth from a singular moment in time. God, the creation of the universe, Adam and Eve, the gods, the Flood, and the lineage of Noah were undeniable key events and figures found in the Bible and most all other ancient cultures from before 1800 BC. Satan could not fabricate new yarns from scratch to deceive people; he was bound to twist the truth instead. He used undeniable facts heard from the flood survivors that correlated with what they had seen and knew from experience, such as remains of civilizations with no inhabitants wherever they ventured, genealogies that stopped at Noah (most of the first kings were the grandsons and great grandsons of Noah), and the extraordinarily long lives of their predecessors that progressive generations didn't enjoy. Noah's family and the several following generations were the source of these stories and were present and accessible to mankind for up to 500 years after the Flood, as collaborated in the story of Gilgamesh in search of Noah. Shem was recorded as living 100 years before the Flood and 500 years after the Flood. The Babel experience was again an undeniable event to the forgers of religious theology in those times, be they the so-called gods inspiring the priests or the priest of the so called gods making it up in their ignorance at the behest of their kings. Most of the kings of the time were the second and third generation from Noah so they established regional and cultural religions congruent with the stories they received from their parents, grandparents, and great grandparents, who were all still very much alive for generations to come. The fascinating and incredible stories of the antediluvian people were sure to be relayed to the children of Shem, Ham, and Jepheth, and obviously written down as found in most of the ancient king lists that were a progressive work. These stories included the rule of the gods, the giants of the land, the miracles and feats performed by the gods, demigods, and the spirits of the dead, such as Hercules, who was half man, half god, and considered a demigod. It would only be natural for the story tellers and scribes wanting to credit a heritage for their new territory or cultures to include these pre-Flood lineages in their own line of descendants in order to claim an unbroken chain of royal blood and to preserve the antediluvian stories for posterity.

Satan and his demons (associate fallen angels) appeared incarnate and portrayed themselves as gods from the heavens (outer space) with all false signs and wonders to secure the devotion, fear, and worship of the sons of men. Every culture from that time to 500 BC worshiped this pantheon of gods in one form or another except the Hebrew line of patriarchs, who worshiped the one true God who manifested his power and glory for the children of Israel to the world to a magnitude unparalleled by any of the so called gods. God choose the Hebrews to be a beacon of light to the world in order for mankind to recognize the glory of God and the source of all truth, to lead men to recognize the person of the son of God, Jesus called Christ, the lamb of God slain before the foundation of the earth when he came into the world. The gods mixed undeniable truths of the time with fabricated theology in order to take glory from God and credit the causes of these truths to themselves and gain the people's devotion. They set themselves up as gods and proceeded to rule over men and even mixed in with man to distort the truth and image of man, who was made in the image of God. They claimed to be gods who caused and commanded nature and human events (the sun god, goddess of the earth, god of the seas, god of war, etc.) to get men to fear adversity from disobedience in their realm of nature. They made fantastic claims, such as the earth was a flat disc made of tin. They claimed creation and societal living for up to 400,000 years before the Flood, exceedingly beyond the archeologically and biblically proven times (about 6,000 years ago). All these theological constraints have been proven false by modern science and physics. On the other hand, the biblical patriarchs with a mandate from God to keep the genealogical records and true historic events were not subject to the deception of the gods and kept to the bare essence of the truth, not adding to the text absurd theology. It is therefore reasonable to conclude that the authors of biblical events held to the truth of His Story; consequently, the Bible is the original and purer theological text. These records that bear antediluvian and post–Flood events in precise detail collaborated in science and history attest to the fact that they were recorded at the times of the events and therefore marks them as the most ancient of all known scripting. All other post flood stories are an echo of the pure text written after the flood event and provide a source of collaboration of the basic facts [13, 14].

If the Bible is a true and accurate historical record regarding these fallen angels manifesting themselves as gods for men to worship during the Antediluvian period, the long lives they lived, the world-wide flood, the Ark with Noah and sons, and so on, then you would expect to find evidence of ancient literature making reference to such.

This is exactly what you find in all the king lists and other literature of all the major cultures in the world before 1800 BC, as a matter of fact!

All the ancient king lists and epic stories such as the Sumerian King List, the Egyptian Kings List, The Chinese King's List, the Indian Vedas, the *Epic of Gilgamesh* and many others have the same exact antediluvian story as each other and the Bible! They all tell of the gods, the long lives and reigns of the time, the Great Flood, and the Ark with Noah and family caricatures. The following are excerpts from several of the king lists in their references to the pre–Flood dynasties.

The Sumerian King Lists;

The Sumerian King Lists are the oldest extant writing in existence (from around 2000BC). The following extant ancient sources contain the Sumerian King List, or fragments of the list [12]:

WB 62 (small clay tablet from 2000BC)
WB 444 (Weld-Blundell Prism) (1827BC)
Kish Tablet (Scheil dynastic tablet) (early 2nd millennium BC)
UCBC 9-1819 ("California Tablet") (1712BC)
Dynastic Chronicle (ABC 18) [5] including copies, K 11261+ and K 12054
Babyloniaca (Berossus) (640BC)
Apkullu-list (W.20030, 7) (165BC)

These manuscripts identified kings that apparently were rulers in the pre-Flood world. These would have to be stories told by the children of Noah who were alive during the time of these dynasties and possibly from writings extant at the time that Noah may have preserved for posterity. These kings were often referred to as gods, demigods, and spirits of the dead by pagan sources and all associated with extraordinarily long lives and reigns.

The Sumerian King List states that eight kings in five cities ruled for 241,200 years before *"the Flood swept over the land"*. Their reigns are measured in *sars* - periods of 3,600 years - and in *ners* - units of 600 - and in *sosses* - units of 60. It is still a mystery as to the actual time span these units refer to but is believed to be connected to the sexagesimal system in some manner. Raul Lopez, a Professor at CSU, believes he has deciphered it. Referring to the total sum of the ages of the biblical antediluvian patriarchs (less Adam and Noah) compared to the sum of the King List, he says, "if the number representing the sum of the ages was wrongly assumed as having been written in the sexagesimal system, the two totals become numerically equivalent" [15].

From the History Files (copied by permission) [16].

> The early city states of Sumer in order of ascendance are as follows: Eridu, Bad-Tibira, Larak, Sippar, Shuruppak, and Nippur (usually without a kingship of its own). Other antediluvian cities existed, but without any known kingships of their own. Instead these flourish later.
>
> City State of Eridu / Eridug
> Situated seven miles south-west of the later city of Ur, Eridu was said to be one of the five cities built before the Flood. According to Sumerian writings, Eridu was founded by the Sumerian deity named Enki, later known by the Akkadians as Ea, god of water and wisdom. It seems to have made the step up from being a village in around 4000 BC. By the time of its kings it had grown into a substantial city of mud brick and reed houses. It was also home to the oldest known temples, dating from the mid-sixth millennium.

1.3 Sandstone tablet with the Sumerian King List

Figure 1.2 Sumerian god with wings

According to the King List, Eridu was host to the First Kingship (of Sumer, before the Flood). 'When kingship was first handed down from Heaven, the city of Eridu was chosen as the seat of kingship.

Ruler	Length of Reign	Secular dates	Inscriptions	Comments
After the kingship descended from heaven, the kingship was in Eridug. *In Eridug, Alulim became king; he ruled for 28800 years*				
Alulim	8 sars (28,800 years)	Between 35th and 30th century BC		
Alalngar	10 sars (36,000 years)			
Then Eridug fell and the kingdom was taken to Bad-tibira				
En-men-lu-ana	12 sars (43,200 years)			
En-men-gal-ana	8 sars (28,800 years)			
Dumuzid	10 sars (36,000 years)		the shepard	
Then Bad-tibira fell and the kingdom was taken to Larag				
En-sipad-sid-ana	8 sars (28,800 years)			
Then Larag fell and the kingdom was taken to Zimbir				
En-men-dur-ana	5 sars & 5 ners (21,000 years)			
Then Zimbir fell and the kingdom was taken to Shuruppag				
Ubara-Tutu	5 sars & 1 ners (18,600 years)			
Then the Flood swept over				

City State of Bad-tibira

Second of the pre-Flood city states, Bad-Tibira (with a probable modern location at Tell al-Madain) was situated on the Iturungal Canal, below Umma. The Bible mentions it as Tubal. The city's main god was Lulal, while the city's temple was E-mush-kalamma, which was mentioned in the tale, *Inanna's Descent to the Underworld*. Bad-Tibira seems to have greatly lost its importance after the Flood, although it was known by the Greeks as Panti-Biblos.

City State of Larak / Larag

The location of Larak has not been identified, but it is believed that the city was on the west bank of the Tigris to the east of Kish. Its patron deity was Pabilsag, god of the trees.

City State of Sippar / Zimbir

Evidence shows that Sippar was occupied from the Uruk Period, although there were actually two cities named Sippar. This one (modern Tell Abu Habbah) was a dual city, half of which was under the protection of the sun-god Utu of Sippar (Shamash in Akkadian), and half under the goddess, Anunit. Sippar is known as Sepharvaim in the Old Testament, which alludes to the city in its dual form. Another Sippar was probably situated to the north, close to or part of early Agade.

City State of Shuruppak / Curuppag

Shuruppak began life near the beginning of the Jemdet Nasr Period, which ended with the Flood. The city was located at modern Tell Fa'rah, situated to the south of Nippur on the banks of the Euphrates. It was also known as Curuppag ('the healing place'). Dedicated to Sud (who was also called Ninlil), the goddess of grain and the air, it became a grain storage and distribution city, with more silos than any other Sumerian city.

Many of the gods depicted in ancient Sumerian art and sculptures have wings (Ereshkigal, Ishtar, Lilith, Marduk, Ninurta, Ashur) as angels do, even fallen angels (Ex 25:20, Ez 10, Is 6, Rev 14:6). This adds another fact that aligns with scripture as an indicator of the origins of these so-called gods.

The Egyptian King Lists

Manetho (Priest & Advisor to Ptolemy in 323 BC) King List

The following are excerpts and comments from LacusCurtius • Manetho's History of Egypt — Book I [17]

> **Fr. 1** (*from the Armenian Version of Eusebius, Chronica*).
> **Dynasties of Gods, Demigods, and Spirits of the Dead.**
>
> From the *Egyptian History* of Manetho, who composed his account in three books. These deal with the Gods, the Demigods, the Spirits of the Dead, and the mortal kings who ruled Egypt down to Darius, king of the Persians.
>
> The first man (or god) in Egypt is Hephaestus, who is also renowned among the Egyptians as the discoverer of fire. His son, Helios (the Sun), was succeeded by Sôsis; then follow, in turn, Cronos, Osiris, Typhon, brother of Osiris, and lastly Orus, son of Osiris and Isis. These were the first to hold sway in Egypt. Thereafter, the kingship passed from one to another in unbroken succession down to Bydis (Bites) through 13,900 years. The year I take, however, to be a lunar one, consisting, that is, of 30 days: what we now call a month the Egyptians used formerly to style a year.

So, the gods and demigods reigned for 1,255 years, then many other kings after that for a total of 3,957 years. Then the spirits of the dead and demigods reigned for 5,813 years for a total of 11,000 years, although the Egyptians reckon it to be 24,900 lunar years, equaling 2,206 solar years. After this Mestraïm, son of Ham, son of Noah, ventured out from Sumer with his clan after the Babel event and set himself as the first pharaoh of Egypt.

> But if the number of years is still in excess, it must be supposed that perhaps several Egyptian kings ruled at one and the same time; for they say that the rulers were kings of This, of Memphis, of Saïs, of Ethiopia, and of other places at the same time. It seems, moreover, that different kings held sway in different regions, and that each dynasty was confined to its own nome: thus it was not a succession of kings occupying the throne one after the other, but several kings reigning at the same time in different regions. Hence arose the great total number of years. But let us leave this question and take up in detail the chronology of Egyptian history [17].

The First Dynasty of Egypt

1. Hêphaestus reigned for 727¾ years.
2. Hêlios (the Sun), son of Hêphaestus, for 80⅙ years.
3. Agathodaemôn, for 56 7/12 years.
4. Cronos, for 40½ years.
5. Osiris and Isis, for 35 years.
6. Typhon, for 29 years.

Demigods:

7. Ôrus, for 25 years.
8. Arês, for 23 years.
9. Anubis, for 17 years.
10. Hêraclês, for 15 years.
11. Apollô, for 25 years.
12. Ammôn, for 30 years.
13. Tithoês, for 27 years.
14. Sôsus, for 32 years.
15. Zeus, for 20 years.

Many of the gods depicted in ancient Egyptian art and sculptures have wings (Isis, Ishtar, Ma'at, Horus, Ashur, Bes) as angels do, even fallen angels (Ex 25:20, Ez 10, Is 6, Rev 14:6). This adds another fact that aligns with scripture as an indicator of the origins of these so-called gods.

Just like the Sumerian King List and the Egyptian King List, there are Chinese antediluvian rulers referred to as the "Three Sovereigns and Five Emperors", of which one is the renowned "Yellow Emperor". The Three Sovereigns were recognized as demigods, offspring of the gods who mated with human women, and they too were accredited for having lived exceptionally long lives. Additionally, the story of the great Flood and the Noah-like character is also recited in their ancient historical records (Gun-Yu) [18].

The Indian Hindu Vedic (*Satapatha Brahmana*) and Puranas (the *Bhagavata Purana, the Matsya Purana*, and the *Mahabharata)* tell of the Gods, the Flood, Noah and sons. From the Ancient Origins;

In the *Satapatha Brahmana* Noah is known as Manu Vaivasvata, a holy man who knew God's favor. He had three sons, just as Noah did, with names very similar to Noah's sons. Ancient Origins cites:

> Also in many other ancient civilizations throughout the world. Accounts of a great deluge are seen in the Deucalion in Greek mythology, the lore of the K'iche' and Maya peoples in Mesoamerica, the stories of the Lac Courte Oreilles Ojibwa tribe of North America, and the stories of the Muisca people, to name but a few [19].

Many of the gods in ancient Chinese, Indian, and other cultures around the world are depicted in art and sculptures as having wings (Sirin, Ekek, Faravahar, Garuda, Huitzilopochtli, Lei Gong, Hermes, Mercury) as angels do, even fallen angels (Ex 25:20, Ez 10, Is 6, Rev 14:6). This adds another fact that aligns with scripture as an indicator of the origins of these so-called gods.

The Collaborating Evidence

These accounts from the Bible, king lists, and ancient chronicles all provide a consensus and a source of evidence that taken together supports and collaborates the basic truths of the Bible. There are no alternate histories to challenge or contradict these accounts. There is no supporting evidence to doubt or classify them as myths other than one's religious beliefs (humanism/atheism) or lack of being able to relate with such an untoward environment. Life before the Flood was quite unlike life as we know it. These seem to be the congruent themes:

1) **The antediluvian tenants lived extraordinarily long lives.**
2) **The manifestations of spiritual beings incarnate was common place.**
3) **Men worshiped these beings as gods.**
4) **Many of these gods had wings as the angels do.**
5) **All acknowledged Noah and the Flood as a demarcation in time and civilizations.**

The feeling we get when we hear these tantalizing accounts are initially counter-wise to our intuitive instincts (based on our entrenched upbringing in a secular world and an un-relatable state of affairs); however, what you have to do is reason outside of your nature affinity to trust in those feelings much like getting turned around in the woods. As a hunter, you often get lost in the woods and that's why you bring a compass. When you break out the compass and see the direction it is pointing, your initial impression is that it is counter-wise to the direction that you are feeling in the pit of your stomach; however, what you have to do is reason outside of your nature affinity to trust in these feelings and trust the compass and move in that direction. Next thing you know you are out of the woods and in the right place every time. This is very much the same thing, you have to reason outside of your nature affinity to trust in these feelings and move in the direction the consensus of the evidence is pointing in. Historical research protocols demands that you have a consensus of the records for it to be considered historically correct or an historical certainty. Here you have a consensus of the main subject matters with the previously reviewed evidence found in all the historical records before 1800 BC and no countering historical evidence. Science dictates that we must proceed in the direction that it is leading us and not trust in our emotions or feelings.

Dinosaurs and Man

Humans and dinosaurs were created in the same week and coexisted in separate habitats until the seasonal changes in environment after the Flood, lack of food sources for the great beasts, and conflict with humans leading to their extinction.

When God commanded Noah to build the Ark, he communicated to him that this would be a grand undertaking. This boat was designed by God to hold "all" the different "kinds" of animals in the world. This was not to include all the variations of animals within a species that were related by micro evolutionary adaptations. For instance, the wooly mammoth, the mastodon, and the elephant are of the same kind. Only one of their kind would have been on the Ark. DNA testing has found that the original progenitor of the elephant kind (species) is the African savanna elephant, of the horse is the zebra, of the domestic dog is the grey wolf, of the domestic cat is the African wild cat, of the pigeon is the rock pigeon, from which all the variations of those kinds of animals we have today originated. All of these original kinds would have come from Noah's Ark in about 2500BC. Furthermore, large beasts and predatory animals such as elephants, hippopotamus, *Tyrannosaurus rex*, stegosaurs, pterosaurs, *Brachiosaurus*, lions, alligators, etc. would have come as either infants or juveniles, thereby conserving room, food, and dangerous happenstance. Small marsupials (rats, rabbits, mice, etc.) would have multiplied quickly to ensure that there were sufficient prey animals during the later stay on the boat and released into the wild to sustain the predatory animals when coming of age. Hibernating animals such as bears, snakes, skunks, bats, groundhogs, and bees would have been in state for the journey. Store rooms for grain and hay and such would be well stocked. There of course would have been milk from cows and goats, as well as eggs from the fowls in abundance. The eight hosts would have been busy but have figured a routine to sustain the lot for the nine months at sea. I am sure they saw their share of miracles as well. Animals came on their own to the Ark lead by the spirit of God, while animals from afar had to have been transported by God to the boat. God closed the door before the rains came and would had to have equally transported the animals back to the habitation he set for them when leaving the Ark.

If the Bible is a true and accurate historic record regarding Noah's Ark, then you would expect to find evidence of dinosaurs such as the *T.rex*, stegosaurs, and pterosaurs.

This is exactly what you find in many epic tales such as *The Epic of Gilgamesh*, and *Beowulf*, in Chinese chronicles and writings of Marco Polo, Herodotus, Alexander the Great, in cave drawings and pottery decor, referred to in history as dragons and flying fiery serpents from every part of the globe, as a matter of fact!

Dinosaurs (Dragons) mentioned in the Bible [1].

Beasts that could only be dinosaurs (the behemoth and leviathan) are described in the chapters 40 and 41 of the book of Job, written about 1900BC.

Job 40:15: Behold now behemoth, which I made with thee; he eateth grass as an ox.

Job 40:16: Lo now, his strength is in his loins, and his force is in the navel of his belly.

Job 40:17: He moveth his tail like a cedar: the sinews of his stones are wrapped together.

Job 40:18: His bones are as strong pieces of brass; his bones are like bars of iron.

Job 40:19: He is the chief of the ways of God: he that made him can make his sword to approach unto him.

Job 40:20: Surely the mountains bring him forth food, where all the beasts of the field play.

Job 40:21: He lieth under the shady trees, in the covert of the reed, and fens.

Job 40:22: The shady trees cover him with their shadow; the willows of the brook compass him about.

Job 40:23: Behold, he drinketh up a river, and hasteth not: he trusteth that he can draw up Jordan into his mouth.

Job 40:24: He taketh it with his eyes: his nose pierceth through snares.

Job 41:1: Canst thou draw out leviathan with an hook? or his tongue with a cord which thou lettest down?

Job 41:2: Canst thou put an hook into his nose? or bore his jaw through with a thorn?

Job 41:3: Will he make many supplications unto thee? will he speak soft words unto thee?

Job 41:4: Will he make a covenant with thee? wilt thou take him for a servant for ever?

Job 41:5: Wilt thou play with him as with a bird? or wilt thou bind him for thy maidens?

Job 41:6: Shall the companions make a banquet of him? shall they part him among the merchants?

Job 41:7: Canst thou fill his skin with barbed iron? or his head with fish spears?

Job 41:8: Lay thine hand upon him, remember the battle, do no more.

Job 41:9: Behold, the hope of him is in vain: shall not one be cast down even at the sight of him?

Job 41:10: None is so fierce that dare stir him up: who then is able to stand before me?

Job 41:11: Who hath prevented me, that I should repay him? whatsoever is under the whole heaven is mine.

Job 41:12: I will not conceal his parts, nor his power, nor his comely proportion.

Job 41:13: Who can discover the face of his garment? or who can come to him with his double bridle?

Job 41:14: Who can open the doors of his face? his teeth are terrible round about.

Job 41:15: His scales are his pride, shut up together as with a close seal.

Job 41:16: One is so near to another, that no air can come between them.

Job 41:17: They are joined one to another, they stick together, that they cannot be sundered.

Job 41:18: By his neesings a light doth shine, and his eyes are like the eyelids of the morning.

Job 41:19: Out of his mouth go burning lamps, and sparks of fire leap out.

Job 41:20: Out of his nostrils goeth smoke, as out of a seething pot or caldron.

Job 41:21: His breath kindleth coals, and a flame goeth out of his mouth.

Job 41:22: In his neck remaineth strength, and sorrow is turned into joy before him.

Job 41:23: The flakes of his flesh are joined together: they are firm in themselves; they cannot be moved.

Job 41:24: His heart is as firm as a stone; yea, as hard as a piece of the nether millstone.

Job 41:25: When he raiseth up himself, the mighty are afraid: by reason of breakings they purify themselves.

Job 41:26: The sword of him that layeth at him cannot hold: the spear, the dart, nor the habergeon.

Job 41:27: He esteemeth iron as straw, and brass as rotten wood.

Job 41:28: The arrow cannot make him flee: slingstones are turned with him into stubble.

Job 41:29: Darts are counted as stubble: he laugheth at the shaking of a spear.

Job 41:30: Sharp stones are under him: he spreadeth sharp pointed things upon the mire.

Job 41:31: He maketh the deep to boil like a pot: he maketh the sea like a pot of ointment.

Job 41:32: He maketh a path to shine after him; one would think the deep to be hoary.

Job 41:33: Upon earth there is not his like, who is made without fear.

Job 41:34: He beholdeth all high things: he is a king over all the children of pride.

Dragons and flying fiery serpents are referred to as a matter of fact throughout the Old Testament.

Dragons in scripture

Deut 32:33: Their wine is the poison of dragons, and the cruel venom of asps.

Neh 2:13: And I went out by night by the gate of the valley, even before the dragon well, and to the dung port, and viewed the walls of Jerusalem, which were broken down, and the gates thereof were consumed with fire.

Job 30:29: I am a brother to dragons, and a companion to owls.

Psalms 44:19: Though thou hast sore broken us in the place of dragons, and covered us with the shadow of death.

Psalms 74:13: Thou didst divide the sea by thy strength: thou brakest the heads of the dragons in the waters.

Psalms 91:13: Thou shalt tread upon the lion and adder: the young lion and the dragon shalt thou trample under feet.

Psalms 148:7: Praise the LORD from the earth, ye dragons, and all deeps:

Isa 13:22: And the wild beasts of the islands shall cry in their desolate houses, and dragons in their pleasant palaces: and her time is near to come, and her days shall not be prolonged.

Isa 27:1: In that day the LORD with his sore and great and strong sword shall punish leviathan the piercing serpent, even leviathan that crooked serpent; and he shall slay the dragon that is in the sea.

Isa 34:13: And thorns shall come up in her palaces, nettles and brambles in the fortresses thereof: and it shall be an habitation of dragons, and a court for owls.

Isa 35:7: And the parched ground shall become a pool, and the thirsty land springs of water: in the habitation of dragons, where each lay, shall be grass with reeds and rushes.

Isa 43:20: The beast of the field shall honour me, the dragons and the owls: because I give waters in the wilderness, and rivers in the desert, to give drink to my people, my chosen.

Isa 51:9: Awake, awake, put on strength, O arm of the LORD; awake, as in the ancient days, in the generations of old. Art thou not it that hath cut Rahab, and wounded the dragon?

Pterosaurs (fiery flying serpent) mentioned in the Bible

Isa 14:29: Rejoice not thou, whole Palestina, because the rod of him that smote thee is broken: for out of the serpent's root shall come forth a cockatrice, and his fruit shall be a fiery flying serpent.

Isa 30:6: The burden of the beasts of the south: into the land of trouble and anguish, from whence come the young and old lion, the viper and fiery flying serpent, they will carry their riches upon the shoulders of young asses, and their treasures upon the bunches of camels, to a people that shall not profit them[26].

Many creationists believe that the stories of dragons could possibly be dinosaurs, as the term "dinosaur" was not used until 1841. Indeed, the multitude of stories and descriptions of these dragons yield in favor of these creatures being living contemporary dinosaurs. Dragons are depicted in stories, art, and drawings on textiles and pottery in most all the countries around the world dated as far back as recorded history. *The Epic of Gilgamesh* and *Beowulf* are both believed to be great battles with predatory dinosaurs [20, 21]. How could so many ancient cultures living as far apart and isolated from each other as the South American natives and peoples of Cambodia depict creatures (dragons) in almost identical features as each other and congruent with the features of dinosaurs? The thunderbird is a good example, as it has been encountered and described in such detail from many diverse cultures though out the world. Without a doubt, the descriptions fit the pterosaurs in almost every aspect – truly a fearful sight to behold.

Based on the fossil record, the majority of larger predatory dinosaurs, such as *T.rex* and *Allosaurus*, lived in remote areas apart from mainstream civilizations in the Midwest of North America (Utah, Arizona, Texas, Wyoming, Dakotas, etc.), East Asia (Mongolia), and possibly Australia before the Flood. In a Pangaea state, that would be the outermost reaches from the interior continent, as separate continents that would be next door via the Bering Strait's land bridge of old. Afterwards, they would have roamed about in isolated areas near the warmer climates for a short span of time. The change in environment (seasonal weather versus greenhouse effect conditions before the Flood), lack of abundant food sources, and human conflict eventually saw their extinction. Evolutionists place these creatures in the Cretaceous period (85-65MM years ago) first discovered in 1902.

Stegosaurus fossils have been found in North America (Colorado, Utah, Wyoming, etc.), China, Mongolia, Africa, and Europe. They would have lasted longer than the larger dinosaurs but appear to have gone extinct due to human hunting. Evolutionists place these creatures in the Jurassic period (156-145MM years ago) first discovered in 1876.

Triceratops fossils have been found in North America in Colorado, Utah, and Wyoming. They would have lasted longer than the larger dinosaurs but appear to have gone extinct due to human hunting. Evolutionists place these creatures in the Cretaceous period (68-65MM years ago), first discovered in 1887.

Brachiosaurus fossils have been found in North America, Portugal, Tanzania, Africa, and Europe. These would have gone extinct quickly with the change in environment after the Flood due their enormous size. Evolutionists place these creatures in the Jurassic period (150-100MM years ago), first discovered in 1914 [8].

Evolutionists claim that the strata show how creatures of one period gave way to the next generation of evolved species and then went extinct because of "natural selection", and that is why they don't normally show up in the next level of strata. Several species (e.g., Coelacanth fish, Jurassic Shrimp, Dawn Redwood, and Gingko Trees) still alive today show up in the fossil records from the Devonian to Cretaceous periods but not in the intermediate periods. Certainly, they did not go extinct then re-emerge. A fossilized cat with a small dinosaur found in its belly was discovered in China in

2003, purported to be from 130 million years ago. This supports the creationist model undergirding the theory that the geological strata represent different habitats caught up in the multiple, sequential cataclysmic events as opposed to living in different time periods. Most modern plants and animals can be found in these fossil records; they have not gone extinct per natural selection. Modern animals and plants such as flamingos, sandpipers, penguins, cormorants, parrots, owls and including numerous types of mammals, reptiles, amphibians, and arthropods are often found with the dinosaur fossils over 65 million years old, which is not supposed to be, as these creatures are supposed to have evolved millions of years after those time periods according to evolution theory [22, 23].

Fossiliferous strata are mostly found near multiple cataclysmic catalysts such as volcanoes, tectonic plates, flood plains, mud slides, and meteor sites, which is why you find them in abundance in select areas. Dinosaurs were probably in many other locations but were not fossilized because of the lack of these catalysts in those areas [8]. It would appear that most fossils found in the rock strata all over the world were the result of the global Flood and ensuing cataclysmic events.

Drawing of dinosaurs in the hunting painting found in Kuwait. Dinosaur bones were also found in the cave along with the drawings. Secular scientists confirmed authenticity with C14 dating.
The scientific community believes these Neanderthals found the bones, pieced them together, and imaged them [24].

Figure 1.4 Cave drawing of dinosaurs in the hunting party

Modern science can barely find enough bones to get a small part of any of these creatures, and yet these Neanderthals could take time from the daily survival to play with bones and have enough wherewithal to piece it together correctly...amazing!

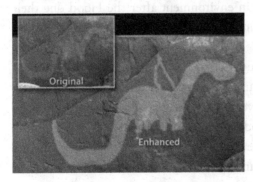

(Left): Figure 1.5 A very distinctive petroglyph of an *Apatosaurus* found at the Natural Bridge Monument in SE Utah (500 to 1500 years old) [25]. The official stance from the scientific communtity on this is that this is a serpent and the legs were stain runs. Really? Four symmetric stain runs where feet normally go, same shade and sharpness as the drawing!

(Right): Figure 1.6 Carvings of a dinosaur in head – to – head combat with a mammoth in Bemifal Cave in S. France. The French government has actually closed this to the public, as well as other caves that apparently have similar depictions with dinosaurs[25].

From GenPack site (reprinted with permission):

> About 4,000 years ago, the Hongshan culture in China produced many wonderful jade dragon carvings (along with other clear animal representations). Over time these dragon productions became highly stylized and were especially popular as pendants. Most of these pieces only resemble dragons in a crude sense, but a few of the older dragon statues appear to be reproductions of certain dinosaurs. Notice the resemblance this jade dragon (lower left) bears to a small *Protoceratops* dinosaur. In the middle is a "baby dragon" carving. It appears to resemble an immature pterosaur, perhaps freshly out of the egg. Its body is still curled and the wings appear immature. Both the baby dragon and the unusual, red carving on the right, are part of the Genesis Park collection.

Protoceratops

www.GenesisPark.com

Figures 1.7a 1.7b 1.7c 1.7d

(Left) Figure 1.8 This "thunderbird" (petroglyph of a pterosaur) was discovered in Black Dragon Canyon, Utah where fossils of the same creature depicted in this cave drawing were discovered close by in Big Ben National Park in the Javelina Formation. This figure, about 7 feet long from wing-tip to wing-tip, is actually painted with a dark-red pigment. Native Americans of the Fremont culture are thought to have inhabited the "Swell" between 700 and 1250 A.D. Black Dragon Canyon is named for the pictograph which resembles a large bat wing reptile with a head crest [25].

A review of numerous historic documentation of encounters with dinosaurs from famous historical charictures will be reviewed in relation to the nations that they are associated with in Parts 4 & 5 of this publications. The writings of Marco Polo, Herodotus the Greek historian, the recordings of Alexander the Great's conquests, and the Chinese chronicles have very detailed descriptions of the beasts and of their interactions with mankind and other animals.

Historical research protocols demand that you have a consensus of the records for it to be considered historically correct or an historical certainty. Here you have a consensus of the main subject matters with the previously reviewed evidence found in historical records.

Zoology – The earth's climate before the Flood had a profound effect on the animal kingdom. With greater carbon dioxide gases in the pre-Flood era causing a worldwide greenhouse effect in the earth, along with a more aligned axis, earth would have been significantly hotter with little variation in season changes. Science has concluded that animals, especially reptilian, grow larger in warmer climates than their cousins do in cooler climates, supporting the theory of microevolution (adaptations within a species based on climatic conditions). Additionally, some animals, especially reptiles, continue to grow as long as they live. Today you will find snakes, turtles, and crocodiles near the equator significantly larger than species of the same kind the farther away you get from the equator. Below is a table comparing extinct species found in the fossil records to living species of the same family. The massive size of the pre-Flood creatures, three times more massive on average, would indicate that it was significantly hotter in the Antediluvian era and testifies to the longer lives they must have lived.

Antediluvian Era Species	Area	Size	Modern Species	Area	Size	Times Larger
Short–faced Bear	S. AM	3.5k lbs.	Brown Bear	N. Am	1.5k lbs.	2.3
Titanoboa	S. AM	2k lbs. x 50'	Giant Anaconda	S. AM	.5k lbs. x 25'	4.0
Croc (*Sarcosuchus*)	Global	17.5k lbs. x 40'	Salty (Crocodylus)	Asia	2k lbs. x 20'	8.8
Turtle (*Archelon*)	N. Am	4.8k lbs.	Leatherback	Global	1.5k lbs.	3.2
Shark (Megalodon)	Global	60'	White Shark	Global	20'	3.0
Giant Sloth	Americas	2.4k lbs.	Three-toed sloth	S. Am	10 lbs.	240.0
Smilodon	Americas	.9k lbs.	Siberian Tiger	Russia	.9k lbs.	1.0

Table References [26, 27, 28, 29, 30, 31, 32, 33, 34, 35, 36, 37]

Historical and Scientific Facts that Support the Creation Model of the Earth.

Radiometric Dating:

All living things take in carbon (C^{12} and C^{14}) from eating and breathing as result of cosmic rays entering into the atmosphere. The ratio of C^{14} to C^{12} is the same as in the atmosphere while an organism is alive. This ratio today is about one C^{14} atom for every 1 trillion C^{12} atoms. This ratio is the basis for determining the age of a fossil. When an organism dies, the amount of C^{12} will remain constant, but the amount of C^{14} will decrease at a predictable rate of degradation. The longer an organism has been dead, the smaller the ratio. The following table shows how the age is estimated using this ratio.

% C14 Remaining	% C12 Remaining	Ratio	Number of 1/2 Lives	Years Dead (Age of Fossil)
100	100	1 / 1T	0	0
50	100	1 / 2T	1	5,730
25	100	1 / 4T	2	11,460
12.5	100	1 / 8T	3	17,190
6.25	100	1 / 16T	4	22,920
3.125	100	1 / 32T	5	28,650

The Decay Factors of the Earth's Core, Magnetic Field, and C^{14} Dating.

The earth's dipole magnetic field has been decaying at approximately 10% over the past 150 years, and the decay rate appears to be on an exponential curve. There is a direct correlation between the strength of the magnetic field around the earth, known as the magnetosphere, and the freely decaying electrical currents found circulating in the earth's core; hence, the magnetic field is decaying congruent with the entropy of the free circulating electrical currents of the earth's molten core.

The sciences behind these assumptions are aligned with both Sir Horace Lamb's 1883 theory and mathematical formula of free electrical current circulating in a conducting sphere and evaluations measuring the magnetic strength and direction of the force by Carl Fredrick Gauss in 1835. Extrapolating the decay rate in reverse on an expected exponential curve would put the optimum strength of the magnetic field in 4000 BC, the approximate time of creation, at such a magnitude that it would virtually reflect most cosmic radiation from entering the earth's atmosphere, resulting in less C^{14} build up in the plants and other living organisms when coupled with the greenhouse effect that existed before the Flood. Based on this evidence, C^{14} based dating is in gross error as used by the secular scientist. The further back in time, the less C^{14} build up is misinterpreted as decay and given extraneous dates. This theory postulated by Dr. Thomas G. Barnes aligns with basic physics of electrical current resistance and entropy. Theories put forth by the secular scientist have to defy or ignore these well-established sciences as they theorize that the present state of the magnetic field is just in a reversal mode based on reversals of magnetic polarizations seen in the earth's strata related data perpetuated by some unknown dynamo source; however, they have no scientific empirical evidence to support the mechanisms for these dynamo postulations. There is therefore no sound scientific reason to believe this is the case, no scientific connection between the two. Dr. Russel Humphreys suggests that at the start of the flood the earth's core experienced some significantly powerful energy surges as "the fountains of the deep were broken up" that produce rapid reversals in the magnet field, which aligns well with the general laws of physics as is exemplified in the reversals measured in the sun in this day and age. These actions would create eddy current moments within the molten core that would produce separate higher-order magnetic components (quadruple, octopole, etc.). These eddy currents would start to dissipate in an attenuating resonance, yielding to entropy and resistance of the more massive flows. The overall dipole orientation would begin to go through reversals based on which subcomponent's total energy were momentarily dominant during the decaying process. The life cycles would of course depend on the size and angular velocities of the subcomponents. These reversals can easily be fitted into the global Flood model as the polarizations found in these strata were formed during rock formations that predominantly resulted from tectonic and volcanic activity. Disruption due to energy surges in the earth's core, free electrical currents, and the tectonic movements within earth's crust on a scale of the catastrophic events of a global Flood could easily account for the reversals evident in these rock strata. Secular scientists believe there must be a dynamo (spinning core) source with-in the earth maintaining a constant energy output for the spinning core velocities and strength of the magnetosphere to have been sustained all these billions of years. Several hypotheses are put forth; however, these hypotheses are without scientific proof or evidence. The empirical evidence to date shows a steady decrease in strength (-10%) over the past 150 years. As a matter of fact, with the discovery of the magnetic field about the planet Mercury, the elements required for the dynamo theory to work are diminished.

	Year	M
1	1835	8.522
2	1845	8.468
3	1885	8.371
4	1900	8.321
5	1905	8.300
6	1910	8.272
7	1915	8.235
8	1920	8.195
9	1925	8.160
10	1930	8.129
11	1935	8.106
12	1940	8.091
13	1945	8.075
14	1950	8.064
15	1955	8.051
16	1960	8.028
17	1965	8.005
18	1970	7.973
19	1975	7.939
20	1980	7.907
21	1985	7.871
22	1990	7.841
23	1995	7.814
24	2000	7.790
25	2005	7.767
26	2010	7.746

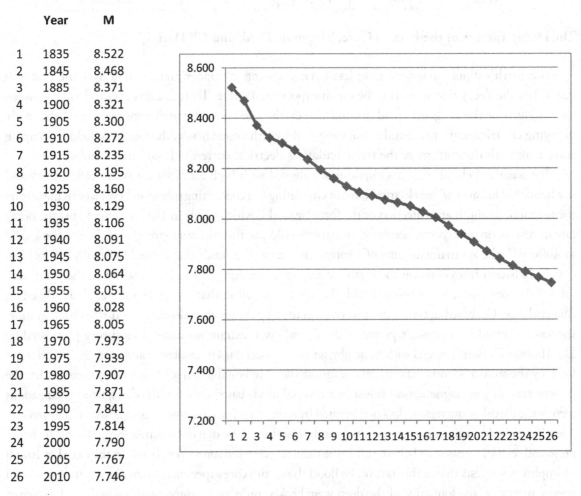

Chart showing the decaying Magnetosphere from 1835 to 2010

The magnetic moment in 1984 was 7.9 x 10^22 Jules per Tesla (1 J/T = 1 Amp-M^2 =1000 Gauss/cm^3)

It was predicted to not have a magnetic field due to its slow rotation, but it does (as expected by the creation model). They have expectations of a reversal or upward moment, in the strength of the earth's magnetic field, happening sometime in the near future based on their dynamo theory; they have had this expectation disappointed for decades. Scientific protocol demands that you have a consensus of the data for it to be considered scientifically valid or a scientific certainty. Where there is no consensus and you inadvertently pick and choose values that agree with your theory or your belief then you have moved into the arena of pseudoscience.

Secular scientists use C^{14} to date subject matters on a linear extrapolation based on the current decay rate without considering the very viable possibility that the magnetosphere was increasingly stronger the further back in time, significantly affecting the magnitude of C^{14} build and estimated decay rate. All secular dates based on C^{14} dating should be adjusted based on the percentage reduction given in the charts below. Even then, there will be a significant margin of error due to unknown environmental factors (magnitude of volcanic activity, cloud coverage, bio population, greenhouse gas percentage, etc.) during the Antediluvian and Ice Age periods [38].

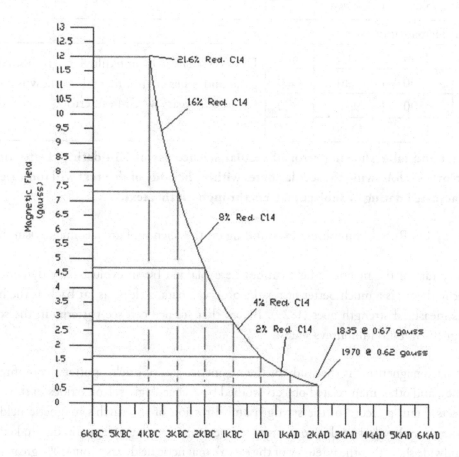

Era	Year	M Strength Gauss	<% C14	
AD	2000	0.62	0.0	Greater margin of error when taking into account unknown environmental conditions affecting the C14 buildup.
	1500	0.81	0.8	
	1000	1.00	1.4	
AD	500	1.35	2.1	The 500 year Ice Age after the Flood would have significant effect on environmental conditions (volcanic aerosols and reflections off the ice).
BC	0	1.70	2.8	
	500	2.30	3.4	
	1000	2.90	4.5	
	1500	3.80	5.5	
	2000	4.70	7.0	
	2400	5.78	7.8	
Flood Demarcation				
	2540	6.05	8.0	Unknown effect of antediluvian greenhouse gases and other environmental unknowns (up to 60K years w/ C14 est. error).
	3000	7.40	12.0	
	3500	9.70	16.0	
BC	4000	12.00	21.6	

Chart and table showing error of secular science use of C14 dating. Dates in parentheses following the secular dates within the body of this text will indicate an adjusted dating of subject matters throughout this text.

In an article by Dr. Russel Humphreys expounding on the science of archaeomagnetism, he points out that [11, 39]:

The decay rate of the magnetic field cannot be explained by an evolutionary dynamo theory. The free-decay theory is a much better fit for the observed data, at least as far back as the historical record of its measured strength goes (1829). Before that science can see patterns in the science of Archaeomagnetism. Dr. Humphreys states:

> "Archaeomagnetism" is the study of the magnetization of bricks, pottery, campfire stones, and other man-related objects studied by archaeologists. Iron oxides in those objects retain a record of the strength and direction of the earth's magnetic field at the time they last cooled to normal temperatures. Archaeomagnetic data taken worldwide show that the intensity of the earth's magnetic field was about 40% greater in 1000 A.D. than it is today, and that it has declined steadily since then.

This decay rate in no way fits into the evolutionary estimate of the age of the earth (4.5by) as it would have been too harmful to the environment at the estimated strength that it would have had to have been at that time.

Creationists of the 1970s extrapolated today's decay back into the past, showing that the field could not be more than about 10,000 years old, assuming a constant decay of intensity.

The archaeomagnetic data actually shows a major fluctuation in the field's surface intensity (and field polarizations) starting in about 2500 BC and slowly attenuating until about the time of Christ where it peaked out at about 50% higher than today. From that time, it shows a steady decrease until it came into balance with the core intensity in about 1000 AD where it has been steadily declining along a calculated exponential curve up to its present magnitude of strength.

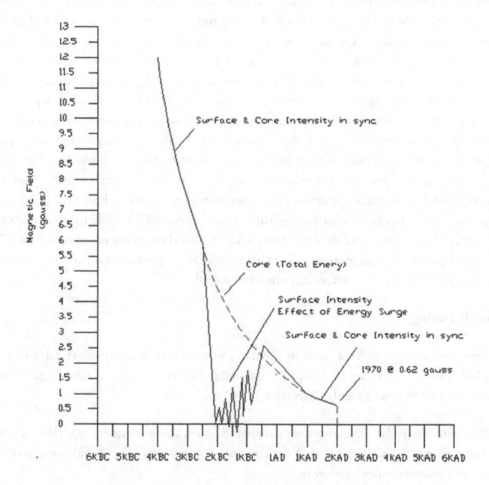

Figure 1 - Magnetic intensities and reversals

These reversals can easily be fitted into a global Flood model as the polarizations found in these strata were formed during rock formations that predominantly resulted from tectonic and volcanic activity during the period of the flood and continental drift that may have progressed until 1000AD. Disruption due to energy surges in the earth's core, free electrical currents, and the tectonic movements within the earth's crust on a scale of the catastrophic events of the global Flood could easily account for the reversals evident in these rock strata. All entropy and electrical resistance norms appear to have continued at a steady exponential decay along the predicted lines of decay and evidently came back to a balance in about 1000AD. The evidence in the archaeomagnetic data in conjunction with the empirical data recorded for the past 150 years collaborates together to confirm:

1) the continuous decay of the magnetosphere over several millennia;
2) the 2500 BC demarcation; and
3) the 6,000 year biblical age of he earth.

The Decay Factors of the Planetary Magnetic Fields

In 1984 Dr. Humphreys took Dr. Barnes' theory on the exponential decay factors of the strength of earth's magnetic field when extrapolated backwards and came up with a model for the life cycle of the Earth's, magnetosphere. This model was based on the age of the universe as given in the Bible, the planetary masses, the atomic spins of H_2O, and a certain k factor (k=0.25 in almost all cases) to apply to other planets in the solar system. He then modeled several planetary magnetic fields such the Sun, Moon, Mercury, Mars, Venus, Jupiter and Saturn. His model not only rightly predicted the known values of the sun, moon, and other nearby planets, it also predicted what we would find when we got close enough to Uranus in 1986 and Neptune in 1989 via the Voyager II and was precisely correct. Secular scientists are not only baffled by what we are finding as opposed to their modeled predictions, they flatly refuse to even acknowledge Dr. Humphreys' keen scientific prowess. Dr. Humphreys' models have made predictions for outer planetary bodies such as certain white dwarf stars, and creationists anxiously wait for the time when science will be able to gather more outer planetary data. These results serve to verify that the creationist theories are based on sound scientific principle, intelligent deduction, more than just chance due the complexity of the model, and are more scientifically valid than the theories secular scientists postulate [40].

Radiometric Dating

Radiometric dating of rocks, as used by secular scientists, does not give dependable or accurate age dates based on linear extrapolation of the decay rates. The basic elements effecting Radiometric dating of rocks are ignored by secular scientists.

a. The system must be a closed system - there is no such thing in nature as a closed system.
b. The rock must initially be void of the daughter components - the initial components of an ancient system cannot be known.
c. The process rate must have always been the same - no process rate is unchangeable.

Uranium 238 decays to lead (Pb) 206 + 8 Helium (He) atoms [1/2 life 4.5 billion years]
Uranium 235 decays to Pb207 + 7He atoms [1/2 life 0.7 billion years]
Thorium 232 decays to Pb208 + 7He atoms [1/2 life 14.1 billion years]

Example of a. [open system] - Uranium can be leachable by ground water, radon gas moves in and out of uranium systems. Uranium and lead both migrate in and out of shales and pitchblende veins and lunar systems in geological times. The "free neutron capture" phenomena can convert lead (e.g.,

Pb206 to Pb207, Pb207 to Pb208) due to free neutrons in the mineral's environment being captured by the lead, which can result in false ages if based on the normal decay factors of uranium or thorium.

Example of b. [daughter comp.]- Modern day rocks formed from magma commonly contain uranium minerals and the radiogenic as well as common lead when the lava cools and crystallizes. Many of these newly formed volcanic rocks have tested to a billion years.

Example of c. [process rate] - Uranium decay rates can be increased by cosmic radiation and its production of neutrinos, this is also the same effect for free neutron capture. Incidences such as these can be caused by reversals in the earth's magnetic fields or supernova explosions from a nearby star.

Based on these factors, the results of testing earth rocks, moon rocks, and meteorites with these radiometric dating methods should not be considered valid. In conclusion, there is to date no reliable, sure, or absolute means of radiometric dating to determine the age of the earth, solar system, or universe[22].

C^{14} testing of dinosaur bones, that are purported to be millions of years old, have been found with significant traces of C^{14} in most all specimens tested. Significant traces are indications that the specimen is less than 50,000 years old based on the half-life decay rate of C^{14}. Secular scientists quickly dismiss these results, claiming they must be contaminated; nevertheless, they hold fast to the uranium/thorium dating methods subject to the same possible contaminations that all open systems may have without missing a beat. Additionally, the majority of the results of C^{14} testing (>50%) are thrown out as skewed because they don't fit the assumed age of a palaeo-sample and will keep testing until they get a result that fits their models (pseudoscience) [22].

The Genome

These basic cells are a combination of interrelated functions of complex molecules (protein/DNA/RNA/carbohydrates) with a sophisticated relationship that cannot exist independently. The basic simplest cell is so complex, being programmed with pre-coded commands that are time released to give the organism its physical appearance and nature, that the basic "life started one stormy night in a primordial soup" is comparable to a tornado sweeping through a junkyard and leaving behind a fully functional Boeing 747, or a hurricane sweeping through a forest and leaving behind a storehouse of dictionaries and encyclopedias complete with deer skin covers and pages full of definitions and subject matter in alpha numeric sequence, which any rational or critical thinker would know to be impossible [2].

Geneticists have concluded that from generation to generation there is a mutation factor in the genetic make-up of living organisms, copying errors in the male DNA and female mtDNA, which can be calculated at over 100 mutations per generation in the DNA and fits well with the entropy or degeneration of aging, health, and other side effects. This allowed for non-harmful results at the beginning of creation with marrying close relatives, such as the sons and daughters of Adam and Eve, before the build-up of deleterious effects of these mutations [5, 6].

Geneticists have concluded that all people alive today come from a specific individual male and female, which is congruent with the Bible. Although their dating of these individuals is not congruent, their dating methods are obviously flawed, as we shall see [4].

Archeology

There are no undisputed examples of transitional species either in the fossil record or in the hundreds of thousands of species alive today. If the theory of evolution were, true there would be an abundance of evidence in the fossil records. Evolutionists now postulate a punctuated equilibrium theory (a negative argument) to account for the missing evidence, saying that the change now happens not over millions of years but quickly, perhaps in a generation or two, and so is not able to be captured in the fossil record. It is worth noting that this has never been witnessed or demonstrated in the past several decades that science has been investigating [22, 41].

Soft tissue was discovered in *T.rex* bone by Mary Schweitzer, and many other dinosaur bones since then. This supports a short time period since the extinction of the dinosaur. Mary believes the soft tissue was preserved for millions of years due to iron elements in the system. [22]

C^{14} testing of coal, diamonds, and dinosaur bones, that are purported to be millions of years old, have been found with significant traces of C^{14} in most all specimens tested. (Significant traces are indications that the specimen is less than 50,000 years old). Secular scientists dismiss these results, claiming they must be contaminated. Informed creation scientists, like members of the RATE (Radioisotopes and the Age of the Earth) team, contend that the modern "AMS measurements carefully eliminate all possible sources of carbon contamination. These include any trace of C^{14} which has possibly entered the samples in recent history, or C^{14} introduction during sample preparation and analysis" [22].

The earmarks of civilizations (community buildings, streets, music, writing, etc.) appear throughout the world in the archeological record just after the biblical time of the Creation ...that is in every region on earth, all congruent with biblical chronology [9].

Examples of archeological pre-Flood versus post–Flood cultures: Note that many of the dates are estimated using the C^{14} dating methods that have been reasonably shown to have gross error. Therefore, the dates are generally off by 50 to 60,000 years, especially if the article was from the Antediluvian period. All these cultures were established after the noted time of creation and came to an abrupt end between 2500 - 2300 BC according to archaeological findings.

Parentheses denote C^{14} adjustment due to the estimated strength of the magnetosphere at that time period in conjunction with biblical chronology not considered by secular scientists [38].

Mesopotamia - Mesopotamia is considered the birthplace of civilization. Most of the ancient writings (the code of Ur-Nammu, The Kish Tablets, the many Sumerian King Lists and *The Epic of Gilgamesh*) that are extant come from that region, supposedly dating as far back as 3500-3000BC (2400-2200BC). Archeologist Ernest Wright states there is an *occupation (gap) between Early Bronze Age and the Middle Bronze Age*. There is a pre/post Flood demarcation in all of the extant Sumerian King Lists. Many of the stories tell of the Creation, the extraordinary long lives and times of the Antediluvian era, the Flood, and Noah's descendants [9, 21, 42].

Palestine – Kathleen Kenyon noted a demarcation (gap) in Jericho (and all of Palestine) occupation continuity.

Finally, cultures with technology to make pottery arrived at Jericho. These Pottery Neolithic A and B peoples (ca. 5200-4000 B.C. [3500-2500 B.C.]) were otherwise unimpressive. The first group lived in pits cut into the ruins of the earlier town, and the second eventually began to build huts and simple houses. A gap in the occupation then proceeded what K called the Proto-Urban Period (ca. 3300-3150 B.C. [2500-2200 B.C.]) but most other archaeologists designated Early Bronze Age I. (Miriam C. Davis book *Dame* Kathleen Kenyon * Digging Up The Holy Land, pg 130)

Egyptian Culture - As with Mesopotamia, there is a demarcation in all of the many diverse king lists of Egypt, with the Pharaoh Narmer listed as the first king after the flood. The historical records show separate kingdoms throughout that region before the Flood and one united kingdom under Narmer's rule after the Flood (between the old and middle Kingdoms). The oldest known historical document in the world is known as the Narmer Palette, which lists Narmer as the oldest verifiable king of Egypt. Narmer was also known as Menes or Mizraim, which was recorded in both the Bible and the Egyptian King Lists as well as other ancient references. The Bible and the king list by Manetho both acknowledge Narmer as the son of Ham, who was the son of Noah. French archaeologist Carl Schaffer also notes the demarcation between the Old and Middle Kingdoms within the strata. [17, 43].

Europe - By 4500BC (3300) farming was widespread throughout Western Europe, Britain, and Scandinavia. Large stone circles, called henges, started showing up in the third millennium, dotting the countryside's in Northwest Europe. These henges are believed to have religious and astronomical functions but may have also provided a central refuge from warring invaders. These were great undertakings that are characteristic of chiefdoms led by powerful ruling elite [9]. French archaeologist Carl Schaffer tells of his discoveries of demarcations from Crete and Ras Shamira (Ugarit) from about 2200 BC that coincided with the same strata of demarcations in the Middle East and Europe.

Figure 1.9   **Figure 1.10**

Skara Brae (Scotland) - Believed to have been established in 3100BC and abandoned for unknown reasons in 2500BC, congruent with the Flood demarcation. It consists of eight clustered houses. There are notable earthwork structures in a circular pattern believed to have been used for religious ceremony[9].

Stonehenge (England) - Believed to have been started building in 3100BC with the latest editions in 2500BC, congruent with the Flood demarcation. It is composed of earthworks with several large standing stones set about in a circular pattern believed to have been used for religious ceremony. Only a global Flood event could have carried these stones off and not leave a clue to where they ended up. Buried beneath the surface in the surrounding countryside are more similar stones and patterns[9].

Figure 1.11 Stonehenge

Cycladic Civilization (Greece) - The chronology of Cycladic civilization is divided into three major sequences: Early, Middle and Late Cycladic. The early period, beginning in 3000 BC, segued into the archaeologically murkier Middle Cycladic, circa 2500-2200BC, reflecting the demarcation congruent with Noah's Flood. By the end of the late Cycladic sequence (1500BC) there was essential convergence between Cycladic and Minoan civilization[44].

The Indus Valley Civilization (NW India & Pakistan) - Signs of life began in 3500BC when the land started being inhabited by scattered farmers and small towns. After the global Flood demarcation point, 2600BC (2300) the first cities were built [9].

East Asian Civilization (China) - Chinese legend has it that civilization began in 2698 with Emperor Huang Di, the "Yellow Emperor", of which there are no archeological finds to date. Just after the global Flood demarcation, the first Dynasty (Xia) was founded by Yu the Great in 2205, which has some archeological backing [9].

Sechin Bajo (Peru) - Believed to have been established in 3500BC based on C14 dating, it now sports the crown for the oldest known settlement. Relatively little is known about the people who lived there. The oldest building was determined with C14 to have stood from 3700BC (3500) to 2900BC (2500), reflecting the demarcation congruent with Noah's Flood. The second and third buildings were found to have been built and used much later, between 1600BC to 1200BC. There are notable earthwork structures in a circular pattern believed to have been used for religious ceremony. Scientists say settlements were beginning to grow in Peru about the time of urbanization in cradles of civilization such as Mesopotamia, Egypt, and India. These temples are very similar to the Sumerian Temples in shape, size, and varying elevations[45, 46].

Scientific protocol demands that you have a consensus of the data for it to be considered scientifically valid or a scientific certainty. Here you have a consensus of the data with the previously reviewed scientific evidence and demarcations in the archeological evidence in and about the time of the flood.

The Final Decree, the wages of sin is death.

The first lesson we learn about the nature of man is that his base nature without limits, without constraint, without the Word of God, is barbaric and knows no bounds to his corruption and evil deeds. Even given a thousand years to find wisdom, understanding, and strength to repent, man fails to do so and falls short of the glory of God.

Psalms 14:1: The fool hath said in his heart, there is no God. They are corrupt, they have done abominable works, there is none that doeth good.

Psalms 14:3: They are all gone aside, they are all together become filthy: there is none that doeth good, no, not one.

Rom 3:10: As it is written, there is none righteous, no, not one:

Rom 3:11: There is none that understandeth, there is none that seeketh after God.

Rom 3:12: They are all gone out of the way, they are together become unprofitable; there is none that doeth good, no, not one.

Gen 6:6-7 And it repented the LORD that he had made man on the earth, and it grieved him at his heart. And the LORD said, I will destroy man whom I have created from the face of the earth; both man, and beast, and the creeping thing, and the fowls of the air; for it repenteth me that I have made them.

Noah and Sons Saved in the Ark.

Gen 6:8-9 But Noah found grace in the eyes of the LORD. These are the generations of Noah: Noah was a just man and perfect in his generations, and Noah walked with God.

The Flood

Gen 6:13: And God said unto Noah, the end of all flesh is come before me; for the earth is filled with violence through them; and, behold, I will destroy them with the earth.

Gen 6:14: Make thee an ark of gopher wood; rooms shalt thou make in the ark, and shalt pitch it within and without with pitch.

Gen 6:15: And this is the fashion which thou shalt make it of: The length of the ark shall be three hundred cubits, the breadth of it fifty cubits, and the height of it thirty cubits.

Gen 6:16: A window shalt thou make to the ark, and in a cubit shalt thou finish it above; and the door of the ark shalt thou set in the side thereof; with lower, second, and third stories shalt thou make it.

Gen 6:17: And, behold, I, even I, do bring a flood of waters upon the earth, to destroy all flesh, wherein is the breath of life, from under heaven; and everything that is in the earth shall die.

Gen 7:11: In the six hundredth year of Noah's life, in the second month, the seventeenth day of the month, the same day were all the fountains of the great deep broken up, and the windows of heaven were opened.

Gen 7:17: And the flood was forty days upon the earth; and the waters increased, and bare up the ark, and it was lift up above the earth.

Gen 7:19: And the waters prevailed exceedingly upon the earth; and all the high hills, that were under the whole heaven, were covered.

Gen 7:20: Fifteen cubits upward did the waters prevail; and the mountains were covered.

Gen 7:21: And all flesh died that moved upon the earth, both of fowl, and of cattle, and of beast, and of every creeping thing that creepeth upon the earth, and every man:

Gen 7:22: All in whose nostrils was the breath of life, of all that was in the dry land, died.

Gen 7:23: And every living substance was destroyed which was upon the face of the ground, both man, and cattle, and the creeping things, and the fowl of the heaven; and they were destroyed from the earth: and Noah only remained alive, and they that were with him in the ark.

Gen 7:24: And the waters prevailed upon the earth an hundred and fifty days.

Gen 8:4: And the ark rested in the seventh month, on the seventeenth day of the month, upon the mountains of Ararat.

Gen 8:5: And the waters decreased continually until the tenth month: in the tenth month, on the first day of the month, were the tops of the mountains seen.

Gen 8:13: And it came to pass in the six hundredth and first year, in the first month, the first day of the month, the waters were dried up from off the earth: and Noah removed the covering of the ark, and looked, and, behold, the face of the ground was dry.

Gen 8:14: And in the second month, on the seven and twentieth day of the month, was the earth dried.

Gen 8:15: And God spake unto Noah, saying,

Gen 8:16: Go forth of the ark, thou, and thy wife, and thy sons, and thy sons' wives with thee.

Gen 8:17: Bring forth with thee every living thing that is with thee, of all flesh, both of fowl, and of cattle, and of every creeping thing that creepeth upon the earth; that they may breed abundantly in the earth, and be fruitful, and multiply upon the earth.

Gen 8:22: While the earth remaineth, seedtime and harvest, and cold and heat, and summer and winter, and day and night shall not cease.

Gen 9:28: And Noah lived after the flood three hundred and fifty years [1].

Historic Facts that Support a World Wide Flood.

Archeology

Archeological evidence supports the fact that all the civilizations throughout the world underwent a demarcation in their cultures in approximately 2500-2350 BC. In virtually every region on earth, the evidence shows that cultures were coming to an unexplainable, abrupt end or were initially established around this time. They also conclude that the culture that replaced the preceding culture was less advanced than the one replaced. This compliments the global Flood scenario as the new occupants would have only had one to three hundred years to develop during repopulation of the earth, compared to their predecessors who had over fifteen hundred years. This along with living longer lives yields to retained knowledge compared to those with lesser longevity, where there is a loss of knowledge with each loss of life [9, 47].

Geology

The geological columns do not reflect millions of years via uniformitarian processes as taught in the school books and by secular scientists. All of the rock formations and fossils found in the earth strata require rapid and cataclysmic circumstances to form, such as in Noah's Flood.

a. Fossils must be buried rapidly and subjected to compression to form.
b. The fossils found in the strata all over the world consist of a jumbled mat of many different types of species apparently overtaken by some oncoming catastrophe.

   c. Igneous rocks (granites, basalts, pumice) formed by upwelling of magmas and cooling on the surface or subsurface of the earth.

   d. Metamorphic rocks converted from sedimentary rocks (e.g., limestone to marble, sandstone to Quartzite, clay or shale to slate) involves tremendous heat and stress.

   e. Sedimentary rocks (sandstone, shale, limestone, etc.) are predominantly mixed with a cementing agent and water and can set within hours under certain prevailing conditions, just as concrete does. Most carbonate cementing agents are associated with sea environments. Fossiliferous sandstone and limestone are associated with rapid formation in order to preserve the fossils, which makes up 95% of the strata found in the Grand Canyon, for an example. Alternately, sandstone can form under tremendous stress (such as hydrostatic pressure) as seen in the recent formation of the Arches Stralec Quarry in the Czech Republic [48, 49].

Rock strata is subsequently dated by the "index" fossils found in a particular stratum. This is solely based on theory and assumption. There is no reliable scientific means to date these rocks or fossils, the naturalist just assumes that the different fossils came from different evolutionary ages because the only alternate theory or model is that of the young earth creationists, which is to them unacceptable. In fact, the different fossils in the different strata actually represent different habitats caught up in different ensuing cataclysmic events, such as an earthquake, upper lake bursting, volcanic eruption, oceanic tidal surges, etc.) along with sediment sorting principles [22, 48, 49, 50, 51].

Fossilized sea creatures and oceanic sediment can be found every place in the world, from the highest mountains in the Himalayas to the valleys farthest from the ocean, which would definitely be an expected result from a worldwide Flood [49, 50].

The earth strata, canyons, and other geological formations (palesols, laterites, ferricretes, siesmites, ripple marks, etc.) that secular scientists have theorized to have taken millions of years have been replicated on a lesser scale in local formations and catastrophic events (e.g., the eruption of Mount Saint Helens and formation of the "Mini Grand Canyon") or proven possible in lab setups in short periods of time (days, weeks, or months) rather than millions of years. Strata, as a result of catastrophic events, is normally found in multiple layers per event, in other words, sediments, volcanic activity, earth quakes and such involve an array of dynamics, such as sources of material, varying flow rates, directional changes, pressure and temperatures, etc. that lay down many layers with diverse matrices per event [49]. Estimating that each layer in a stratum represents millions of years does not conform to the predominant processes of known geological sciences. As a matter of fact, geologists and scientists coming to this realization out of a need to force fit these formations into an evolutionary model are now claiming that the millions of years are now represented in the interfaces between the strata layers, again, against the known scientific evidence.

With the aforementioned events and lab results, it is easy to see how such a thing as the Grand Canyon could have been formed in just months from the magnitude of the events that occurred during the global Flood, which would have included gradual and dynamic flooding, earthquakes, volcanic activity, and even a possible meteor strike.

Figure 1.12 Grand Canyon S. Rim

Figure 1.13 Mount St Helen
Mini Grand Canyon

Mount Saint Helen and Catastrophism by Steven A. Austin, PhD.

Austin reports that deposits forming geological strata from the dynamic activity accompanying the eruption of Mount Saint Helen accumulated up to 400 feet from pyroclastic flows, mudslides, steam water, waves on the lake, and other mechanisms. It appeared that the pyroclastic flows contributed much to the accumulation with fine pumice, ash, and laminae – and all within minutes. Modern science books teach that strata formations that have these same matrices formulated over long periods of time due to seasonal changes. These formations should now best be associated with catastrophic events rather than uniformitarian processes as a lesson demonstrated by nature. Austin also adds:

> A mudflow on March 19, 1982, eroded a canyon system up to 140 feet deep in the headwaters of the North Fork of the Toutle River Valley, establishing the new dendritic pattern of drainage. The little "Grand Canyon of the Toutle River" is a one-fortieth scale model of the real Grand Canyon. The small creeks which flow through the headwaters of the Toutle River today might seem, by present appearances, to have carved these canyons very slowly over a long time period, except for the fact that the erosion was observed to have occurred rapidly! Geologists should learn that, since the long-time scale they have been trained to assign to landform development would lead to obvious error on Mount St. Helens, it also may be useless or misleading elsewhere [51].

The Mount St. Helens eruption was a local catastrophic event. Noah's Flood was of a magnitude of incalculable proportions in comparison. Waters receding during Noah's Flood would have easily cut through the largely soft sandstone formations that makeup the Grand Canyon.

Canyon formations in a global Flood event would be unique to mitigating circumstances dependent on cataclysmic elements such as number and size of nearby volcanoes, (e.g., Yellowstone Grand Canyon carved out by nearby mega volcano under Yellow Stone Park), tectonic movement, meteor bombardment (e.g., crater in Winslow AZ), local flooding sources (freshwater lakes), global (oceanic) flooding and sediment sources, relative eco systems, erosion effects, sequence, and magnitude of events. No two locations would be the same. The area around the Grand Canyon has evidence of many various and monumental cataclysmic events that combined to create one of the world's most unique wonders that appeared as a result of the global Flood. Could the Colorado River have truly carved the canyon at a greater rate than the uplift of the ground swell during the tectonic collision that formed the Rockies and surrounding geology over a period of 25 million years and then at a substantially slower rate carve the canyon over 55 million years to where it is today? That's twice the time period. Lake Mead, the source of the Colorado River, is at 2,200 feet from sea level, and the canon rim is at 8,000 feet from sea level. In actuality, there was probably no uplift at all, as can be observed through the strata layers that are all horizontal with no planar tilt, but rather a compiling of strata due to the many tidal surges that would have accompanied the dynamic turbulence during a global flood of such magnitude.

If the Bible is a true and accurate historical record regarding Noah's World Wide Flood, then you would expect to find massive fossiliferous strata made of sandstone from a distant oceanic basin source, with predominantly oceanic sea creatures and cementing agents, laid down with multiple layers due to the continental drifting and nature of catastrophic events of that magnitude. You should also find evidence of oceanic sea creatures in every place in the world, including the top of mountains.

This is exactly what you find around the world with 95% of the strata made of fossiliferous sandstone from an oceanic source as can be clearly seen in the Grand Canyon, the fossiliferous Morrison formation spread out from Texas to Canada covering 580,000 square miles and has an average of 328 feet thick, the source for the Navajo Sandstone layer in southern Utah coming from the Appalachian Mountains over 1,200 miles away, and sea creatures such as trilobites at the top of Mount Everest, as a matter of fact!

ROCK STRATA IN THE GRAND CANYON

Kaibab Limestone
Toroweap Formation
Coconino Sandstone
Hermit Shale
Supai Formation
Redwall Limestone
Temple Butte Limestone
Tonto Group
Late Pre-Cambrian Rocks

Figure 1.14 Rock Strata in the Grand Canyon

Kaibab Limestone (Permian) - This layer is composed primarily of a sandy limestone with a layer of sandstone below it. In some places, sandstone and shale also exist as its upper layer. It is highly metamorphosed, and also known as Kaibab Marble. This formation extends across northern Arizona, southern Utah, east-central Nevada, and southeast California. Fossils that can be found in this layer are brachiopods, coral, mollusks, sea lilies, worms, and fish teeth. Cementing agents: carbonates and little silica.

Toroweap Formation (Permian) - This layer is composed of the same material as the Kaibab Limestone above and contains a similar fossil history, likely the probably same source under a different deposition flow rate.

Coconino Sandstone (Permian) - This layer is composed of pure quartz sand, which are essentially petrified sand dunes. This Permian formation spreads across northern Arizona, northwest Colorado, Nevada, and Utah. No skeletal fossils have yet to be found, but numerous invertebrate tracks and fossilized burrows exist. Silica cementing agent.

Hermit Shale (Permian) - This layer is composed of soft, easily eroded shales which have formed a slope. Fossils found in this layer consist of ferns, conifers and other plants, as well as some fossilized tracks of reptiles and amphibians.

Supai Formation (Pennsylvanian) - This layer is composed primarily of shale that is intermixed with some small amounts of limestone and capped by sandstone. The limestone features become more and more prominent in the western regions of the canyon, leading one to believe that that region was originally more marine. It covers northwest Arizona and southwest Utah. Numerous fossils of amphibians, reptiles, and terrestrial plants exist in the eastern portion which are replaced by marine fossils as you move westward.

Redwall Limestone (Mississippian) - This layer is composed of marine limestones and dolomites. This is probably the most prominent rock layer in the canyon, as it usually forms a sheer cliff ranging from 400-500 feet in height, which has become a natural barrier between the upper and lower regions of the canyon. Numerous marine fossils can be found in the Redwall Limestone including brachiopods, clams, snails, corals, fish, and trilobites (many millions of nautiloids). Many caves and arches can also be seen in the Redwall. Carbonate cementing agents.

Temple Butte Limestone (Devonian) - This layer is composed of freshwater limestone in the east and dolomite in the west. In the eastern Grand Canyon this layer occurs irregularly and only then by way of limestone lenses that fill stream beds that have been eroded into the underlying Mauv Limestone. The only fossils to be found in the eastern region are bony plates that once belonged to freshwater fish. In the western region there are numerous marine fossils. Carbonate cementing agents.

Tonto Group (Cambrian)

Muav Limestone - This layer is composed primarily of limestone that is separated by beds of sandstone and shale. The Mauv Limestone layer is much thicker in the western areas of the canyon than it is in the east. It does not have much in the way of fossils, though there are some trilobites and brachiopods. Carbonate cementing agents.

Bright Angel Shale - This layer is composed primarily of mudstone shale. It is also interbedded with small sections of sandstone and sandy limestone. Fossils found in this layer consist of marine animals such as trilobites and brachiopods.

Tapeats Sandstone (Cambrian) - This layer is composed of medium-grained and coarse-grained sandstone. Ripple marks formed by ocean waves of an early Cambrian sea are common in the upper layer. It contains fossils of trilobites, brachiopods, and trilobite trails. Silica cementing agent.

Great Unconformity - This non-layer indicates an age in which no sediments can be found. It is indicative of a time when an advancing sea eroded away the sediments that should be here.

Late Pre-Cambrian Rocks

Chuar Group - These layers are composed of the following:
Sixtymile Formation - This layer is composed primarily of sandstone with some small sections of shale.
Kwagunt Formation - This layer is composed primarily of shale and mudstone with some limestone. Fossils to be found in this layer are those of stromatolites, the oldest fossils to be found anywhere in the Grand Canyon.
Galeros Formation - This layer is composed of interbedded sandstone, limestone, and shale. Fossil stromatolites also exist in this layer.
Nankoweap Formation - This layer is composed of a coarse-grained sandstone.

Unkar Group
Cardenas Lavas - This dark brown layer is composed of basaltic lava flows.
Dox Sandstone - This layer is composed of sandstone interbedded with shale and occurs primarily in the eastern regions of the canyon. Its fossil record contains stromatolites and algae.
Shinumo Quartzite - This layer is composed of sandstone.
Hakatai Shale - This layer is composed primarily of shale with some sandstone.
Bass Formation - This layer is composed primarily of limestone with some interbedded shale. Its fossil record consists of stromatolites, first laid down from shallow ocean waters.
Pre-Cambrian Unconformity - This non-layer supposedly represents a time where the mountains that had grown here were gradually eroded away to form a plain.
Early Pre-Cambrian Rocks
Vishnu Schist and Zoroaster Granite - This layer consists of mica schist. These were originally sediments of sandstone, limestone, and shale that were metamorphosed and combined with metamorphosed lava flows to form the schist [50].

Grand Canyon's Three Sets of Rocks

Layered Paleozoic Rocks

1. Kaibab Formation (Fm)
2. Toroweap Formation
3. Coconino Sandstone
4. Hermit Formation
5. Supai Group
6. Surprise Canyon Fm
7. Redwall Limestone
8. Temple Butte Fm
9. Muav Limestone
10. Bright Angel Shale
11. Tapeats Sandstone

Grand Canyon Supergroup Rocks

12. Sixtymile Formation
13. Chuar Group
14. Nankoweap Fm
15. Unkar Group

Vishnu Basement Rocks

16. Schists
17. Granites
18. Elves Chasm Gneiss

Layer age in millions of years	Layer thickness in feet
270	350
273	250
275	300
280	300
285-315	1,000
320	0-75
340	500
385	0-50
505	450
515	350
525	0-200
<740	200
740-770	5,200
900	370
1,100-1,200	6,800
1,680-1,840	Unknown

The Great Unconformity

Layered Paleozoic Rocks

Tonto Group

Grand Canyon Supergroup Rocks

Vishnu Basement Rocks

Period	Era
	Paleozoic
Permian	Major Extinction
	Reptile Diversity
Pennsylvainian	First Reptiles / Scale Trees, seed ferns
Mississippian	
Devonian	Amphibians / Jawed fish / Metazoin Families
Cambrian	Fish & Chordates / **Explosion of Novel Creatures**
Great Unconformity (transitional fossils missing)	
Pre-Cambrian	**Proterozoic**
	Microbial Fossils

Figure 1.15 Evolution eras next to Grand Canyon Strata and Elevations

Summary of comments from John D. Morris, Ph.D., former president of ICA, on the Grand Canyon:

Geologists have historically interpreted the geological stratum as the result of uniformitarian process that accumulated over long periods of time, millions of years. As our knowledge of geological processes has increased, and in view of the now many witnessed and recorded natural catastrophic events, geologists are reinterpreting geological stratum as the result of catastrophic "water-related processes". Morris points out: *"Evidence of underwater turbidity currents is found in the Tapeats Sandstone, the Redwall Limestone, and others"*. These strata are made up of uniform deposits that cover massive areas, some from Mexico to Canada, and therefore cannot be attributed to local catastrophic events. Morris adds: *"The Supai Formation has traditionally been interpreted as a delta deposit, but has laterally extensive thin members, unlike modern deltas"*. The fossils in these Grand Canyon stratum are out of sequence with the ideal progressive complexity espoused by evolution with such examples as the more complex trilobites at the bottom and less complex corals at the top. There is little evidence of erosion of the Colorado Plateau's upper most stratum after a supposed 70my. The erosion of the canyon walls show evidence of having been subjected to a rapid turbulent flow with the mostly soft sandstone sediment being carried off to the west, as opposed to the theory that is was eroded by the Colorado River over eons of time flowing to the east. Dating efforts indicate that it occurred more recently in time than traditional evolutionary estimates. One example Morris sites is that the "*volcanic basalts on the rim date as older than the deeply buried Cardenas Basalts*" [52].

Coal and oil deposits most certainly formed from cataclysmic events of massive earth movement, overturning trapping organic matter, and then subjecting them to the months of hydrostatic pressures from the height of the flood waters. This is being reproduced in labs all over the world these days [22, 48].

DNA Evidence

Geneticists from the University of Adelaide Australian Center for Ancient DNA have studies that suggest that people alive before the demarcation of 2500BC have a distinctively different genetic makeup compared to the culture that replaced the preceding cultures.

> They say the rapid expansion of the Bell Beaker culture, which is believed to have been instrumental in building the monoliths at Stonehenge, could hold the key.

> 'What is intriguing is that the genetic markers of this first pan-European culture, which was clearly very successful, were then suddenly replaced around 4,500 years ago, and we don't know why,' study co-author Alan Cooper of the University of Adelaide Australian Center for Ancient DNA said.

> 'Something major happened, and the hunt is now on to find out what that was.'[53]

Cultures since that time have a mix of the preceding cultures as the invading culture usually takes some percentage of the women and children captive and also settles among the existing inhabitants. The various computations of the earth's population along the time line are congruent with the allotted time since the Flood.

When interrogating the genome from a biblical perspective, the DNA relationship agrees more with the biblical model than the evolutionary model and puts it within the 6K to10K years of earth history. An article from *Science* looking at demographics of diverse cultures over time and location shows a marked bottleneck in the history of humankind about 5,000 years ago and confirmed in the genome. Excerpts from an ICR article states the following [54]:

> The authors wrote, "The maximum likelihood time for accelerated growth was 5,115 years ago." Old-earth proponents now have a new challenge: to explain why—after millions of years of hardly any genetic variation among modern humans—human genomic diversity exploded only within the last five thousand years?

Literary Sources

There are hundreds of cultures with stories of the "Great Flood" in their histories. Most all of the ancient writings dated before 1800 BC in the form of king lists (Mesopotamia, Egypt, Briton, Wales, etc.) and epic tales (such as *The Epic of Gilgamesh*) all include the global Flood and Noah's decedents in these lineages, as a matter of fact.

The Conclusion

The Antediluvian period, from all indications, was without a doubt, a fearful and strange world compared to our world today. The size and type of the creatures, the manifestations of spiritual beings, and the savage environments were the results of man living apart from God, which had no place in God's plan for man and so had to end. God allowed this period to show the end of man's ways without a savior, a lesson to be observed throughout time, not to be dismissed as just a child's story. The biblical account that was once dismissed as a myth by the leading experts in science and academia in the mid 19th century has indeed been vindicated with the myriads of evidence discovered in the past 150 years. All the sciences, literature, artifacts, and cave drawings collaborating the chronology and events of the Bible, even its most extraordinary claims, form a consensus that the testimony of the Bible is more trustworthy than any conflict brought about by future discoveries. As history has shown us in the past, where there is a conflict, time has repeatedly shown the error to be with the contradicting entity or science due to unknown or ignored factors at the time of the initial conclusion. It is not logical to take one piece of doubtful evidence that amounts to <.1% of all the evidence as a basis to discard the remaining abundant hard evidence. As in all sciences, you must base your conclusions on the consensus of available data, not the exceptions. Scientific protocol demands that you have a consensus of the data for it to be considered scientifically valid or a scientific certainty. Here you have a consensus of the data with the previously reviewed subject matters in the various scientific and historical disciplines that include dozes of points of facts that indeed establishes a scientific/historical certainty.

REFERENCES

1   Biblical References from: The Holy Bible (1913). King James Version. Chicago, Ill. John A. Dickson Publishing Co.

2   Human Genome Project Information Archives (2003). Retrieved from http://web.ornl.gov/sci/techresources/Human_Genome/project/info.shtml

3   Panspermia-Theory.com. Retrieved from http://www.panspermia-theory.com/

4   Ghose, Tia (2013). Livescience. Genetic 'Adam' & 'Eve' uncovered. Retrieved from http://www.livescience.com/38613-genetic-adam-and-eve-uncovered.html

5   Maran, Laurence (2013). Sandwalk. Estimating the human mutation rate: Direct method. Retrieved from http://sandwalk.blogspot.com/2013/03/estimating-human-mutation-rate-direct.html

6   Williams, Alex. Creation.com. Mutations: evolution's engine becomes evolution's end. Retrieved from http://creation.com/mutations-are-evolutions-end

7   Missler, Chuck. Koinonia House. A hidden message: The gospel in Genesis. Retrieved from http://www.khouse.org/articles/1996/44/

8   Brett-Surman, M.K. (2000). *Dinosaurs: Revised & updated*. San Francisco, CA: Fog City Press.

9   Wolf, A. (2008). *A short history of the world: The story of mankind from prehistory to the modern day*. New York, NY: Metro Books by arrangement with Arcturus Publishing Limited.

10   GeoScience. A geological trip to Yass. Retrieved from http://www.geosci.usyd.edu.au/users/prey/FieldTrips/Yass04/Devonian.html

11   Humphreys, D. R. 1993. The Earth's magnetic field is young. *Acts & Facts*. 22 (8). Retrieved from http://www.icr.org/article/earths-magnetic-field-young/

12   Crystal Links. Sumerian king list. Retrieved from http://www.crystalinks.com/SumerianKingList.html

13   Real History World Wide. Ancient man and his first civilizations. Sumerian religion. Retrieved from http://realhistoryww.com/world_history/ancient/Misc/Sumer/Sumerian_Religion.htm

14   Crystalinks. Ancient astronaut theory. Retrieved from http://www.crystalinks.com/ancient_aliens.html

15   Lopez, R (1998). Answers in Genesis. The antediluvian patriarchs and the Sumerian king list. Retrieved from https://answersingenesis.org/bible-history/the-antediluvian-patriarchs-and-the-sumerian-king-list/

16   History Files. Middle East kingdoms. Ancient Mesopotamia. Retrieved from http://www.historyfiles.co.uk/KingListsMiddEast/MesopotamiaSumer.htm

17   LacusCurtius • Manetho's History of Egypt — Book I. Retrieved from http://penelope.uchicago.edu/Thayer/E/Roman/Texts/Manetho/History_of_Egypt/1*.html

18   Learn Chinese History. History of Chinese Emperors – names, dynasties & reins. Retrieved from http://www.learnchinesehistory.com/history-chinese-emperors/

19   Ancient Origins. Reconstructing the story of humanity's past. Retrieved from http://www.ancient-origins.net/human-origins-religions/startling-similarity-between-hindu-flood-legend-manu-and-biblical-020318

20   Breeden, D. Ph. D, (2011). *The adventures of Beowulf*. Seattle, WA: CreateSpace Independent Publishing Platform.

21   The Epic of Gilgamesh. Assyrian International News Agency. Books Online. www.aina.org. Retrieved from http://www.aina.org/books/eog/eog.htm

22   Morris, H. M. (1985). *Scientific creationism*. Green Forrest, AR: Master Books.

23   Verrengia, Joseph (2005). Livescience. Dinosaur fossil found in mammal's stomach. Retrieved From http://www.livescience.com/3794-dinosaur-fossil-mammal-stomach.html.

24   World News Daily Report. Prehistoric cave art depicting humans hunting dinosaurs discovered in Kuwait. Retrieved from http://worldnewsdailyreport.com/prehistoric-cave-art-depicting-humans-hunting-dinosaurs-discovered-in-kuwait/

25   History's Evidence of Dinosaurs and Men. Retrieved from http://historysevidenceofdinosaursandmen.weebly.com/

26 Dell'Amore, Christine (2011). Biggest bear ever found. National Geographic News, National Geographic. Retrieved from http://news.nationalgeographic.com/news/2011/02/110203-biggest-bear-largest-giant-short-faced-animals-science/

27 Wikipedia. Brown bear. Retrieved from https://en.wikipedia.org/wiki/Brown_bear

28 Strauss, Bob (2016). Dinosaur Expert. Titanoboa, the world's biggest prehistoric snake. About education. Retrieved from http://dinosaurs.about.com/od/otherprehistoriclife/ss/10-Facts-About-Titanoboa.htm#step1

29 Our Planet (2015). World's top 5 largest crocodiles ever recorded. Retrieved from https://ourplnt.com/worlds-5-largest-crocodiles-ever-recorded/

30 Switek, Brian (2016). National Geographic. Monster-size marine crocodile discovered. Retrieved from http://news.nationalgeographic.com/2016/01/160111-ancient-crocodile-marine-largest-paleontology/

31 Wikipedia. Archelon. Retrieved from https://en.wikipedia.org/wiki/Archelon

32 Wikipedia. Leather back sea turtles. Retrieved from https://en.wikipedia.org/wiki/Leatherback_sea_turtle

33 Schiavo, Amanda (2013). Megalodon vs great white shark. Latin Times. Retrieved from http://www.latintimes.com/megalodon-vs-great-white-shark-how-does-prehistoric-beast-stack-against-feared-white-death-video.

34 San Diego Zoo (2009). Extinct ground sloth, Tardigrada. Retrieved from http://library.sandiegozoo.org/factsheets/_extinct/sloth_extinct/extinct_sloth.htm

35 World Animal Foundation. Sloth fact sheet. Retrieved from http://www.worldanimalfoundation.net/f/sloth.pdf

36 Wikipedia. Smilodon. Retrieved from https://en.wikipedia.org/wiki/Smilodon

37 Earth Rangers (2011). Top 10 biggest cats. Retrieved from http://www.earthrangers.com/wildwire/top-10/top-10-biggest-cats/

38 Barnes, T. G. Ph.D, (1983). *Origin and destiny of the Earth's magnetic field* (2nd Ed.). El Cajon, CA: Institute for Creation Research.

39 D. Russell Humphreys, Ph.D. 1989. The mystery of Earth's magnetic field. *Acts & Facts*. 18 (2). Retrieved from http://www.icr.org/article/mystery-earths-magnetic-field/

40 Humphreys, R. D. Dr. (1984). Creation Research Society. The creation of magnetic planetary fields. Retrieved from http://www.creationresearch.org/crsq/articles/21/21_3/21_3.html

41 Gingerich, P.D. (2007). Palaeontologia Electronica. Punctuated equilibrium. Retrieved from http://palaeo-electronica.org/2007_3/books/equal.htm

42 Assyrian International News Agency. Books online. The Epic of Gilgamesh. Retrieved from http://www.aina.org/books/eog/eog.pdf

43 Ancient Egypt Site. Narmer palette. Retrieved from http://www.ancient-egypt.org/history/early-dynastic-period/1st-dynasty/horus-narmer/narmer-artefacts/narmer-palette.html

44 The Modern Antiquarian. Cycladic culture. Retrieved from http://www.themodernantiquarian.com/site.php/10854/knossos.html#fieldnotes

45 James Q. Jacobs (2000). Earl monumental architecture on the Peruvian coast. Retrieved from http://www.jqjacobs.net/andes/coast.html#1

46 National Geographic News. Sechin Bajo. Retrieved from http://news.nationalgeographic.com/news/2008/02/080226-peru-oldest.html

47 Renfrew, C & Cooke, K. (1979). *Transformations: Mathematic approaches to cultural change*. New York, NY: Academic Press Inc.

48 Lovett, R. A. (2014). Nature. Sandstone arches form under their own stress. Retrieved from http://www.nature.com/news/sandstone-arches-form-under-their-own-stress-1.15590

49 Froede, Carl (2007). Geology by design. Green Forest, AR: Master Books.

50 Grand Canyon Explorer. Grand Canyon rock layers. Retrieved from http://www.bobspixels.com/kaibab.org/geology/gc_layer.htm

51 Austin, S.A. Ph.D. Mt. St. Helens and catastrophism. Institute for Creation Science. Retrieved from http://www.icr.org/article/mt-st-helens-catastrophism/

52 Grand Canyon: Is it really "exhibit a" for evolution and the old Earth? Institute for Creation Research. Retrieved from http://www.icr.org/article/grand-canyon-it-really-exhibit-a-for-evolution-old/

53   American Renaissance. Why did European DNA suddenly change 4,000 years ago? Retrieved from http://www.amren.com/news/2013/04/why-did-european-dna-suddenly-change-4000-years-ago/

54   Tomkins, J.P. Ph.D. ICR. Human dna variation linked to biblical event timeline. Retrieved from http://www.icr.org/article/human-dna-variation-linked-biblical

PART 2

Post Flood Ice Age

The continental land masses appeared to be in one supercontinent state before the Flood, known as Pangaea. The present location of the continents may have started their drifting at an initially accelerated rate during and immediately after the Flood to the present state of global position. The archaeomagnetic data (reference discussion in Part 1) supports the massive movements of the earth crusts from about 2500 BC to 750 BC, with the greater magnitude at the start and then an attenuating cycle afterwards, until it came back into balance with the entropy curve of the earth's electromagnetic generating core in about 1000 AD. That the earth was in a super continent state at one time is supported by geological evidence found at locations where scientist estimate the lands split along the tectonic plates. There are fossils of like species, contours of continental shelves, certain geological formations, such as rocks of similar matrices and paleomagnetism of rocks, and oil fields of similar slates that match up at the coast lines at points where they are presumed to have originated from, mainly from the east coast of the Americas and Canada, matching the points along the west coast of Europe and Africa [1,2]. The earth's axis may have shifted due to the magnitude of tidal and earth crust movement during the Flood causing more drastic seasonal changes than what was known before the Flood.

It appears that the American continents slipped away at a much more accelerated rate of movement from the more stable continents of Europe, Africa, Asia, and so on. This is supported by the more catastrophic aftermath seen in the strata of the American continents' interior compared to other continents. The tidal actions and underwater currents during the height of the flood waters on the American continents produced much more dynamic effects (canyons, mesas, buttes, mountain ranges, deep stratification, etc.) with the ocean's massive wave and underwater current actions compared to the more gradual flood waters and wave actions of a lesser magnitude in the European, African, Mesopotamian, and Asian interiors. The mesas and buttes originated from the many oceanic mega waves and underwater currents during the initial accelerated drifting of the continent where some localized cementing of the sandstone formations occurred. This, along with other dynamic results of earthquakes, volcanic activity, and such added to the geological formations such as conglomerate, quartzite, basalt, chert, limestone, lava flows, and sills. This would have given them the needed stability to withstand the erosion effect from the receding tides and currents that took away the surrounding loose deposits leaving behind these monuments. The mesas and buttes throughout the Midwest are at about 5,000 to 8,000 ft above sea level and stand about 450 ft to 2,000 ft higher than the surrounding grade level. They are made of mostly sandstone strata with carbonate cementing agents, which are associated with oceanic organics. These same formations can also be found in the coastal lands of many other nations including Spain, Sardinia, North and South Africa, Arabia, India, and Australia. These areas would have been hit the hardest with more massive tidal actions due to mega water displacement during the initial accelerated movement of the American continents. The interiors of these continents would have had a more gradual increase in the water levels with some tidal activity of lesser magnitude [3, 4].

The mountain ranges on the east and west coast may have been created when the American continents started hitting resistance that caused the momentum of the tectonic plates to collide, causing the earth to heave up like a child running and sliding on a loose carpet. Major mountain ranges in the European, African, and Asian mainland continents were created from the displacement surges against both east and west sides from the movement of the American continents, such as the creation of the Himalayas caused by the collision between the Indian and the Eurasian plates. Many mountains were also created from other means as well, such as volcanic activity, upwarping from underground magma displacement, and erosion of surrounding earth that were all elements within the cataclysmic events of Noah's Flood [5].

Oil fields were created along the coast lines where the continents were separating, causing the earth to fold over and trapping the organic mass within earthen pockets. This also occurred where mountains were toppled by the forces of the massive tidal surges, again, trapping the organic mass within earthen pockets. Such massive upheaval of upper crust and seas, tectonic movements of the earth's crust, magma flows, and earth turning events on a worldwide scale caused disruptions due to energy surges in free electrical currents the earth's core. Eddy currents within the molten core realigned and captured the residual magnetic north and south orientations in the rocks and cooling magma flows. Virtually all the oil fields tested for remnants of C^{14} have tested positive, qualifying these oil deposits to have been created within the past 60,000 years (4,500 years ago by the biblical time line).

Two thirds of the animal species from the past have gone extinct due to the dramatic change in the environment and oceans, which went from extreme high temperatures to an ice age environment [6].

Many of the fossils found in the strata hold near photocopy images of the creatures that once lived on the earth that didn't have time for some bit of microevolution to adapt to the new conditions. Many life forms became extinct due to the traumatic forces experienced during the great Flood such as crushing pressures due to the displacement of earth and water in reaction to movements of the continents, the heating of the oceans from the release of hydrogen sulfide due to massive magma flows above and below the water, and the more frigid waters experienced after the Flood. The food chain would have been disrupted on a massive scale with the loss of smaller creatures due to the rise and fall of the water temperatures, causing a domino effect up the food chain. The larger beasts that may have survived the trauma of the flood event such as the *Thalassomedon*, *Tylosaurus*, Megalodon, and the ichthyosaurs would have eventually starved to death due to lack of abundant food sources. It is obvious from the groupings of the animals (size, type, natural habitat, and place in the food chain) normally associated with the Cambrian, Ordovician, Silurian, Devonian, Carboniferous, or Permian period, that these creatures appear in their perspective strata as representing different environments. These animals were caught in the sediments from those environments during the ensuing cataclysms (near shore, off shore, deep sea, shorelines, inlands, etc.) as these events occurred around the world.

Many fossils being tested for remnants of C^{14} have tested positive, qualifying these deposits to have been created within the past 60,000 years (4,500 years ago by the biblical timeline). Additionally, many of the dinosaur fossils being tested are finding soft tissue, favoring these relics to be less than 10,000 years old.

Precambrian Fossils -4 billion to 541 million years BC period of earth history [7, 8,9]

Most of the fossils from the Precambrian period are microorganisms (cyanobacteria) and have parallel phylum found in modern times. There are no examples in the fossil records to link any of the Precambrian forms from any origin, but there are plenty of make believe theories such as the various endosymbiotic theories, with the still and ever present mark of pseudoscience and no empirical evidence (*De Novo* magic moments). As can be surmised, these fossils are found in mostly igneous and metamorphic rocks from oceanic sources and particularly from about underwater volcanoes and magma fumes where the water is acidic and not suitable for other types of marine life. They are the microbial fauna found in what is considered by evolutionists the oldest strata of any rock.

Archea are single celled organisms that have no nucleus and exist today in several forms. They are very robust and can survive environmental extremes of temperatures and salinity found in many forms in modern environments.

Chemotrophs are organisms that obtain energy by the oxidation of electron donors in their environments. These molecules can be organic (chemoorganotrophs) or inorganic (chemolithotrophs). The chemotroph designation is in contrast to phototrophs, which utilize solar energy. Chemotrophs can be either autotrophic or heterotrophic. Chemoautotrophs are commonly found in ocean floors where sunlight cannot reach them because they are not dependent on solar energy. Ocean floors often contain underwater volcanoes that provide heat in order to substitute sunlight for warmth.

Stromatolites - Paleoproterozoic (2.3 bya) are calcareous mounds (bio-chemical structures) formed from lime-secreting cyanobacteria trapped in sediment rocks that can be found forming today in lagoons in Australia.

Ctenophores (Comb Jellies) (700 mya) is a phylum of invertebrate animals that live in marine waters worldwide. Their most distinctive feature is the 'combs' – groups of cilia which they use for swimming – they are the largest animals that swim by means of cilia (Wikipedia). These animals are still alive today in basically the same well–marked forms as found in the fossil records. The Comb Jelly has even a grander surprise. It does not fit in the Pre-Cambrian period with its more complex organization. It has nerves and muscle cells that coexisting creatures do not, and on the flip side lacks genes thought essential for animals that low on the evolutionary scale. It was generally thought that sponges were the original progenitor of many a species, but now the Comb Jelly is throwing conventional evolutionary theology a curve ball.

The majority of the fossiliferous rocks from the Precambrian era are igneous and metamorphic with a small amount of sandstone [10]. Archeologists date rocks based on the fossils found in the rock.

Finding these Stromatolites, Archea, and Chemotrophs microorganisms in abundance by themselves in a given strata, archeologists assume that the layer is between 4 billion to 541 million years old.

Excerpts from Answers in Genesis: [11].

> A while ago, evolutionists would not have expected to find any fossils in rocks that they thought were, say, three billion years old; life supposedly hadn't evolved yet. However, fossils of bacteria kept turning up in progressively older rocks (no surprise to creationists), which allowed less and less time for the first life to evolve in the hypothetical, oxygen-free early atmosphere. Now an Austrian/Swiss team of scientists has looked at rock from Western Australia's Pilbara region, supposedly around 3.5 billion years old, and found what appear to be fossilized cyanobacteria. These appear to be indistinguishable from the same (oxygen-producing) creatures making the mat structures called stromatolites in the shallows of Shark Bay, some 500 kilometers away on the coast.

These microorganisms, supposedly the oldest form of life found in the earth's strata, have thousands of organized arrangements of encoded programming stored in their genomes. As an article from Nature put it, "encoded by operons that have an extraordinarily diverse architecture and a high rate of evolution for both the *cas* genes and the unique spacer content" [12]! There are no preceding forms of life or organisms found in the fossil records to support an evolutionary process. The existence of such a complex molecule (an interdependent system of protein/DNA/RNA/carbohydrate combinations) in the most basic of phylum precludes any evolutionary process, as the odds of such complex molecules being spontaneously developed in some primordial soup is beyond the given mathematical possibility of arrangements, earth time period, or possible "chance" environmental conditions to auto develop without an architect, designer, or creator!

In an article from the Oxford Journals regarding the studies of bacterial and archaeal genomes, the authors concluded that the findings "[undermine] the 'Tree of Life' model of evolution", and that genomes "are built according to the same, simple 'master plan' with wall-to-wall protein-coding and RNA-coding genes". The authors also noted that "it could be hard even to identify a set of genes that have a coherent history over a substantial evolutionary span", "the emerging complexity of the prokaryotic world is currently beyond our grasp", and that "We have no adequate language, in terms of theory or tools, to describe the workings and histories of the genomic network". Excerpts from the cited article:

> The first bacterial genome was sequenced in 1995, and the first archaeal genome in 1996. Soon after these breakthroughs, an exponential rate of genome sequencing was established, with a doubling time of approximately 20 months for bacteria and approximately 34 months for archaea. Comparative analysis of the hundreds of sequenced bacterial and dozens of archaeal genomes leads to several generalizations on the principles of genome organization and evolution. A crucial finding that enables functional characterization of the sequenced genomes and evolutionary reconstruction is that the majority of archaeal and bacterial genes have conserved orthologs in other, often, distant organisms. However, comparative genomics also

shows that horizontal gene transfer (HGT) is a dominant force of prokaryotic evolution, along with the loss of genetic material resulting in genome contraction. A crucial component of the prokaryotic world is the mobilome, the enormous collection of viruses, plasmids and other selfish elements, which are in constant exchange with more stable chromosomes and serve as HGT vehicles. Thus, the prokaryotic genome space is a tightly connected, although compartmentalized, network, a novel notion that undermines the 'Tree of Life' model of evolution and requires a new conceptual framework and tools for the study of prokaryotic evolution.

Indeed, in terms of general organization, the great majority of the archaeal and bacterial genomes are notably similar, and are built according to the same, simple 'master plan' with wall-to-wall protein-coding and RNA-coding genes, preferentially organized in directions, typically, with a single origin of replication. Most of the archaeal and bacterial genes are simple units, with uninterrupted coding sequence and short regulatory regions.

The virtually unlimited flexibility of the architecture of prokaryotic genomes owing to extensive rearrangements, which create diverse variations on the themes of conserved operons, and the discovery of previously unsuspected signaling, regulatory and defense systems, only a few of which are briefly discussed in this article, add to the complexity of the prokaryotic genomescape that is revealed by comparative genomics.

From a complementary, genome-centric perspective, the results of comparative genomics indicate that the genes in any genome are far from having the same history, and it could be hard even to identify a set of genes that have a coherent history over a substantial evolutionary span.

The paradox of today's state of the art is that, despite the tremendous progress—but also owing to these advances—the emerging complexity of the prokaryotic world is currently beyond our grasp. We have no adequate language, in terms of theory or tools, to describe the workings and histories of the genomic network. Developing such a language is the major challenge for the next stage in the evolution of prokaryotic genomics [13].

The conclusion of this research is a revelation of truth in spades. The super computers used today in the research and study of the genome are inadequate tools. The most advanced super computer is no match for these Mega Super Nova Genome Bio-computers. The most sophisticated state of the art technology cannot come close to the Mega Super Nova Genome Bio-computers found in the simplest of creatures (microbes) known to science. This which begs the question, how can a computerized system developed by an intelligent agent be out gunned by a computerized system that happened by random chance? This is way beyond evolution. This is way beyond physics as we know it. This is God saying, "Hello...I'm here...can you hear me now?" How any intelligent scientist cannot stop, take pause, and contemplate the weight of this matter and come to any other conclusion is beyond reason. Their conclusions are born out of prejudice. If something does not align with their humanistic theology, it is not accepted at any cost. It is not possible to find an answer in evolution. This is way beyond time and chance, as will be concluded in the Cambrian section of this part. To construct a Mega Super Nova Genome Bio-computer that is as small as a molecular cell requires an intelligent designer, a Genome Bio-computer engineer to create such a phenomenon of biblical proportions as they say. There is too much coded information, computed logic (algorithms), organized sequencing systems, and biological blueprints to have developed from nothing by chance happenstance as the Darwinian Theory would have us to believe. That would be like saying a wholly functional computer more advanced than the most state of the art computer of today could have come out of a primordial soup by chance.

Cambrian Explosion - Fossils from 542 to 490 million years BC period of earth history

The Cambrian explosion, or less commonly known as the Cambrian radiation, was a relatively short evolutionary event compared to the Pre-Cambrian epoch. It began around 542 million years ago in the Cambrian period, during which most major animal phyla appeared, as indicated by the fossil record. Among the animals found in this period were the oceanic chordates, animals with a dorsal nerve cord (subphyla Vertebrata, which include fish, amphibians, reptiles, birds, and mammals); hard-bodied brachiopods, which resembled clams; and arthropods ancestors of spiders, insects, and crustaceans. As few as 19 and as many as 35 well-marked species of animals suddenly appeared in these fossil records. Amongst these phyla are clams, sponges, jellyfish, jawless fish, worms, trilobites, and the nautilus that is still alive today in basically the same well-marked forms as found in the fossil records [14, 15].

Excerpts from Answers in Genesis: text parentheses are the author's comments [11].

> Far from showing organisms changing, the fossil record is very static—organisms appear fully formed and then disappear or remain today. The lack of change recorded in the fossil record is used by some evolutionists to support the idea of punctuated equilibrium. This hypothesis suggests that evolution happened in rapid bursts over short periods. The lack of transitional forms and the sudden appearance of new organisms in sedimentary layers are used to support this idea. (Punctuated equilibrium is in direct opposition to Darwin's theory that the process would have to happen over millions of years in response to environmental mechanisms and chance - that would also imply that all species everywhere on earth underwent metamorphic changes in the same instants in times between each epoch, not possible or believable, but very desperate as time reveals evidence in opposition of evolution and ever-increasing support of creationism).

> The presence of living fossils is another quandary for those who interpret the fossil record from an evolutionary perspective. Thousands of organisms have remained virtually unchanged over alleged millions of years of earth's history. One of the most famous accounts is that of the coelacanth. The coelacanth was believed to be extinct as none had been found in the fossil record in the last 65 million years of sediments. Then, in 1938, a living specimen was caught off of the coast of South Africa. Since

then, another species in Indonesia has been found. How does something avoid being discovered in the fossil record over 65 million years?

The evolutionary sequence of plants is not displayed in the fossil record even though the story is told in textbooks. At least four different evolutionary lines are supposed to have emerged from prehistoric green algae, the common ancestor of all plants. In a recent text on plants, not a single fossil series is provided to support the phylogenetic tree diagrams that supposedly explain the evolutionary history of plants. The grand claims are laced with words like "probably," "apparently," and "presumably." The places where the fossil record is the most complete should provide the clearest picture of evolution, but this is where many evolutionists disagree. The lack of fossil ancestors for the major groups would seem to be important, but the evolutionists fill in the gaps with imagination, not science. The evidence clearly points to diverse groups created in the supernatural events described in the opening chapter of Genesis.

In the theory of evolution, spawned from Darwin's book *The Origins of the Species* published in 1859, adherents believe that life evolved from simple to complex species through chance, natural selection, and survival of the fittest. After approximately 160 years of research in the sciences of archeology, geology, anthropology, zoology, and genetics, they still have no actual scientific evidence to prove it as would be expected from the proposed models (no undisputed transitional examples in the fossil records). The model would predict that there should be an equal amount of evidence in the fossil records to support those presuppositions due to the significant amount of time and incremental forms involved. To date, scientists have not found the missing strata containing the missing links that Darwin so hoped would validate his theory.

In an effort to justify the theory of evolution, scientists claiming they have supporting evidence of transitional forms have periodically announced the discovery of the odd species here and there to give the public a case for argument against creationism. These animals are supposed to be representative of an intermediate step in the transformation from one species to another based on their appearance (they seem to have characteristics of two types of species) with no consecutive species before or after showing changes in an incremental process. Most of these are species with minor variations within a family, which is expected in the creation model. Two of the most popular are the *Anchiornis* and *Archaeopteryx*, the supposed link between dinosaurs and birds. These animals are as well marked a species as any other fossilized animal, they just have similarities of two different species, which is a common appearance in nature (e.g., the bearcat, ostrich, hyena, etc.). The "list of transitional fossils" found in Wikipedia is misleading. They are not intermediate transitional fossils at all; they are all well–marked species placed in a sequential order from simple to complex forms to appear to be part of an evolutionary tree. There are no undisputed intermediate transitional forms in that list.

An excerpt from a parley between the late Dr. Patterson, senior paleontologist at the prestigious British Museum of Natural History, and Luther Sunderland from Creation.com [16]

In Luther Sunderland's book *Darwin's Enigma*, he recounts writing the Dr. Patterson of the British Museum to ask him why he had not shown any photographs of transitional fossils in the book *Evolution* that he had written. Dr. Patterson replied thusly:

> 'I fully agree with your comments on the lack of direct illustration of evolutionary transitions in my book. If I knew of any, fossil or living, I would certainly have included them. You suggest that an artist should be used to visualize such transformations, but where would he get the information from? I could not, honestly, provide it,…

He went on to say:
> 'Yet Gould [Stephen J. Gould—the now deceased professor of paleontology from Harvard University] and the American Museum people are hard to contradict when they say there are no transitional fossils. … You say that I should at least "show a photo of the fossil from which each type of organism was derived." *I will lay it on the line—there is not one such fossil for which one could make a watertight argument.*'[3] [Emphasis added].

He had also written:
> 'The reason is that statements about ancestry and descent are not applicable in the fossil record. Is *Archaeopteryx* the ancestor of all birds? Perhaps yes, perhaps no: there is no way of answering the question.

The total representative examples of these supposed transitional forms amount to about <.01% of what the evolutionary model would predict due to the long periods required for chance and natural selection to produce these transformations. Such examples are pushed to the public as a diversion while ignoring that 99.99% short fall. Since when did science start establishing fact on <.01%. Any other area of science normally looks for a consensus from repeated test sampling with the same end results in the >95% category. The repeated results in this category come up a consensus of 0% findings. There have been no strata with intermediate transitional forms between sequential strata in any given rock formation in any discovery from before or after Darwin first proposed the theory.

Darwin's Doubt [15]

During this supposed evolutionary period, almost all of the modern phyla suddenly appeared. The vast diversity and disparity of fauna that just suddenly appeared in the fossil record with no trace of transitional fossils has been the plague of the Darwinian Theory since day one. The following summarizations and commentary from Stephen Meyer's book *Darwin's Doubt* best describes the fallacy of this theory and the birth of today's pseudoscientific approach to establishing historical processes setting precedence for future evolutionists.

Only isolated segments of the supposed "tree of life" that Darwin proposed show up in the fossil records, and these are in a fully developed novel stasis. The roots are missing, no branching is found anywhere (intermediate transitional forms), intermediate transitional forms of organisms for thousands to millions of generations of the first stages of branching aftermath are missing (not considering the time it would take for the genome to evolve to such a complex state), and intermediate transitional forms of organisms for thousands to millions of generational stages of branching aftermath are missing between segments thereafter as was keenly pointed out to Darwin by his professor Adam Sedgwick. When Darwin first wrote his book *The Origins of the Species*, he sent copies to several leading experts in the fields of paleontology, including Adam Sedgwick, Roderick Impey Murchison (who named the Silurian Period after an ancient Welsh tribe), and one Louis Agassiz, a Harvard University professor who had the reputation of "knowing the fossil record better than any man alive", was considered a genius, and who named the Cambrian Period. All three of these prominent naturalist of their times returned a "thumbs down" verdict after reading the book. Agassiz was quick to point out "then we should find not just one or a few missing links, but innumerable links shading almost imperceptibly from alleged ancestors to presumed descendants. Geologists, however, had found no such myriad of transitional forms leading to the Cambrian fauna". This was from a time when there were few major exemplary fossil sites that all collaborated the same findings in consecutive strata. Murchison rejected the theory on the basis of the complexity of design of the creatures, like the compound eyes of the trilobite, saying, "The earliest signs of living things, announcing as they do a high complexity of organization, entirely excludes the hypotheses of a transmutation from lower to higher grades of being". This statement by the prominent naturalist was made before the discovery of the super complex genome, which further compounds Murchison's statement due to the amount of programmed code bits in a gene sequence, as compared to the components that makeup the eye. His own professor, Adam Sedgwick, replied back saying, "You have deserted-after a start in that tram-road of all solid physical truth-the true method of induction". And so the diversion from true methodologies of evaluating evidence based on collaborating themes succumbed to accepting make believe theories without evidence, putting them into school books and teaching them as "fact" in support of one's theological beliefs. Humanism, as it was with Catholicism in yesteryear, once again propagated man–made theology for their own advantage. The younger sect of up and coming humanistic scientists looking for an alternative to biblical creationism eagerly grasped onto Darwin's theories, willfully ignoring the preponderance of evidence and establishing a new pseudoscience that accepted theories without empirical evidence. Even when the surmounting collaboration of evidence surrounding a subject matter emphatically supports an alternate theory, it is rejected if it in any way aligns with biblical or creation chronology, the truth be damned. Darwin himself had his doubts and rested his hopes on the future of discovery to vindicate his claims. After the feedback from his peer reviews, Darwin stated, "The difficulty of understanding the absence of vast piles of fossiliferous strata, which on my theory were no doubt somewhere accumulated before the Silurian (i.e. Cambrian) epoch, is very great." He also wrote, "I allude to the manner in which the numbers of species of the same group suddenly appear in the lowest known fossiliferous rock". Since that time there has been a vast array of discovery and fossil sites that not only fail to bring to fruition Darwin's hope that future discoveries would validate his theories but also greatly increased the chasm, as there are more and more complete and diverse creatures now in the list of the Cambrian explosion with no transitional specimens and with insufficient time to product such an array of diversity and disparity (large differences in forms of life) according to the Darwinian theory.

In 1909 Charles Doolittle Walcott discovered the Burgess bestiary in Mount Wapta of the Canadian Rocky Mountains between Emerald Lake and Yoho Valley in Yoho National Park, located in British Columbia, Canada. The Burgess bestiary is a rock outcrop of shale in Mount Wapta brimming with Cambrian fossils where even the soft parts have been preserved. This discovery subsequently dispelled the notion theorized by some (the **artifact hypotheses**) that the Precambrian transitional fauna were not preserved due to their soft body state. Walcott's team collected over 65,000 specimens, thereby increasing the diversity and disparity many times more than what was originally known in Darwin's day. Walcott, a humanist and Darwinian, was also disappointed that there were no transitional forms discovered. He, like Darwin hoping against all hope, came up with another pseudoscientific theory referred to as the "**Lipalian interval**", a negative argument that attempts to explain away the absence of evidence. This has become the hallmark of today's pseudoscientific theories, especially when new discoveries obliterate previous extraneous theories. He postulated that the reason the transitional creatures are not showing up in the fossiliferous strata is due to certain geological processes. He noted that the Precambrian period was a time of great uplift from the continental shifting, and he suggested that the transitional ancestors of the Cambrian epoch happened at a time when the seas were receding from the land masses and therefore, must be in strata at the bottom of the oceans. This was before offshore drilling came into existence. After offshore drilling made its debut in the 1940s-60s, the Lipalian interval theory was quickly scuttled. The deep-sea core samples only reinforced the existing data where there was hardly any evidence of fossils whatsoever, much less the rich treasure trove the Darwinists hoped for.

The next major discovery to disappoint the evolutionist was made in 1995 by renowned Chinese paleontologist Professor J.Y. Chen in the town of Chengjiang, located in the Kunming Province in southern China. Again, the fossils found in the Maotianshan shale showed more diversity and disparity of species than what was found in the Burgess bestiary in a more photographic sharpness than any other find to date. Chen is not a creationist but rather an orthodox scientist of the "old school", using reasonable deductive analysis in his research apart from humanistic philosophical guidelines. He was invited to give a lecture in the spring of 2000 at the University of Washington's geological department. Chen, in the presentation of his discoveries and what his research has yielded to the scientific community highlighted the, apparent contradiction between the Chinese fossil record and the Darwinian orthodoxy. This prompted an attending professor to respond, in an admonishing tone, asking if he wasn't nervous about expressing his doubt about Darwinism so freely, especially in light of China's reputation for suppressing dissenting opinions. Chen responded saying, "In China, we can criticize Darwin, but not the government. In America you can criticize the government, but not Darwin". Apparently, there are still some scientists that maintain their objective integrity despite the consequences.

Again, the conclusion of this study is that the diversity and disparity amidst the lack of transitional strata has reached epic proportions, and it must now be accepted that the supporting evidence just does not exist after an exhaustive and noble effort. It is time to stop agreeing with theological apparitions that are beyond redemptive resources. Scientific protocol demands that you have a consensus of the data for it to be considered scientifically valid or a scientific certainty. Where there is no consensus and you inadvertently pick and choose values that agree with your theory or your belief then you have moved into the arena of pseudoscience.

The Genomic Evidence [15]

Evolutionists such as evolutionary biologist Richard Dawkins, professor of biology Jerry Coyne from the University of Chicago, Oxford University chemist Peter Atkins, and others make statements to the effect that both the physical evidence, as found in Precambrian and Cambrian fossiliferous strata, and the genetic evidence together positively bridges the gap for the substantial collaborating evidence needed to once and for all establish the evolutionary "tree of life" model as fact. They make these statements with the utmost confidence and authoritative composure, and in the case of Richard Dawkins, infer that if you believe otherwise you're a quack and should be subjected to public humility, shame, and insults for your ignorance. They bank on their standing and confident air to persuade the public that these statements are facts, are based in science, and are accepted by experts, when in fact, just the opposite is true. Mr. Dawkins and others of his persuasion are either ignorant (have not done their research) or willfully ignorant (having knowledge of the facts but are not willing to accept them as a whole, just those data that favor their theology), no doubt the latter in Mr. Dawkins' case. They believe that if they stand together as supposed experts in their fields and affirm these statements and one another that the public will buy into their propaganda and stand with them, or else shut up and go way from public debate, so as to allow them full reign to progress their humanist agenda and pseudoscience.

The genomic sciences have sought to confirm the theory of evolution and the "tree of life" model through the expected results that should be yielded from the research and study of the genome. After years of research by many independent organizations, most of the experts have concluded that not only does the evidence not support the "tree of life" model but that we do not even have the tools to analyze the genome to any significant degree.

The Divergence Hypothesis

Several attempts have been undertaken to track a genetic evolutionary divergent point, known as the "**deep-divergence hypothesis**", a point in time when a genesis creature or universal common ancestor existed, from which all animals have emerged. This theory begins with the assumption of evolution and predicts that by analyzing the anatomical and molecular similarities, biologists can reconstruct the tree of life during the Precambrian and Cambrian periods. These studies use a method of analysis referred to as the "molecular clock". Molecular clock studies are based on an assumption that the magnitude of difference between genetic similarities in two or more animal genes, RNA, or proteins reflects the amount of time that has passed during their evolution from a common ancestor. Thus, the greater the difference, the greater the time, and vice versa. These lengths of times are determined by their place in the rock strata compared to assumed earlier ancestors of both subject species, such as birds and mammals from an earlier reptile. Biologists then estimate the number of mutations from the divergent point by genetic comparisons. This, in conjunction with the dating of the rock strata, helps them determine an evolution rate of transformation. Needless to say, this scientific undertaking has yielded a wide range of results from the participating independent studies, anywhere from 274 million years ago (mya) to 14.2 billion years ago (bya) when applied to the Cambrian animals to determine when they diverged from a Precambrian ancestor (a phylum that is missing from the Precambrian strata). Since there can be only one true divergent point from which the tree of life has generated from, the multitude and wide range of results bear witness that there is no consensus and therefore cannot be determined by the tools and the state of art technology of modern science. Additionally, the proponents for these assumptions hold to the previously discussed "artifact theory" for why these ancestors have no evidenced in the fossil record which, as previously concluded, has been disproved from the many Cambrian strata discoveries in the past 150 years.

In 1999, evolutionary biologists G.A. Wray, J.S. Levinton, and L.H. Shapiro compared the difference between the amino-acid sequences of seven proteins and the nucleotide base sequences of a ribosomal RNA molecule for several modern animals representing Cambrian phyla. This study resulted in the universal common ancestor that lived 1.2bya.

Evolutionary biologist D. Erwin and colleagues compared the difference between the sequences of 7 nuclear housekeeping genes and 3 ribosomal RNA genes across 113 species of living Metazoa (creatures with differentiated tissue). This study resulted in a universal common ancestor that lived 800mya. In 1999, Erwin admitted that "attempts to date those branching[s] by using molecular clocks have disagreed widely".

In 1997, a study by Japanese biologist N. Nikoh and colleagues resulted in the universal common ancestor that lived 940mya.

In 1999, a study by B. Wang, S. Kumar, and S.B. Hedges resulted in the universal common ancestor that lived 1.2 - 1.5 bya.

One study actually reported that the divergent date fell between a range of 274mya and 1.6bya. The 274 date is 250my after the Cambrian explosion! They decided to split the difference and concluded that the date was 830mya.

Another study by S. Aris-Brosou and Z. Yang reported that the divergent date could fall between a range of 452mya and 2bya, depending on which genes were studied and which estimate method was used. The 452 date is 72my after the Cambrian explosion!

A survey by D. Graur and W. Martin published in *Trend in Genetics* titled "Reading the Entrails of Chickens: Molecular Timescale of Evolution and the Illusion of Precision" cited one study that claimed to be 95% certain that the divergent date fell within a 14.2bya range (the earth is only 4.5bya).

One paper in the journal *Molecular Biology and Evolution* states, "The rate of molecular evolution can vary considerably among different organisms, challenging the concept of the "molecular clock".

A. Smith and K. Peterson note: "Molecular clocks are not error-free and come with their own suite of problems...the accuracy of the technique depends upon having an accurate calibration point or points (correctly estimating the strata ages between ancestral subject phyla 1 and 2), and a reliable phylogeny with correct branching-length estimates (phyla that are actually close relatives)."

The oldest fossilized organism dates to about 3.5bya. The latest documentaries place the universal common ancestor at about 3.9bya, not based on any consensus of lab testing results (actually ignoring the scientific method), as there were no collaborating results and therefore nothing on which to base a consensus, but rather because it is the best fit for the theory placing it before the oldest known fossil and after a time when the earth was in a state not suitable for life to emerge. When you hear a secular scientist such as Neil deGrasse Tyson infer that geneticists can trace the DNA back to a universal common ancestor, they are not telling you the truth! Scientific protocol demands that you have a consensus of the data for it to be considered scientifically valid or a scientific certainty. When there is no consensus, and you decide to inadvertently pick and choose values that agree with your theology or your belief, then you have moved into the arena of pseudoscience.

Phylogenetic Reconstruction (Molecular Sequences)

The study of molecular sequencing attempts to track the animal genetic tree of life by assessing the magnitude of related characteristics to establish branching (divergent) points along the trees branches back to the trunk, especially among the major Cambrian groups. In the final analysis, the story the body of evidence tells, like the deep-divergence hypothesis, results in a multitude of conflicting patterns.

Molecule vs Molecule

A 2009 edition of *Trends in Ecology and Evolution* included a paper that notes "evolutionary trees from different genes often have conflicting branching patterns".

A 2009 edition of *New Scientist*'s cover story notes that the tree of life's molecular sequences "lies in tatters, torn to pieces by an onslaught of negative evidence ", "many biologists now argue that the tree of life concept is obsolete and needs to be discarded", and "the evolution of animal and plants isn't exactly tree-like".

A 2012 edition of *Biological Review* included a paper that notes "phylogenetic conflict is common and frequently the norm rather than the exception ".

An article in the *New Scientist* reported a story on the research and study by M. Syvanen on 2,000 genes of six very diverse animals saying, "In theory, he should have been able to use the gene sequences to construct an evolutionary tree showing the relationship between the six animals. He failed. The problem was the different genes told contradicting evolutionary stories." Syvanen himself confessed "We've just annihilated the tree of life. It's not a tree anymore, it's a different topology entirely. What would Darwin have made of that?"

Leading biologist Atonis Rokas of Vanderbilt University also echoes that sentiment, after 150 years of the acceptance of Darwin's *Origin of the Species*, saying "a complete and accurate tree of life remains an elusive goal", and that "despite the amount of data and breadth of taxa analyzed, relationships among most metazoan phyla remain unresolved".

A year later, A. Rokas and S.B. Carroll of the University of Wisconsin reiterated this disparity, saying "certain critical parts of the tree of life may be difficult to resolve, regardless of the quantity of conventional data available" and concluded from their extended study that "inferences from these two independent lines of evidence (molecules and fossils) support a view of the origin of the Metazoa as a radiation compressed in time".

So, instead of establishing the tree of life that geneticists initially hoped for, they have unanimously concluded that it not only shows the error of that assumption, it inversely well establishes the sudden appearance of the countless species in the Cambrian era, confirming the findings in the fossil record! So why do we encounter such arrogance in Richard Dawkins and company, and where does it come from? Scientific protocol demands that you have a consensus of the data for it to be considered scientifically valid or a scientific certainty. Where there is no consensus and you inadvertently pick and choose values that agree with your theory or your belief then you have moved into the arena of pseudoscience.

Molecule vs Anatomy

In 1965, L. Pauling and E. Zuckerkandl suggested that a study comparing anatomy and DNA sequencing should result in similar phylogenetic trees, saying "the best available single proof of the reality of macroevolution would be furnished", and "only the theory of evolution...could reasonably account for such a congruence between lines of evidence obtained independently". Following that notion, D. Theobald made a comparative study leading to assertions in his "29+ Evidence for Macroevolution" that "well-determined phylogenic trees inferred from the independent evidence of morphology and molecular sequencing match with an extremely high degree of statistical significance".

Studies made over the years by many different organizations since then have ultimately proved just the opposite. The technical data from the studies of molecular homologies often fail to confirm the evolutionary tree. Much of the results coming out in the 1990s showed conflicting phylogenetic trees derived from anatomical and molecular evolutionary studies.

One anatomical study that received much acclaim during this period was the "Coelomata hypotheses". The Coelomata hypotheses takes bilaterian animals and divides them into three classifications; Acoelomata, Psuedocoelomata, and Coelomata, wherein is found several different types of bilaterian animals. Their grouping was based on similar anatomy, such as the arthropods and annelids with their segmented body plans. After a study referred to as the "Ecdysozoa Hypotheses", which looked at the molecular presence (the 18S ribosomal RNA) in each of these animals, they were rearranged in different groupings based on the presence of "coeloms", their central body cavity. These molecular and anatomical groupings of course did not match each other as the predicted hypotheses would expect. Advocates for the Coelomata hypotheses, a classic pillar in the house of Evolution, opposed the claims of the Ecdysozoa hypotheses, citing some supporting molecular data as well, but the Ecdysozoa defenders contend that there is much more supporting data for the Ecdysozoa hypotheses.

Many other studies since that time have also come to bear ill tidings for the Pauling / Zuckerkandl assumption. There was a paper in the journal *Science* by L. Maley and C. Marshall that noted, "Animal relationships derived from these new molecular data sometimes are very different from those implied by older, classical evaluations on morphology."

Valentine, Jablonski, and Erwin, referring to sponges that are traditionally placed at the bottom of the animal tree with progressively more complex phyla (e.g., cnidarians, flatworms, nematodes) branching off, noted that molecules "indicate a very different configuration" where some higher deuterostome phyla branch off very early and some lesser complex phyla branch very late. Some sponges were found to be more closely related to jellyfish than they were to other sponges.

The anatomical body plan of Cnidarian and ctenophores are similar and so are believed to be close in morphological ascendance, but molecular data shows that they are quite distant based on conclusive findings from papers by A. Rokas et al, "Conflicting Phylogenic Signals at the base of the Metazoan Tree" and Halanych "The New View of Animal Phylogeny".

Larger datasets only serve to further increase the chasm between the two instead of closing the gap, as was hoped for. A paper in 2012 by Davalos et al reports "Incongruence between phylogenies derived from morphological versus molecular analyses and between trees based on different subsets of molecular sequences has become pervasive as datasets have expanded rapidly in both characters and species".

Finally, J. H. Schwartz, and B. Maresca wrote in the journal *Biological Theory*: "This assumption derives from interpreting molecular similarities (or dissimilarities) between taxa in the context of a Darwinian model of continual and gradual change. Review of the history of molecular systematics and its claims in the context of molecular biology reveals that there is no basis for the 'molecular assumption'".

The results of the three previously reviewed case studies and even in the anatomy versus anatomy studies (such as germ cell formation) have been ether inconclusive or contradictive to the theory of evolution, which reflects well on the creation model. If in truth there is no "tree of life" history then there can be no collaborating evidence, which is true for all three cases. These results, taken in hand with the missing transitional strata and fossils, serve to collaborate and form a consensus that the theory of evolution is not an acceptable theory at all, and should even be rejected as a competing theory! Scientific protocol demands that you have a consensus of the data for it to be considered scientifically valid or a scientific certainty. When there is no consensus, and you decide to inadvertently pick and choose values that agree with your theology or your belief, then you have moved into the arena of pseudoscience.

Combinational Inflation

In 1966, a convention was held at The Wistar Institute in Philadelphia, PA. The convention was held to bring together leading scientists to discuss the "mathematical challenges to the Neo-Darwinian interpretation of evolution". Attending this conference were prominent scientists of the time such as Marcel-Paul Schutzenberger (mathematician and physician), Stanislaw Ulam (co–designer of the hydrogen bomb), Murray Eden (engineering and computer science professor from MIT), Ernst Mayr (biologist and leading architect of modern Neo-Darwinism), Richard Lewontin (genetics and evolutionary biology professor from U of C), and Sir Peter Medawar (a Nobel laureate and director of the N. London Med. Research Council's Laboratories) who chaired the meeting.

With the discovery of the DNA structure, testing the outcome of random chance as proposed by the theory of evolution could now yield more concise results. The DNA coding system can be compared to the English language, or rather text, in the way DNA communicates, signals, and processes material resources to the building of a creature. Minor mutations within a text (removing a letter or replacing one with a random alternative) may be forgiven, but the more singular components (letters or words) that get replaced or removed at random, the more distorted the meaning gets and the less likely the communication will be successful. The same is true of randomly combining or recombining genetic "text" without intelligent direction. Marcel-Paul Schutzenberger noted at the convention that in computer language, which DNA codes mostly resemble, if there are just a few random changes, the system jams up and there is no output. The chances are less than $1/10^{10000}$ per these the aforementioned mathematicians. They conclude that random mutation will result in a distortion or lethal outcome and that nature would eliminate the negative mutated creature (survival of the fittest). The possibility of combinational outcomes renders the chances of a favorable mutation nil. The more transformational changes required to generate a new novelty, say an eye, the more inflated the negative outcomes become and the less the chances are of randomly combining in the perfect sequence. For example, a chain of 2 amino acids could have 20^2 (400) possible combinations, 3 amino acids could have 20^3 (8,000) possible combinations, 4 amino acids could have 20^4 (160,000) possible combinations, and so on.

The DNA and epigenetic systems (extraneous information, data, instructions, algorithms found in the structure of the genome apart from the DNA) of the genome function much like the intricate systems of electrical circuitry hardware (with wiring, transmitters, transistors, capacitors, diodes, switches, etc.) in conjunction with computerized software, only they are much more sophisticated and much more sensitive to changes. You could not randomly remove or replace ether the hardware components with other components of differing functions or replace code bits in the software with random text and expect the piece of equipment to function at full capacity – if at all. All the case studies of the predicted theoretical outcomes by secular scientists as to the mechanisms that could cause evolutionary changes have shown that just as in the analogies of the electrical circuitry, the software, the English text, and the components of a particular function have to be placed in specific order by an entity that has a specific plan in mind. The electrical circuitry, hardware, and software of a modern day laptop computer could in no way come to exist by random chance! But that is what evolutionists want you to believe regarding the genome.

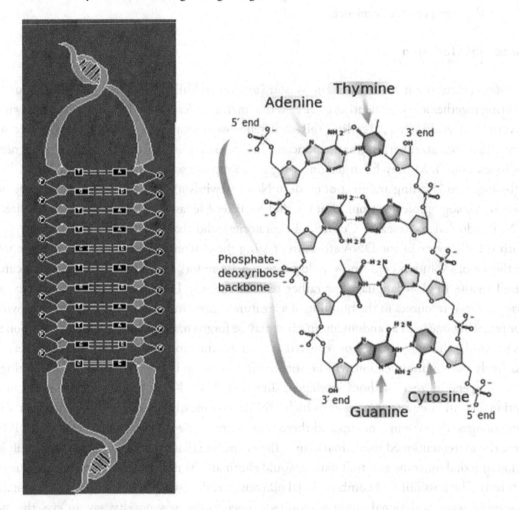

Figure 2.1 The DNA molecule depicting the nucleotide base stored along the sugar-phosphate backbone of the molecule that functions much like the hardware and software of a computer.

When statisticians estimate an event happening by chance, they often use what is called "*conditional probability*". If they calculate the chances are less than half, they deem the results as implausible and vice versa. If the chances are greater than half, the event is deemed plausible. Douglas Axe, a Ph.D. student in chemical engineering, estimated the chances for a modest length of protein folds (150 residues) that perform a specific function via any folded structure compared to the whole set of possible amino-acid sequences of that size to be $1/10^{77}$, indubitably less than $1/2$ probability, not plausible, and in actuality, impossible.

The pseudoscience that plagues the theory of evolution, as well as the make believe theories that supplement the missing empirical data (e.g., the Dynamo theory, the Oort cloud, punctuated equilibrium, the artifact hypotheses, etc.) is, not surprisingly, extended to the battle of the genomic evolution on the side of the secular humanist as well. On one side, you have representatives of the secular humanist theology such as Richard Dawkins (author of *The Blind Watchman*), Jerry Coyne, Peter Atkins, and company that base their arguments on supposed scientific publications that have been generated to defend the genetic tree of life based on "real" science. These publications are in truth based on the hypothetical scenarios of evolution and presupposition of a genesis creature that underwent morphological changes paralleling supposed anatomical transformation and evolution of phylum. The body of proof within these papers is based on theory alone (hypothetical scenarios) with no consensus of supporting empirical data, lab test results, or other scientific data of consequence. On the other hand, geneticists that have tested these same theories in the lab have all come back with a consensus of negative results, which of course are ignored by the Dawkins of the world.

Steven Meyer's book *Darwin's Doubt* has well established the scientific facts concerning any possibility that chance and natural selection could be a cause for the evolution of life (nil). Meyer's assertions are based on multiple independent laboratories and scientists putting all the Darwinian, neo-Darwinian, evo-devo, self-organization theorists, or any other Johnny–come–lately theories to the test. All of them have come back with a consensus of negative results that chance or random natural selection could possibly yield anything resembling the Darwinian "tree of life". As previously discussed, conventions held by top mathematicians revealed the odds of such coincidence to be at "0" in all possible scenarios (1 in 10^{77} at best). Every possible scenario to simulate any natural happenstance that could produce macro evolutionary transformation, one novel species from another novel species, or even a step in the direction of a transition toward another species, has failed momentously in all instances, just as the Wistar convention mathematicians predicted. Richard Dawkins, however, continues confidently espousing that his model shows how it works in nature, except that, as Douglas Axe points out, at the critical moment (the 1 in 10^{77} moment) he intelligently directs the model to accept the data, glossing over the chance that would be needed for that moment to happen. Wala! You have evolution at work, except it really is the result of intelligent design (his intellectual input), not chance happenstance as in nature. Again, the consensus of redundant and well established lab results conclude this a matter of fact!

The pseudoscientific rebuttals in all cases against Meyer's conclusions that are based on the empirical evidence resort to *"de novo" (anew)* at the critical core of their arguments, as if *de novo* was some sort of information generating mechanism, which sells well to the general public due to their lack of technical understanding. In essence, they are saying that it just appeared for the first time out of nowhere, as if by magic (very scientific). Evolutionary biologist's use of *"de novo origination"* is void of any known mutational process. This brings these arguments and references to supporting publications to nothing but theory and conjecture with no supporting facts or empirical evidence. It is becoming apparent that the secular scientists of today have become acclimated to an environment that accepts scientific theory based on the *de novo* at the critical moment in place of empirical evidence as fact. They live in a world where they produce hollow papers, accept each other's theories as if sufficient for proof, and ignore the consensus of empirical evidence (redundant collaborating lab testing results) that emphatically debunks their theories. They then impetuously discourage any inference to intelligent design, and even punish the violators.

The following are peer-reviewed publications and theories cited by secular scientists that oppose Meyer's conclusions and were used in court cases, such as defense attorney Long's references in the 2005 *Kitzmiller v. Dover* trial. They defer to *de novo* as the evolutionary mechanism at the critical moment in place of any consensus of empirical evidence or lab test results.

Nurminsky et al, "Selective Sweep of a Newly Evolved Sperm-Specific Gene in Drosophila" 574.

"This unusual regulatory region did not really "evolve", "it was aboriginal, created *de novo* by the fortuitous juxtaposition of suitable sequence".

Chen, DeVreis, and Chengl, "Evolution of Antifreeze Glycoprotein Gene from a Trypsinogen Gene in Antarctic Notothernioid Fish" 3816.

In an explanation regarding the origins of human genes involved in neurodevelopment the publication suggested "*de novo* generation of building blocks — single genes or gene segments coding for protein domains" where an exon spontaneously "originated from a unique non-coding sequence".

Article in PLos Genetics by Wu, Irwin, and Zhang, "De Novo Origen of Human Protein-Coding Genes".

"60 new protein-coding genes that originated *de novo* on the human lineage since the divergence from chimpanzees".

Stuart Kauffman, Self-Organization Theorists, Lecture at MIT.

"Life bubbles forth in a *natural magic* beyond the confines of entailing law, beyond mathematization" saying that self-organization theory allows us to be "reenchanted" with nature and to "find a way beyond modernity". Basically, he is saying let's forget true science and the need for the underlying scientific principle of Vera causa (true cause). It's time to move deeper into our make believe (pseudo) science and leave the truth and real world behind.

So it appears that when secular scientists run out of theories or options, they would rather believe in *magic* rather than concede to *intelligent design*. What ever happened to "everything has a physical explanation" a *Vera causa*? None of these or any other publication typically referenced by the defenders of evolutionary biology makes any reference to the mechanisms behind the "new genetic information" found in animals of diverse species along any evolutionary lineage. Any reference to "existing genetic information" supposedly passed from one species to others along an evolutionary lineage either refers to the *de novo* "magic moment" or to a process that has been satisfactory and repeatedly tested and found false.

End summary and commentary of Stephen Meyers book "*Darwin's Doubt*".

Geological Strata

The fossils found in strata are segmented to varying degrees and assortments. During the Flood, waters reached tremendous heights and brought sediment and sea creatures inland and deposited them together in strata, which make up the majority of fossils. The dynamics in which the strata were built were an amalgamation of many differing physical actions. These included varying flow rates, tectonic vibrations, volcanic eruptions, large volume displacement of land and water mass, and so on. Much of the sorting of phylum in the strata were influenced by environmental sources, particle sifting during tectonic vibrations, deposition fallout rates due to varying sizes of the particles/species, flow rates and temperatures, and erosion during flow changes and regression, to name a few.

Secular geologists have organized earth's strata (rock formations) as if it represents geological time periods and epochs, each representing millions of years. Since there is not an absolute means to date rocks, geologists devised a system to estimate the age of a given rock strata based on what fossils they find in it, purely assumption based on evolutionary theory with no scientific supporting data (pseudoscience in action). The fossils found in segmented strata were placed in a chronological order and a logical appearance in time based on the evolutionary process of uniformitarianism theory. These segments were placed in an order considering environmental factors, size, and natural progression from simple to complex fauna. Geologists, looking at the variations of a particular species found in the fossil records, will determine the ages within an epoch based on their judgement as to the progression they believe the variations show. This is all in disregard to scientific analogy of modern-day depictions. For instance, if a worldwide catastrophic flood event happened today, there would be strata in different locations depicting variations of the same species. The ponies found in Chincoteague strata would be interpreted as an earlier variation for the mustang found in a stratum from Wyoming and assigned an earlier age by millions of years, even though they are contemporary. The same would be true for all species throughout the world, but this logic is ignored by the secular scientist to make the evidence fit the evolutionary model.

This evolutionary progression was assumed to have started in the seas with microorganisms, then to fish and plankton, then to amphibian and vascular land plants, then to small land bound reptiles and vegetation, to increased sized reptiles (dinosaurs) and trees, and then to mammalian type creatures, and so on, with supplemental periods of extinction events (cosmic rays, volcanism, meteor strike) over millions of years. Progression was determined by "natural selection", that is environmental factors that weed out lesser adapted creatures, choose the fitter specimens, and promote physical transformation through cellular mutation (survival of the fittest). Geologic time is divided into named groupings according to six basic units, which are (in order of size from longest to shortest) eon, era, period, epoch, age, and chron. There is no absolute standard for the length of any unit; rather, it takes at least two ages to make an epoch, at least two epochs to compose a period, and so on. The dates for specific eons, eras, periods, and so on are usually given in relative terms [17].

Periods/Systems of the Paleozoic Era/Erathem

- **Cambrian** (about 545 to 495 Ma): Cambria, the Roman name for the province of Wales
  Fossils: Chordates and fish
- **Ordovician** (about 495 to 443 Ma): Ordovices, the name of a Celtic tribe in ancient Wales
  Fossils: Diverse metazoan families
- **Silurian** (about 443 to 417 Ma): Silures, another ancient Welsh Celtic tribe
  Fossils: Vascular land plants
- **Devonian** (about 417 to 354 Ma): Devonshire, a county in southwest England
  Fossils: Amphibians and diverse jawed fish
- **Mississippian** (a sub period of the Carboniferous period, about 354 to 323 Ma): the Mississippi River

Fossils: Seed ferns

- **Pennsylvanian** (a sub period of the Carboniferous, about 323 to 290 Ma): the state of Pennsylvania
  Fossils: Reptiles and scale trees
- **Permian** (about 290 to 248.2 Ma): Perm, a province in Russia
  Fossils: Reptiles/major extinction

Periods/Systems of the Mesozoic Era/Erathem

- **Triassic** (about 248.2 to 205.7 Ma): a tripartite, or threefold, division of rocks in Germany
  Fossils: Dinosaurs and mammals
- **Jurassic** (about 205.7 to 142 Ma): the Jura Mountains of Switzerland and France
  Fossils: Diverse dinosaurs and birds
- **Cretaceous** (about 142 to 65 Ma): from a Latin word for "chalk," a reference to the chalky cliffs of southern England and France
  Fossils: Flowering plants, primates, extinction of dinosaurs

Epochs/Series of the Cenozoic Era/Erathem

- **Paleocene** (about 65 to 54.8 Ma): "early dawn of the recent"
- **Eocene** (about 54.8 to 33.7 Ma): "dawn of the recent"
- **Oligocene** (about 33.7 to 23.8 Ma): "slightly recent"
- **Miocene** (about 23.8 to 5.3 Ma): "less recent"
- **Pliocene** (about 5.3 to 1.8 Ma): "more recent"
- **Pleistocene** (about 1.8 to 0.01 Ma): "most recent"
- **Holocene** (about 0.01 Ma to present): "wholly recent"
  Phylum: Diverse mammals and humans

This order is never really seen in nature and in many cases the strata has missing segments that are referred to as "unconformities". Most examples only have a portion of the full spectrum of strata layers, and much of it is out of sequence from the model but in relative agreement with each other when comparing strata found in different locations around the globe.

Geologists agree that most of the earth's strata was formed underwater. Most secular geologists will argue that it was laid down by slow uniformitarian processes with some localized catastrophes/flooding events; however, the evidence says otherwise. Sedimentary rocks laid down by massive movement of water make up 75% of the earth's surface with the remaining left to igneous and metamorphic rock formations. Being that the sedimentary depositions only amount to 5% of the volume of the earth's crust, they are spread out as relatively thin layers over the surface. The matrix material for these layers come from many different sources and directions. Based on the mass or quantity of material, they could only have been deposited by massive movement of water in a global catastrophic event. Strata around the world appears to have the same "stratification", which are layers of the same consecutive order and make up (environment, source material, and similar fossils). Professor Derek Ager (1923-1993) was a British paleontologist, former president of the British Geological Association, and Emeritus Professor of Geology at the University College of Swansea, Wales. Ager argued that the rock strata around the world underwent periods of slow deposition punctuated by major catastrophic events that account for the sediment strata found around the world. He cites locations in Britain, the Canadian Rockies, Greenland, and Australia that have fossiliferous lower Cambrian strata that conformably overlay a type of fossil free sandstone layer known as quartzite. This layer in turn overlays a great variety of different types of Precambrian strata in an unconformable manner. This layer of quartzite is found throughout the world along with other associated strata combination such as basal conglomerate, followed by marine shale, and thin limestone. Layers of rock laid down around the world with such conformity, patterns, and order cannot be accredited to slow process or localized flooding events that happened at different geological ages; however, this can easily be accounted for by a singular worldwide event. The amount of material found in sandstone depositions in these massive areas that are covered by laminar layers would require an incredible hydraulic force that can only be explained by movement of water on the magnitude of a global flood scenario. The Shinarump conglomerate that can be seen in the Zion National Park in Utah, for example, is a fossil bearing (land animal) sandstone rock formation. It is a 100-ft. thick uniform layer, spread out over 97,000 square miles. Shinarump conglomerate is a part of the Chinle formation that is spread over an estimated 310,000 to 890,000 square miles. Then there is the Morrison formation, a dinosaur's fossil bearing sandstone rock formation spread out from Texas to Canada and covering 580,000 square miles and is an average of 328 feet thick. These strata could not have been accumulated by slow uniformitarian process as they are fossiliferous, which requires quick burying and pressurization processes, then there is the magnitude of forces required to lay down such mass which puts it outside the realm of localized catastrophic events. Additionally, much of the sand is from oceanic sources, inferring that it had to come from a great distance. The source of sand that makes up most of these strata cannot be positively identified; however, the source for the Navajo sandstone layer in southern Utah is believed to have come from the Appalachian Mountains, from a stretch between Pennsylvania to New York, over 1,200 miles away. This connection was made by matching elements such as small amounts of zirconium with inclusion of uranium found in the sand. When accounting for the multitude of strata, science cannot overlook the fact that geological formations such as strata are laid down in multiple layers at a time as seen and recorded in present day formations. In light of these facts the geological science favors the hypotheses that much of the world's strata were also laid down in the same catastrophic geological event, which in turn supports a flood of epic (biblical) proportions to have supplied the great mass of material for all the associated strata [18].

(NOTE: the following C[14] dating needs to be adjusted for gross error due to strength of the magnetosphere, the greenhouse effect, and other environmental factors neglected to be considered by the secular scientific community). Dates in parentheses are the author's based on these assumptions.

Water levels before the Flood, by all indication, were much lower than today's levels. The waters would have receded from the land when the continents spread out, opening gaps in the sea floor in combination with the climatological cycles. Much of the moisture would have accumulated as snowfall in the poles during the Ice Age. Water levels continued to increase in the several hundreds of years after the Flood due to melting ice from the post–Flood Ice Age. Remains of ancient cultures and cities are found underwater in many diverse locations.

Atlit-Yam Haifa, Israel - C[14] dated to 6200-6700 BC (2500). Lies between 26 and 39 ft. below the water surface. Abandoned suddenly (such as with Skara Brae, Scotland), human remains, square buildings, artifacts such as axes, sickle-blades, and arrow heads were found in pristine condition. Stone semi-circles with 1,300-pound megaliths used for a worship center was found to echo the many similar centers in virtually all the ancient cities of the Antediluvian era [19].

Greek Underwater City (Aegean Sea) - Dated to 2500BC. Depths below the water surface not given. Artifacts included stone defensive structures, paved surfaces, pathways, towers, pottery, tools, and other artifacts [20].

Doggerland (N. Sea off coast of England, stretching from Scotland to Denmark) - Dated to 6200BC (2500). Lies between 49 and 118 ft. below the water surface. Vessels have dragged up remains of mammoth, lion, and other land animals, as well as small numbers of prehistoric tools and weapons. Amongst the structures is Seahenge [21].

Dwarka, Gulf of Cambay, India lies between 65 and 130 ft. below the water surface (from about 2500-2000 BC). The structures (regularly spaced dwellings, a granary, a bath, a citadel, and a drainage system) resembled Harrapan civilization dating to 2000BC. Artifacts recovered included pieces of wood, pottery shards, weathered stone hand tools, fossilized bones, microliths, wattle and daub remains, and hearth material [22].

Archaeological Demarcation at the time of the Flood

The Antediluvian era is referred to as the Early Bronze Age by historians in reference to the era's characterization. Archeologists from around the world have noted a definite demarcation in the geological record between the Early and Intermediate Bronze age.

Highlights from Bob Maddison's" second edition of "Now and Then regarding these demarcations [23].

The Catastrophic End of the Early Bronze Age

Testimonials from renown archaeologists Kathryn Kenyon, Ernest Wright, Claude Schaeffer, John Garstung, Paolo Matthiae, Carl Blegen, and Michael Rice appear to agree that there was a definite demarcation in all the archaeological excavations around the world in about 2500-2200 BC from a natural disaster of a magnitude not seen in any other strata. These "gaps" in the occupation between cultural residents are global and appear between the Early and Intermediate Bronze Age. The geographical areas include Europe, Asia Minor, Indus Valley, China, and the Americas.

Maddison relays that French archaeologist Carl Schaffer tells of his discoveries of demarcations from Crete and Ras Shamira (Ugarit) from about 2200 BC that coincided with the same strata of demarcations in the Middle East and Europe:

> *"There is not the slightest doubt that the conflagration of Troy II corresponds to the Catastrophe that made an end to the Habitations of the Early Bronze Age of Alaca Huyuk, of Alisair of Tarsus, of Tepe Hissar [in Asia Minor] and to the Catastrophe that burned ancient Ugarit (II) in Syria, the city of Byblos that flourished under the Old Kingdom in Egypt, the contemporaneous cities of Palestine, and that it was among the causes*

that terminated the old Kingdom of Egypt". In the same Catastrophe was destroyed the civilizations of Mesopotamia and Cyprus."

From Kathryn Kenyon, excavator of both Jericho and Jerusalem, he quotes:

"The final end of the early Bronze Age civilization came with catastrophic completeness... Jericho...was probably completely destroyed... Every town in Palestine that has so far been investigated shows the same break... All traces of the early Bronze Age civilization disappeared." (Archeology in the Holy Land [London, 1960], p134).

From Ernest Wright, he quotes:

"One of the most striking facts about the Early Bronze Age civilization is its destruction, one so violent that scarcely a vestige of it survived. We do not know when the event took place; we only know that there is not an Early Bronze Age city excavated or explored in all Palestine which does not have a gap in its occupation between Early Bronze Age III and the Middle Bronze Age. To date this gap, we know that it must approximately contemporary with a similar period in Egypt called the First Intermediate period between dynasties XI and XI (Ca. 22nd and 21st Century B.C.)." ("The Archeology of Palestine" in The Bible and the Ancient Near East, Essays in Honor of William Foxwell Albright [1961], p103).

From Maria Gimbutas, he quotes:

"The destruction of the early Helladic II town at Lerna in the Eastern Peloponnese is an example of the widespread and violent destruction that occurred Ca. 2300 B.C. in the Aegean and East Mediterranean."

Historical research protocols demand that you have a consensus of the records for it to be considered historically correct or an historical certainty. Here you have a consensus of renown archaeologists around the world testifying to the obvious demarcation in the archeological record in and about 2500BC, which has all the characteristics that parallel a global catastrophic event in both the time period and totality of the event around the world, and yet it is a great mystery to these secular archeologists – they haven't a clue as to what could have caused it.

THE ICE AGE

An estimated 500-year ice age immediately followed the Flood due to the cataclysmic interruption of the climatological cycle and sudden change in climate and seasons that it brought about. An article by Michael Oard from the ICR website has the best technical explanation of the post–Flood Ice Age [24]: (copied by permission)

The origin of the ice age has greatly perplexed uniformitarian scientists. Much cooler summers and copious snowfall are required, but they are inversely related, since cooler air is drier. It is unlikely cooler temperatures could induce a change in atmospheric circulation that would provide the needed moisture. As a result, well over 60 theories have been proposed. Charlesworth states:

"Pleistocene phenomena have produced an absolute riot of theories ranging 'from the remotely possible to the mutually contradictory and the palpably inadequate.'"

A uniformitarian ice age seems meteorologically impossible. The necessary temperature drop in Northern Canada has been established by a sophisticated energy balance model over a snow cover. Summers must be 10 degrees to 12 degrees C cooler than today, even with twice the normal winter snowfall.

The Milankovitch mechanism, or the old astronomical theory, has recently been proposed as the solution to the problem. Computer climate simulations have shown that it could initiate an ice age, or at least glacial/interglacial fluctuations. However, an in-depth examination does not support this. The astronomical theory is based on small changes in solar radiation, caused by periodic shifts in the earth's orbital geometry. It had been assumed too weak to cause ice ages by meteorologists, until the oscillations were "statistically" correlated with oxygen isotope fluctuations in deep-sea cores. The latter cycles are believed related mostly to glacial ice volume, and partially to ocean paleotemperature, although the exact relationship has been controversial. The predominant period from cores was correlated to the 100,000-year period of the earth's eccentricity, which changes the solar radiation at most 0.17%. This is an infinitesimal effect. Many other serious problems plague the astronomical theory. Although models can test causal hypotheses, Bryson says they ". . . are not sufficiently advanced, nor is our knowledge of the required inputs, to allow for climatic reconstruction."

A POST-FLOOD MODEL

The climate change following the Genesis Flood provides a likely catastrophic mechanism for an ice age. The Flood was a tremendous tectonic and volcanic event. Large amounts of volcanic aerosols would remain in the atmosphere following the Flood, generating a large temperature drop over land by reflecting much solar radiation back to space. Volcanic aerosols would likely be replenished in the atmosphere for hundreds of years following the Flood, due to high post-Flood volcanism, which is indicated in Pleistocene sediments. The moisture would be provided by strong evaporation from a much warmer ocean, following the Flood. The warm ocean is a consequence of a warmer pre-Flood climate and the release of hot subterranean water during the eruption of "all the fountains of the great deep" (Genesis 7:11). The added quantity of water must have been large to cover all the pre-Flood mountains, which were lower than today. Evaporation over the ocean is proportional to how cool, dry, and unstable the air is, and how fast the wind blows. Indirectly, it is proportional to sea surface temperature. A 10 degree C air-sea temperature difference, with a relative humidity of 50%, will evaporate seven times more water at a sea surface temperature of 30 degrees C than at 0 degrees C. Thus, the areas of greatest evaporation would be at higher latitudes and off the east coast of Northern Hemisphere continents. Focusing on northeast North America, the combination of cool land and warm ocean would cause the high-level winds and a main storm track to be parallel to the east coast, by the thermal wind equation. Storm after storm would develop near the eastern shoreline, similar to modern-day Northeasters, over the continent. Once a snow cover is established, more solar radiation is reflected back to space, reinforcing the cooling over land, and compensating the volcanic lulls.

The ice sheet will grow as long as the large supply of moisture is available, which depends upon the warmth of the ocean. Thus, the time to reach maximum ice volume will depend upon the cooling time of the ocean. This can be found from the heat balance equation for the ocean, with reasonable assumptions of post-Flood climatology and initial and final average ocean temperatures. However, the heat lost from the ocean would be added to the atmosphere, which would slow the oceanic cooling with cool summers and warm winters. The time to reach maximum ice volume must also consider the heat balance of the post-Flood atmosphere, which would strongly depend upon the severity of volcanic activity. Considering ranges of volcanism and the possible variations in the terms of the balance equations, the time for glacial maximum ranges from 250 to 1,300 years.

The average ice depth at glacial maximum is proportional to the total evaporation from the warm ocean at mid and high latitudes, and the transport of moisture from lower latitudes. Since most snow in winter storms falls in the colder portion of the storm, twice the precipitation was assumed to fall over the cold land than over the ocean. Some of the moisture, re-evaporated from non-glaciated land, would end up as snow on the ice sheet, but this effect should be mostly balanced by summer runoff. The average depth of ice was calculated at roughly half uniformitarian estimates. The latter are really unknown. As Bloom states, "Unfortunately, few facts about its thickness are known . . . we must turn to analogy and theory. . .."

The time to melt an ice sheet at mid-latitudes is surprisingly short, once the copious moisture source is gone. It depends upon the energy balance over a snow or ice cover. Several additional factors would have enhanced melting. Crevassing would increase the absorption of solar radiation, by providing more surface area. The climate would be colder and drier than at present, with strong dusty storms that would tend to track along the ice sheet boundary. The extensive loess sheets south of and within the periphery of the past ice sheet attest to this. Dust settling on the ice would greatly increase the solar absorption and melting. A mountain snowfield in Japan was observed to absorb 85% of the solar radiation after 4000 ppm of pollution dust had settled on its surface.

ONE ICE AGE

Earth scientists believe there were many ice ages—perhaps more than 30—in regular succession during the late Cenozoic based on oxygen isotope fluctuations in deep-sea cores. However, the ocean results have many difficulties, and sharply conflict with the long-held four ice-age continental scheme. Before the early 20th century, the number of ice ages was much debated. Some scientists believed in only one ice age, but the sediments are complex and have evidence of anywhere from one to four, or possibly more till sheets, separated by non-glacial deposits. Four ice ages became established mainly from gravel terraces in the Alps, and reinforced by soil stratigraphy. Much has been learned about glacial behavior and sedimentation since then. The Alps terraces are now viewed as possibly ". . . a result of repeated tectonic uplift cycles—not widespread climatic changes per se." Variously weathered "interglacial soils" between till sheets are complex, and practically always have the top organic horizon missing. It is difficult to know whether they are really soils. Besides, the rate of modern soil formation is unknown, and depends upon many complex factors, like the amount of warmth, moisture, and time. Therefore, the number of glaciations is still an open question.

There are strong indications that there was only one ice age. As discussed previously, the requirements for an ice age are very stringent. The problem grows to impossibility, when more than one is considered. Practically all the ice-age sediments are from the last, and these deposits are very thin over interior areas, and not overly thick at the periphery. Till can sometimes be laid down rapidly, especially in end moraines. Thus, the main characteristics of the till favor one ice age. Pleistocene fossils are rare in glaciated areas, which is mysterious, if there were many interglacials. Practically all the megafauna extinctions were after the last—a difficult problem if there was more than one.

One dynamic ice age could explain the features of the till along the periphery by large fluctuations and surges, which would cause stacked till sheets. Organic remains can be trapped by these oscillations. Large fluctuations may be caused by variable continental cooling, depending upon volcanic activity. In addition, most of the snow and ice should accumulate at the periphery, closest to the main storm tracks. Large surface slopes and warm basal temperatures at the edge are conducive to rapid glacial movement.

In summary, the mystery of the ice age can be best explained by one catastrophic ice age as a consequence of the Genesis Flood.

Editorial notes: **Beth Mull, Senior Editor** Institute for Creation Research

1. Uniformitarian scientists now claim that there were about 50 ice ages in the late Cenozoic, not just 30. [see 1st sentence under *One Ice Age*]. A reference for this is

Walker, M. and Lowe, J. 2007. Quaternary science 2007: a 50-year retrospective. *Journal of the Geological Society, London* 164: 1073-1092.

2. Rapid seafloor spreading due to catastrophic plate tectonics would have also greatly contributed to the warming of the oceans. This could possibly be included under 'the release of hot subterranean water during the eruption of "all the fountains of the great deep" (Genesis 7:11).' [1st paragraph under *A Post-Flood Model*].

3. Regarding the sentence in the 3rd paragraph, 'It [the Milankovitch theory] had been assumed too weak to cause ice ages by meteorologists, until the oscillations were "statistically" correlated with oxygen isotope fluctuations in deep sea cores.' Although Mike doesn't cite a reference for this, he is referring to the "Pacemaker of the Ice Ages" paper that I just refuted.

Hayes, J. D., J. Imbrie, and N. J. Shackleton. 1976. Variations in the Earth's Orbit: Pacemaker of the Ice Ages. *Science* 194, no. 4270 (December 10): 1121-1132.

Ice core dating by secular scientists neglects to take into account the effect that a global Flood would have to the climate variables, accumulation and precipitation rates, or seasonal layering. Many of these layers that are counted as annual indicators could very well have been laid down by individual storms. It has been suggested that 95% of the ice near the poles was accumulated within the 500 years following the Flood [25].

Civilization from Here

From the time Noah and his family left the Ark and began to repopulate the earth till the time of the birth of nations was about 200 to 250 years. By 100 years after the Flood, the average life span for the next three to four generations was quickly degrading from the 1,000 years antediluvian to about 230 years, no doubt due to the environmental changes brought about by the Flood. It is evident not only from the biblical account, but from historical accounts as well, that during this period of decline the manifestations of spiritual beings, God and the gods, were declining as well. The gods still appeared to communicate with men and were still worshiped by man, but there was an evident limitation to their physical appearances, to the point that men erected representative idols and statues in their places. From this time, civilization was ruled by mortal man (with the exception Melchizedek, King of Salem) and was held to the warmer regions of the hemisphere due to the Ice Age ice caps for next 500 years. A race by the immerging populace to dominate and rule what areas were habitable was apparent first in Mesopotamia, where they first migrated from the Ark, then to the warmer climate to the southeast in Egypt. Records of conquest and war are in all the literature of the times.

Tower of Babel and Birth of the Nations

We know from Genesis 11:1-9 that as the population grew they migrated east from the highlands of Armenia where they settled in the land of Shinar. All the peoples spoke the same language. At this time Nimrod, the son of Kush, the son of Ham, the son of Noah, rose up and became the first king in the land of Shinar, subjecting men unto his rule. Nimrod, looking to make a name for himself, put the people to work to build a city and a great tower (ziggurat) that could reach into the heavens.

God came down and looked over the city and tower and commented on their combined efforts, saying that as one people speaking the same language nothing could stop them from doing anything they set their minds to. God then altered their speech so different people groups started speaking different languages. The city was from then on known as Babel. Out of the confusion, the people separated and began a migration throughout the world. It was about this time that Mezriam, Nimrod's uncle, took his people to the land of Egypt to make a name for himself as well, and began to build an empire of his own. As the glacial ice receded, others set out to establish their own kingdoms to rule in other parts of the globe, even taking to ships to reach the farthest shores such as North and South America.

A Sumerian story with some similar elements, such as confusion of languages, is told in *Enmerkar and the Lord of Aratta*. The ruins of the city of Babylon are near Hillah, Babil Governorate, Iraq.

Flavius Josephus, a Jewish-Roman historian, recounted these events as found in the Hebrew Bible and mentioned the Tower of Babel in his *Antiquities of the Jews* (94 AD). He asserted that it was Nimrod (the grandson of Ham, the son of Noah) who built the tower. He goes on to say that Nimrod was a tyrant who tried to turn the people away from God. In this account, God confused the people instead of destroying them because the flood event hadn't taught them to flee idolatry. This information would have been from resources extant at the time of Josephus.

The oldest known written documents [26]

The Kish tablet is a limestone tablet found at Tell al-Uhaymir, Babil Governorate, Iraq - the site of the ancient Sumerian city of Kish. It is dated to 3500 BC, which is in the middle Uruk period, or more aptly 2300 to 2100 BC due to errors with dating methods. Today, a plaster cast of the artifact is in the collection of the Ashmolean Museum in Oxford.

Figure 2.2 The Kish tablet is inscribed with proto-cuneiform signs and may be considered the oldest known written document. The writing is still purely pictographic and represents a transitional stage between proto-writing and the emergence of the partly syllabic writing of the cuneiform script proper. The "protoliterate period" of Egypt and Mesopotamia is taken to span from about 3500 to 2900 BC (2500 to 2200). The Kish tablet is thus more accurately identified as the first document of the Mesopotamian protoliterate period. Several hundred documents dating to about the thirty–second century BC have been found at Uruk. The administrative texts of the Jemdet Nasr period (3100–2900 BC) (2300), found among other places at Jemdet Nasr and Tell Uqair represent a further stage in the development from proto-cuneiform to cuneiform, but can still not be identified with certainty as being written in Sumerian, although it is likely.

The oldest writings known from Egypt and India (which has evidence of Sumerian origin) are placed at about the same period, 3200BC (2100). The oldest known civilization in South America, located in Peru, is also dated between 3000-2500 BC (2300-2000) with the oldest extent writing being from around 900BC [27].

The first substantiated king list of China begins in 2205 with Yu the Great, interesting enough he is known for his efforts to control flooding [28].

All the ancient texts written from 2400 to 1700 BC (e.g., all the king lists of antiquity, *The Epic of Gilgamesh, Atra-Hasis* and the *Eridu Genesis)* include the great Flood in the narrative. The Great Flood must have been recent event if the story tellers had to include it, as its magnitude and devastating effects were well known facts at the time related by all the great bards, story tellers, and historians of the period. The sources of these stories, Noah and his sons and their wives, were still alive and only a couple of generations away from every living being at the time. The Flood event was not specific to one local region in the ancient texts, but included worldwide in most all cultural recounts of history [29].

The significance of these facts is that they fit well and are congruent with the biblical account of the Flood and origins of the nations. All the peoples of all the world in antiquity acknowledged the flood event and the nations originating from Shinar (Sumer of Mesopotamia), which is now modern-day Iraq.

One of the oldest stories in the world to date is *The Epic of Gilgamesh*. The last adventure told in the story was his search for the man that was attributed to having received immortality from "the gods". This man turned out to be the biblical Noah. Upon finding Noah, Noah tells him the story of God's judgment of mankind, the building of the Ark, and the Great Flood that wiped out all living creatures. Apparently, the pagans of the time attributed immortality to Noah because he was probably well over 700 or even 800 years old at this time. (Noah lived to 950 years and was alive during half of Abraham's life). One of the epic adventures of Gilgamesh appears to include a battle with a dinosaur–like creature [29].

One of the oldest Egyptian artifacts to be discovered is the Narmer Pallet, dating to about 3000BC (2100). The Narmer Pallet was discovered in the Temple of Horus in 1897 by British archeologists James E. Quibell and Frederick W. Green. It is believed that Narmer, or Misraim as he is also referred to in other ancient texts of that same period, was the grandson of Noah via Ham, which aligns with the Biblical record listing Misriam as the grandson of Noah. Narmer was the first verified king of Egypt. Pallets were normally used to grind cosmetics; however, this one was so large and heavy that it was thought to be used to grind cosmetics for the gods. This pallet depicts the conquests of King Narmer, animals of sorts, and two long–neck beasts (referred to as serpopards, meaning "serpent" and "leopard") that could have been modeled after a brachiosaur of some type (*Mamenchisaurus, Massospondylus,* or *Camarasaurus)*. The same beasts are also found on many ancient Mesopotamian and Egyptian artifacts of that same period. The pallet is on display in the Egyptian Museum in Cairo. It is made of a flat, soft, dark-green siltstone in raised relief [30].

Ceremonial palette of King Narmer, archaic period. A votive offering recording a history of the king, who wears the crown of Upper Egypt.

Figure 2.3 Narmer Pallet dating to about 3000BC (2300)

It was in this period that the Bible gave us the generations of Noah down to Abraham, the father of many nations and most significantly the nation of Israel.

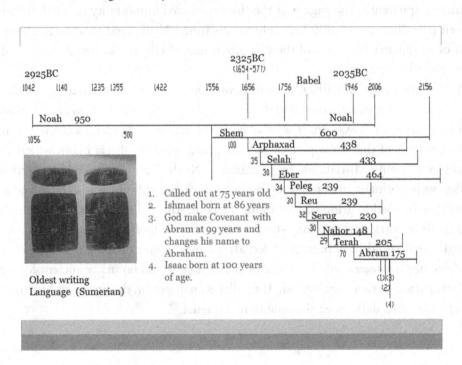

Figure 2.4 Generations from Noah to Abram

The Neanderthals

An excellent article by Ann Habermehl in Answers in Genesis explains who the Neanderthals were and their place in the biblical record (copied by permission) [31].

> Cuozzo's work represented a new research concept with regard to the scientific methods used in the study of ancient fossils. Whereas everybody else merely examined the Neanderthal skulls as they were at a point in time, Cuozzo looked at the skulls (using X-rays) as changing continuously from the moment of birth right on through to death. He had come to some radical conclusions: Neanderthals were ancient people who had developed their unique morphological characteristics (appearance) because they lived to an age of several hundred years, and, in addition, they had matured to adulthood very slowly. The significance of Cuozzo's work did not appear to sink in among creationists, who have largely ignored his ideas. Creationists who have taken heed include Beasley (1992), Murdock (2004), and Robbins (2009).
>
> Of course, we don't have to look very hard to find extraordinarily long-lived people, because they are in plain view in the early historical Genesis accounts. Between Creation and the Flood, there were people like Adam who lived 930 years and Methuselah who lived 969 years, to pick two examples out of the genealogy of *Genesis 5*. Noah lived 950 years in all, 600 before the Flood and 350 after it ({% scripture "Genesis 7:11, 9:28, 29" %}). Lifespans were still quite long for some time after the Flood; generations of people after Noah lived for hundreds of years (*Genesis 11:10–22*). If we accept the Bible literally, we have to believe that these people actually lived that long. From this we can deduce that, according to Cuozzo's studies, all the ancient long-lived people of early Genesis who lived for hundreds of years could be classified as Neanderthals, including everyone from Adam through to the Flood and for some generations after the Flood.
>
> If browridges were the result of old age, it naturally follows that Neanderthal children did not have them. This is indeed the case, as is shown in Fig. 7. Although creationists might think that the subject of facial bone changes with age is new, the medical scientific community at large has been quite aware of this for a long time; surveys of the literature on the subject go back as far as the 1860s (Albert, Ricanek, and Patterson 2007; Behrents 1985; Guagliardo 1982). Israel (1977), for instance, pointed out that as people age, different parts of the craniofacial skeleton will grow at different rates. It may be surprising how wide the subject is of interest.
>
> The biggest puzzle, that neither the majority of creationists nor the evolutionists have been able to solve, is why the Neanderthals disappeared. The robust Neanderthals appeared to have everything going for them, all agree, and there is no visible reason why they should not have survived (Trinkaus 1978). Nonetheless, disappear they did, rather suddenly, before the end of the post-Flood Ice Age or, as evolutionists call it, the end of the last ice age (Van Andel and Davies 2004). However, the problem of

the demise of the Neanderthals goes away entirely if we accept that Cuozzo is correct in his conclusions that the Neanderthals were the post-Flood long-lived people who spread out from Babel in all directions. Their "disappearance" would have occurred when they no longer lived long enough to develop the distinctive Neanderthal characteristics.

The modern humans who supposedly "replaced" the Neanderthals would be the descendants of the latter, who did not live as long as their ancestors. This not only makes the matter of the Neanderthal disappearance very simple and straightforward, it also explains why it happens that modern humans arose at around the same time as the Neanderthals disappeared; furthermore, this would be true in all parts of the world. Proponents of Occam's razor (Occam's razor 2009), often stated as "The simplest explanation is usually the best," would recognize the Cuozzo explanation of the Neanderthal demise as a good one.

DNA is one area where Cuozzo and Lubenow agree. The latter's Chapter 23, "Technical Section: mtDNA Neandertal Park—A Catch 22," is an excellent overview of the matter of DNA, including the political implications of the struggle that he calls "the molecules" versus "the fossils" (this chapter is not very technical in spite of its title) (Lubenow 2004). The bottom line is that Lubenow does not consider DNA to be a reliable source of scientific information. Cuozzo does not put any weight on the mtDNA results, either, stating that there are changes in mtDNA over a person's lifetime, so that the old Neanderthals would have different mtDNA than the young ones; the genome of the ancient people would have been far less devolved than ours; and genetic mutations in mtDNA have been occurring much faster than previously believed (Cuozzo 2009). This theme of continuous human physical degeneration from the earliest people to the present has been ably developed by Sanford (2008), who attributes the shortening of our lifespan throughout the millennia to accumulation of damaging genetic mutations.

One more thing should be mentioned here. If these Neanderthals were extremely old when they died, it would not be surprising if they showed some old-age characteristics, such as arthritis, and some signs of trauma such as healed broken bones (Trinkaus 1978). Indeed, it is surprising that the skeletons of these old people were in such good shape overall at the time of their death. Writers go on and on about how strong these people were (for example, Trinkaus 1978). By comparison, we can see how much we humans have degenerated in the thousands of years since then; our own old people, who do not live nearly as long, show many signs of disease and deterioration in their old age. Degeneration of our genome has taken its very visible toll.

It is hard for us to imagine what the world must have been like during the catastrophic period of the melting of the great continental ice sheets and the glaciers in high mountains. Enormous amounts of water were released from the melting ice, causing flooding and great changes in the landscape, and raising world ocean levels from their minimum at the height of the glaciation to approximately their level today (Lamb 1997, pp. 114–116).

The dispersion of the Neanderthal after the Flood coincides with the post–Flood Ice Age based on location where Neanderthal remains have been discovered, the warmer regions in Europe, Asia and Africa [15].

The Ancient Warrior [32, 33, 34]

The Ice Man known as Ötzi was found frozen in the Swiss Alps and is one of the world's oldest mummified remains to have survived buried and preserved in the ice fully intact with clothes, weapons, food, and tools dating from the later part of the Ice Age. Hikers discovered his mummified corpse in 1991 in a rocky hollow high in the Ötztal Alps on Italy's border with Austria. His age is (C14) dated from 3300-3000BC (2000BC), about 350 years after the Flood. His DNA was related to a people group from Sardinia, an island off the west coast of Italy (confirming post–Flood). His DNA also resembled the DNA of the farmers of Bulgaria and Sweden. Additionally, it appears he had a higher percentage of Neanderthal related DNA than modern Europeans (again, reflecting post–Flood). On September 24, the find was examined there by archaeologist Konrad Spindler of the University of Innsbruck. He dated the find to be "about four thousand years old" (2000BC), based on the typology of an axe among the retrieved objects (again, confirming post–Flood Ice Age). Ötzi was of small stature in mid 40s. He possessed a copper-bladed ax, flint-tipped dagger, fire-starting kit, birchbark container holding embers wrapped in maple leaves, half-finished arrows in his deerskin quiver, and a stalk of yew—an unfinished longbow. Ötzi had an arrowhead in his shoulder and appeared to have suffered from blunt force trauma. It is this author's belief that he was a casualty of war even though he was identified as a farmer through DNA and isotope analysis. Warring tribes could have pulled him into a conflict to defend his lands. He was armed with bow and unfinished arrows (apparently stripped of his good arrows by the enemy) and had a brass cutting tool that could be used for many domestic occasions but also hand–to–hand combat, and he had been mortally shot with an arrow in his left shoulder. Additionally, there was blood from four other men on his clothes, probably men he had encountered earlier in hand–to–hand combat. It appears that he was stripped of his warmer outer garments by his foes as well. Note that the DNA testing associating him with a post antediluvian culture, the dating of the artifacts to 2000BC by Spindler, and the adjusted C14 dates are all collaborative whilst the secular C14 testing results are about 1,000 years in error.

The conclusion

History aligns well with the biblical chronology during this period. Sumer of Mesopotamia is well established as the birthplace of civilization, where city–states emerged and from which the ideas of civilization expanded and spread throughout the world, even as the ice receded for the next 300 to 500 years after the Flood. It is notable that inventions such as the wheel, chariots, ships, storage facilities, fire, writing, art, mathematics, public buildings, irrigation systems, community living, and government (legislation) all appeared throughout the world suddenly in a moment of time about 4000BC. The evolutionary model would have had these varying concepts and ideas progressively cultivated and built upon each other over long periods of time. As the abundance of historical evidence supports the biblical account, it throws in sharp relief the error of the dating methods used by the secular scientific community. The C^{14} dating is the basis for calibrating most all the dating methods used and has been reasonably shown to be in gross error considering the very real possibility of the effects that the environment would have had on the C^{14} buildup in the plants and animals due to the reflective characteristics of ice coverage, volcanic aerosols in a very active post–Flood Ice Age, and protective strength of the magnetosphere. The people groups were divided in Babylon around 2350 to 2200 BC, from which came the migrations of the people throughout the world. Historical records and artifacts from this era such as the Sumerian and Egyptian King Lists, *The Epic of Gilgamesh*, the story of Enmerkar and the Lord of Aratta, and Narmer's Pallet collaborate the biblical text bearing the names, places, and events that were originally known only from the Bible and discarded as myth until the discovery of Sumer in recent times.

Neil deGrasse Tyson lays down the scientific method in his series COSMOS: A Space Time Odyssey, stating that searchers need to ***strictly*** adhere to a simple set of rules:

1) test ideas by experiment and observation,
2) build on those ideas that pass the test,
3) reject the ones that fail,
4) follow the evidence wherever it leads,
5) question everything.

To recount the facts and observed patterns of evidence to this point:

1) The Bible attests to a young earth (6,000 years old) and a global flood demarcation in a biblical time range (BTR) between 2500 and 2200 BC by the biblical genealogical chronologies.
2) All the ancient writings (king lists, epic stories, genealogical chronologies) discovered dating prior to 1800 BC denote the global flood as a demarcation in every culture from all corners of the globe, which attests to a young earth (6,000 years old) and a global flood demarcation in a biblical time range (BTR) between 2500 and 2200 BC.
3) Historians in antiquity attest to a young earth (6,000 years old) and a global flood demarcation in about 2500 to 2200 BC.
4) Most all the leading archeologists attest to a global catastrophic demarcation in every culture from all corners of the globe between the early and middle Bronze Age in about 2500 BC.
5) The decay of the earth and planetary magnetospheres and the archeomagnetic records attest to a global catastrophic demarcation in all corners of the globe starting in about 2500 BC.
6) DNA Evidence indicates a definite demarcation in about 2500 BC in both cultural characterizations and population bottleneck.
7) All the anthropological artifacts, remains, and other evidence align well with the biblical chronologies.
8) The geological records (stratum and fossils) and known rock formations and processes reflects the expected aftermath of a global flood.
9) Significant amounts of C^{14} found when age dating petroleum, dinosaur bones, and other ancient artifacts testify to a young earth.
10) Patterns in the ice caps favor to a single and recent ice age supporting a young earth.

At this point it is blatantly obvious that the idea that the biblical chronologies may be literally true, as Isaac Newton believed, has been tested by experiment and observation from multiple historical and scientific fields of study. All the results are congruent with the biblical chronologies. We shall now build on those ideas that pass the test and continue to reject the ones that fail and follow the evidence wherever it leads, questioning everything.

REFERENCES

Biblical References from: The Holy Bible (1913). King James Version. Chicago, Ill. John A. Dickson Publishing Co.

1   Encyclopedia Britannica. Pangaea. Retrieved from https://www.britannica.com/place/Pangea

2   Schlische, R. The breakup of Pangaea: The North America - African connection. Retrieved from http://www.rci.rutgers.edu/~schlisch/103web/Pangeabreakup/breakupframe.html

3   National Park Service. Scotts Bluff. Geographic land forms. Retrieved from https://www.nps.gov/scbl/planyourvisit/upload/Geographic-Landforms.pdf

4   Science Clarified. Mesa & butte. Retrieved from http://www.scienceclarified.com/landforms/Faults-to-Mountains/Mesa-and-Butte.html

5   Science Clarified. Mountain. Retrieved from http://www.scienceclarified.com/landforms/Faults-to-Mountains/Mountain.html

6   GeoScience. A geological trip to Yass. Retrieved from http://www.geosci.usyd.edu.au/users/prey/FieldTrips/Yass04/Devonian.html

7   Fossil Museum. Precambrian fossils. Retrieved from http://www.fossilmuseum.net/Paleobiology/Precambrian-Fossils.htm

8   Fossil Museum. Precambrian era paleobiology. Retrieved from http://www.fossilmuseum.net/Paleobiology/Preambrian_Paleobiology.htm

9   The Burgess Shale. The microbial world. Retrieved from http://burgess-shale.rom.on.ca/en/science/origin/02-microbial-world.php

10 Geology Class. The Precambrian. Retrieved from http://www.geologyclass.org/Precambrian%20Concepts.htm

11 Patterson R. (2011). Answers in Genesis. Evolution exposed: Earth science. Chapter 7: The fossil record. Retrieved from https://answersingenesis.org/fossils/fossil-record/the-fossil-record-1/

12 Nature (2011). Microbiology. Retrieved from http://www.nature.com/nrmicro/journal/v9/n6/abs/nrmicro2577.html

13 Koonin E.V. and Wolf, Y.I. (2008). Genomics of bacteria and archaea: the emerging dynamic view of the prokaryotic world. Retrieved from http://nar.oxfordjournals.org/content/36/21/6688.full.pdf

14 Fossil Museum. Cambrian Explosion. Retrieved from http://www.fossilmuseum.net/Paleobiology/CambrianExplosion.htm

15 Meyers, S.C. (2013). *Darwin's doubt*. New York, NY: HarperCollins Publishers.

16 Bates, G. Creation.com. That quote about the missing transitional fossils. Retrieved from http://creation.com/that-quote-about-the-missing-transitional-fossils

17 Encyclopedia.com. Stratigraphy. Retrieved from http://www.encyclopedia.com/topic/stratigraphy.aspx

18 Ashton, J.F. Phd. (2012). *Evolution impossible: 12 reason why evolution cannot explain the origin of life on Earth*. New York, NY: HarperCollins Publishers

19 Ancient Origins. AtlitYam. Retrieved from http://www.ancient-origins.net/ancient-places-asia/9000-year-old-underground-megalithic-settlement-atlit-yam-001579

20 Holloway, April (2015). Ancient Origins. Huge ancient Greek city found underwater in the Aegean. Retrieved from http://www.ancient-origins.net/news-history-archaeology/huge-ancient-greek-city-found-underwater-aegean-sea-003709

21 Kuschk (2012). The Basement Geographer. Doggerland: Ancient Europe underwater. Retrieved from http://basementgeographer.com/doggerland-ancient-europe-underwater/

22 Archeology Online. Gulf of Cambay. Retrieved from http://archaeologyonline.net/artifacts/cambay

23 Maddison, B (2012). "Now and Then" Second Edition (pgs 126 to 128). Retrieved from https://books.google.com/books?id=fSzsAwAAQBAJ&pg=PA127&lpg=PA127&dq=Archaeologist+Ernest+Wright+states+there+is+an+occupation+(gap)+between+Early+Bronze+Age+and+the+Middle+Bronze+Age.&source=bl&ots=daVONbF

li2&sig=_FadWWwwqOhusIQiNWT9xG74RPY&hl=en&sa=X&ved=0ahUKEwjs_9SdlYf
WAhUG7CYKHRyTD_8Q6AEIKTAA#v=onepage&q=Archaeologist%20Ernest%20Wright%20states%20
there%20is%20an%20occupation%20(gap)%20between%20Early%20Bronze%20Age%20and%20the%20
Middle%20Bronze%20Age.&f=false

24 Oard, M. (1987). The ice age and the genesis flood. *Acts & Facts*. 16 (6). Copyright © 1987 Institute for Creation Research, www.icr.org. Used by permission. Retrieved from http://www.icr.org/article/ice-age-genesis-flood/

25 Vardiman, L. Ph.D. Ice cores and the age of the earth. Institute of Creation Research. Retrieved from http://www.icr.org/article/ice-cores-age-earth/

26 Wikipedia. Kish tablet. Retrieved from https://en.wikipedia.org/wiki/Kish_tablet

27 Wikipedia. History of Writing. Retrieved from https://en.wikipedia.org/wiki/History_of_writing

28 The History Files. Far east kingdoms, China. Retrieved from http://www.historyfiles.co.uk/KingListsFarEast/ChinaDynasties.htm

29 The Epic of Gilgamesh. Assyrian International News Agency. Books Online. www.aina.org. Retrieved from http://www.aina.org/books/eog/eog.htm

30 Ancient Egypt Site. Narmer palette. Retrieved from http://www.ancient-egypt.org/history/early-dynastic-period/1st-dynasty/horus-narmer/narmer-artefacts/narmer-palette.html

31 Habermehl, A. (2010). Answers in Genesis. Those enigmatic Neanderthals. What are they saying? Are we listening? Retrieved from https://answersingenesis.org/human-evolution/neanderthal/those-enigmatic-neanderthals/

32 Hall, Stpehen S (2007). Last hours of the iceman. National Geographic. Art by Kazuhiko Sano. Retrieved from http://ngm.nationalgeographic.com/2007/07/iceman/hall-text

33 Wikipedia. Ötzi. Retrieved from https://en.wikipedia.org/wiki/%C3%96tzi

34 DNA Explained - Genetic Genealogy (2012). Otzi was a brown eyed left handed farmer. Retrieved from https://dna-explained.com/2012/11/21/otzi-was-a-brown-eyed-left-handed-farmer/

PART 3

The Supporting Sciences

A Case for New Evidence

As concluded in Part 1, any new discoveries that appear to be contradictory to the biblical text must be deemed flawed due to insufficient data, unknown past conditions, or assumptions in error. Scientific claims that some new evidence proves that man is millions of years old does so in the face of the consensus of empirical evidence that concludes otherwise. It is neither logical nor prudent to discard large amounts of scientific and historic evidence that supports creationism and the bible for a singular bit of new evidence that supposedly refutes creationism or the bible. It should be assumed that the dating methods behind the new evidential phenomena are flawed, just as time has shown us about other dating methods such as the C^{14} dating, radiometric dating, ice core dating, Egyptological dating methods, and genome dating. Establishing the facts of science, engineering, medical principles, justice systems, etc. has to proceed based on the consensus of data/evidence (the 95%) not the exceptions to the rule (the 5%). In engineering, tensile stress values are established for a material property based on the breaking point of repeated tests of the material of interest. A test piece that breaks substantially below the value that is set for that material is considered flawed and upon investigation has always proved so. Time and advances in science and technology will continue to reveal the flaws prevalent in the evolutionary model and yield in favor of the creation model, just as it has for the past 300 years with previous scientific claims that refuted the truth of biblical histories.

Dating Methods

Be careful what you read from secular sources regarding dating methods and their reliability. I've heard many proponents claim that age dating subject matter is usually completed by several different reliable methods that all collaborate and establish a solid age range. This is simply not true! Archeologist are free to pick and choose which test results fit their assumptions. Sometimes peer reviews are missed before the articles make to the public domain which inadvertently reveals this madness (pseudoscience).

Cases in point:

A. Mungo Woman, skeletal remains found in the Lake Mungo sand dunes in Australia. Dating efforts initially yielded an age date of about 19,000 years on a bone apatite and 27,000 years on the soft tissue when tested with the C^{14} dating method. Of course, they chose to believe the older date as the official age and discarded the earlier date). Next, C^{14} dating of some charcoal that was found in a layer above the skeleton yielded a date of 26, 500 years, so naturally they concluded that the skeleton, being in a lower stratum, had to be older. That date then became the official age of the remains. Mungo Man was later discovered in the same sand bed (stratigraphic horizon) and assumed to be of the same age. This time the sand that the Mungo Man was found in was tested with the thermoluminescence (TL) method, which resulted in a date of 42,000 years old. Based on this new and more reliable age dating method, the C^{14} dates were abandoned and the new official date was assigned based on the new TL results. Many secular scientists did not accept the latter results, as they basically pick and choose the results they feel best fit their presumptions [1].

B. Jinmium, Australia – The dating of the aboriginal sandstone rock art by the (TL) method in 1996 resulted in an estimated age of 116,000 to 176,000 years. Later tests on these same stones with an optically-stimulated luminescence (OSL) method resulted in an estimated age of 10,000 to 22,000 years. Fragments of charcoal from the site were tested with the C^{14} dating method and yielded dates around 4,000 years old. Consequently, a retraction had to be published for the earlier erroneous extraneous test results of the TL method and an official date was decided to be between 6,000 and 10,000 years. Basically, they discarded the holy grail of C^{14} dating and the TL dating methods claiming that the OSL method (in this case as it best fit their presumptions) had the most reliable test results [2].

C. Dwarka, Gulf of Cambay, India lies between 65 and 130 ft. below the water surface. The structures (regularly spaced dwellings, a granary, a bath, a citadel, and a drainage system) resembled Harrapan civilization dating to 2000BC. Artifacts recovered included pieces of wood, pottery shards, weathered stone hand tools, fossilized bones, microliths, wattle and daub remains, and hearth material. Several dating methods (C^{14}, TL & OSL) produced wide and varying results of the different artifacts, which was interpreted as the artifacts showing a very old and maintained civilization with each varying result, proving a different stage of habitation along a timeline (1,000BC to 29,300BC). One piece of wood tested to 7500 BC by two labs and to 6500 BC by a third (1,000 yrs. difference). Pottery just below that stratum was tested to 11000 BC. Other clay specimens tested at 18K and 14K (4k dif.) and yet another piece sent to two different labs came up with 5.5K, 4K, and 2.3K (3.2K dif.). Still other samples from the same strata yielded results at 29.3K, 23.7K, 22.6K (6.7K def.). That would make this small community not only the oldest civilization in the world but the longest lasting one as well (28.3K yrs.), which is in no way a reasonable consideration. It would most likely be from about 2500 to 2000 BC based on their resemblance to the Harrapan civilization and be a result of either the flood or the Ice age meltdown [3]. The claims of these submarine archeological sampling are refuted by the scientific community as being ill managed and reported to the public without peer review. They are not pleased that a piece of wood was reported as having been tested with C^{14} testing with two wide ranging results (7500 yrs. and 5500 yrs.). Additionally, many of the artifacts were judged as being not manmade and the claims are extraordinarily out of sequence with the larger known history of the area [4]. Scientists and dating methods run amuck. Had the archeologist first submitted his findings for peer review, he or she would have been advised to pick and choose the more agreeable test results and discard the rest as contaminated so that only those that provided a consensus would be put forth into the public domain. This is done so the proponents for secular humanism can say it was all validated by several different dating methods with collaborating results and therefore is an historical certainty.

D.   In an article by Don Patten, Ph.D. he concludes[5]:

Tree ring chronologies are not a reliable dating method. He cites the publication of two tree-ring chronologies from European and subsequent retractions due to inaccuracy of the tests that brought them into conflicting results. He cites David Rohl in pointing out:

> the Sweet Track chronology from Southwest England was 're-measured' when it did not agree with the published dendrochronology from Northern Ireland (Belfast). Also, the construction of a detailed sequence from southern Germany was abandoned in deference to the Belfast chronology, even though the authors of the German study had been confident of its accuracy until the Belfast one was published. It is clear that dendrochronology is not a clear-cut, objective dating method despite the extravagant claims of some of its advocates.

E.   An excerpt from an article by Creation Worldview Ministries, titled "Carbon-14 Dating Technique Does Not Work!", shows the conflict between stratification dating and C^{14} dating methods, which is very typical of what you find more often than not when testing carbon based samples in supposed 250-65 million-year-old strata [6].
Burnt wood was found within Cretaceous Limestone, supposedly 65 to 140 million years old. The C^4 content was dated by Dr. Rainer Berger, Geophysics Department, University of California, Los Angeles (UCLA), and reported on November 6, 1978. **"We have dated this sample as UCLA-2088 and found it to be 12,800+/-200 years old."** Dinosaur, bear, large cat and human footprints have been found in the same layer. This means that none of these footprints could be older than about 13,000 years according to the Carbon-14 dating technique.

Scientific protocol demands that you have a consensus of the data for it to be considered scientifically valid or a scientific certainty. When there is no consensus, and you decide to inadvertently pick and choose values that agree with your theology or your belief, then you have moved into the arena of pseudoscience.

CREATION.com evaluation of dating methods [1] (reprinted by permission), 3

- **Carbon-14** dates are determined from the measured ratio of radioactive carbon-14 to normal carbon-12 (C^{14}/C^{12}). Used on samples which were once alive, such as wood or bone, the measured C^{14}/C^{12} ratio is compared with the ratio in living things today. The date is calculated by assuming the change of C^{14} in the sample is due entirely to radioactive decay. It is also assumed that carbon has been in equilibrium on the earth for hundreds of thousands of years. Wrong dates are usually caused by assuming a wrong initial C^{14}/C^{12} ratio, contamination or leaching. Samples from before the Flood, or from the early post-Flood period, give ages that are too old by tens of thousands of years. This is because the Flood buried lots of C^{12}-rich plants and animals. This would result in a lower C^{14}/C^{12} ratio, which is wrongly interpreted as great age.

- **Thermoluminescence (TL)** dates are obtained from individual grains of common minerals such as quartz. When such grains are heated, they emit light, and this is related to the radiation 'stored' in the crystal structure. It is assumed that the radiation was slowly absorbed from the environment, building up from zero at a certain time in the past (perhaps when the grain was last exposed to sunlight). A date is calculated by measuring the light emitted from the mineral grain when it is heated, and measuring the radiation in the environment where the grain was found.

  Unfortunately, there are many unknowns and many assumptions need to be made, including the amount of radiation 'stored' in the mineral at a certain time in the past, that the change in radiation has only been affected by the radiation in the environment, that the radiation in the environment has remained constant, and that the sensitivity of the crystal to radiation has not changed. All these factors can be affected by water, heat, sunlight, the accumulation or leaching of minerals in the environment, and many other causes.

- **Optically-stimulated luminescence (OSL)** dates are based on exactly the same principle as TL. But instead of heating the grain, it is exposed to light to make it emit its 'stored' radiation. The calculated date is based on the same assumptions, and affected by the same uncertainties, as for TL.

- **Electron-spin resonance (ESR)** dates are based on the same principles as TL and OSL. However, the 'stored' radiation in the sample is measured by exposing it to gamma radiation and measuring the radiation emitted. The measuring technique does not destroy the 'stored' radiation (as does TL and OSL), so the measurement can be repeated on the same sample. The calculated date is based on the same assumptions, and affected by the same uncertainties, as for TL and OSL.

- **Thorium-uranium (Th/U)** dates are based on measuring the isotopes of uranium and thorium in a sample. It is known that uranium-238 decays radioactively to form thorium-230 (through a number of steps, including through uranium-234). The dating calculation assumes that the thorium and uranium in the sample are related to each other by radioactive decay. Furthermore, before a date can be calculated, the initial ratios of $^{30}Th/^{38}U$ and $^{34}U/^{38}U$ need to be assumed, and it is also assumed that there has been no gain or loss of uranium or thorium to/from the environment—i.e., that the system is 'closed'. However, the bone and soil must have been 'open' to allow these elements to enter and accumulate.

- **Protactinium-uranium (Pa/U)** dates are based on similar principles as Th/U dating, but use uranium-235 and protactinium-231 instead. The isotope ^{35}U decays radioactively to form ^{231}Pa. Again, it is assumed that the isotopes in the sample are related to each other by radioactive decay. Also, the initial ratio of ^{31}Pa/^{35}U has to be assumed, and it is assumed that there has been no gain or loss of uranium or protactinium to/from the environment—i.e., that the system is 'closed'. Again, any bone sample containing uranium must have been 'open' to allow it to accumulate in the first place.

- **Tree Ring Count (Dendrochronology)** dates are based on overlapping rings when comparing older dead trees to living tress in the same area matching the overlaps using the C14 dating. Additionally, the rings are assumed to be the result of annular seasonal changes, so each ring represents a year. C14 dating has been reasonably shown to be flawed with organic objects greater than 3000 years old so the assumption that matching tree rings using C14 is not scientifically viable. Additionally, tree rings in the 500 year post–Flood era would be greatly affected by that environment producing false rings (maybe up to five rings annually) due to the mass of ice coverage at that time resulting in lesser seasonal temperature changes and a wetter environment from the continuous melting.

Reference

1. Details about dating methods may be obtained from such sources as: Smart, P.L. and Frances, P.D. (Eds.), *Quaternary Dating Methods—A User's Guide*, Quaternary Research Association, Technical Guide No. 4, Cambridge, 1991, or Faure, G., *Principles of Isotope Geology*, 2nd edition, John Wiley & Sons, New York, USA, 1986.

In an article by Dr. Jason Lisle in regard to dating the age of the universe, he states [7]:

Magnetic Fields Confirm Recent Creation

Dr. Russell Humphreys (a Ph.D. physicist and biblical creationist) has produced a model of planetary magnetic fields which can explain their present strengths in terms of biblical creation. In essence, the model estimates the initial strength of each magnetic field at the moment of its creation, then the model computes their present strengths based on 6,000 years of decay from electrical resistance. Impressively, this biblically based model is able to account for the present measured magnetic fields of all the known planets and even many of the moons as well.

Of course, almost any model can be "adjusted" to fit existing data, so it is perhaps even more impressive that Dr. Humphreys' model successfully predicted the present magnetic field strengths of the planets Uranus and Neptune before they were measured by the *Voyager* spacecraft. Specific, successful predictions are the mark of a good scientific model. Dr. Humphreys also predicted that Mars would have remnant (permanent) magnetism, which has now been confirmed. Remnant magnetism occurs in rocks which cooled and solidified in the presence of an external magnetic field. Such remnant magnetism is also found on the moon. This confirms that both the moon and Mars once had strong magnetic fields as expected in the Humphreys model. Planetary magnetic fields strongly support the biblical age of the solar system.

Comets

A comet's tail (or tails) is an indication that comets cannot last forever. The tail means that the comet is losing material; a comet gets smaller every time it orbits the sun. It has been estimated that a typical comet can only orbit the sun for about 100,000 years at most before completely running out of material. (This is an average figure, of course; the exact life span would depend on how big the comet is to begin with, and the parameters of its orbit.) Since we still have a lot of comets, this suggests that the solar system is much younger than 100,000 years. This agrees perfectly with the Bible. Clearly, 4.5 billion years would be an absurdly inflated age for comets.

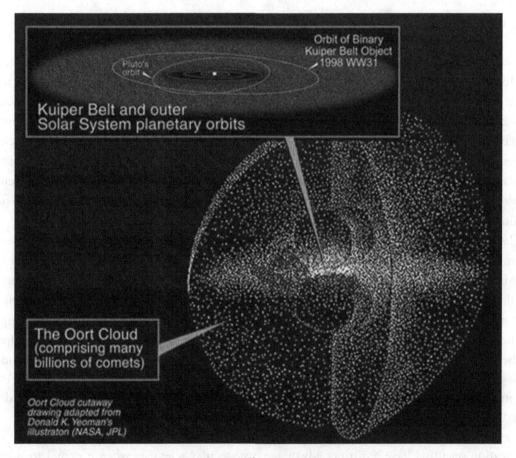

Figure 3.1 The Oort Cloud

How do secular astronomers attempt to reconcile this with their belief in billions of years? Since comets can't last that long, secular astronomers must assume that new comets are introduced to the solar system to replace those that are gone, so they've invented the idea of an "Oort cloud." This is supposed to be a vast reservoir of icy masses orbiting far away from the sun. The idea is that occasionally an icy mass falls into the inner solar system to become a "new" comet. It is interesting that there is currently no evidence of an Oort cloud, and there is no reason to believe in one if we accept the creation account in Genesis. Comets are consistent with the fact that the solar system is young.

Why can we not observe them? We can observe planets of other stars millions of light years away because they pass in front of their suns which can be observed. Would not trillions of comets that are only about 1mly away not be observed in the same manner when they inadvertently pass between us and any line of sight of all the other lights coming to us from every vector in the universe? This theory cannot be tested by any experiment nor, as Tyson in his Cosmos Series admits, is it observable to date…so why is it being taught as fact? (a handful of new comets showing up every now and then does not support an Oort cloud as there are many possible alternate explanations).

Scientific Models

Distinguishing between models based on empirical data and models based on theoretical premise.

Historical empirical data models (EDM) take trending data as it is found in studies of a particular subject matter of interest, usually over time and/or space, and use it to explain present conditions or to construct a model to predict past or future trending or configurations. Empirical data models predicting trends or conditions are proven right or wrong when an investigation into those sciences exposes trending data or conditions that were not previously known. (Models that predict accurately are a rare occurrence). This can be in the form of what conditions are today based on past trending models, in regard to similar time/space/matters of interest, or in the form of time laps for future trending observation of the unfolding patterns or trends.

Historical theoretical premise models (TPM) start with a theory of unknown processes based on patterns or configurations found in nature and use it to construct a model of past or future trending or configurations that may answer the cause of known patterns or configurations. Theoretical premise modules of past trending cannot be proven, as it cannot be witnessed or observed and the models were developed to fit existing conditions. However, theoretical premise modules of future trending will be exposed in time. Theoretical premise models normally make presumptions beyond the empirical data because it does not fit into a base model. (This is a common element in the evolution model).

Planetary Magnetospheres by Dr. Humphreys & Dr. Barnes [8, 9] (Example of EDM w/ predictive results)

Creation scientists have a distinct advantage over secular scientists when it comes to scientific modeling – the Word of God. There are clues given in the Bible that would never be considered by the secular scientist. One of the most exemplary EDM models of creation science is the planetary magnetosphere model developed by Dr. Russell Humphreys in 1984. Using the clues given in the Bible, he was able to make accurate predictions based on assumptions and deduced processes that would not have been known from any other scientific or historical resource.

Key Scriptures on the Process of Creation:

Ge:1:2: And the earth was without form, and void; and darkness was upon the face of the deep. And the Spirit of God moved upon the face of the waters.

Ge:1:6: And God said, let there be a firmament in the midst of the waters, and let it divide the waters from the waters.

Ge:1:7: And God made the firmament, and divided the waters which were under the firmament from the waters which were above the firmament: and it was so.

Gen:1:9: And God said, let the waters under the heaven be gathered together unto one place, and let the dry land appear: and it was so.

Ge:1:10: And God called the dry land Earth; and the gathering together of the waters called he Seas: and God saw that it was good.

2Pe:3:5: For this they willingly are ignorant of, that by the word of God the heavens were of old, and the earth standing out of the water and in the water:

These scriptures describe a process by which God first made all astrological objects as bodies of water (the earth, sun, moon, stars, et al) with all the physical properties of water, mass, and motion, including molecular structure (H_2O), gravity, orbits, rotation, and magnetospheres. Then he created the solid matters and associated elements (dry land). So in six days, God created the earth within a solar system of many, within a galaxy of many, within a grand universe.

Time of creation: The approximate year of creation can be determined by formulating a time line based on the genealogies and chronological events given in Old Testament (as displayed throughout this text in segments found in associated sections/chapters of interest) which comes to about 6000 years from 2000 AD.

Based on this knowledge, the following assumptions were made for the basis of this model:

A. The earth was created about 6,000 years ago.

B. While yet in the watery state God created atomic nuclei with their spins pointing in the same direction, thereby creating the force of the original magnetosphere.

C. Once the solids and other elements were created, the alignments would immediately decay to random order due to natural thermal collisions; however, large electrical currents (billions of amperes) would be generated due to the laws of electricity and magnetism in the planets' interior iron core, reproducing the magnetosphere at near the same strength.

D. At this point, the electrical currents in the core would start to decay exponentially due to the laws of electrical resistance and entropy.

This expected decay rate is reflected in the empirical data recorded over the last 150 years, as shown in the chart below.

There are four possible arrangements of the molecules that God could have started with but only three, in an ortho state known as an ortho molecule, would have produced the magnetic moments needed to begin with while in the H_2O state. The magnetic moments of the 10 elections in the water molecule cancel each other out, so their total contribution equals zero. The magnetic moment of the oxygen nucleus is similarly zero. But the two hydrogen nuclei (protons) in the molecule have a magnetic moment of 1.41×10^{26} J/T. An external magnetic field, however slight, normally lines each pair of nuclei in one of four possible arrangements. It is not known from scripture what fraction of protons God aligned in each case to produce the magnet moment. Dr. Humphreys used a k factor from 0 to 1 (1/4, 1/2, 3/4, & 1) to apply to the formula. The k factor of 0.25 was assumed for the earth.

	Year	M
1	1835	8.522
2	1845	8.468
3	1885	8.371
4	1900	8.321
5	1905	8.300
6	1910	8.272
7	1915	8.235
8	1920	8.195
9	1925	8.160
10	1930	8.129
11	1935	8.106
12	1940	8.091
13	1945	8.075
14	1950	8.064
15	1955	8.051
16	1960	8.028
17	1965	8.005
18	1970	7.973
19	1975	7.939
20	1980	7.907
21	1985	7.871
22	1990	7.841
23	1995	7.814
24	2000	7.790
25	2005	7.767
26	2010	7.746

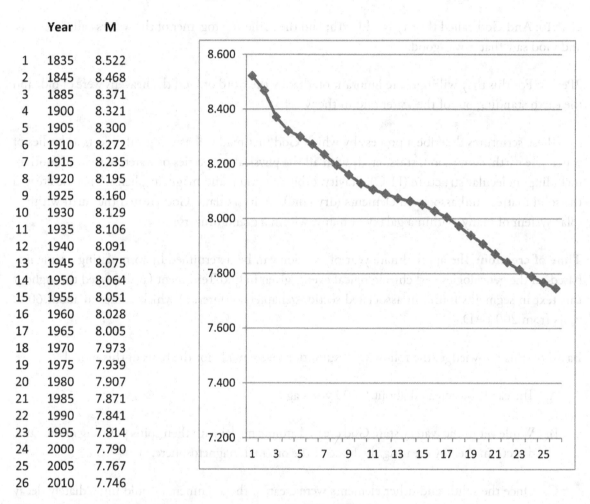

Chart showing the decaying magnetic moment (M) of the Magnetosphere from 1835 to 2010

Applied Physics: Quantum Physics (QP), Solar Physical Data (SPD) Electrical Currents (EC) (V, I, Ω), Entropy (En) (decay on an exponential curve).

(QP) The spinning characteristics of the nucleus of many atoms, such as hydrogen, emit a small dipole magnetic field in line with the spinning axis. God appears to have created atomic nuclei with aligned spins that would have produced a magnetic field (the magnetosphere) about the earth while in the initial H_2O state. In the finished state of creation, the spinning quickly gets distorted by the thermal collisions of the atoms. This starts generating electrical currents in the earth's iron core, which in turn maintains the magnetic field. The nuclei are completely disoriented within a few seconds after creation. The currents are now fully stabilized establishing a magnetosphere of nearly the same magnitude.

(EC & En) Refer to the second edition of Dr. Thomas Barnes' book *Origin and Destiny of The Earth's Magnetic Field*) for a detailed analysis of empirical data based on known physical principles of electrical currents and entropy (decay on an exponential curve) [9.]

Table 1
Planetary Physical Data (1984)

No.	Body	Mass	Avg. Radius	Avg. Density	Rotation Period
		(kg)	(km)	(g/cm^3)	(days)
1	Sun	1.991×10^{30}	695,950	1.410	24.66
2	Mercury	3.181×10^{23}	2,433	5.431	58.82
3	Venus	4.883×10^{24}	6,053	5.256	244.59
4	Earth	5.979×10^{24}	6,371	5.519	1.00
5	Moon	7.354×10^{22}	1,738	3.342	27.40
6	Mars	6.418×10^{23}	3,380	3.907	1.03
7	Jupiter	1.901×10^{27}	69,758	1.337	0.41
8	Saturn	5.684×10^{26}	58,219	0.688	0.43
9	Uranus	8.682×10^{25}	23,470	1.603	0.45
10	Neptune	1.027×10^{26}	22,716	2.272	0.66
11	Pluto	$(1.08 \pm 1) \times 10^{24}$	5,700	1.65 ± 1.57	6.41

Formula and Variables

Earth's magnetic moment at creation

(k.9425m)

μw	m	mw	k	Mc	Mc
2.8E-26	5.979E+24	2.992E-26	0.25	1.4E+24	1.41E+24
J/T	kg	kg		J/T	J/T

μw	magnetic moment of an ortho molecule, 2.8×10^{-26}, J/T
m	mass of the planet, kg
mw	mass of a water molecule, 2.992×10^{-26}, kg
k	fraction of aligned molecules (1/4, 1/2, 3/4, 1)
Mc	planet's mag. moment at creation, $k(m/mc)\mu w$, J/T

Earth's magnetic moment at a time after creation (1980)

μo	R	π	δ	T	t	M	
1.25664E-06	3480	3.1416	1329	2049	5980	7.94E+22	Known
henry/M	km		mhos/M	2075	Years	7.61E+22	Calculated
				Years		J/T	

μo   magnetic permeability, $4\pi \times 10^{-7}$, henry/meter

R   planetary core radius, km

π   Pi, 3.1416

δ   uniform electrical conductivity, $\pi^2 T/\mu o R^2$, mhos/meter

T   time it takes any given field to decay to 36.8% of any given value, $t/\ln(Mc/M)$ $(\mu o \delta R^2/\pi^2)$, years

t   time after creation, years

M   planet's mag. moment at a time after creation, $Mc \exp(-t/T)$, J/T

Note that the T and M calculated values produced by the model are within 5% of the known values, which is within the tolerance of any acceptable scientific modeling (T = 99%, M = 96% accurate).

Data table resulting from Dr. Humphreys' model

Table 2
Solar System Magnetic Data (1984)

No.	Body	Mag. Mo. @ Creation	Present Mag. Mo.	Decay Time	Core Radius	Core Conductivity
		(J/T)	(J/T)	(Years)	(km)	(mho/M)
1	Sun	4.7×10^{29}	3.5×10^{29}	19,000		
2	Mercury	7.5×10^{22}	4.8×10^{19}	810	1,800	60,000
3	Venus	1.2×10^{24}	$<1 \times 10^{19}$	<510	2,700	<17,000
4	Earth	1.4×10^{24}	7.9×10^{22}	2,075	3,480	42,000
5	Moon	1.7×10^{22}	$<1.3 \times 10^{15}$	<360	350	<30,000
6	Mars	1.5×10^{23}	$<2.1 \times 10^{18}$	<540	1,750	<43,000
7	Jupiter	1.8×10^{27}	1.6×10^{27}	>41,000	56,000	>3,000
8	Saturn	1.3×10^{26}	4.3×10^{25}	5,300	35,000	>1,100
9	Uranus	2.1×10^{25}	3.0×10^{4} (1986)			
10	Neptune	2.4×10^{25}	1.5×10^{24} (1989)			
11	Pluto	2.6×10^{24}				

The Decay Factors of the Planetary Magnetic Fields

In 1984, Dr. Humphreys took Dr. Barnes' theory based on the exponential decay factors of the strength of earth's magnetic field when extrapolated backwards and came up with this model based on the approximate age of the universe as given in the Bible, the planetary masses, and a certain k factor (k=0.25 in almost all cases) to apply to other planets in the solar system. He then modeled several planetary magnetic fields such as the Sun, Moon, Mercury, Mars, Venus, Jupiter, and Saturn. He not only rightly predicted the known values of the sun, moon, and planets, he also predicted what we would find when we got close enough to Uranus in 1986 and Neptune in 1989 via the Voyager II and was precisely correct. Due to the uncertainties of the planets' interiors, Dr. Humphreys predicted that the magnetic moments of both planets would be between 1×10^{23} and 1×10^{25} A m². On January 20, 1986, Voyager II passed by Uranus and measured Uranus's magnetic moment at 3.0×10^{24} A m². On August 25, 1989, Voyager II passed by Neptune and found that it has a magnetic moment of 1.5×10^{24} A m². Both actual values are approximately in the middle of Dr. Humphreys' estimates[10,11,12]. Additionally, Dr. Humphreys' model accurately predicted Mercury's decaying magnetosphere. In 1974 & 75, to the surprise of NASA scientists, the Mariner 10 Spacecraft measured Mercury's magnetic moment at 4.8×10^{22} gauss CM³. In 1984 Dr. Humphreys published his Magnetic Field Model which included the predicted decay factors for Mercury's magnetic field. In 2008 Messenger flew by Mercury and found the magnetic moment had decayed as the model had predicted[13]. NASA scientists had predicted that there would be no magnetic field due to its size, whereas Dr. Humphreys' model would have predicted it would have a magnetic field, its original strength, and the approximate strength at any given time, just as it did with the Uranus and Neptune magnetic fields. The actual measured magnetic strength is not a precise science, and scientists are not in agreement as to the magnitude of decay of Mercury, as the data interpretation ranges from 0%, 4%, 27%, to 40% decay. Being that Dr. Humphreys' model has been accurate in all other instances, there is no reason not to believe that his predicted calculation is probably the most accurate at 4%.

From Wikipedia [14]:

> Before 1974, it was thought that Mercury could not generate a magnetic field because of its relatively small diameter and lack of an atmosphere. However, when *Mariner 10* made a fly-by of Mercury (somewhere around April 1974), it detected a magnetic field that was about 1/100th the total magnitude of Earth's magnetic field. But these passes provided weak constraints on the magnitude of the intrinsic magnetic field, its orientation and its harmonic structure, in part because the coverage of the planetary field was poor and because of the lack of concurrent observations of the solar wind number density and velocity. Since the discovery, Mercury's magnetic field has received a great deal of attention, primarily because of Mercury's small size and slow 59-day-long rotation.
>
> Before the discovery of its magnetic field in 1974, it was thought that because of Mercury's small size, its core had cooled over the years. There are still difficulties with this dynamo theory, including the fact that Mercury has a slow, 59-day-long rotation that could not have made it possible to generate a magnetic field.

From MIT News

An article on the MIT website comments that the discovery of Mercury's magnetic field, the residual magnetism found in planetesimals, meteors, and moon rocks, has complicated their understanding of the dynamo theory.

> It had been thought that smaller bodies couldn't have dynamos because they cool more rapidly and are therefore more likely to have metallic cores that do not stay in liquid form for very long.

> the finding suggests that sustaining a magnetic field like the one on Earth might not require a large, cooling core that constantly moves liquid and creates currents, [15]

As it stands today, all the measured planetary magnetospheres appear to be on a decaying slope, all are aligned with the predictions of the Model, and there is no indication of any upward trending in any astrological body that has been examined that would support the dynamo theory. The secular scientists are not only baffled by what we are finding as opposed to their modeled predictions, they flatly refuse to even acknowledge Dr. Humphreys' keen scientific prowess. Dr. Humphreys' models have made predictions for outer planetary bodies, such as certain white dwarf stars, and creationists anxiously wait for the time when science will be able to gather more outer planetary data. These results serve to verify that creationist theories are rooted in sound scientific principle and intelligent deduction. Due to the complexity of the model, creationist theories are based on more than just chance and more scientifically valid than the theories that secular scientists postulate.

This is an excellent example of a true scientific model based on the consensus of empirical data, physical science, and biblical truths. The model showed accurate results of known values in diverse conditions and has had the most successful predictions of unknown values of planets before they were examined. The basic scientific principle that the testing of a hypothesis should always come up with positive results and have a proven track record to be accepted as a favorable theory applies most ardently here. Dr. Humphreys' planetary magnetic fields model is not perfect but has earned the standing to be further tested and refined under the auspices of mainline science. The possibilities to refine this model and advance the sciences in these areas of interest are unlimited, as further research yields more data and applicable related physics are discovered.

In an article by Dr. Humphreys, he quotes from a prominent scientist, Dessler, as follows [10,16]:

> "Predictions have value," writes a prominent space scientist about planetary theories. "The classic test of a theory," he says, "is its ability to predict. Successful predictions are so rare that they are usually regarded as compelling evidence in favor of the underlying theory." If that is so, then the Voyager II space probe has provided "compelling evidence" in favor of the creationist's theory of the origin of planetary magnetic fields by confirming two of its predictions. A main tenet of consequence of creationist theory is that planetary magnetic fields must be much younger than the billions of years required by evolutionary theory.

Based on the complexity and accuracy of this model, the following can be concluded:

A. The 150 years of empirical data on the decaying magnetic strength about the earth is a segment of a decaying magnetosphere on an exponential curve that is about 6,000 years old. This, along with the empirical data of other astrological bodies, serves to debunk the earth's (planetary) core dynamo theory and most certainly does not fit into a 4 billion-year-old earth model.

B. Dr. Barnes' "free decay" theories, based on the physics of entropy and electrical current resistance in the earth's core, are accurate.

C. The age and process of creation described in the Bible is accurate or else this model would not work.

D. The universe and everything in it was created about 6,000 years ago, debunking the theory of evolution.

E. The use of C^{14}/C^{12} ratio (C^{14}) as a dating method is limited to about 3,000 years based on the fact that the strength of the magnetosphere would have significantly affected the magnitude of C^{14} build up in the environment before that time, along with other environmental conditions both known and unknown. All other dating methods that are calibrated using C^{14} as a base line are thereby held to be in gross error as well (the domino effect). Any dates ascribed to periods, events, objects, et al, before 1000BC are in gross error and must be re-dated to align with more reliable and accurate biblical chronology.

F. The Bible can and should be used for guidance for future scientific investigation and modeling.

The Lunar Origins Theories, Moon's recession rate moving away from the earth (Example of EDM vs TPM)

Another bit of empirical scientific trending data that fits perfectly into the EDM creation model of the universe is the observed recession rate of the moon moving away from the earth and how it fits within lunar origins theories. Recent scientific measurements show the moon moving away from the earth at approx. 3.82cm/Year (1.5"). This fits perfectly into the 6,000-year age of the earth that the creation model is based on, without significantly affecting the earth's tidal movements or the habitability of the earth. Because this in no way fits "as is" into the evolutionary model, several TPM evolutionary models are proposed, all with significant drawbacks conflicting with known sciences [17]. One of the most defended models is expounded upon by Tim Tomas, a physicist at a MS degree level whose professional interests have been in astronomy, astrophysics, and atmospheric physics. Key excerpts from his argument are as follows [18]:

> Slichter (1963) reanalyzed the Earth-moon torque by devising a new way to use the entire ellipsoid of Earth rather than treating it as a series of approximations. He decided that, depending on the specifics of the model, the moon would have started out very close to Earth anywhere from 1.4 billion to 2.3 billion years ago, rather than 4.5 billion years ago. Slichter remarked that if "for some unknown reason" the tidal torque was much less in the past than in the present (where "present" means roughly the last 100 million years), this would solve the problem.

Lambeck noted that after the struggles of Slichter, Goldreich, and others, the observed and modeled values for tidal dissipation were finally in agreement (*Lambeck, 1980, page 286*). However, this still left a time scale problem. According to Lambeck, "*...unless the present estimates for the accelerations are vastly in error, only a variable energy sink can solve the time-scale problem and the only energy sink that can vary significantly with time is the ocean.*" (*Lambeck, 1980, page 288*). In section 11.4, "*Paleorotation and the lunar orbit*", Lambeck explicitly points out that paleontological evidence shows a much slower lunar acceleration in the past, and that this is compatible with the models for continental spreading from Pangea (*Lambeck, 1980, pages 388-394*). It is important to remember that by 1980, Lambeck had pointed out the essential solution to Slichter's dilemma - moving continents have a strong effect on tidal dissipation in shallow seas, which in turn dominate the tidal relationship between Earth and the moon.

Hansen's models assumed an Earth with one single continent....His continent doesn't move around as a model of plate tectonics would do it, but Hansen was the first to make a fully integrated model for oceanic tidal dissipation directly linked to the evolution of the lunar orbit. As Hansen says, his results are in "sharp contrast" with earlier models, putting the moon at quite a comfortable distance from Earth 4.5 billion years ago.

Although it may seem to the casual reader that the Earth-moon system is fairly simple (after all, it's just Earth and the moon), this is only an illusion. In fact, it is frightfully complicated, and it has taken over 100 years for physicists to generate the mathematical tools, and physical models, necessary to understand the problem. ***Slichter's dilemma, as I called it, was a theoretical one.*** Slichter's dilemma is today, essentially a solved problem. Once all of the details are included in the physical models of the Earth-moon system, we can see that there is no fundamental conflict between the basic physics and an evolutionary time scale for the Earth-moon system.

Based on the assumptions of this model, the following can be concluded:

A. The author is relying on the 100 years of work for creating a model that aligns with the evolutionary theory, hence the difficulty in making the empirical evidence (the actual known rate of moon recession from the earth) fit their model. *In actuality, the earth-moon system is quite simple. It fits perfectly in the creation model and only becomes complicated when you have to force it to fit into an evolutionary model.*

B. The model, no matter how complicated and mathematically sound it is, is still only theory and not fact, that is, not an observable science. It only shows a possibility, not an absolute conclusion.

C. Circular reasoning is used in selling the model. They had the patterns and estimates they needed the TPM model to conform to, which they succeeded in doing. Then they run the model and say, "See, it shows the exact patterns we find in the paleontological evidence."

D. If the model is correct in the relationship between the recession rate and tidal patterns in paleontological evidence, it assumes that only the evolutionary model has the continents in the Pangaea state to begin with; whereas in fact, so does the creation model. A slower recession rate caused by the tidal patterns found in the paleontogical evidence would uphold the creation models as well.

E. The worldwide Flood of Noah's time would also have had a great magnitude of effect on the geological landscape and could account for some or most of the paleontological evidence and patterns. Due to the negligence of the evolutionist to even consider an alternate chain of events (even when the evidence is so abundant and clear) cataclysmic happenstance with varying conditions and formations is often misinterpreted as having taken eons of time within uniformitarian processes.

Big Bang Model vs. Humphreys Creation Model [19,20] (Example of opposing TPMs with best fit scenarios)

Dr. Russell Humphreys, a prominent nuclear physicist and geophysicist who earned an award for excellence for his contributions to light ion–fusion target theory from the Sandia National Laboratories in New Mexico, is a creationist who formulated a model of the origins of the universe based on the processes espoused in the Bible, laws of physic and general relativity. His model aligns well with astrophysics science with little to no ad hoc theories or conflicting opposing physics that the big bang is plagued with.

Naked observations about universe.

The observable universe appears to be a spherical entity homogenous in all directions. In other words, the density of stars, the relative temperatures and cosmic microwave background radiation (CMBR), the redshift of light from galaxies at the various distances away from earth, the speed at which the surrounding galaxies are speeding away from the earth (the further in any direction the faster [71km/sec per mega parsec], and equal at any specified distance in any direction) are all generally of equal magnitude and measurement. The Bible infers that the earth is the center of creation due to man's presence here as the object of God's love and attention. The process of creation that is described in the Bible starts with a watery object, a sphere in space and time, that God made to separate when stretching out the heavens from the earth. One body of water, the second heaven, comes out above the expanse (the universe with it celestial bodies in a watery state also), and an earthly body of water appears under the expanse (the earth in its initial state according to Dr. Humphreys). This would appear as a snow globe, or rather a star globe, from God's point of view where the outer "crystal" that surrounds the universe is made of water, probably frozen 3/4 of the way from the inside and liquid on God's side, but could be some other solid matter converted at the same time the earth and galaxies were created. That is exactly how it appears, as a matter of fact. Secular scientists have concluded the following specifications in regard to our universe from Wikipedia: the diameter is approximately 93 billion light years across, the volume = 4×10^{80} m^3, its mass at 1.5×10^{53} kg, its density at 9.9×10^{-30} c/gm^3, average temperature at 2.72548 K, and the age estimated at between 13 and 17 billion years. It appears that the galaxies at the outer rim of the universe (46.5 billion light years from earth in any direction) are traveling at approximately $3.37*10^5$ km/sec/MP (4740 megaparsecs x 71 km/s at this time in history based on the red shift of the most critical galaxy where light will reach us before going dark due to the faster than light speeds) [19] in a continuing expansion from the initial "big bang" or "stretching out". These values are most likely based on or influenced by evolutionary time elements and so are probably not reliable. The best that science can reliably determine is that the universe appears to be spherical with a radius of 12 billion light years [7.] It is theorized that the expansion is increasing as time marches on, not slowing down as expected. The reason for this expansion has got the secular scientists baffled because their big bang model initially had it slowing down to revert and begin a collapsing segment of an ongoing cycle. This has led scientists to make up extraneous theories to account for the forces that cannot be detected presently due to lack of energy signatures (such as heat, radio waves, or electromagnetic telltale signs), that is the theories of dark matter and dark energy. This author's theory about this subject is that the accelerated expansion is being caused by the gravitational pull of the outer barrier (God's star globe water crystal). This "star globe" would have to be massive enough in any radial segment to have a greater pull on the universe than the gravity of the universe that would be pulling together the mass within to cause it to collapse. The star globe would have had to have been far enough away from the outer rim of the universe to start with to have allowed it to continue expanding for the past 6,000 years. As the Bible indicates that we are in the last days, I would surmise the space between the outer rim and the boundary is decreasing rapidly and may be less than 25% to 10% of its starting distance due to the acceleration of the expansion. This theory should be explored and tested in the mainstream astrophysical sciences.

Figure 3.2 Full-Sky Image of the Oldest Light in the Universe (13 bya),
colors indicate "warmer" (red) and "cooler" (blue) spots.

The Big Bang Theory [18]

The most outstanding contradiction of the big bang theory (BBT) is that it presumes to explain the origins of the universe as we know it today when in actuality it does not address the origins of the universe but rather a process from an existing state to its present state. Dr. Humphreys' creation model (HCM) explains the origins and the process by which the universe came to be.

The following is an overview of the BBT and the major problems with known physics.

The big bang theory (BBT) starts some 13 to 17 billion years ago with a singularity that contained all the mass and energy in the universe in an entity smaller than the size of an atom within an unbound space. Where this singularity comes from is not really explained. Therefore, the BBT is really only an explanation of the beginning of the universe as we know it today, starting at a random point in time (many believe within a cyclical process). Scientists conclude it started with a singularity based on reversing the expansion that they are measuring today along a linear path, as if laid out on a hypersphere. This would be similar to existing on the surface of a balloon as it is being filled with gas and expanding, or more precisely, raisins in a lump of dough as it expands when baked. Scientists have no explanation as to what caused the initial explosion and expansion from the original singularity or the immediate secondary expansion with a very precise energy surge and orderly distribution of material and energy that resulted in the present state of this universe. It is noted that this expansion, by chance, was of a precise balance. With too much energy the planets and stars could not be formed due to spatial difficulties with the gravity of clustered gases, energy balances, and conditions producing matter from energy. Too little energy would cause the expansion to collapse back into a singularity due to the gravity of the whole, all by pure chance and contrary to the normally expected mass disarray of energy and widespread chaotic aftermath of any typical explosion. They assume that the initial state of the universe was made up primarily of hydrogen gas with some elements of helium, deuterium, and lithium gas in an extremely hot environment via a process called quantum pair production as a result of the explosion. Quantum pair production is a process that requires ideal conditions for photons to produce matter from energy in particle/antiparticle pairs based on Einstein's formula $E=Mc^2$ (where E=Energy, M=Mass, c^2=speed of light). Theoretically, for every particle of matter that was generated via this process, there should be a partnering antimatter particle, but in truth...there is not! So, the big bang theory depends on believing that these ideal conditions emerge throughout the universe by chance to create the equally distributed density of galaxies we see in any direction we look, even though it is contradicted by natural expectations and the lack of evidence of the predicted 50% antimatter. There was an expectation in the BBT of some evidence of the initial heat present after the initial explosion, which was discovered in the form of cosmic microwave background radiation (CMBR) (i.e., predictions by George Gamow in 1962 to be approximately 50,000). The expectation of CMBR is not exclusive to the BBT, though proponents like to claim it is and is proof of concept. It is found as an expectation in preceding and post theories of the beginnings of the universe as well (predicted to be at 3,000 by K. Eddington in 1926 on a non-BBT theory and Dr. Humphreys' creation model). It was measured at 2,700 in 1964. As these gases began to cool, they began to contract in local formations, forming stars and planets within individual galaxies, approximately 2 trillion galaxies. Here again there is no scientific backing but rather ad hoc theory. For example, in regard to star formations, the BBT theorizes that most stars were created from groups of gas clusters; however, computer models do not produce globular clusters. Population II & I stars, which comprise most of our stars today, are said to be made of gas clouds forced to condense in the wake of a supernova explosion and resulting solar winds. This theory does not align with known physics. In nature, gas in a vacuum in an open system will disperse in the wake of solar winds and not condense. There would need to be a means of trapping or boxing in the gases for even the minutest chance of such a result. Additionally, the concentration of condensed gases would have to have formed a nucleus with a mass of 10,000 solar masses (SM) (1 SM = Size of our sun) before gravity would overcome the natural expansion caused by gas partial pressures and induced magnetic fields to the point that it will draw other surrounding gases together to form a celestial body (star). The largest stars observed are only about 120 SM. So in conclusion, the BBT is riddled with chances of conditions that are not supported by scientific evidence and are even in defiance of known physics in many points of theory. The more happenstance a theory depends upon, the greater the likelihood that it is not an acceptable theory. The chances for just one star system to come out of the big bang are astronomical; the chances for our universe to come out of the BBT is not even calculable. How come this sounds familiar? Because the theory of evolution rests on the same perfect dance and fairy tale happy ending.

Dr. Humphreys' White Hole Cosmology Theory [17]

Dr. Humphreys' theory [7] is based on Einstein's theory of general relativity (GR), which among other things, addresses the space/time delineation based on the gravitational pull of planets, etc. Within this framework is the theory behind anomalies that occur around black holes. It is believed that black holes are created around the dying and collapsing of a star. The black hole draws in all matter and energy (including light) that gets near the event horizon (the point where escape is impossible and matter degrades to atomic particles that accelerate to greater than light speeds) into a single ball of energy (a singularity in the shape of a sphere due to gravity). Nothing can be observed in a black hole beyond the event horizon because light cannot escape; therefore, no one knows what goes on within a black hole. Any object being drawn into a planetary or sun size black hole gets virtually torn apart. As the object starts to pass over the event horizon, that point starts to accelerate on an atomic level up to and much faster than the speed of light, whereas the parts still yet further away from the event horizon are moving at the original velocity (say 30k M/H). Time begins to slow down to nothing. The difference is hardly noticeable to the person standing at the event horizon, all would seem to be at a normal pace. A black hole will grow in proportion to the matter and energy it eats.

By the same principle, Dr. Humphreys' theory is based on GR principles as it relates to theories of black holes and white holes. A white hole is basically the opposite of a black hole. It expels matter and energy from within, and it too has an event horizon. According to Dr. Humphreys' theory, God's first creation was a body of water that held all the mass in the universe (that would have been held together by gravity in a sphere greater than 2 million light years in diameter) within a black hole. God then made the waters to separate when stretching out the heavens from the earth being expelled through a white hole. One body of water, the second heaven, comes out above the expanse (the universe with its celestial bodies in a watery state also), and an earthly body of water appears under the expanse (the earth in its initial state).

Ge:1:6: And God said, let there be a firmament in the midst of the waters, and let it divide the waters from the waters.

Ge:1:7: And God made the firmament, and divided the waters which were under the firmament from the waters which were above the firmament: and it was so.

These scriptures describe a process by which God first made all astrological objects (the earth, sun, moon, stars, etc.) as bodies of water with all the physical properties of water, mass, motion, and so on (e.g., molecular structure [H_2O], gravity, orbits, rotation, magnetospheres, etc.). He then created the solid matters and associated elements (dry land). So in six days, the first week in time, God created the earth within a solar system of many, within a galaxy of many, within a grand universe.

Dr. Humphreys surmises that the initial creation of the liquid waters in a black hole precipitated the resulting compaction, which transformed the water to various elements, and the rapid gravitational collapse to heat the waters to the point where nucleosynthesis would occur, and finally on the second day converting the black hole to a white hole by beginning the rapid expansion of space. The high temperatures, followed by the expansion, would produce the CMBR. So, on or about the second day until about the fourth day, God "stretched out the heavens" as it says in Job 9:8, Psalms 104:2, Isaiah 40:22, Isaiah 42:5, Isaiah 44:24, Jeremiah 10:12, Zechariah 12:1. We can take this to mean that at this time the heavenly bodies were in a solid state of creation and started to be expelled through the event horizon. This would in turn cause time to speed up to many millions and possibly billions of light years within seconds, even though it would seem to anyone living on one of these planets, experiencing this phenomena, as if all things were carrying on at a normal (earth time) pace. This white hole would be the size of the universe, as opposed to a planetary sized black hole, so the acceleration would not have such a great effect in different parts of an object. In other words, the object would stretch a bit, but not pulled apart, and would reshape due to gravity once it was outside the event horizon. The event horizon would start to shrink in proportion to the diminishing mass within the hole until it vanished completely. Dr. Humphreys assumes that our solar system would be at the center of the universe due to the many inferences in the Bible, which also fits what we observe in the universe.

A. The density of the galaxies is approximately the same in any direction you look.
B. All objects in the universe appear to be moving away (expanding out from our location) as evidenced in the various magnitudes of red shift (light spectrum of objects moving away from a central location) of stars in any direction at their perspective distances from earth.
C. Due to the GR time delineation of the stars traveling past the event horizon, we can see the light of the stars even though they may be billions of light years away from the earth, even from the first day of creation some 6,000 years ago. This can only be true if we were at the center of the universe; otherwise, light from stars passing after the earth would not have reached us as of yet, and we would see a dark portion of the sky without any significant mass of starlight.

The BBT assumes the universe has no boundaries, no edge, and no center. In contrast, the Humphreys model assumes a spherical boundary (referred to as the second heaven in scripture, which may be made of water) all within God's abode (referred to as the third heaven in scripture). The assumption that matter was first created as water molecules approximately 6,000 years ago is affirmed by Dr. Humphreys' acutely predictive planetary magnetosphere model. Humphreys' model, which bases its assumptions on the atomic nuclei with aligned spins of H_2O molecules and the estimated short time period from the creation of the universe [12].

The strata of make believe theories of secular humanists amount to a modern-day Tower of Babel, reaching even to the heavens (outer space). Built upon the original pseudoscientific theory of evolution are the latest unsupported theories of punctuated equilibrium: the pseudoscientific use of C14 dating methods, the pseudoscientific use of radiometric dating methods, the pseudoscience of the dynamo theory as an engine powering the magnetosphere of planets and stars, the pseudoscientific theory of the geological ages applied to the earth's strata, the pseudoscience used to model lunar origins, erroneous historical chronologies, erroneous dinosaur ancestry, and the pseudoscience of the comet generating Oort cloud. All of these have no verifiable scientific evidence and even defy well established physical sciences. I suppose having a generation that grew up in today's secular academic system being fed on pseudoscience (calling unsubstantiated theory fact apart from any scientific evidence) along with watching the pseudoscientific feats of traveling through space at warp speeds in *Star Trek* and *Star Wars* makes it easy to feed them this fairytale laden pseudoscience. Scientific protocol demands that you have a consensus of the data for it to be considered scientifically valid or a scientific certainty. When there is no consensus, and you decide to inadvertently pick and choose values that agree with your theology or your belief, then you have moved into the arena of pseudoscience. None of these theories have a shred of evidence but are born out of the need for the evolutionary model to work. If we strip all these make-believe theories away, it is clear that the creation model is well supported based on the consensus of the empirical evidence alone without extraneous theories needed to "make it work".

Theory of Evolution vs Biblical Creation Account

The following table shows the weight of the evidence of the theory of evolution compared to the biblical creation model. The weight of each score is based on evidence found in all science, history, and literature as previously reviewed. The final score based on the preponderance of the evidence resulted in:

Theory of Evolution Model: 19.8 **Biblical Creation Model:** 92.2

Scoring Guidelines:

No Empirical Evidence = 0

If the model has a theory that is not backed up with empirical evidence, and does not fall under any of the following categories, the score for the model making the prediction gets a weight of "0". The opposing model will get a weight of "100" if a theory is needed for the support of the one model and is not needed for the support of the opposing model.

Some Inferring Evidence = 25

Theory based on not so much empirical evidence but some inferring evidence can receive a weight of "25".

Theoretically Possible = 50

If there is no empirical evidence, but the theory aligns well with known physics, it can receive a weight of "50".

Theoretically Possible w/ some inferential evidence = 75

If there is no empirical evidence but some inferring evidence, and if the theory aligns well with known physics, it can receive a weight of "75".

Supported by empirical evidence alone = 100

If the empirical evidence "as is" fits reasonably within a given model, with no additional theories required to "make it fit", that particular model gets a weight of "100".

Count	Theory of Evolution	Score	Count	Biblical Creation Model	Score
A	**Theory of Evolution**	19.8	B	**Biblical Creation Model**	92.2
	Based on Darwinian theory (1859) no evidence (trans. forms) / contrary to laws of entropy	Ave. Wt.		Based on the biblical historical record (from 4000 BC) & wt of scientific and historical evidence	Avg.Wt.
1	**Microevolution**	100	1	**Microevolution**	100
	Supported by empirical evidence within species			Supported By empirical evidence within species	
2	**Macroevolution**	0	2	**Macroevolution**	100
	No evidence / only needed to make the evolutionary model work			Genome reproduces only like kind w/ degenerative component	
3	**Artifact Hypotheses**	0	3	**Artifact Hypotheses**	100
	Disproved w/ Burgess bestiary & Maotianshan shale discoveries			Only needed to make the evolutionary model work	
4	**Lipalian Interval**	0	4	**Lipalian Interval**	100
	Disproved w/ deep core drilling			Only needed to make the evolutionary model work	
5	**Punctuated Equilibrium**	0	5	**Punctuated Equilibrium**	100
	No evidence / neg. argument / contrary to natural expectation			Only needed to make the evolutionary model work	
6	**Panspermia Theory**	0	6	**Panspermia Theory**	100
	No evidence / neg. argument / prob nil w/ known physics			Only needed to make the evolutionary model work	
7	**Decay of Planetary Magnetic Fields**	0	7	**Decay of Planetary Magnetic Fields**	100
	Dynamo theory /no evidence / contrary examples (Mercury)			Empirical evidence aligns perfectly with model	
	Only needed to make the Evolutionary Model Work				
8	**Archaeomagnetism**	75	8	**Archaeomagnetism**	75

	Earth core reversals /ignoring scientific data that affect results			Disruption due to energy surges in the earth causing eddy	
				current moments within the molten core	
9	**Planetary Magnetospheres**	25	9	**Planetary Magnetospheres**	100
	Poor NASA model / ignoring Dr. Humphreys predictive model			Empirical evidence aligns perfect with Humphreys' predictive model	
10	**Rock Formation and Fossilization**	0	10	**Rock Formation and Fossilization**	100
	Uniformitarianism- Contrary to science of geology & natural exp.			Empirical evidence aligns perfectly with catastrophism model	
11	**Comet Life Cycle**	0	11	**Comet Life Cycle**	100
	Oort Cloud /no evidence / neg. argument / contrary evidence			Empirical evidence aligns perfectly with model	
	Only needed to make the evolutionary model work				
12	**Lunar Origins Theories**	0	12	**Lunar Origins Theories**	100
	No empirical evidence / circular reasoning models			Empirical evidence aligns perfectly with model	
	Only needed to make the evolutionary model work				
13	**Big Bang Theory**	25	13	**Dr. Humphreys' Creation Model**	50
	Mostly contrary to known physics & natural examples			Theory aligns well with physics & theory of general relativity (GR)	
	Only needed to make the evolutionary model work			Aligns well with the observable universe	
14	**Sudden Appearance of Civilization (Time & Place)**	50	14	**Sudden Appearance of Civilization (Time & Place)**	100
	No argument (coincidence)			Empirical evidence aligns perfectly with model	
15	**Babel Event / Cultures**	25	15	**Babel Event / Cultures**	100

	Alternate origins hypotheses (evidence to the contrary)				Empirical evidence aligns perfectly with model	
	(time & place)				(Time & Place)	
16	**Ancient Writings of Flood/Noah**	0	16		**Ancient Writings of Flood/Noah**	100
	Ignoring multi sources (dismissed as myth)				Historical evidence aligns perfectly with model	
17	**Coexistence of Dinosaur with Man**	0	17		**Coexistence of Dinosaur with Man**	100
	Denying evidence of multi sources (dismissed as myth)				Historical evidence aligns perfectly with model	
18	**Origin of Genome**	0	18		**Origin of Genome**	100
	Panspermia theory/ Neg. argument / probability nil				Empirical evidence aligns perfectly with creation model	
19	**C^{14} Dating - Quantification vs Qualification**	50	19		**C^{14} Dating - Quantification vs Qualification**	75
	Ignores scientific data that affect results				Scientific evidence aligns perfectly with model	
20	**C^{14} Testing of Coal & Dinosaur Bones**	0	20		**C^{14} Testing of Coal & Dinosaur Bones**	100
	Ignores results in the blind (no refuting data)				Scientific evidence aligns perfectly with model	
21	**Dating Methods**	0	21		**Dating Methods**	100
	Ignores scientific data that affect results				Not depended on	
22	**25-2300BC Demarcation Arch/Genome**	0	22		**25-2300BC Demarcation Arch/Genome**	100
	Denies the evidence (coincidence)				Historical/scientific evidence aligns well with model	
23	**Ice Ages**	50	23		**Ice Ages**	50

	Ignores scientific data that affect results				Scientific evidence aligns perfectly with model	
24	**Neanderthal Man**	50		24	**Neanderthal Man**	50
	Ignores scientific data that affect results				Scientific evidence aligns perfectly with model	
25	**Biblical Arch. Discovery**	25		25	**Biblical Arch. Discovery**	75
	Ignores/Minimizes magnitude of evidence				Historical/scientific evidence Aligns perfectly with model	
26	**Pangaea**	100		26	**Pangaea**	100
	Historical/scientific evidence Aligns perfectly with model				Historical/scientific evidence Aligns perfectly with model	
27	**Cambrian Explosion**	0		27	**Cambrian Explosion**	100
	Sudden appearance of novel creature				Sudden appearance of novel creature	
	w/ no transformational predecessors				w/ no transformational predecessors	
28	**Genome Lab Testing**	0		28	**Genome Lab Testing**	100
	Results across the board negative to chance and nat. selection				Too complex to have happened naturally.	
	Could not reproduce evolutionary transformation in lab testing.				Results across the board negative to chance and nat. selection	
29	**Mathematical Possibility**	0		29	**Mathematical Possibility**	100
	Chances for evolution determined to be $1/10^{77}$				Results are particular to evolutionary model	
	Statisticians "conditional probability" <1/2				Statisticians "conditional probability" >1/2	
Weight based on evidence found in all science, history and literature						

The conclusion based on the naked facts obviously favor the creation model. Based on statisticians' *"conditional probability"*, the **theory of evolution model** is less than 1/2 probability (19.8/100, or < 20%), not plausible. The **biblical creation account model** comes out well over 1/2 probability (92.2/100, or >90%) and therefore would be considered the favorable model.

The Darwinian Tree of Life Model and State of the Science Today

A simple Google search using the following (independent genome tree of life lab results) will return a slew of sources that are congruent in their conclusions that the Darwinian Tree of life (ToL) model is obsolete based on the genomic sciences. The following review is a summary of what is being reported from the scientific community.

There are two basic cell structures found in living organisms, the *eukaryotes* and the *prokaryotes*. *Eukaryotes* (that includes fungi, plants and animal) have a nucleus where they store DNA. *Prokaryotes* (bacteria) do not have a central nucleus for storing DNA.

Prokaryotic species can live in a diverse range of ecological environments as opposed to *eukaryotes*. Certain *organotrophic species* feed off organic matter such as sugars, amino acids, hydrocarbons, and methane gas. Other *phototrophic species* feed off light energy. Then there are the *lithotrophic species* that feed on inorganic diets such as CO_2, H_2S, H_2, Fe^2, elemental sulfur, and a wide variety of other environmental chemicals.

The hypothetical Tree of Life (ToL) branches into three basic classifications: bacteria, archaea, and eukaryotes. The traditional means of drawing the ToL has been to look at the similarities of creatures found in the fossil record and compiling them into a graduating order from simple to complex based on the physical appearances. This method becomes problematic when the unique differences (disparities) between *eukaryotes* found in the same strata is of a great magnitude; for example, is a fungus related more to a plant or animal? *Prokaryotes* are even more difficult to place in a ToL–like model due to the incredible variety. It is difficult to know which differences truly reflect differences of evolutionary history, as they appear in the fossil record all at once (as a radiation or explosion) with no trace of diverging branches.

The genomic sciences have now compounded the problem. First, it now appears that the *prokaryote* must now be divided into two distinct groups, **bacteria** and **archaea**. **Archaea,** classified as a *prokaryote* due to the lack of a nucleus, have some traits that follow the *prokaryote* structure and other traits that resemble the *eukaryote* structures. Second, the placement within a traditional ToL is found to be more complicated based on cataloged genomic similarities/differences between one possible related species and another species not initially associated based on physical and cellular characteristics. And third, the missing data to identify any divergent branch is much more poignant than ever before.

The four mechanisms that naturalists believe play a part of the evolution of one species to another species lacks the ability to obtain new DNA coding, all variable traits within the species have to come from existing data.

> *The raw material of evolution is the DNA sequence that already exists: there is no natural mechanism for making long stretches of new random sequence. In this sense, no gene is ever entirely new. Innovation can, however, occur in several ways:*

- *Intragenic mutation: an existing gene can be modified by mutations in its DNA sequence.*
- *Gene duplication: an existing gene can be duplicated so as to create a pair of closely related genes within a single cell.*
- *Segment shuffling: two or more existing genes can be broken and rejoined to make a hybrid gene consisting of DNA segments that originally belonged to separate genes.*

- *Horizontal (intercellular) transfer:* a piece of DNA can be transferred from the genome of one cell to that of another—even to that of another species. This process is in contrast with the usual vertical transfer of genetic information from parent to progeny.

Mutation is mostly benign, deleterious, or fatal. Very rarely will a mutation actually benefit the host, and that is usually restricted to a specific community and is without any supporting scientific experimental evolutionary assenting qualities outside of theoretical assumptions.

Horizontal transfer and segment shuffling depend on existing data and cannot be a mechanism for evolution, as there could only have been one original common ancestor and therefore no source to receive a horizontal transfer of DNA data. Even if there were multiple original common ancestors, as some want to believe, it still could not account for new DNA material for the higher order of phyla.

Gene duplication involves a supposed mutation process that could occur during the duplication process, giving rise to an evolutionary transformation; however, observation of the adaptations in nature resemble more of a preprogramed genomic algorithm that cause these changes, step for step, providing the phyla the ability to adapt to the changes within its environment and has only been observed at the species level. Random "accidental" mutations would not have the response time or the chances in its favor to keep up with the needed timely responses in all of God's creatures, as has been observed since Darwin brought it to our attention. These supposed mutations are actually the result of a preprogramed algorithm that pulls on a resource of stored (latent) information/data/ instructions that inserts that data in a placement unique within the genome during the duplication process in response to sensory input [21].

In an article from the Oxford Journals regarding the studies of bacterial and archaeal genomes, the authors concluded that the findings *"[undermine] the 'Tree of Life' model of evolution"*, and that genomes *"are built according to the same, simple 'master plan' with wall-to-wall protein-coding and RNA-coding genes"*. The authors also noted that *"it could be hard even to identify a set of genes that have a coherent history over a substantial evolutionary span"*, *"the emerging complexity of the prokaryotic world is currently beyond our grasp"*, and that *"we have no adequate language, in terms of theory or tools, to describe the workings and histories of the genomic network"*. [22]

A recent article from *Nature concluded the following* [23]:

> *"Gene surveys suggest the existence of an enormous number of branches, but even an approximation of the full scale of the tree has remained elusive"*

> *"The results reveal the dominance of bacterial diversification and underline the importance of organisms lacking isolated representatives, with substantial evolution concentrated in a major radiation of such organisms. This tree highlights major lineages currently underrepresented in biogeochemical models and identifies radiations that are probably important for future evolutionary analyses."*

The follow clip of an article from NCBI, titled *Mapping the Tree of Life*, relays that the ToL structure remains controversial and obscure [24].

"Although the three-domain structure of the ToL is established, the deep phylogenetic structure of each of the domains remains murky and sometimes controversial. Obstacles to accurate inference of deep phylogenetic relationships are both systematic, in molecular phylogenetic calculations, and practical, due to a paucity of sequence representation for many groups of organisms."

"All molecular phylogenetic trees have systematic limitations that cloud our view of the deeper branches in the tree of life (ToL). Consequently, I discuss the building of phylogenetic trees and emphasize the intrinsic limitations of any results. Progress toward assembly of a universal phylogenetic ToL also relies on how comprehensive is our knowledge of the extent and the richness of life's diversity. Therefore, I show how the recent explosion of environmental sequences has heavily influenced the patterns seen in the trees. I conclude that we have in place the outlines of a universal ToL, but the details of the patterns of deep evolution in all the phylogenetic domains remain obscure."

The Wired website reports "New Algorithms Force Scientists to Revise the Tree of Life" [25]:

Despite the surmounting abundance of data available with the advances of the genomic sciences, the conflicts and debates as to the alignment of phylum in the ToL have risen exponentially in proportion to these advances. Evolutionary biologist Michael Donoghue concedes that they cannot place 20 different types of yeast in the ToL much less be able to resolve the 1.8 million species that are could possibly be misplaced presently in the Darwinian ToL. He states;

For example, it's not clear whether snails are most closely related to clams and other bivalves or to another mollusk group known as tusk shells, said Rokas. And we have no idea how some of the earliest animals to branch off the tree, such as jellyfish and sponges, are related to each other. Scientists can rattle off examples of conflicting trees published in the same scientific journal within weeks, or even in the same issue.

These scientist tried to produce phylogenetic trees based on yeast genes using an information theory algorithm to match up the phylum in a sequential order based on data sets that aligned the closest within the a ToL model. Donoghue confessed;

The result, published in Nature in May, was unexpected. Every gene they studied appeared to tell a slightly different story of evolution.

"Just about all the trees from individual genes were in conflict with the tree based on a concatenated data set," says Hilu. "It's a bit shocking."

"I am not so sure we know what the true relationships are," he said. "If we aren't sure what the truth is, we can't tell if we have the right tree."

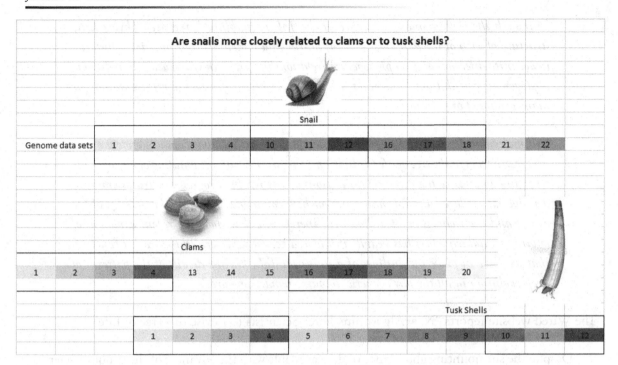

Figure 3.3 Example of genome ToL conflict

Despite the abundance of technical scientific literature easily found on the internet, proponents for the traditional Darwinian evolutionary ToL model aggressively contend for its continued representation in public schools and other public venues. David Hillis speaking to the Texas State BoE in 2009 claimed he was one of the "world's leading experts on the tree of life" and stated that in reconstructing the ToL model using biological molecules there is "overwhelming agreement correspondence as you go from protein to protein, DNA sequence to DNA sequence" which is far removed from the realities being communicated in the technical journals based on the state of the art within the genomic sciences. Evolutionist get away with this because of the closed doors to the creationist in public forums and no one to fact check these supposed "experts", the blind leading the blind [26].

Academia continues to teach evolution with the traditional Darwinian ToL model, which basically ignores the progress of genomic sciences and changing model for the past century that only show the radiation (as in the Cambrian explosion) of phyla in each geological period congruent with the fossil record.

> *"How do we build a phylogenetic tree? The underlying principle is Darwin's idea of "descent with modification." Basically, by looking at the pattern of modifications (novel traits) in present-day organisms, we can figure out—or at least, make hypotheses about— their path of descent from a common ancestor."[27]*

Basically, this is done by organizing phyla from simple to complex and then determining the years between them based on evolutionary assumptions and their place in the fossil records/strata assumed periods which has no supporting scientific empirical evidence (only circular reasoning, fossils dated by position in strata, strata dated by type of fossils found in the strata). There is no real science behind tracing or connecting these assumed morphological changes, pure assumption, hypotheses, inference, and conjecture, because there is no physical/cellular/genomic data to support or link them to a ToL Model. The consensus among genomic scientists today agree that the origins of life should now be modeled more as a "bush" to represent a radiation or explosion. These bushes would only contain branches (variations) within the species (such as Darwin's diversity of finches and pigeons) and not be connected to other species although evolutionist will extend it beyond the species based on pure assumption, hypotheses, inference, and conjecture. Science has once again come around to more closely agree with the Creation model of the history of life based on the empirical evidence just as the magnetosphere, geological and archeological sciences have. The secular humanist have no other option but to continue to propagate a failed theology which they apparently get away with.

How to Teach Evolution as a Matter of Fact [28,29,30]

First, remember to teach it under one umbrella, solely under the subject heading of "evolution". Do not mention, or if you do, just skim over the subdivisions of microevolution and macroevolution.

Microevolution: comparatively minor evolutionary change involving the accumulation of variations in populations usually below the species level - Merriam Webster's Dictionary
Macroevolution: evolution that results in relatively large and complex changes (as in species formation) - Merriam Webster's Dictionary.

Microevolution describes adaptive changes or genomic variations that occur within a species in response to changes within its environment (such as temperatures, predation, food resources, etc.), genomic influences (diets, parental matches/mismatches, chemical intake, etc.), or other unknown influences. These are not true "mutations" as they are often referred to but rather the redirection or wakening of existing, stored DNA data/information/instructions that were input by the creator to help the animals to adapt to their changing environment over time and do generally follow the basic "survival of the fittest" or "natural selection" principles espoused by Darwin, without which all species would have become extinct eons ago.

So, it is best to teach this strictly under the heading of evolution. Make sure you refer to these changes as "chance mutations", "survival of the fittest" or "natural selection". Never refer to them as pre-existing DNA encoded data/information/instructions directed by complex algorithms. There is plenty of empirical evidence to show the science behind these "evolutionary changes", such as Darwin's finches with beaks that have changed due to wet vs dry weather, sheep where the wooliest survive allowing for woolier offspring, and many others [31]. Remember not to emphasize that these changes and examples are all within the species with no evidences of changes from one species to another; you want them to think singularly. Don't let on that there is a difference between micro and macro evolution. If you can get the students thinking that these principles are universal, you can segue into macroevolution from microevolutionary principles and processes without them suspecting a thing, believing that it all works within these same scientific protocols.

Don't explain to them that macroevolution requires DNA encoded data/information/instructions /algorithms that is not preexisting and therefore requires some mutation that has a mechanism to acquire that DNA data/information/instructions from some external source. Do not teach them that there are two immutable facts in regard to acquiring DNA encoded data/information/instructions/

algorithms from some external source, 1) there is no known source or mechanism that has been found to reasonably explain where the original DNA encoded data/information/instructions/algorithms came from and 2) there is no known source or mechanism found to reasonably explain where additional DNA encoded data/information/instructions/algorithms could possibly come from. So, be sure to avoid any mention of that to the students.

Make sure you do not distinguish between adaptive changes, "survival of the fittest", or "natural selection" on a microevolutionary scale and mutations required for macroevolution. Refer to all changes as "mutations" as defined in the Merriam Webster's Dictionary, no matter what mechanism is the cause behind the changes.

Mutations: a significant and basic alteration, a relatively permanent change in hereditary material that involves either a change in chromosome structure or number (as in translocation, deletion, duplication, or polyploidy) or a change in the nucleotide sequence of a gene's codons (as in frameshift or missense errors) and that occurs either in germ cells or in somatic cells but with only those in germ cells being capable of perpetuation by sexual reproduction - Merriam Webster's Dictionary

Second, segue into the macroevolution aspect, but don't make that distinction, just refer to it as a continuation of evolution. Make comparisons of the species in a progressive alignment, putting them in an order that shows progressive complexity so as to provide "proof of concept". Basically, you want to build on the foundation you laid using microevolutionary processes to extend to the changes at a macroevolution level, so the students can understand how these changes occurred between the species – as a response to environmental changes, predation, and natural selection over millions of years due to small incremental adaptations. Make a comparison of anatomies of similar use and function. Explain how the genome sets being so closely related tell the story that this is a result of evolutionary processes. Don't let on that it is just as likely that it is because they are creatures close in anatomy and that their organs and appendages serve the same or close to the same function, so whether it was from evolution or special creation, obviously they are going have genome sets closely related.

Third, make all the empirical evidence that doesn't fit "as is" into the evolutionary timeline to fit by adding extraneous theory to the evidence to force it to fit into the evolutionary model. Once you have decided on the most believable theory, hide it in the midst of real facts and teach it along with those facts as if it were fact too. No one will know the difference. For example, when you teach earth science to students, teach them about gravity, general relativity, and about the dynamo engine powering the earth's magnetosphere. Don't let them know that that the dynamo engine is just a theory and that the empirical evidence does not align with the theory: the record of decay over the past 150 years as opposed to cyclical data record that would be the result of a dynamo engine; the rotation of Mercury being too slow to support a dynamo, residual magnetism discovered (to the surprise of NASA) in the moon, Mars, and other planetesimals that were predicted to have never had a magnetosphere; and the fact that all known planets to date are on a decaying slope and none show the cyclical data that should support a dynamo engine. Don't mention the fact that scientists have not found the missing strata containing the missing links that Darwin so hoped would validate his theory. Minimize the missing transitional fossils. Don't let on that they are the impetus for all the failed theories since the dawn of the theory of evolution (e.g., the **artifact hypotheses, Lipalian Interval,** and the most recent **punctuated equilibrium).** Definitely emphasize the transitional fossils that are in the table listing the species in progressive complexity and refer to them as "transitional fossils" so they think the matter is settled, even though they are all species in stasis with no trace of species with transitional variations connecting them in any of the given examples.

Do not share with the class the following facts. Here are some excerpts from actual studies that pretty much conclude the opposite of the claims of these evolutionary publications.

In an article from the Oxford Journals regarding the studies of bacterial and archaeal genomes, the authors concluded that the findings "[undermine] the 'Tree of Life' model of evolution", that genomes "are built according to the same, simple 'master plan' with wall-to-wall protein-coding and RNA-coding genes", that "it could be hard even to identify a set of genes that have a coherent history over a substantial evolutionary span", and that "the emerging complexity of the prokaryotic world is currently beyond our grasp". The also noted that they "have no adequate language, in terms of theory or tools, to describe the workings and histories of the genomic network" [22].

Chen, the scientist studying the fossils found in the Maotianshan Shale, is not a creationist but rather an orthodox scientist of the "old school" using reasonable deductive analysis in his research apart from humanistic philosophical guidelines. He was invited to give a lecture in the spring of 2000 at the University of Washington's geological department. Chen, in the presentation of his discoveries and what his research has yielded to the scientific community, highlighted the apparent contradiction between the Chinese fossil record and the Darwinian orthodoxy. This prompted an attending professor to respond, in an admonishing tone, asking if he wasn't nervous about expressing his doubt about Darwinism so freely, especially in light of China's reputation for suppressing dissenting opinions. Chen responded saying, "In China, we can criticize Darwin, but not the government. In America you can criticize the government, but not Darwin". Apparently, there are still some scientists that maintain their objective integrity regardless of the consequences [28,32].

The Divergence Hypothesis [28]

Needless to say, this scientific undertaking has yielded a wide range of results from the participating independent studies anywhere from 274 million years ago (mya) to 14.2 billion years ago (bya) when applied to the Cambrian animals to determine when they diverged from a Precambrian ancestor (a phylum that is missing from the Precambrian strata). Since ***there can be only one true divergent point*** from which the tree of life has generated from, the multitude and wide range of results bear witness that **there is no consensus and therefore** *it cannot be determined* by the tools and the state of art technology of modern science contrary to the claims in all the documentaries, defending publication and evolutionary scientist. Additionally, the proponents for these assumptions hold to the "artifact theory" (discussed earlier) for why these ancestors have no evidence in the fossil record, which, as previously concluded, has been disproved from the many Cambrian strata discoveries in the past 150 years.

In 1997 a study by Japanese biologist N. Nikoh and colleagues resulted in the universal common ancestor that lived 940mya. In 1999 a study by B. Wang, S. Kumar, and S.B. Hedges resulted in the universal common ancestor that lived 1.2 - 1.5 bya. One study actually reported that the divergent date fell between a range of 274mya and 1.6bya. The 274 date is 250my after the Cambrian explosion! They decided to split the difference and concluded that the date was 830 mya. Another study by S. Aris-Brosou and Z. Yang reported that the divergent date could fall between a range of 452mya and

2bya depending on which genes were studied and which estimate method was used. The 452 date is 72my after the Cambrian explosion! A survey by D. Graur and W. Martin published in *Trend in Genetics* titled "Reading the Entrails of Chickens: Molecular Timescale of Evolution and the Illusion of Precision" cited one study that claimed to be 95% certain that the divergent date fell within a 14.2bya range (the earth is only 4.5bya).

The oldest fossilized organism dates to about 3.5 bya. The latest documentaries place the universal common ancestor at about 3.9 bya, not based any of the lab testing results (because there is no consensus), but rather because it is the best fit for the theory placing it before the oldest known fossil and after a time were the earth was in a state not suitable for life to emerge [25]. Scientific protocol demands that you have a consensus of the data for it to be considered scientifically valid or a scientific certainty. When there is no consensus, and you decide to inadvertently pick and choose values that agree with your theology or your belief, then you have moved into the arena of pseudoscience.

Phylogenetic Reconstruction (Molecular Sequences) [28]

The study of molecular sequencing attempts to track the animal genetic tree of life by assessing the magnitude of related characteristics to establish branching (divergent) points along the trees branches back to the trunk, especially among the major Cambrian groups. In the final analysis, the story the body of evidence tells, like the deep-divergence hypothesis, results in a multitude of conflicting patterns (no consensus therefor no conclusion that supports that hypothesis).

A 2009 edition of *Trends in Ecology and Evolution* included a paper that notes "evolutionary trees from different genes often have conflicting branching patterns". A 2009 edition of a *New Scientist* cover story notes that the tree of life molecular sequences "lies in tatters, torn to pieces by an onslaught of negative evidence ", that "many biologists now argue that the tree of life concept is obsolete and needs to be discarded", and that "the evolution of animal and plants isn't exactly tree-like". An article in the *New Scientist* reported a story on the research and study by M. Syvanen on 2,000 genes of six very diverse animals saying, "In theory, he should have been able to use the gene sequences to construct an evolutionary tree showing the relationship between the six animals. He failed. The problem was the different genes told contradicting evolutionary stories." Syvanen himself confessed, "We've just annihilated the tree of life. It's not a tree anymore, it's a different topology entirely. What would Darwin have made of that?" Leading biologist Atonis Rokas of Vanderbilt University also echoes that sentiment, after 150 years of the acceptance of Darwin's Origin of the Species, saying, "a complete and accurate tree of life remains an elusive goal", and "despite the amount of data and breadth of taxa analyzed, relationships among most metazoan phyla remain unresolved". A year later A. Rokas and S.B. Carroll of the University of Wisconsin reiterated this disparity saying, "certain critical parts of the tree of life may be difficult to resolve, regardless of the quantity of conventional data available" and concluded from their extended study "inferences from these two independent lines of evidence (molecules and fossils) support a view of the origin of the Metazoa as a radiation compressed in time".

Do not share with the students that instead of establishing the tree of life that geneticists had hoped for going into these studies, they have unanimously concluded that it not only shows the error of that assumption (no consensus therefor no conclusion that supports these hypothesis), it inversely well establishes the sudden appearance of the myriads of species in the Cambrian era confirming the findings in the fossil record (and fitting well in the creation model)! Scientific protocol demands that you have a consensus of the data for it to be considered scientifically valid or a scientific certainty. When there is no consensus, and you decide to inadvertently pick and choose values that agree with your theology or your belief, then you have moved into the arena of pseudoscience.

Let us now review a popular documentary that embodies these quintessential teachings and apply our understanding of evolution being taught as fact.

Analysis of the COSMOS: A Space Time Odyssey - Hosted by Neil deGrasse Tyson

S1E1: Tyson begins the series by explaining the scientific method, searchers *strictly* adhering to a simple set of rules:

6) test ideas by experiment and observation,
7) build on those ideas that pass the test,
8) reject the ones that fail,
9) follow the evidence wherever it leads,
10) and question everything.

Accept these terms and the cosmos is yours.

Tyson goes on to teach the Big Bang (BBT) as a matter of fact, ignoring all the physics problems that plague the theory. One of the elements of the scientific method is to "reject the ones that fail". If a theory cannot be tested by experiment and observation and it defies known physics, how can it be taught as fact? The more happenstance a theory depends upon, the greater the likelihood that it is not an acceptable theory. The theory espouses a perfect song and dance – everything in optimum placement, under ideal circumstances, with the exact energy inputs, in billions of circumstances all produced from chaotic mechanisms. Remember Tyson's advice…question everything. His supposed "strong observational evidence" fits into other theories just as well so they cannot be held to give credence to the BBT alone when accounting for all the relative evidence. Scientific certainties must be based on the consensus of the evidence. You cannot just pick and choose evidence that favors your hypothesis and ignore the other pertinent data.

Tyson infers that life started from a primordial soup and may have originally come to the earth from another part of the Milky Way (the panspermia theory). Instead of addressing the sheer impossibility of the genome being developed under primitive conditions, he just says, "we still don't know how life got started". How easy it is to teach evolution as fact when you don't have to address the major difficulties with the theory, just brush it off and go on your way. He states, "the origin of life is one of the greatest unsolved mysteries of science" and then carries on from there, explaining how life started cooking its brew under ideal circumstances by accident. He does not relay that this process that happened by accident cannot be repeated in a laboratory on purpose from supposed intelligent beings. So much for testing ideas by experiment and observation before building on those ideas that pass the test.

S1E2: Tyson referred to the mechanism for the change in the brown bear to the polar bear as a "mutation". Teaching that an *accidental error* in the copying process of the DNA (an entirely random mutation) was the *Vera causa,* the mechanism of change, is not a true representation of what happened. It is the goal of the evolutionist to equate a mutational cause (as proposed by Darwin) to a micro-evolutionary adaptation in order to segue into the pan evolutionary theory not distinguishing the difference between micro & macro evolution. With the advances in the genomic sciences, it is now an academic certainty that the causes behind micro-evolutionary changes are the result of genomic algorithms that retrieve encoded data/information/instructions that are stored in the DNA to give phyla the ability to adapt to its changing environment. These are incredible mechanisms that God input into his creation to allow for phyla to be able to adapt to changes in its environment without which phyla would not survive. These genomic algorithms receive data input of pertinent information from its environment through its senses such as sight, sound, feel, smell, taste, along with other physiological inputs from living organisms such as stress hormone levels (adrenaline, cortisol, norepinephrine), mating contributions, etc. These preprogrammed algorithms digest and process this information to cause slight variations in the offspring to progress it to a creature better fit to survive a new environment. These changes are a natural part of life (not a mistake as a mutation in a DNA molecule infers) and can be seen in many diverse creatures that exemplify the ability to sense its changing environment and react to it for survival on a hyper scale. Take the chameleon, monarch butterfly, and the Galapagos finches. The chameleon can change its skin tones to match the surrounding environment as a camouflage instantaneously, it is not mutating every time it changes. The ability to do this originated in the genome that built the cells upon genomic algorithms, basically taking functionality that normally happens on a genomic level and inflating them to respond on a cellular level. [34]. The genomic algorithms in the monarch butterfly are programmed to sequentially pass on coded information for a migratory progression that spans from Canada to Mexico and back through four generations of offspring. An algorithm that is passed on to the offspring and senses where it is geographically and in a progressive series is not a mutation but rather a preprogram DNA molecule written by an intelligent designer [35,36]. Darwin uses the Galapagos finches as an example of survival of the fittest. He studied how they adapted when their habitat went from a wet environment to a dry environment. He observed how the birds' overall body size and their beak size changed as well as the shape of the beaks attributing the changes to mutational adaptations. Had he spent more time (note that we have the advantage of hindsight), he would have discovered that when their habitat went back from a dry environment to a wet environment that the birds' overall body size, beak size, and shape changed back to the original condition. Was this de-evolution? Were the mechanisms for change random mutations? No, they were pre-encoded DNA molecules being executed by genomic algorithms written by an intelligent designer. First, the chances according to the consensus of scientist from the Wistar convention put it in the $1/10^{77}$ of any changes happen by chance to begin with, then to keep up step for step with the ebb and flow of the changing environment certainly could not be by chance (random) mutations [37,38]. Just like the Galapagos finches, the polar bears will most likely change into a subspecies of Ursidae such as the brown bear (or new variation) to adapt to their new environment as a result of global warming. The polar bear is a variation or subspecies of the species Ursidae. To characterize the polar bear as a new species, as Tyson puts it in his Cosmos documentary, is misleading with the intent to segue into the pan theory of evolution based on the same mechanisms (mutations) ignoring the scientific method he espoused at the start of series [39]. To take for granted that the monarch butterfly will go extinct due to climate changes (global warming) as espoused in many concerning articles seems shortsighted from an evolutionary stand point. Based on the scientific evidence, they should either go extinct or adapt in keeping with the rhythm of nature. Evolutionists claim that fossil remains of butterflies can be found in strata dating to 66mya [0,41]. If they survived the mean environmental changes (ice ages and global warming) for the past 66my, why would this episode be any different? You would think that the odds were in their favor.

Another clear example of this genetic response of phyla to its environment on a hyper scale is found in Genesis 30, where Jacob was enabled by God to get the sheep and the cattle to produce offspring of a certain coloration that he might inherit them.

Gen 30:31: And he said, What shall I give thee? And Jacob said, Thou shalt not give me any thing: if thou wilt do this thing for me, I will again feed and keep thy flock:

Gen 30:32: I will pass through all thy flock to day, removing from thence all the speckled and spotted cattle, and all the brown cattle among the sheep, and the spotted and speckled among the goats: and of such shall be my hire.

Gen 30:33: So shall my righteousness answer for me in time to come, when it shall come for my hire before thy face: every one that is not speckled and spotted among the goats, and brown among the sheep, that shall be counted stolen with me.

Gen 30:34: And Laban said, Behold, I would it might be according to thy word.

Gen 30:35: And he removed that day the goats that were ringstraked and spotted, and all the she goats that were speckled and spotted, and every one that had some white in it, and all the brown among the sheep, and gave them into the hand of his sons.

Gen 30:36: And he set three days' journey betwixt himself and Jacob: and Jacob fed the rest of Laban's flocks.

Gen 30:37: And Jacob took him rods of green poplar, and of the hazel and chesnut tree; and pilled white strakes in them, and made the white appear which was in the rods.

Gen 30:38: And he set the rods which he had pilled before the flocks in the gutters in the watering troughs when the flocks came to drink, that they should conceive when they came to drink.

Gen 30:39: And the flocks conceived before the rods, and brought forth cattle ringstraked, speckled, and spotted.

Gen 30:40: And Jacob did separate the lambs, and set the faces of the flocks toward the ringstraked, and all the brown in the flock of Laban; and he put his own flocks by themselves, and put them not unto Laban's cattle.

Gen 30:41: And it came to pass, whensoever the stronger cattle did conceive, that Jacob laid the rods before the eyes of the cattle in the gutters, that they might conceive among the rods.

Gen 30:42: But when the cattle were feeble, he put them not in: so the feebler were Laban's, and the stronger Jacob's.

Apparently, the stripping of the bark on the almond, hazel, or chestnut branches could have exposed the water to many possibilities, be it some basic chemical (amino acids) from the type of tree or possible from some type of fungi beneath the bark. Science has shown that these mechanisms can influence the algorithms of the genome to produce alternate fur coloration of animals when the mother ingests it while mating [2,43]. Another theory that aligns well with the ability of the genome to detect its surroundings via sensory input and the need for camouflage is speciation. Jacob came from a long line of husbandry and probably learned a thing or two about the ability of animals to produce varied coloration based on their habitat. Like the polar bear, the arctic fox and hare adapted to the sheer white background as they migrated northward toward the poles. The sight of striped coloration before the sheep while they mated may have been a signal to the genomic algorithm to produce a more varied fur coat to enhance its survival in a perceived habitat of varied coloration. The God who formulated the genomic algorithms would certainly know how to manipulate them. After all the theorizing, we were not there and it will probably remain a mystery but I am confident that there was some input that these genomic algorithms responded to that were very similar to the adaptations affected by the Galapagos finches and polar bears [44].

Tyson infers that if you go back far enough in the DNA comparisons, you will find that we share a common ancestor with the butterfly, grey wolf, mushrooms, shark, bacterium, and sparrow. He then says, "Science has made it possible to reconstruct this family tree for all the species of life on earth". Following Tyson's scientific method, let's see where we go from here… test ideas by experiment and observation, build on those ideas that pass the test, reject the ones that fail, follow the evidence wherever it leads, and question everything.

1) Test ideas by experiment and observation,
   a. **The Divergence Hypothesis**
      i. This scientific undertaking has yielded a wide range of results from the participating independent studies anywhere from 274 million years ago (mya) to 14.2 billion years ago (bya) when applied to the Cambrian animals to determine when they diverged from a Precambrian ancestor (a phyla that is missing from the Precambrian strata).
      ii. In 1997 a study by Japanese biologist N. Nikoh and colleagues resulted in the universal common ancestor that lived 940mya. In 1999 a study by B. Wang, S. Kumar, and S.B. Hedges resulted in the universal common ancestor that lived 1.2 - 1.5 bya., One study actually reported that the divergent date fell between a range of 274mya and 1.6bya. The 274 date is 250my after the Cambrian explosion! Another study by S. Aris-Brosou and Z. Yang reported that the divergent date could fall between a range of 452mya and 2bya depending on which genes were studied and which estimate method was used. A survey by D. Graur and W. Martin published in *Trend in Genetics* titled "Reading the Entrails of Chickens: Molecular Timescale

of Evolution and the Illusion of Precision" cited one study that claimed to be 95% certain that the divergent date fell within a 14.2bya range (the earth is only 4.5bya).

iii. The oldest fossilized organism dates to about 3.5 bya. The latest documentaries place the universal common ancestor at about 3.9 bya, not based any of the lab testing results (because there is no consensus), but rather because it is the best fit for the theory, placing it before the oldest known fossil and after a time when the earth was in a state not suitable for life to emerge. The Scientific method demands that you have a consensus of the data for it to be considered scientifically valid or a scientific certainty. When there is no consensus, as it is so in these studies, and you decide to inadvertently pick and choose values that agree with your theology or your belief, then you have moved into the arena of pseudoscience.

b. **Phylogenetic Re construction (Molecular Sequences)**

i. The study of molecular sequencing attempts to track the animal genetic tree of life by assessing the magnitude of related characteristics to establish branching (divergent) points along the trees branches back to the trunk, especially among the major Cambrian groups. In the final analysis, the story the body of evidence tells, like the deep-divergence hypothesis, results in a multitude of conflicting patterns (no consensus therefore no conclusion that supports that hypothesis).

ii. In an article from the Oxford Journals regarding the studies of bacterial and archaeal genomes, the authors concluded that the findings "[undermine] the 'Tree of Life' model of evolution", that genomes "are built according to the same, simple 'master plan' with wall-to-wall protein-coding and RNA-coding genes", that "it could be hard even to identify a set of genes that have a coherent history over a substantial evolutionary span". A 2009 edition of *Trends in Ecology and Evolution* included a paper that notes "evolutionary trees from different genes often have conflicting branching patterns". A 2009 edition of a *New Scientist* cover story notes that the tree of life molecular sequences "lies in tatters, torn to pieces by an onslaught of negative evidence ", that "many biologists now argue that the tree of life concept is obsolete and needs to be discarded", and that "the evolution of animal and plants isn't exactly tree-like". An article in the *New Scientist* reported a story on the research and study by M. Syvanen on 2,000 genes of six very diverse animals saying, "In theory, he should have been able to use the gene sequences to construct an evolutionary tree showing the relationship between the six animals. He failed. The problem was the different genes told contradicting evolutionary stories." Syvanen himself confessed, "We've just annihilated the tree of life. It's not a tree anymore, it's a different topology entirely. What would Darwin have made of that?" Leading biologist Atonis Rokas of Vanderbilt University also echoes that sentiment, after 150 years of the acceptance of Darwin's Origin of the Species, saying, "a complete and accurate tree of life remains an elusive goal", and "despite the amount of data and breadth of taxa analyzed, relationships among most metazoan phyla remain unresolved". A year later A. Rokas and S.B. Carroll of the University of Wisconsin reiterated this disparity saying, "certain critical parts of the tree of life may be difficult to resolve, regardless of the quantity of conventional data available" and concluded from their extended study "inferences from these two independent lines of evidence (molecules and fossils) support a view of the origin of the Metazoa as a radiation compressed in time".

2) build on those ideas that pass the test,
   a. None of these ideas passed the test.
   b. Evolutionists build on those ideas anyway.
   c. The scientific method demands that you have a consensus of the data for it to be considered scientifically valid or a scientific certainty. When there is no consensus, and you decide to inadvertently pick and choose values that agree with your theology or your belief, then you have moved into the arena of pseudoscience.

3) reject the ones that fail,
   a. All these tests failed, therefore we should reject the evolutionary tree of life model and the ideal of a universal common ancestor.

4) follow the evidence wherever it leads,
   a. the evidence supports the intelligent design and sudden creation models.
   b. the fossil records and genomic sciences appear to support the sudden appearance of novel creatures as in the Cambrian radiation.
   c. The scientific method demands that you have a consensus of the data for it to be considered scientifically valid or a scientific certainty. Since there is a consensus, we need to follow the evidence.

5) and question everything.
   a. On what experiments and observations are we believing in evolution? On what basis are we ignoring the myriads of test results and observations that testify against the theory of evolution?

S1E3: Tyson talks about the Oort cloud as if it is a fact, not referring to it as a theory based on an evolutionary model. We have never observed these "trillions of frozen comets, left over from the formation of the solar system nearly 5 billion years ago". A spherical image is shown giving a hazy view of our solar system. He admits (surprisingly) that no one has seen it based on the distances they are from each other and lack of light at that distance from earth (about 1ly from earth). He explains why scientists believe that there is an Oort cloud, referencing some calculations by Oort based on the rate that new comets appear. Observable comets only have an average life span of about 100,000 years, which means they could not have been around for the 5-billion-year existence of the solar system unless there is a reserve from which they come from, hence the theory of the Oort Cloud. Why can we not observe them? We can observe planets of other stars millions of light years away because they pass in front of their suns, which can be observed. Would not trillions of comets that are only about 1mly away not be observed in the same manner when they inadvertently pass between us and any line of sight of all the other lights coming to us from every vector in the universe? This theory cannot be tested by any experiment nor, as Tyson admits, can it be observed…so why is it being taught as fact? (A handful of new comets showing up every now and then does not support an Oort Cloud as there are many possible alternate explanations). Remember Tyson's advice…question everything. The Oort Cloud is only needed to support an evolutionary model but the observable evidence fits the creation model perfectly. Science should build on that and follow the evidence wherever it leads and not imagine things into existence that cannot be proved just to satisfy one's religious beliefs, and certainly should not be teaching unsubstantiated theory as fact in defiance of the scientific method.

Tyson asserts that Isaac Newton's lifelong research of alchemy and biblical chronology never lead anywhere. That is not the truth, Tyson just did not like the conclusions it led him to. Newton was a devout Christian and he not only studied the biblical chronologies, but also all the ancient texts available at the time and made several absolute conclusions.

From Answers in Genesis, he made these claims about his findings based on records available at the time [45]:

- He wrote, 'I have a fundamental belief in the Bible as the Word of God, written by men who were inspired. I study the Bible daily.'
- God's Word is correct in every detail, including its history, so it must be our starting point.
- Except for the Bible itself, the other histories of early nations were not recorded until well after the events had passed. For example, the first historian to write about ancient Egypt (apart from Moses) was Herodotus.
- Most records of early history were lost or distorted as a result of repeated foreign invasions.
- Ancient peoples were not averse to making big assumptions to fill in the gaps.
- Scientific investigation leads to a greater knowledge of God, the Creator of the universe.

REFERENCES

Biblical References from: The Holy Bible (1913). King James Version. Chicago, Ill. John A. Dickson Publishing Co.

1   Walker, T. CREATION.com. The dating game. Retrieved from http://creation.com/the-dating-game

2   CSIRO Australia (1998). Tests reveal true age of controversial Jinmium aboriginal rock shelter. ScienceDaily. Retrieved from www.sciencedaily.com/releases/1998/05/980527184936.htm

3   Archeology Online. Gulf of Cambay. Retrieved from http://archaeologyonline.net/artifacts/cambay

4   Frontline. Questionable claims. Retrieved from http://www.frontline.in/navigation/?type=static&page=flonnet&rdurl=fl1905/19050670.htm

5   Patten, D Ph.D. CREATION.com. Tree ring dating (dendrochronology). Retrieved Ffom http://creation.com/tree-ring-dating-dendrochronology

6   Creation Worldview Ministries. Carbon-14 dating technique does not work! Retrieved from https://www.creationworldview.org/articles_view.asp?id=6

7   Lisle, J. Dr. (2008) Answers in Genesis. The age of the universe part 2. Retrieved from https://answersingenesis.org/answers/books/taking-back-astronomy/the-age-of-the-universe-part-2/

8   Humphreys, R. Ph.D. CRS Quarterly Journal. The creation of planetary magnetic fields. Retrieved from http://www.creationresearch.org/crsq/articles/21/21_3/21_3.html

9   Barnes, T. G. Ph.D, (1983). *Origin and destiny of the earth's magnetic field* (2nd Ed.). El Cajon, CA: Institute for Creation Research.

10 Humphreys, R. Ph.D. Institute for Creation Research. Beyond Neptune: Voyager II supports creation. Retrieved from http://www.icr.org/article/beyond-neptune-voyager-ii-supports-creation/

11 NASA. Voyager Interstellar Mission. Uranus magnetosphere. Retrieved from http://voyager.jpl.nasa.gov/science/uranus_magnetosphere.html

12 NASA. Voyager Interstellar Mission. Neptune's magnetic environment. Retrieved from http://voyager.jpl.nasa.gov/science/neptune_magnetic.html

13 Thomas, B. M.S. (2011). Mercury's fading magnetic field fits creation model. Retrieved from http://www.icr.org/article/mercurys-fading-magnetic-field-fits/

14 Wikipedia. Mercury's magnetic field. Retrieved from https://en.wikipedia.org/wiki/Mercury%27s_magnetic_field

15 MIT News. Retrieved from http://news.mit.edu/2010/explained-dynamo-0325

16 Dessler, A.J. "The Neptune challenge," Geophysical *Research Letters,* 14 (September 1987), 889.Retrieved from http://onlinelibrary.wiley.com/doi/10.1029/GL014i009p00889/pdf

17 Jonathan H. Ph.D., (2005). The moon's recession and age. Retrieved from http://creation.com/the-moons-recession-and-age

18 Thomas T. MS, (2000) The recession of the moon. Retrieved from http://www.talkorigins.org/faqs/moonrec.html

19 Williams, A. and Hartnett, J. Ph.D., (2005). *Dismantling the big bang: God's universe rediscovered.* Green Forest, AR. Master Books, Inc.

20 Humphreys, R. Ph.D., (1994) (11th print 2010). *Starlight & time: Solving the puzzle of distant starlight in a young universe.* Green Forest, AR. Master Books, Inc.

21 NCBI. (2002). *Molecular biology of the bell.* (4th ed). The diversity of genomes and the tree of life. Retrieved from https://www.ncbi.nlm.nih.gov/books/NBK26866/

22 Koonin E.V. and Wolf, Y.I. (2008). Genomics of bacteria and archaea: The emerging dynamic view of the prokaryotic world. Retrieved from http://nar.oxfordjournals.org/content/36/21/6688.full.pdf

23 Hug, L.A., Baker, B.J., Anantharaman, K., Brown, C.T., Probst, A.J., Castelle, C.J., ...Banfield, J.F. (2016). A new view of the tree of life. *Nature Microbiology, 1* (16048). doi:10.1038/nmicrobiol.2016.48

24   NCBI. (2009). Mapping the tree of life: Progress and prospects. Retrieved from https://www.ncbi.nlm.nih.gov/pmc/articles/PMC2786576/

25   Wired. (2013). New algorithms force scientists to revise the tree of life. Retrieved from https://www.wired.com/2013/06/algorithms-revise-tree-of-lif/

26   Evolution News. A Primer on the Tree of Life (Part 2): Conflicts in the Molecular Evidence. Retrieved from https://evolutionnews.org/2009/05/a_primer_on_the_tree_of_life_p_1/

27   Khan Academy. Building a phylogenetic tree. Retrieved from

28   https://www.khanacademy.org/science/biology/her/tree-of-life/a/building-an-evolutionary-tree

29

30   Meyers, S.C. (2013). *Darwin's doubt.* New York, NY: HarperCollins Publishers.

31   Darwin, C (1859). *The Origins of the species.* John Murray, London.

32   Illinois State University. Twelve lines of evidence for the evolution of humans and other primates. Retrieved from http://www.indiana.edu/~ensiweb/nick.he.html

33   McGraw Hill Education. 21 evidence for evolution. Retrieved from http://www.mhhe.com/biosci/genbio/raven6b/graphics/raven06b/other/raven06b_21.pdf

34   Virtual Fossil Museum. Chengjiang Maotianshan shales fossils. Retrieved from http://www.fossilmuseum.net/Fossil_Sites/Chengjiang.htm

35   Darwin was Right.org. The Evidence for Evolution. All species share a common descent. Retrieved from http://www.darwinwasright.org/common_descent.html

36   Wikipedia. Chameleon. Retrieved From https://en.wikipedia.org/wiki/Chameleon

37   Earth Justus. Monarch butterfly. Retrieved From http://earthjustice.org/irreplaceable/monarch-butterfly?gclid=EAIaIQobChMI25XDjrDm1QIVTTuBCh2R0gzxEAAYAyAAEgJkEvD_BwE

38   National Aquarium (2014). The all day relay race. Retrieved From http://aqua.org/blog/2014/november/monarchs-ultimate-race?gclid=EAIaIQobChMI25XDjrDm1QIVTTuBCh2R0gzxEAAYAiAAEgK1mfD_BwE

39   Answers in Genesis. Evolution of finch beaks again. Retrieved From https://answersingenesis.org/natural-selection/adaptation/evolution-of-finch-beaks-again/

40   Answers in Genesis. Reverse evolution causes Darwin's finches to go missing Retrieved From https://answersingenesis.org/natural-selection/reverse-evolution-causes-darwins-finches-to-go-missing/

41   a-z Aminals. Retrieved From https://a-z-animals.com/animals/bear/

42   Answers in Genesis. Marvels of the Monarch. Retrieved From https://answersingenesis.org/creepy-crawlies/insects/marvels-of-the-monarch/

43   Wikipedia. Butterfly. Retrieved From https://en.wikipedia.org/wiki/Butterfly

44   Jacob and the Spotted Sheep. Retrieved From jbq.jewishbible.org/assets/Uploads/364/364_sheep.pdf

45   Gene Imprint. Retrieved From http://www.geneimprint.com/site/press/12861015-1154826620

46   HHS Public Access. POPULATION GENOMICS REVEAL RECENT SPECIATION AND RAPID EVOLUTIONARY ADAPTATION IN POLAR BEARS. Retrieved From https://www.ncbi.nlm.nih.gov/pmc/articles/PMC4089990/

47   Answers in Genesis. Sir Isaac Newton (1642/3–1727). Retrieved From https://answersingenesis.org/creation-scientists/profiles/sir-isaac-newton/

PART 4

Descendants of Ham

The Babel Event

Gen 10:32: These are the families of the sons of Noah, after their generations, in their nations: and by these were the nations divided in the earth after the Flood. **(Total of 79 original people groups/ nations)** [7, 31]

Japhethic Nations:

Gen 10:2: The sons of Japheth; 1.Gomer (Cimmeria, Germany), and 2.Magog (Russia), and 3.Madai (Medes, Indian), and 4.Javan (Greece), and 5.Tubal (Russia), and 6.Meshech (Russia), and 7.Tiras (Trace, Etrusca).

Gen 10:3: And the sons of Gomer; 8. Ashkenaz (Germany), and 9.Riphath, and 10.Togarmah (Armenia).

Gen 10:4: And the sons of Javan; 11. Elishah, and 12.Tarshish, 13.Kittim, and 14.Dodanim (Dardanians).

Gen 10:5: By these were the isles of the Gentiles divided in their lands; everyone after his tongue, after their families, in their nations. **(Total of 14 Nations from Japheth)**

Hametic Nations:

Gen 10:6: And the sons of Ham; 1.Cush (Ethiopia), and 2.Mizraim (Egypt), and 3.Phut (Libya), and 4.Canaan (Canaanites, Phoenicians, Hittites).

Gen 10:7: And the sons of Cush; 5.Seba, and 6.Havilah, and 7.Sabtah, and 8.Raamah, and 9.Sabtecha: and the sons of Raamah; 10.Sheba, and 11.Dedan.

Gen 10:8: And Cush begat 12.Nimrod: he began to be a mighty one in the earth.

Gen 10:9: He was a mighty hunter before the LORD: wherefore it is said, Even as Nimrod the mighty hunter before the LORD.

Gen 10:10: And the beginning of his kingdom was Babel, and Erech, and Accad, and Calneh, in the land of Shinar.

Gen 10:11: Out of that land went forth Asshur, and builded Nineveh, and the city Rehoboth, and Calah,

Gen 10:12: And Resen between Nineveh and Calah: the same is a great city.

Gen 10:13: And Mizraim begat 13.Ludim, and 14.Anamim, and 15.Lehabim, and 16.Naphtuhim,

Gen 10:14: And 17.Pathrusim, and 18.Casluhim, (out of whom came 19.Philistim,) and 20.Caphtorim.

Gen 10:15: And Canaan begat 21.Sidon his firstborn, and 22.Heth,

Gen 10:16: And the Jebusite, and the 23.Amorite, and the 24.Girgasite,

Gen 10:17: And the 25.Hivite, and the 26.Arkite, and the 27,Sinite (Chinese's),

Gen 10:18: And the 28.Arvadite, and the 29.Zemarite, and the 30.Hamathite: and afterward were the families of the Canaanites spread abroad.

Gen 10:19: And the border of the Canaanites was from 31.Sidon, as thou comest to 32.Gerar, unto 33.Gaza; as thou goest, unto 34.Sodom, and 35.Gomorrah, and 36.Admah, and 37.Zeboim, even unto 38.Lasha.

Gen 10:20: These are the sons of Ham, after their families, after their tongues, in their countries, and in their nations. **(Total of 38 Nations from Ham)**

Semite Nations:

Gen 10:21: Unto Shem also, the father of all the children of 1.Eber (Hebrews) brother of Japheth the elder, even to him were children born.

Gen 10:22: The children of Shem; 2.Elam (Persia), and 3.Asshur (Assyria), and 4.Arphaxad, and 5.Lud, and 6.Aram (Syria).

Gen 10:23: And the children of Aram; 7.Uz, and 8.Hul, and 9.Gether, and 10.Mash.

Gen 10:24: And Arphaxad begat 11.Salah; and Salah begat 12.Eber.

Gen 10:25: And unto Eber were born two sons: the name of one was 13.Peleg; for in his days was the earth divided; and his brother's name was 14.Joktan.

Gen 10:26: And Joktan begat 15.Almodad, and 16.Sheleph, and 17.Hazar-maveth, and 18.Jerah,

Gen 10:27: And 19.Hadoram, and 20.Uzal, and 21.Diklah,

Gen 10:28: And 22.Obal, and 23.Abimael, and 24.Sheba,

Gen 10:29: And 25.Ophir, and 26.Havilah, and 27.Jobab: all these were the sons of Joktan.

Gen 10:30: And their dwelling was from Mesha, as thou goest unto Sephar a mount of the east.

Gen 10:31: These are the sons of Shem, after their families, after their tongues, in their lands, after their nations. **(Total of 27 Nations from Shem)**

A total of 79 original people groups/nations.

At the time of the Babel event, approximately 2345-2100 BC, the people had one language and worked together to build up the cities and cultural infrastructures to include the infamous "Tower of Babel" ziggurat under the rule of King Nimrod, grandson of Ham. The scripture tells us they were all together in unity in the land of Shinar and not yet at war. When God first "confused" their language, it would have affected the family tribes or people groups. A people (ethnic) group would have made up about 1/79 or 1.3% of the total population of an estimated 175,200 people in that center (Sumer or Shinar). The Bible records the generations from Noah averaged between 4 and 12 male descendants per generation. It is a reasonable assumption that each generation had an equal amount of female offspring. Splitting the difference would be a conservative estimate to assume that each generation had an average of eight (8) couples (male/female children). The average count was probably higher with the mandate to repopulate the earth and wanting more descendants in order to have the greater influence in the community. With the long lifespans at this time. Having more children beyond the 35 year generation would be natural. Based on that assumption, the following calculation for the populace at the time of Babel would have been about 175,200 people:

Where:
Generation (Gen) = 35 years
Non-Producing Generations (NP) = previous generations before the last (still living) no longer producing offspring
Mortality Rate (MR) (based on max 40% mortality rate), **natural causes (NC)** mortality rate [20%] = 1 gen out of 5 (avg. life span at 230 years during this period), cost of human lives due to **wars (W)** [15%], due to **diseases (D)** (and other: accidents, hippopotamus & dragon attacks) [5%].
Flood to Babel = 175 years (5 Gens): MR = D = 5%
Babel to 105 years = 3 Gens: MR = W+D = 20%

Gen1 = 3 Cpls x 8 = 24 x .95(MR) = 23 Cpls,
Gen2 = Gen1 x 8 x .95(MR) = 173 Cpls,
Gen3 = Gen2 x 8 x .95(MR) = 1,317 Cpls,
Gen4 = Gen3 x 8 x .95(MR) = 10,009 Cpls,

Gen5 = Gen4 x 8 x .95(MR) = 76,006 Cpls,

World Population = Gen5 + NP x 2 = (76,066 Cpls + 11,525 Cpls) x 2 = **175,200 individuals**.
People Group Population = 175.2K / 79 original nations = 2.2K people in each ethnic group on average.

All these "couples" lived in and about Sumer up to the time of the Babel event. All the people groups were affected by the change in their language and cultures. It appears that the change even included the outward physical appearances that we see today in different cultures. After the change, they would have woken up the next morning hearing, seeing, and believing that they had always spoken the language they were now speaking with the physical appearance as such, be it Sumerian, Egyptian, Hebrew, Chinese, Indian, etc. Initially, they would have thought everything was normal, having conversation while eating breakfast with the family, walking to work with their brothers, sisters, and neighbors, jesting and laughing. To their utter dismay, they would have found it very strange and confusing as to why, when they got to work that morning, the project manager of the construction site was now speaking gibberish and the people all appeared physically altered. They would have sought out their other siblings and returned home with the strangest tales to relay to the rest of the family, who would also have the same tales from their visit to the market center and such. This would have prompted an emergency meeting with the tribal elders to contemplate the meaning and limits to this phenomenon. They would come to perceive that this phenomenon had affected all the other tribes but not theirs for some reason. Realizing that they were in the minority, not being able to do business in the city for lack of communication, and feeling the squeeze of overpopulation for that region, and as human nature is, the tribal leaders of these people groups saw an opportunity to establish a kingdom and rule apart from subjugation to King Nimrod. They would have been motivated to move far from the land of their birth and find a suitable country where they could stake a claim on the land and establish their own kingdoms where all spoke the same language. They would have traveled though the remains of former civilizations but seen no inhabitants, thereby confirming the Flood stories told by their ancestors. Many of these travelers would have encountered the "terrible lizards" of legend (dragons such as *T.rex*, *Allosaurus*, pterosaurs, stegosaurs, etc.). They would have most likely picked a spot that looked good for crops or raising livestock. They may have chosen a spot with some remains of a former civilizations as an indicator of the usefulness of the land and to use the material and foundations to build on. This would be an ideal setting to be able to adapt the antediluvian ascension stories to their newly established culture's heritage. The next three generations would have increased the world populace, taking into account the average mortality rates (MR), to about **45.82 million (MM) individual people** 105 years after Babel (BTR 2245-2040 BC):

Gen6 = Gen5 x 8 x .80(MR) = 486,821 Cpls,
Gen7 = Gen6 x 8 x .80(MR) = 3,115,654 Cpls,
Gen8 = Gen7 x 8 x .80(MR) = 19,940,183 Cpls,

World Population = (Gen7 + [NP-Gen1]) x.8 (MR) x 2 = (19.94MM Cpls + 2.97MM Cpls) x 2 = **45.82MM**
People Group Population = 45.82K / 79 original nations = **580K people in each ethnic group on average**.

Secular estimates put the world population between 72MM and 27MM in 2045 BC [1]. This would again inspire further expansion due to overpopulation and warring conflicts of a region for centuries to come. Wars over land boundaries would have started immediately when one people group would settle too close to another, starting feuds over the rights to the land and conquest to dominate and rule larger territories and people. In some cases, the first residents (small people groups) were driven out by larger invading groups and forced to move on to new territories rather than lose people to fighting. For example, the Chinese people may have initially settled in Egypt then moved to their present location when the warlord Mizraim came into Egypt on his tour of world conquest.

Historical evidence shows that the major cultures around the world were unanimously established after the time indicated in the Bible of the Babel event (2350 - 2145 BC). It also reveals that the cultures appeared on the scene suddenly with completely developed infrastructure, governments, buildings, written and spoken languages, scripts, and religious doctrine. All these ancient cultures from before 1800BC have overt indications of their Mesopotamian roots as reflected in much of the artifacts, drawings, and of course, the basic Genesis story in their recorded histories. Anthropological science has no reasonable explanation for the evidence on an evolutionary scale. There is no evidence of transitional or developmental stages from one language to another from one culture to another during this time period, especially considering the short time span for it to have to fit into, as opposed to the ascending sub cultures where there is much supporting evidence to track the original language (e.g., Japanese subculture from the Chinese culture based on the Chinese Hanzi script). Major cultures coming out of Babel between 2350 and 2000 BC had completely developed infrastructure, governments, buildings, written and spoken languages, scripts, and religious doctrine [2]:

Shinar (Sumer) – Known as the birthplace of civilization. The Sumerian King List would have started at about 2400 BC. The oldest script containing the king list is WB 62, a small clay tablet from 2000BC. The Kish tablet is inscribed with proto-cuneiform signs and may be considered the oldest known written document (2350 BC).

Africa, Egypt & Cush – The Egyptian King List starts at about 2350 BC. The oldest script is the Narmer Pallet, secular date at about 2300 BC, depicting his world conquest.

China – The Chinese King List starts with Emperor Yu and is estimated to be from 2250BC. The oldest Scripts are inscriptions on oracle bones, primarily ox scapulae and turtle shells from 1200 BC [3]. Originally a peace-loving people that may have initially settled in the land of Egypt, then forced out by the warlord Namar to the present location.

India – In about 2300 BC, the Aryans settled in the Punjab in Northern India, establishing the first post–Flood civilizations. The oldest writings known from India are placed at about 2600 BC. These are known as the Harappan Writings, which has not been deciphered and are believed to be from the Antediluvian period. After that, the oldest extant written records are known as the Vedas. Extant copies only go back to 500 BC but are estimated to have originated in between 2300 - 2000 BC.

S. America – The oldest known civilization in S. America lies in Peru. It is dated between 2300-2000 BC with the oldest extant writing being from around 900BC.

Europe – The **Minoan civilization** appears to have been the first post flood culture that existed in that region before being destroyed by a massive volcano. The **Mycenaean (Greece)** (or **Mycenaean civilization**) is believed to be the most ancient civilization in Europe after the Minoans (c. 1600–1100 BC)

Hebrew Culture – The cultural, religious doctrines and practices started with Adam and maintained by the patriarch lineage of Abraham as moved by the spirit of God. As the Hebrew script does not align with any other antediluvian script, it is a safe assumption that the Hebrew language was new from the Babel event along with the rest and not the original language. Abraham was called out of Babylon by God and led to what would become the Israelite nations in about 1960 BC. The Dead Sea Scrolls are the most abundant, ancient Hebrew scripts we have. The consensus is that the Qumran Caves Scrolls date from the last three centuries BC. There are pieces of the Torah manuscripts that have been discovered from 700 and 600 BC to include the Book of Numbers and Leviticus [4].

Sumer of Mesopotamia (Shinar) is well established as the birthplace of civilization, where city-states emerged and from which the ideas of civilization expanded and spread throughout the world, even as the Ice Age was coming to a close between 2350BC and 2000BC. Many of the nations of the world have king's lists and genealogies that trace their ancestry back to this time period. All nations today are the descendants of the three sons of Noah: Japheth, Ham and Shem. Europe is made up largely of Japheth's descendants, which includes the Germans, British, Irish, Italian, Spanish, and so on. African, Asian, Filipino, Indian, and American Indian groups come from Ham's lineage. The Semitic tribes such as the Hebrews, Levantine Arabs, Assyrians, Samaritans, Syriacs-Arameans, Maronites, Druze, Mandaeans, and Mhallami, come down from Shem's line.

Ham's descendants.

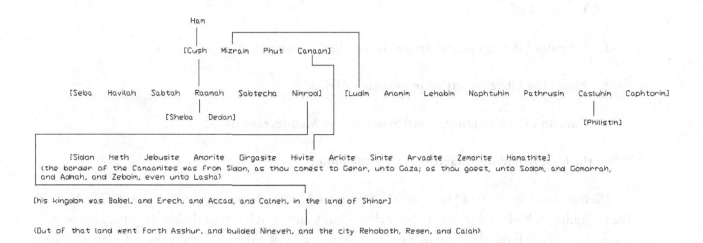

Biblical Reference: Genesis 10: 6-20. These were the sons of Ham according to their families, according to their language, in their lands, and in their nations.

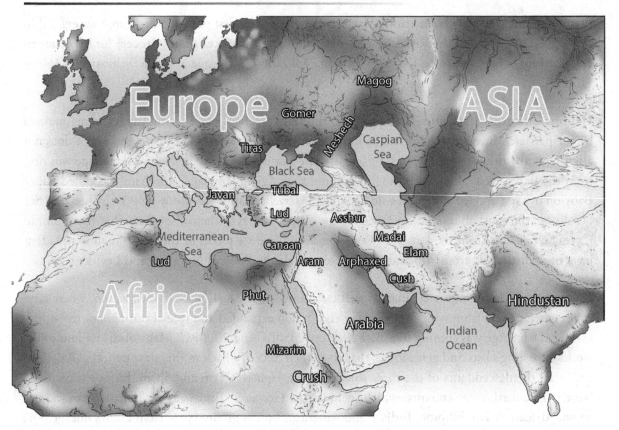

Figure 4.1 Table of Nations Map

The Four Predominant Hamitic Nations:

1. **Cush (The Ethiopians) settled in Ethiopia, south of Egypt, and an area north of the Persian Gulf.**

2. **Mizraim (The Egyptians) settled in northeast Africa.**

3. **Phut (The Libyans) settled in northern Africa.**

4. **Canaan (The Canaanites) settled east of the Mediterranean.**

Babel, the First Kingdom Established after the Flood

Nimrod, son Cush, son of Ham, was the first to establish his kingdom after the Flood. Gen 10: The beginning of his kingdom was Babel, Erich (Uruk), Accad (Akkad), and Calneh in the land of Shinar. Gen 11-12: From that land he went to Assyria and built Nineveh, Rehobeth, Ir, Calah, and Resen.

The most ancient chronologies in the world are out of ancient Sumer in the form of Kings Lists. These king lists are found in several independent sources, of which one main script is the Kish tablet, found at Tell al-Uhaymir, Babil Governorate, Iraq - the site of the ancient Sumerian city of Kish. It is dated to 3200 BC to 2900 BC. With obvious errors in the dating methods this date would then be more aptly in and about 2100BC. The Kings List is estimated by secular sources as based on a chronological sum of the reins where as it has been reasonably shown that many of these kings were actually contemporary rulers of more local areas (and probably blood related per dynasty). The majority of these names and kingships have been archeologically confirmed. The last king's reign on the list according to secular reckoning appears to be in about 1674BC. Note the similarities of the Bible and Kings List in respect to the longevity of lives/reins during the antediluvian period and up to 600 years after the flood with a more relative life span after that period, if these dynasties were contemporary rulers per dynasty then it would be a parallel pattern in a general sense [5].

The Sumerian King List post–Flood Era **(Dynasties' overall time spans cannot be sufficiently estimated, maybe from 2500BC to 1600BC with many of the kings contemporary instead of successive)** [5, 6];

FIRST DYNASTY OF KISH

Ruler	Length of Reign	Secular Dates	Inscriptions	Comments
After the Flood had swept over, and the kingship had descended from heaven, the kingship was in Kish				
Jushur	1,200 yrs.			
Kullassina-bel	960 yrs.			
Nangishlishma	670 yrs.			
En-tarah-ana	420 yrs.			
Babum	300 yrs.			
Puannum	840 yrs.			
Kalibum	960 yrs.			
Kalumum	840 yrs.			
Zuqaqip	900 yrs.			
Atab	600 yrs.			
Mashda	840 yrs.		the son of Atab	
Arwium	720 yrs.		the son of Mashda	
Etana	1,500 yrs.		the shepherd who ascended to heaven and consolidated all the foreign countries	Names before Etana are not archeologically verified and do not appear on any other king list
Balih	400 yrs.		the son of Etana	
En-me-nuna	660 yrs.			
Melem-Kish			the son of En-me-nuna	
Barsal-nuna	1,200 yrs.		the son of En-me-nuna	
Zagmug	140 yrs.		the son of Barsal-nuna	
Tizqar	305 yrs.		the son of Zagmug	
Ilku	900 yrs.			
Iltasadum	1,200 yrs.			
En-me-barage-si	900 yrs.	2600 BC	who made the land of Elam submit	1st ruler confirmed apart from epigraphical evidence
Aga of Kish	625 yrs.	2600 BC	son of En-me-barage-si	Mentioned in *The Epic of Gilgamesh*
Then Kish was defeated and the kingdom was taken to E-ana				

FIRST DYNASTY OF URUK

Ruler	Length of Reign	Secular dates	Inscriptions	Comments
Mesh-ki-ang-gasher	324 yrs.	2600 BC	son of Utu, Mesh-ki-ang-gasher entered the sea and disappeared	
Enmerkar	420 yrs.		son of Mesh-ki-ang-gasher, the king of Unug, who built Unug (Uruk)	
Lugalbands	1200 yrs.		the shephard	
Dumuzid	100 yrs.	2600 BC	the fisherman whose city was Uara, he captured En-me-barage-si single-handedly	
Gilgamesh	126 yrs.	2600 BC	whose father was a phantom, the lord of Kulaba	of *The Epic of Gilgamesh*, the oldest epic story
Ur-Nungal	30 yrs.		son of Gilgamesh	
Udul-kalama	15 yrs.		son Ur-Nungal	
La-ba'shum	9 yrs.			
En-nun-tarah-ana	8 yrs.			
Mesh-he	36 yrs.		the smith	
Melem-ana	6 yrs.			
Lugal-kitun	36 yrs.			
Then Unug was defeated and the kingdom was taken to Urim (Ur)				

FIRST DYNASTY OF UR

Four Kings - *Then Urim was defeated and the kingdom was taken to Awan*

DYNASTY OF AWAN

Three Kings - *Then Awan was defeated and the kingdom was taken to Kish*

SECOND DYNASTY OF KISH

Eight Kings - *Then Kish was defeated and the kingdom was taken to Hamazi*

DYNASTY OF HAMAZI

One King - *Then Hamazi was defeated and the kingdom was taken to Uruk*

SECOND DYNASTY OF URUK

Three Kings - *Then Uruk was defeated and the kingdom was taken to Ur*

SECOND DYNASTY OF UR

Three Kings - *Then Ur was defeated and the kingdom was taken to Adab*

DYNASTY OF ADAB

One King - *Then Adab was defeated and the kingdom was taken to Mari*

DYNASTY OF MARI

Six Kings - *Then Mari was defeated and the kingdom was taken to Kish*

THIRD DYNASTY OF KISH

Queen Kug-Bau - the only woman in the kings list - *Then Kish was defeated and the kingdom was taken to Akshak*

DYNASTY OF AKSHAK

Six Kings - *Then Akshak was defeated and the kingdom was taken to Kish*

FOURTH DYNASTY OF KISH

Eight Kings - *Then Kish was defeated and the kingdom was taken to Uruk*

THIRD DYNASTY OF URUK

One King - *Then Uruk was defeated and the kingdom was taken to Akkad*

DYNASTY OF AKKAD

Eleven Kings - *Then Akkad was defeated and the kingdom was taken to Urik*

FOURTH DYNASTY OF URUK

Five Kings - *Then Uruk was defeated and the kingdom was taken to the Army of Gutium*

GUTIAN RULE

No famous kings for 3 years, then 17 kings reigned - *Then Gutian was defeated and the kingdom was taken to Uruk*

FIFTH DYNASTY OF URUK

One King - *Then Uruk was defeated and the kingdom was taken to Ur*

THIRD DYNASTY OF UR

Five Kings - *Then Ur was defeated and the very kingdom of Sumer was torn out. The kingdom was taken to Isin*

DYNASTY OF ISIN - Fifteen kings

As concluded in the article from Answers in Genesis written by R.E. Lopez [5],

> The Sumerian King List records in a chronological succession the names of most of the kings of Sumer and the lengths of their reigns. The composition is based on the theory that there was always only one king at a time for all of Babylonia, and a single capital. A few of the existing manuscripts of the List have an initial section dealing with kings before the Flood that is significantly different from the rest of the list. This antediluvian section was a later addition written by a person different from the one who composed the postdiluvian section of the list. This scribe appears to have adapted an earlier list of antediluvian kings to conform to the style and philosophy of the document he was bringing up to date. However, it is evident that his source for the antediluvian kings did not claim that the different kingships were successive. The original King List was probably composed during the reign of Utu-hegal of Uruk (2119–2112 BC) and the antediluvian section added after the reign of Sin-magir (1827–1817 BC) of the Isin dynasty.

Nimrod has yet to be identified in archeological discoveries. Jushur, the first name listed on the Sumerian King List, may well have been Nimrod, as there has been no archeological discoveries made verifying his existence. This is likely due to invading kingdoms destroying previous kings' legacies; and it was also a common practice to change one's name when one became king. Take for example the case with one of sons of Ham, Mizraim. Later known as Narmer, Mizraim was the first King of Egypt whose name and place in history have been verified by archeological discoveries from the same time period. Narmer and Nimrod were the immediate relatives of Ham (son and grandson), who probably would have lived some 600 years as of the first and second generation from Noah. Nimrod's reign and influence in Shinar was cut short when God confused the languages at Babel. He migrated along with a certain people group to continue his kingship in Assyria and built Nineveh, Rehobeth, Ir, Calah, and Resen.

The Epic of Gilgamesh [7]

One of the oldest epic tales in the world, *The Epic of Gilgamesh,* is from Mesopotamia from the third dynasty of Ur (oldest fragment from 2100BC [1850*]). Gilgamesh is listed in the Sumerian King List as the fifth king of Uruk (modern day Iraq) in 2600BC (2250*). There are several tales told in the epic from unknown authors. Written in Sumerian, it is the oldest surviving epic in Babylonian literature. The Gilgamesh epic is found in many different sources from different periods throughout Mesopotamia. The "Old Babylonian Tablets" from 1800BC (1670*) are the oldest complete version extant to date. The standard Akkadian version was discovered by Hormuzd Rassam in Nineveh in 1853 in the library of Ashurbanipal[7,8].

* w/ C14 correction factor due to the estimated strength of the magnetosphere at that time period not considered by secular scientists or correction factor based on the biblical chronology that is the most accurate[9].

The first episode of the epic tells of the initial conquests, might, and heroism that made King Gilgamesh famous among men. The king took all the young men in his realm into his army and had a rule that he was to sleep with all new brides on their wedding nights. All in all, he was an oppressive ruler. Gilgamesh was born of a mother said to be a goddess, Ninsun, and a mortal father. He built an abode in a walled city where they worshipped pagan gods such as Enlil, the father of the gods; Shamash, the highest of the gods; Eanna, that he built a temple to; Anu, god of the firmament; and Ishtar, the goddess of love and war. The people of Uruk cried out to Anu for relief from the oppression of the king.

The second episode of the epic tells how the goddess Anu created an adversary (Enkidu) of equal strength to stay Gilgamesh's unrestrained passions. Enkidu was born in the wild and lived as an animal until he was beguiled by a temple prostitute and tamed by the trappers in the region. One night Gilgamesh was going into a new bride's chamber when Enkidu confronted him for his evil, to which the two proceeded to do battle. After a weary time of it, Enkidu conceded and the two became best friends for life.

In the third episode, Gilgamesh and his army along with Enkidu, out of boredom, went in search of a savage beast that was reported to be terrorizing the forest in the outskirts of his domain. After a bit of a hike, they found the beast Humbaba in the cedar forest. The beast struck fear into both Enkidu (his knees buckled) and Gilgamesh (brought to tears). Gilgamesh cried out to Shamash, his god, who brought eight dragons as the raging winds to attack the beast gouging at his eyes. Gilgamesh, Enkidu, and his men advanced on him. Humbaba, wounded and severely beaten, started his retreat turning seven times along the way to go on the offense, only to fail to get an advantage and so continued his retreat until he reached his layer. Gilgamesh could read sorrow in his eyes and could sense him pleading in his heart, and so thought to capture him alive and make him a beast of burden. Enkidu however, had no compassion, knowing that the beast was untamable and would turn on them at the first chance and urged Gilgamesh to kill it. Gilgamesh, heeding his companion, struck him once with his axe and then gave a blow to the neck with his sword. Enkidu then followed with the second and third blow with his sword, and Humbaba fell to the ground dead. They returned home with his head.

In the fourth episode, Gilgamesh refused the advances of the goddess Ishtar who then turns the bull of heaven loose on earth. The bull intended to kill Gilgamesh, only to be killed by Gilgamesh after it had killed several of his men and nearly took Enkidu. Then, by judgment of the gods for killing Humbaba and the bull of heaven, he is made to suffer through the agonizing and lingering death of his best mate Enkidu. This created a fear of death in him that shook him to the core.

In the fifth episode, Gilgamesh, urged on by the agonizing death of Enkidu, went in search of a man that he heard tell the gods granted immortality. Gilgamesh resolved to seek eternal life for himself so as not to endure the same fate as his best mate. After an exhaustive investigation and search, he was told the man lived on the other side of a certain sea that no man could cross save one –Urshanabi. Gilgamesh joins with Urshanabi and makes the crossing successfully to find the famed Utnapishtim, whom he believed the gods had granted immortality. Utnapishtim tells him of the life before the Flood, the judgment of the gods, and the Flood. Utnapishtim tells him there is no everlasting life, and even he will eventually die. On the return home, Urshanabi the boat man tells Gilgamesh of a plant that grows on the bottom of the sea that will give him back his youth. Gilgamesh ties rocks to his legs, sinks to the bottom, and finds the plant. Unfortunately, it was thieved by a serpent on his journey home. Gilgamesh returns home, finally dies, and is lamented by all great and small alike[6].

Humbaba is described as:

(1) Being a ferocious monster whose name means "hugeness" or fierce giant;
(2) Being a terror to all flesh, his charge is the rushing of the flood, with his looks he crushes alike the trees of the forest and reeds of the swamp;
(3) Roaring like the torrent of a storm;
(4) Having breath that is like fire;
(5) Having jaws that are death itself, his teeth are dragon's fangs, his continence like a lion;
(6) Behaving like a battering ram, he nodded his head and shook it;
(7) Having acute hearing, he can hear a heifer stirring at sixty leagues;
(8) Coming out at night, alluding to him being nocturnal, which befits a large predator to hunt under the cloak of darkness;
(9) Having tracks easily followed (clearly visible) probably due its distinct shape, large size, and deep imprint; and
(10) Making his abode in a layer in the midst of a cedar forest.

This story was told at a time when, according to evolution, there were no dinosaurs; therefore, these people should not have knowledge of any of the distinct characteristics of dinosaurs. On the contrary, all these descriptive narratives can easily be used to describe large predatory dinosaurs. It is safe to assume from the location that this was probably an *Allosaurus* (or another similar creature such as *Albertosaurus, Cryolophosaurus, Megalosaurus*, or Carnotaurus) as opposed to a *T.rex*[10]. From the description of leviathan in the Bible and the story of Beowulf, we gather that a mature *T.rex* would not be susceptible to ordinary weaponry such as swords and axes as this creature was [11]. This creature would have had to have a smaller frame than *T.rex*, as he had a hide more susceptible to sharp steel blades. He appeared to be intimidated by the crowd, causing him to retreat to his layer. This beast has at least ten general characteristics that coincidently mirror an extinct creature. *Allosaurus* is supposed to have been extinct for more than 150 million years. For the author to describe these features, having no knowledge of a dinosaurs, is rather remarkable.

Figure 4.2 Allosaurus

The author alluded many times to human qualities such as: "Humbaba heard the noise far off he was enraged", "he cried out, Who is this that has violated my woods and cut down my cedars?", "Gilgamesh, let me speak"...telling a sad story and pleading for his life, "Humbaba said Enkidu, what you have spoken is evil; you, a hireling, dependent for your bread! In envy and for fear of a rival you have spoken evil words". Personification is conventional in epic story telling when the foe is a monstrous beast. The author could not have any knowledge of how Humbaba must have felt and what he would say if he could speak. The author took poetic liberties, as authors will do, to give the creature more personable human qualities, giving it the ability to speak in order for the reader to relate to his point of view. The author of Gilgamesh described his features as that of a monster but is interpreted by many as a humanoid, probably because of the humanlike qualities the author gives him.

The eight dragons that attacked Humbaba in answer to Gilgamesh's prayers are described by the bard at first by the terrible spirits by which they were possessed, as types of stormy winds, probably because of their aggressive spirit in combination with the beating of their massive wings. Associating spirits with the wind is a poetic analogy used quite often in antiquity and in present day. The dragons were hitherto associated with fire and serpents in their physical appearance, which is common of dragon stories throughout history. This fits the description of possibly several species of pterosaurs, extinct flying reptiles also described as thunderbirds in Native American lore and cave drawings (petroglyphs).

Figure 4.3 Flying Pterosaurs

As previously noted, this event may be an instance of the manifestation of the spiritual world interfacing with the physical world to a much greater degree than we know today. The gods (spiritual beings, demons) whom the Sumerians communed with and worshiped could very well have worked together to possess these creatures to further capture the devotion of these pagan worshipers. Demonic possession of men and animals is evidenced throughout history. The snake in the Garden of Eden, the Gerasene man that confronted Jesus and the pigs possessed by Legion, and the two lions of Tsavo, Africa in the late nineteenth century that terrorized and killed over a hundred men [12] are all examples of spiritual beings manifesting through physical hosts.

The initial story was evidently recorded by a very skilled, colorful bard and scribe appointed by the king. As such, he would have the stories align with the king's religious beliefs and would have elements of the events embellished to interject mystery and extraordinary heroism. The aim of all appointed royal scribes in antiquity would be to leave an impressive legacy, as it is in the nature of men to do so. Utnapishtim was most certainly Noah based on his intricate knowledge of the flood events and reputation of being immortal due to his extreme age. He would have been about 850 years old at this time, while Noah lived to be 950 years old. This very talented bard retold Noah's tale with Gilgamesh's gods being the authors of the events rather than Noah's God to satisfy the expectations of the king and to give glory to these gods.

Lastly, the story is based on real historical characters. This gives the story a solid foundation and suggests that the events have some basis in truth. The monsters were most likely actual creatures of some sort, even if exaggerated to some extent. There are several references in the text to Noah's persona that align with biblical history at a time when they were not exposed to Christian or Jewish influences. The inferences in this most ancient of epic tales collaborate the biblical accounts of the Flood, the person of Noah, man coexisting with dinosaurs, and manifestations of spiritual beings as gods to be worshiped.

Egypt

The next dominant kingdom to be established after Sumer was Egypt. The first historically verifiable king of Egypt was Mizraim (Menes), son of Ham, who was referred to as Narmer once he established his throne in Egypt. There are Egyptian king's lists from several sources from different time periods. The names vary slightly, but that is not uncommon in ancient cultures. It was not uncommon for kings to be referred to by many different names for different reasons, many times their names were changed when they became king. Different cultures referring to kings from other kingdoms will have a slight variance in the pronunciation. We see that in more recent history with the emperors of Rome and the popes.

Egypt's Sumerian roots has academic standing as well. Professor Waddell, an explorer and amateur archaeologist, who has studied Sumerian and Sanskrit and published many books on ancient history, very clearly shows how all the kings lists, pictographs, monument carvings, and artifacts are of Sumerian origins. Dr. Waddell also specifically explains how many of the first listed kings of the Sumerian, Egyptian, Indus (Vedas) and Minoan Kings Lists are actually the same persons. He states, "yet who the conquerors were and when the invasions took place has remained unknown owing to lack of evidence on which to base a judgment, and a like absence of evidence in regard to chronology has made the dating of the early and most of the later Pharaohs an affair of guesswork, and lead equally able and conscientious inquirers to fix the period of Menes and his first dynasty at dates differing from one another by as much as two millenniums of years." [13]

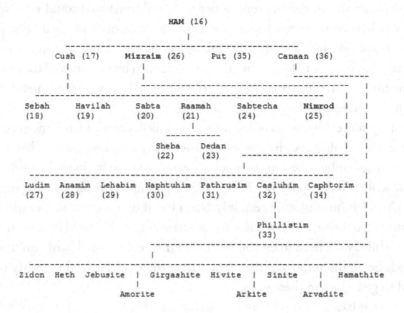

The Egyptian King Lists [14]

The ancient Egyptians maintained the king lists themselves, but they come down to us in fragments. The most popular are the Palermo Stone, the Abydos King list, and the Turin Canon.

Many of the King Lists, and especially the Egyptian King list, have been the casualties of historical chronology wars. Many historians in the centuries before Christ began to doctor their Kings list to be able to claim that their cultures were the most ancient of cultures. Egypt has about (10) major King Lists that are incongruent to the point of utter confusion as to the true history and time periods.

Isaac Newton tried to make sense of it in his time. From Answers in Genesis, he made these claims about his findings based on records available at the time:

- God's Word is correct in every detail, including its history, so it must be our starting point (par. 410–415).
- Except for the Bible itself, the other histories of early nations were not recorded until well after the events had passed (par. 483–484). For example, the first historian to write about ancient Egypt (apart from Moses) was Herodotus (c. 484–425 BC).
- Most records of early history were lost or distorted as a result of repeated foreign invasions (par. 517).
- Ancient peoples were not averse to making big assumptions to fill in the gaps (par. 193).

It has been very well established that the beginning of the post–flood dynasties started with Narmer (son of Ham, son of Noah), who was also known as Mestraim, Menes, or Min. He was the first pharaoh or king of Egypt in about 2300 -2000BC (BTR) [200 to 500 years after the Flood]. In Sumerian he was often referred to as Manj-the-Warrior (Aha-Manj), in Egyptian as Manis-the-Warrior (Manis Tusu), and in Indian as Manja-the-Shooter (Asa-Manja).

Mizraim and his people came from Sumer, where he may have started out as a Sumerian Emperor, and ended up occupying Egypt. Indeed, Mizraim is still the Israeli name for the nation of Egypt. The name is also preserved in the Ugaritic inscriptions as msrm, the Amar tablets as Misri, and in the Assyrian and Babylonian records as Musur and Musri. Modern Arabs still know it as Misr. Professor Waddell asserts that Menes first extended his kingdom from Sumer to India conquering the first Indus Valley colony (decedents of Madai of Japheth) and then to Crete conquering the Greeks and establishing the Minoan culture. After that he made his way towards Egypt to conquer the Sinites (Chinese), who had settled in Egypt after the Babel event for the past several hundred years. Apparently the Sinite emperor, knowing of Narmer's conquests and hearing that he was making his way to Egypt, gathered his people and headed off to the other side of the Himalayas to preserve his kingdom, an area that was uninhabited up to then and with a natural barrier against the likes of Narmer. Menes, being the son of Ham, could have potentially lived to 450 years old – plenty of time for world conquest. Many of the artifacts and text of this Bronze Age period appear to support these underlying assumptions. Josephus relates a curious episode that he called the Ethiopic War, an incident that was apparently well known throughout the ancient world. According to this account, some six or seven nations descended from Mizraim were destroyed, clearly a major conflict that would have had profound and far-reaching repercussions on the world of those times. Josephus lists those nations that were destroyed as the Ludim, the Anamim, the Lehabim, the Naphtuhim, the Pathrusim, the Casluhim, and the Caphtorim. In the end, Menes was reported to have been carried off by a hippopotamus. Professor Waddell believes that this was misinterpreted, and that the inscriptions on his tomb indicated a "piercing fly" (Kheb), which he believes was a wasp that came up from the waters of the Nile. That too may have been misinterpreted, as the flying creature was probably a pterosaur being misinterpreted as an insect or hippopotamus for lack of relative identity of the beast. (That often happens with extinct animals that the translator is not knowledgeable of). Kheb is identified in the Sumerian glossary as a "voracious and wolfish insect of the field". Although a hippopotamus can be described as voracious and wolfish, and could come up out of the Nile, it certainly doesn't have wings, and I don't know of any wasp or hornet that could be described as voracious and wolfish, could come out of the Nile, and be able to carry off a human being. In contrast, a pterosaur can be described as voracious and wolfish, does have wings, has been known to hide in river waters to ambush elephants, and can carry off a full-grown adult. [13]

The changing culture of Egypt [2]

The Battle of Pelusium took place in 525BC between the Achaemenid Empire (Cambyses II King of Persia) and ancient Egypt (Pharaoh Amasis II). Egypt became a province of Persia until the conquest of Alexander the Great in 332BC.

Alexander the Great overtook Egypt in 332 BC. He was received as a liberator and pronounced son of the deity Amun Re at the Oracle of Siwa Oasis in the Libyan Desert, after which he referred to Zeus-Ammon as his true father. He founded the city of Alexander in Egypt at this time.

Ptolemy I Soter I was a general under Alexander the Great and close friend. He usurped the Egyptian throne after Alexander's death and retained the title Pharaoh of Egypt to start the Ptolemy dynasty in 323 BC that lasted till 30 BC. He built the Library of Alexander. The Ptolemy dynasty ended with the suicides of Cleopatra the VII and her Roman ally Mark Anthony after losing the Battle of Actium to Octavian's forces and the death of her son Caesarion during the Roman Conquest, after which it became a providence of Rome under Gaius Julius Caesar Octavianus (later known as Augustus).

Famous persons of history document encounters with extraordinary beasts (pterosaurs) in ancient Egypt [15].

The Assyrian monarch Esarhaddon (689-661BC) describes marching south into the desert to fight against Tirhaka, the king of Egypt and Nubia, *"where serpents and scorpions cover the plain like ants"* and even recalls *"seeing yellow serpents that could fly"*. The Greek historian, Herodotus (500Bc to 400BC), known as "the Father of History", writes,

> There is a place in Arabia, situated very near the city of Buto, to which I went, on hearing of some winged serpents; and when I arrived there, I saw bones and spines of serpents, in such quantities as it would be impossible to describe. The form of the serpent is like that of the water-snake; but he has wings without feathers, and as like as possible to the wings of a bat.

> Herodotus, in speaking of Egypt, talks about the ibis, a bird held in high esteem there. The reason the ibis is so revered in Egypt is because of its habit of killing snakes - particularly nasty snakes, in fact. And not just regular snakes, but flying snakes. According to Herodotus, these snakes come flying into Egypt every year from the east (i.e., the Arabian Peninsula or Sinai wilderness), but the ibises catch them as they fly through a rocky pass, and slaughter the flying snakes there, so that they do not invade Egypt (Herodotus 2.75-76). This is all to the good, as Herodotus reports that these snakes only live in the Middle eastern deserts, perching in trees in large numbers, and happen to be very vicious and poisonous. They also happen to be cannibalistic in reproducing, as the female consumes the male in the style of the praying mantis, and then when the young are born (live, not from eggs), they eat their way out of their mother's belly. (3.107-110)

Prosper Alpin wrote a book on the natural history of Egypt in 1580s. In it, he described the flying serpents that lived there. He described their head crest, a small piece of skin on the head, their length as long as palm tree, and their leaf-shaped tail being "thick as a finger". This description fits the modern fossil record of pterosaurs, plus details you could not get from the fossil record.

It is believed Moses and Israel encountered these "fiery serpents" during their forty years in the Sinai desert across from Egypt (in about 1450BC), as it was at the same place as described by Herodotus and Esarhaddon. The abundance and ferocity of these beasts fit the bill perfectly.

Num 21:6: And the LORD sent fiery serpents among the people, and they bit the people; and much people of Israel died.

Num 21:7: Therefore the people came to Moses, and said, We have sinned, for we have spoken against the LORD, and against thee; pray unto the LORD, that he take away the serpents from us. And Moses prayed for the people.

Num 21:8: And the LORD said unto Moses, make thee a fiery serpent, and set it upon a pole: and it shall come to pass, that every one that is bitten, when he looketh upon it, shall live.

Num 21:9: And Moses made a serpent of brass, and put it upon a pole, and it came to pass, that if a serpent had bitten any man, when he beheld the serpent of brass, he lived.

The "winged snake" actually shows up in many of the Egyptian artifacts and hieroglyphics, such as in the "Book of the Dead". Also, the arm rest of King Tut's throne is actually a winged snake.

China

The next dominant culture to emerge in antiquity are the Chinese with their successive dynasties believed to be the Sinite people group, descendants of Canaan and Ham. Just like the Sumerian King List and the Egyptian King List there are antediluvian rulers referred to as the "Three Sovereigns and Five Emperors", of which one is the renowned "Yellow Emperor". The Three Sovereigns were recognized as demigods, and they too were accredited for having lived exceptionally long lives. Additionally, the story of the great Flood and the Noah–like character is also recited in their ancient historical records [16].

Some years after the Babel dispersion, the first kingdom of China was established. There are records from the first dynasty all the way down through time to current day. In a story by Ricardo Lewis about a lecture given by a geochemist named Sun Weidong to an audience of laymen, students, and professors at the University of Science and Technology in Hefei, the following was reported: [3]:

> He also cited several ancient Chinese classics, at one point quoting historian Sima Qian's description of the topography of the Xia empire — traditionally regarded as China's founding dynasty, dating from 2070 to 1600 B.C. "Northwards the stream is divided and becomes the nine rivers," wrote Sima Qian in his first century historiography, the *Records of the Grand Historian*. "Reunited, it forms the opposing river and flows into the sea."
>
> In other words, "the stream" in question wasn't China's famed Yellow River, which flows from west to east. "There is only one major river in the world which flows northwards. Which one is it?" the professor asked. "The Nile," someone replied. Sun then showed a map of the famed Egyptian river and its delta — with nine of its distributaries flowing into the Mediterranean.
>
> In the past year, Sun, a highly decorated scientist, has ignited a passionate online debate with claims that the founders of Chinese civilization were not in any sense Chinese but actually migrants from Egypt. He conceived of this connection in

the 1990s while performing radiometric dating of ancient Chinese bronzes; to his surprise, their chemical composition more closely resembled those of ancient Egyptian bronzes than native Chinese ores. Both Sun's ideas and the controversy surrounding them flow out of a much older tradition of nationalist archaeology in China, which for more than a century has sought to answer a basic scientific question that has always been heavily politicized: Where do the Chinese people come from?

That Egypt has its root from Sumer is again, academic. The above sited scientific and historical evidence along with the typical foundational antediluvian genesis story and the time period overwhelmingly establishes the roots of the Chinese culture. The expansion process from Sumer to all the cultures in the world took on many forms and avenues.

Xia dynasty (2070 - 1600 BC)

King Yu the Great was the first ruler of China that has some archeological verification. At this time in history, the world was coming to the end of the Ice Age. Rising water levels and flooding had been a mounting problem for the past 300 years. Yu became famous for the introduction of flood control methodologies. New archeological discoveries support the stories of flood control during the time of the first dynasty [17]. It is recorded that after the Flood Yu surveyed the land and then sectioned it out. He then built the channels needed to drain water off to recover the land and make it usable for farming. It is noted that many snakes and dragons were driven out as well [12].

> The Shan-hai-king [is] a Chinese work of extreme antiquity. The Chinese say that the record was compiled by the great Yu, at the time when he was minister under the Emperor Shun, prior to the time when he himself was Emperor. Geographers and historians alike acknowledge the Shan Hai King to be the world's oldest geography. The following text [states]: *"The Pa snake swallows elephants, after three years it ejects the bones; well-to-do people, eating it, are cured of consumption."* [12].

Other Asian cultures such as Japan, Korea, Cambodia, Vietnam, Singapore, and Malaysia; Taiwan, Hong Kong, Macau appeared to have expanded out from China to form subcultures in the original Chinese civilization, as can be concluded from the basic Chinese Hanzi script in an attenuated form found in most all the Asian languages along with other obvious signs . [18, 19, 20, 21].

Confucius - September 28, 551 – 479 BC) was a Chinese born teacher, politician, and world renown philosopher whose teachings were given sanction and a place in the Chinese culture during the Han Dynasty. It is believed that he authored many of the Chinese classic texts. He coined the well-known saying, "Do not do to others what you do not want done to yourself" [22].

Famous persons of history document encounters with extraordinary beasts (pterosaurs and dragons [dinosaurs]) in ancient China [15].

Marco Polo (travel period 1271-1291 AD) published a book in 1300 AD titled *The Travels of Marco*

Polo. He was an adventurer that traveled through Persia, Asia, Indonesia, and China and recorded the unique customs of the different cultures along with the different types of plants and animals that he encountered on his journeys. In his journal, Marco Polo tells of dragons he encountered in Karajan and how the people would defend against them. From chapter 49 of his journal:

"Leaving the city of Yachi, and traveling ten days in a westerly direction, you reach the province of Karazan, which is also the name of the chief city....Here are seen huge serpents, ten paces in length (30 feet), and ten spans (8 feet) girt of the body. At the fore part, near the head, they have two short legs, having three claws like those of a tiger, with eyes larger than a forepenny loaf and very glaring.

The jaws are wide enough to swallow a man, the teeth are large and sharp, and their whole appearance is so formidable, that neither man, nor any kind of animal can approach them without terror. Others are met with of a smaller size, being eight, six, or 5 paces long; and the following method is used for taking them. In the day-time, by reason of great heat, they lurk in caverns, from whence, at night, they issue to seek their food, and whatever beast they meet with and can lay hold of, whether tiger, wolf, or any other, they devour;

After which they drag themselves towards some lake, spring of water, or river, in order to drink. By their motion in this way along the shore, and their vast weight, they make a deep impression, as if a heavy beam had been drawn along the sands. Those whose employment is to hunt them observe the track by which they are most frequently accustomed to go, and fix into the ground several pieces of wood, armed with sharp iron spikes, which they cover with sand in such a manner as not to be perceptible.

When therefore the animals make their way towards the places they usually haunt, they are wounded by these instruments, and speedily killed. The crows, as soon as they perceive them to be dead, set up to scream; and this serves as a signal to the hunters, who advance the spot, and proceed to separate the skin from the flesh, taking care immediately to secure the gall, which is most highly esteemed in medicine.

In cases of the bite of a mad dog, a penny weight of it, dissolved in wine, is administered. It is also useful in accelerating parturition, when the labor pains of women have come on. A small quantity of it being applied to carbuncles, pustules, or other eruptions on the body, they are presently dispersed; and it is efficacious in many other complaints.

The flesh also of the animal is sold at a dear rate, being thought to have a higher flavor than other kinds of meat, and by all persons it is esteemed a delicacy."

Marco Polo lived in China for about 17 years and wrote about the emperor of China raising dragons and using them to pull his chariots in parades.

There are entries in the official Chinese records from 1611 that established a post for a "Royal Dragon Feeder" and tell of dragons pulling the emperors' chariots just as described by Marco Polo. There are many books from ancient China that tell of Chinese families that raised dragons to use their blood for medicines and harvesting eggs. These records can be found in ancient texts up to as late as the sixteenth century AD (reference the prescription narrative by Pan Ts'ai Kang Mu).

The Sung Dynasty (960-1279 AD) used the saliva of the purple dragon to engrave the stories and epitaph of dignitaries onto tablets of gold, jade, and crystal. Buddhist records from this era maintain that dragon feeding was a common practice throughout the orient. The Chinese medical scholar **Lei Xiao** (420-477 AD) recorded the following:

> *"For using dragon's bones, first cook odorous plants; bathe the bones twice in hot water, pound them to powder and put this in bags of gauze. Take a couple of young swallows and, after taking out their intestines and stomach, put the bags in the swallows and hang them over a well. After one night take the bags out of the swallows, rub the powder and mix it into medicines for strengthening the kidneys. The efficacy of such a medicine is as it were divine!"*

El Edrisi (1099–1165 or 1166) was a Muslim geographer, cartographer, Egyptologist and traveler who lived in Sicily. He says that it is a large island on the confines of China towards India, and that among other remarkable features is a mountain called Nacan, or Kini Balu, on which are serpents of such magnitude as to be able to swallow oxen, buffaloes, and even elephants. Masudi includes Zanig, Kalah, and Taprobana among the islands constituting the territory of the Mahraj.—P. Amédée Jaubert, Géographie d'Edrisi, vol. i. p. 104; Paris, 1836 [15].

There is no mistaking the Chinese reference to dragons as dinosaur–like beasts as there are numerous sketches, idols, drawings, and literary descriptions to establish the range of dinosaurs that they are likened to.

(Right): Figure 4.4 Statues of Chinese dragons

(Left): Figure 4.5 A very distinctive carving of a *Stegosaurus* found in the ancient ruins discovered in the 1800s at Ta Prohm, Cambodia (700 to 1200 AD).

Africa

Cush, the son of Ham, established a kingdom in Africa just south of Egypt (Ethiopia). Cush and Egypt had wars for some time, and Cush even ruled over Egypt for a season. The descendants of Cush continued to push southward and eventually occupied all of Africa, the interior was either densely forested or desert and seething with predators and could not be densely populated.

Most languages spoken in Africa belong to one of three large language families: Afro-asiatic, Nilo-Saharan, and Niger–Congo. Another hundred belong to small families such as Ubangian (sometimes grouped within Niger-Congo) and the various families called Khoisan, or the Indo-European and Austronesian language families which originated outside Africa; the presence of the latter two dates to 2,600 and 1,500 years ago, respectively. In addition, African languages include several unclassified languages and sign languages [23].

Famous persons of history document encounters with extraordinary beasts, dinosaurs in ancient India (pterosaurs and dragons) [15].

Titus Livius Patavinus (Livy) [59 BC - 17 AD], a Roman historian, wrote a monumental history of Rome and the Roman people. He wrote an account about an African reptile that attacked the Roman Army under the command of General Regulus.

"After many soldiers had been seized in its [the dragon's] mouth, and many more crushed by the folds of its tail, its hide being too thick for javelins and darts, the dragon was at last attacked by military engines and crushed by repeated blows from heavy stones."

Antonio Pigafetta, a sixteenth century Italian explorer, reported on creatures he had seen in the African Congo:

"There are also certain other creatures which, being as big as rams, have wings like dragons, with long tails, and long chaps, and divers rows of teeth, and feed upon raw flesh. Their colour is blue and green, their skin painted like scales, and they have two feet but no more. The Pagan negroes used to worship them as gods, and to this day you may see divers of them that are kept for a marvel. And because they are very rare, the chief lords there curiously preserve them, and suffer

151

the people to worship them, which tendeth greatly to their profits by reason of the gifts and oblations which the people offer unto them." (Pigafetta, Filippo, The Harleian Collections of Travels, vol. ii, 1745, p. 457.)

The Americas

Sechin Bajo (Peru) - believed to have been established in 3500BC based on C14 dating. It now sports the crown for the oldest known settlement. Relatively little is known about the people who lived there. The oldest building was determined with C14 to have stood from 3700BC (3000) to 2900BC (2500), reflecting the demarcation congruent with Noah's Flood. The second and third buildings were found to have been built and used much later, between 1600BC (1200) to 1200BC (700). There are notable earthwork structures in a circular pattern believed to have been used for religious ceremony. Scientists say settlements were beginning to grow in Peru about the time of urbanization in such cradles of civilization as Mesopotamia, Egypt, and India. These temples are very similar to the Sumerian temples in shape, size, and varying elevations[24, 25].

Major Ancient Civilizations in S. America and Mexico [2].
First Civilization - Peru - 1600 BC
Olmec People - Gulf Coast of Mexico - 1400 BC - 300 BC
Mayan Civilization started in the Highlands of Guatemala - 1200 BC - 800 AD (expanded throughout S. America)
Chavin Culture - Peru - 800 BC - 200 BC
Zapotecs - Southern Mexico - 500 BC - 1 BC
Tikai - Guatemala - 300 AD - 700 AD
Teotihuancan - Central Mexico - 300 BC - 750 AD
Moche - Peru - 200 BC - 500 AD
Nazca - Peru - 200 AD - 800 AD (Known for the Nazca lines and advanced technology in medicine, engineering, hand gliding)
Toltechs - Central Mexico - 950 AD - 1160 AD (The ruler Topilzin-Quetzalcoatl was associated with and named after a legendry flying serpent who was worshiped as a god)
Aztechs - Valley of Mexico - 1300 BC - 1520 (also worshiped flying serpent Quetzalcoatl; Aztech civilization ended with Spanish invasion of conquistador Hernan Cortez.)
Huari /Tiahuanaco - (Wari Peoples) Peruvian Andes/Lake Titicaca - 400 AD - 1100 AD
Inca Indians - S. American West coast and mountains - 1430 AD to 1532 AD (ended with Spanish invasion)
Spanish Territories / Wars of Independence - S. America became the territory of Spain from the 1500s until the wars of Independence in the 18th centuries, sparked by the American and French Revolutions, of the different nations now established.

AN ACCOUNT OF THE ANTIQUITIES OF PERU. JESUS MARIA [26].
Don Juan de Santa Cruz Pachacuti, descendent of the Incas and Spaniards, wrote in 1632:

> I affirm that I have heard, from a child, the most ancient traditions and histories, the fables and barbarisms of the heathen times, which are as follows; according to the constant testimony of the natives touching the events of past times.

They say that, in the time of *Purun1-pacha,* all the nations of Ttahuantin-suyu came from beyond Potosi in four or five armies arrayed for war. They settled in the different districts as they advanced. This period was called **Ccallac-pacha~** or *Tutayac-pacha.* As each company selected suitable places for their homes and lands, they called this *Purunpacharacyaptin.* This period lasted for a vast number of years. After the country was peopled, there was a great want of space, and, as the land was insufficient, there were wars and quarrels, and the nations occupied themselves in making fortresses, and every day there were encounters and battles, and there was no rest from these tumults, insomuch that the people never enjoyed any peace. Then, in the middle of the night, they heard the *Hapi-iiuiios* disappearing, with

mournful complaints, and crying out-"We are conquered, we are conquered, alas that we should lose our bands!" By this it must be understood that the devils were conquered by Jesus Christ our Lord on the cross on Mount Calvary. **For in ancient times, in the days of *Purun-pacha,* they say that the *Hapi-fiufius* walked visibly over the land, and it was unsafe to go out at night, for they violently carried off men, women, and children, like infernal tyrants and enemies of the human race as they are. Some years after the devils called *Hapi-iiuiius Achacallas* had been driven out of the land,** there arrived, in these kingdoms of *Ttahuantinsuyu* a bearded man, of middle height, with long hair, and in a rather long shirt. He was called *Tonapa Uiracocha nipacachan;* but was he not the glorious apostle St. Thomas?

Famous documented encounters with extraordinary beasts, dinosaurs in Native American history (pterosaurs and dragons) [15]**.**

"An ancient Mayan relief sculpture of a peculiar bird with reptilian characteristics (archaeornis & archaeopteryx) has been discovered in Totonacapan, in northeastern section of Veracruz, Mexico. José Diaz-Bolio, a Mexican archaeologist-journalist responsible for the discovery, says there is evidence that the serpent-bird sculpture, located in the ruins of Tajín, is not merely the product of Mayan flights of fancy, but a realistic representation of an animal that lived during the period of the ancient Mayans — 1,000 to 5,000 years ago. If indeed such serpent-birds were contemporary with the ancient Mayan culture, the relief sculpture represents a startling evolutionary oddity. Animals with such characteristics are believed to have disappeared 130 million years ago." (Anonymous, "Serpent-Bird of the Mayans," *Science Digest,* vol. 64, Nov., 1968, p. 1.)

Figure 4.6 Sketch of a Mayan figurine that appears to be carrying a pterodactyloid pterosaur on his shoulders. The image has such detail that there is no question as to what it is with the distinct head

crest, large eye, and leathery wing with its claws ("Serpent-Bird of the Mayans," Science Digest, vol. 64, Nov., 1968, p. 1.).

Genesis Park - Dragons in History [27]

The story of a couple of cowboys who happened upon and shot down a "winged dragon" was run in a local Arizona newspaper, *The Tombstone Epitaph*, on April 26, 1890. It was described as resembling a pterodactyl, only much larger. They described the creature as being 93 ft. long and 4 ft. wide with a wingspan of 160 ft. This appears to be the North American pterosaur Quetzelcoatlus, one of the largest known flying creatures of all time, whose fossils were found in Texas (Gish, Dinosaurs by Design, 1992, p. 16.). This is believed to be the thunderbird (Wakinyan), the jagged-winged, fierce-toothed flying creature that appears in the legends of Sioux American Indian who lived in a cave on the top of the Olympic Mountains. (Geis, Darlene, Dinosaurs & Other Prehistoric Animals, 1959, p. 9.) It was associated with its piercing cry and thunderous beating wings (Lame Deer's 1969 interview) and seen in the day only when it was dark, thundering, and lighting, hence the name "thunderbird" [15].

Evolutionist Adrienne Mayor spent considerable time researching the possibility that Native Americans dug up dinosaur fossils. But some of the reports she received make a lot more sense if these early Americans interacted with actual dinosaurs, not yet extinct. There is no evidence for sophisticated Ancient Paleontologists. An old Assiniboine story tells of a war party that "traveled a long distance to unfamiliar lands and [saw] some large lizards. The warriors held a council and discussed what

Figure 4:7 Indian vs Dinosaur

they knew about those strange creatures. They decided that those big lizards were bad medicine and should be left alone. However, one warrior who wanted more war honors said that he was not afraid of those animals and would kill one. He took his lance [a very old weapon used before horses] and charged one of the large lizard type animals and tried to kill it. But he had trouble sticking his lance in the creature's hide and during the battle he himself was killed and eaten." (Mayor, *Fossil Legends of the First Americans*, 2005, p. 294.) This story conjures up credible visions of the scaly hide of a great reptile, something Native Americans would not know from mere skeletons. It was once thought that Woolly Mammoths had flourished in North America prior to the arrival of humans. But the discovery of sites where many mammoths were killed and butchered has established the co-existence of men and mammoths. Perhaps similar evidence involving dinosaurs will be forthcoming.

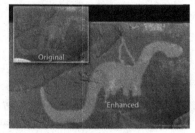

(Right): Figure 4:8 A very distinctive petroglyph of an *Apatosaurus* found at the Natural Bridge Monument in SE Utah (500 to 1,500 years old). The official stance from the scientific community on this is that this is a serpent and the legs were stain runs. Really? Four symmetric stain runs where feet normally go, same shade and sharpness as the drawing!

REFERENCES

Biblical References from: The Holy Bible (1913). King James Version. Chicago, Ill. John A. Dickson Publishing Co.

1   Wikipedia. World population estimates. Retrieved from https://en.wikipedia.org/wiki/World_population_estimates

2   Wolf, A. (2008). *A short history of the world: The story of mankind from prehistory to the modern day*. New York, NY: Metro Books by arrangement with Arcturus Publishing Limited.

3   Lewis, R. (2016). FP. Does Chinese civilization come from Egypt? Retrieved from http://foreignpolicy.com/2016/09/02/did-chinese-civilization-come-from-ancient-egypt-archeological-debate-at-heart-of-china-national-identity/

4   Evans, C.A. (2010). Holman Quick Source™ Guide to: *The Dead Sea Scrolls*. North Nashville, TN: B&H Publishing Group.

5   Answers in Genesis. The Antediluvian Patriarchs and the Sumerian king list. https://answersingenesis.org/bible-history/the-antediluvian-patriarchs-and-the-sumerian-king-list/

6   The History Files. Middle East kingdoms: Ancient Mesopotamia. Retrieved from http://www.historyfiles.co.uk/KingListsMiddEast/MesopotamiaSumer.htm

7   The Epic of Gilgamesh. Assyrian International News Agency. Books Online. www.aina.org. http://www.aina.org/books/eog/eog.htm

8   Wikipedia. Epic of Gilgamesh. Retrieved from https://en.wikipedia.org/wiki/Epic_of_Gilgamesh

9   Barnes, T. G. Ph.D, (1983). *Origin and destiny of the earth's magnetic field* (2nd Ed.). El Cajon, CA: Institute for Creation Research.

10   Brett-Surman, M.K. (2000). *Dinosaurs: Revised & updated*. San Francisco, CA: Fog City Press.

11   Breeden, D. Ph.D, (2011). *The adventures of Beowulf*. Seattle, WA: CreateSpace Independent Publishing Platform.

12   Discover Magazine. Tsavo man-eaters. Retrieved from http://blogs.discovermagazine.com/notrocketscience/2009/11/02/how-many-people-did-the-man-eating-lions-of-tsavo-actually-eat/#.WYiSBIjyvIU

13   Waddell, L.A. (1930). Egyptian civilization: Its Sumer origins & real chronology. Retrieved from http://www.thechristianidentityforum.net/downloads/Egyptian-Chronology.pdf

14   Answers in Genesis. Chronology Wars. Retrieved from https://answersingenesis.org/bible-history/chronology-wars/

15   History's Evidence of Dinosours and Men. Retrieved from http://historysevidenceofdinosaursandmen.weebly.com/written.html

16   New World Encyclopedia. Three Sovereigns and Five Emperors. Retrieved from http://www.newworldencyclopedia.org/entry/Three_Sovereigns_and_Five_Emperors

17   Wade, N. (2016). Science. Scientific evidence of flood may give credence to legend of China's first dynasty. Retrieved from http://www.nytimes.com/2016/08/05/science/china-great-flood-xia-emperor-yu.html?_r=0

18   Stearns, P. (2000). The spread of Chinese civilization to Japan. Retrieved from http://history-world.org/Chinese%20Civilization%20To%20Japan.htm

19   Dagmara, C. (2014). Quora. Which Asian ethnicity or culture came first? Chinese, Japanese, or Korean? Retrieved from https://www.quora.com/Which-Asian-ethnicity-or-culture-came-first-Chinese-Japanese-or-Korean

20   Britannica. Cambodia. Retrieved from https://www.britannica.com/place/Cambodia

21   Ancient History. Chinese characters. Retrieved from http://www.ancient.eu/Chinese_Writing/

22   Britannica. Confucius. Retrieved from https://www.britannica.com/biography/Confucius

23   Wikipedia. Languages of Africa. Retrieved from https://en.wikipedia.org/wiki/Languages_of_Africa

24 Jacobs, James Q. (2000). Earl monumental architecture on the Peruvian coast. Retrieved from http://www. jqjacobs.net/andes/coast.html#1

25 Ancient Origins. Sechin Bajo. Retrieved from http://www.ancient-origins.net/ancient-places-americas/ sechin-bajo-peru-location-oldest-man-made-structure-new-world-005845

26 Maria, J. An account of the antiquities of Peru. Retrieved from http://www.sacred-texts.com/nam/inca/rly/ rly2.htm#page_112_fr_3

27 Genesis Park. Dragons in history. Retrieved from http://www.genesispark.com/exhibits/evidence/historical/ dragons/

PART 5

Descendants of Jepheth

Japheth's descendants.

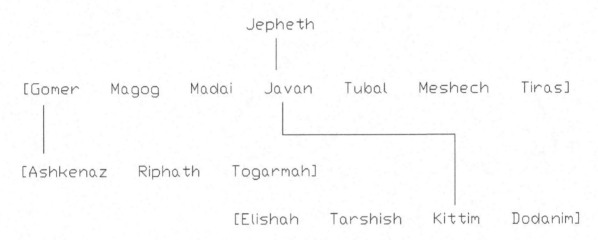

Biblical Reference: Ge:10:5: By these were the isles of the Gentiles divided in their lands; every one after his tongue, after their families, in their nations.

The European Nations

1. Gomer (the Cimmerians) settled north of the Black Sea, but then expanded to settle Germany, France, Spain, and the British Isles.
2. Magog (the Scythians, Russians) settled the land north of the Caspian Sea.
3. Madai (the Medes, India) settled the land south of the Caspian Sea and Northern India.
4. Javan (the Ionians or Greeks).
5. Tubal (the Turks) settled the land south of the Black Sea.
6. Meshech (the Slavs) settled between the Black and Caspian Seas.
7. Tiras the (Etruscans) settled the land west of the Black Sea.

Europe

Some of the most valued European documents are the Anglo-Saxton Chronicles, or as Professor L.A. Waddell referred to them, the "British Chronicles".

Key documents

Cin Dromma Snechta as preserved by Keating (fifth century AD)
Saltair of Cashel (seventh century AD)
History of the Britons by Nennius (eighth century AD)
History of the Kings of Britain by Geoffrey of Monmouth (tenth century AD)
Chronicum Scotorum (fifteenth century AD)
Ussher's chronology (seventeenth century AD)

Within the folds of these and other historical documents are the genealogies of the European nations that trace their lineage back to the sons of Noah.

The following excerpt is from the Nennius *History of the Britons* (700 AD) [1].

> "17. I have learned another account of this Brutus from the ancient books of our ancestors. After the deluge, the three sons of Noah severally occupied three different parts of the earth: Shem extended his borders into Asia, Ham into Africa, and Japheth into Europe.
>
> The first man that dwelt in Europe was Alanus, with his three sons, Hisicion, Armenon, and Neugio. Hisicion had four sons, Froncus, Romanus, Alamanus, and Brutus. Armenon had five sons, Gothus, Valaothus, Cibidus, Burgundus, and Longobardus. Neugio had three sons, Valdalus, Saxo, and Boganus. From Hisicion arose four nations—the Franks, the Latins, the Germans, and Britons: from Armenon, the Gothi, Valagothi, Cibidi, Burgundi, and Longobardi: from Neugio, the Bagari, Vandali, Saxones, and Tarinegi. The whole of Europe was subdivided into these tribes.
>
> Alanus is said to have been the son of Fethuir; Fethuir the son of Ogomuin, who was the son of Thoi; Thoi was the son of Boibus, Boibus of Semion, Semion of Mair, Mair of Ecthactur, Ecthactur of Aurthack, Aurthack of Ethec, Ethec of Ooth, Ooth of Aber, Aber of Ra, Ra of Esraa, Esraa of Hisrau, Hisrau of Bath, Bath of Jobath, Jobath of Joham, Joham of Japheth, Japheth of Noah, Noah of Lamech, Lamech of Mathusalem, Mathusalem of Enoch, Enoch of Jared, Jared of Malalehel, Malalehel of Cainan, Cainan of Enos, Enos of Seth, Seth of Adam, and Adam was formed by the living God. We have obtained this information respecting the original inhabitants of Britain from ancient tradition.
>
> 18. The Britons were thus called from Brutus: Brutus was the son of Hisicion, Hisicion was the son of Alanus, Alanus was the son of Rhea Silvia, Rhea Silvia was the daughter of Numa Pompilius, Numa was the son of Ascanius, Ascanius of Eneas, Eneas of Anchises,

Anchises of Troius, Troius of Dardanus, Dardanus of Flisa, Flisa of Juuin, Juuin of Japheth; but Japheth had seven sons; from the first, named Gomer, descended the Galli; from the second, Magog, the Scythi and Gothi; from the third, Madian, the Medi; from the fourth, Juuan, the Greeks; from the fifth, Tubal, arose the Hebrei, Hispani, and Itali; from the sixth, Mosoch, sprung the Cappadoces; and from the seventh, named Tiras, descended the Thraces: these are the sons of Japheth, the son of Noah, the son of Lamech."

The following are excerpts and commentary from Bill Cooper's book *After the Flood*[2]:

Modern historians often retort that the Genesis story has no basis in the historical records. Cooper shows that just the opposite is true and states:

This portion of Genesis in particular is fully corroborated by an overwhelming richness of documentary and other historical evidence so vast that it is unique in recorded history! No other document enjoys such a wealth of detailed corroboration from such a wide-ranging variety of sources.

Cooper goes on to demonstrate that there are genealogies and king lists of the early Celts and Saxons that pre-date Christianity and that these peoples were very much aware of their heritage and descendants from the Babel dispersing and lineage of Jephthah. Cooper reiterates:

Again, we shall see how these ancient and unique records are dismissed by the modernist school with a readiness that is astonishing in its unthinking disregard for the historical method.

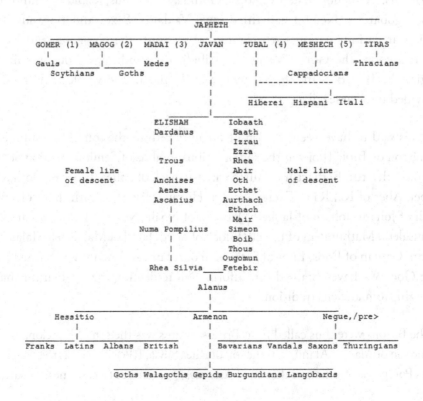

Ireland.

Using Ussher's chronology, Cooper deduced that the Flood event happened about 2348 BC and that Partholan's colony arrived in Ireland 864 years after the Flood. This is collaborated by many other histories of Europe and the Middle East. Next came the colonization of Ireland by the Milesians in 504 BC.

Event	Date Anno Mundi	Date BC	Date PD
The Creation.	0000	4004	—
The Flood.	1858	2348	0000
First colonization of Ireland by Partholan.	2520	1484	864
Death of Partholan.	2550	1454	894
End of First Colony.	2820	1184	1164
Second colonization of Ireland under Nemedh.	28501145	1203	
Third colonization of Ireland under the Tuatha De Dananns.	3303	701	1647
Fourth and final colonization of Ireland under the Milesians.	3500	504	1844

Many of the Irish pre-Christian genealogies have records of clans and tribes tracing back to those same patriarchs whose names appear in the Genesis record:

> It thus becomes clear the Irish genealogies were compiled at a time when it would have been beyond all possibility for the Christian monks to have influenced or altered them in any way, and we are left with the simple conclusion that these genealogies owed their existence to the preservation of records that was entirely independent of either the Jewish or Christian churches; and we see that the ancient Irish, in common with their forebears in the Middle East, preserved records of events that significantly confirm the Genesis account concerning the descent and dispersal of the nations.[2]

One of the most outstanding epic tales from the Scandinavians, descendants of Magog, son of Jepheth, son of Noah, is the story of **Beowulf** from the sixth century AD. The story from an unknown author was written in old English and is the oldest surviving epic in British literature. It survived the destruction of religious artifacts during the reign of King Henry the VIII and a fire that destroyed the library of Sir Robert Bruce Cotton (1571-1631). This manuscript can be found today in the British Library in London.[3]

The story tells of **Hrothgar the Great, king of the Danes**, who built the then famous mead hall he named **Heorot** (the Heart (as a stag), a wine hall of great space and height) from which a great sound of rioting and uproar reached out to the nearby moor, catching the attention of a great beast of terror that they called **Grendel**. Grendel would come in the middle of the night, break through the hall's doors, and quickly devour the many sleeping or passed out drunk men and women he found there. The story goes on to tell of the exploits of the men from Geat, amongst whom was the most famous hero of all, Beowulf. Beowulf, who hears of the plight of the king through the tales and "the sad songs of poets heard throughout the world", comes to the mead hall with his band of warriors seeking fame and fortune. Hrothgar was offering a rich bounty to anyone who could defeat the beast that had cursed his land for twelve years. Beowulf regales the king and his audience with tales of battles with sea monsters, then beds down with his warriors for their first night in the hall. Grendel arrives on scene, as expected, and proceeds to eat every bit of a sleeping warrior in several quick gulps. Beowulf attacks the beast and overcomes him without sword, shield, or weaponry. He uses just his bare hands as it was found that no weapon could penetrate Grendel's thick hide when his companions tried to take him on, joining Beowulf in the battle. The battle between the beast and Beowulf comes to an end when Beowulf twists Grendel's arm off and he retreats to his lair in the moors and dies. A surprise awaits Beowulf and the king when **Grendel's mother** shows up the next night to once again eat one of the warriors. She flees back to her lair, which she enters through a pool under a waterfall with troops in hot pursuit. Surrounding the pool are ravenous water monsters that hasten to flee from the menacing mob, of which one is killed and hauled up to the top of a mountain to be laid out and studied by the band. Beowulf, the king, and their troops pursue the beast when Beowulf alone enters the lair and commences the battle. Using a sword given to him as a gift from one of the king's top officers, he fails to penetrate the hide. He then tries to wrench off her arm as he did Grendel's but gets pinned down, failing again to get the upper hand. Finally, our hero finds a sword left behind by the giants that once lived there, and proceeds to hack into the back of her neck. Suddenly, a bright flash lights up the cave and melts the sword. Beowulf returns to his home in Scandinavia triumphant and soon becomes the king of the Geats, where he reigns for fifty years. At the end of his life, a **dragon** comes and starts harassing his people and burning their villages with fire. It is found that the dragon's lair is in a cave where there are hoards of treasure left behind by former kings. Beowulf and his trusted warriors meet with the dragon in the cave where the beast fends them off with flames of fire from his mouth. He and his best mate, **Wiglaf**, advance on the beast whilst his troops head for cover without the cave. In the end, Beowulf and his faithful companion are burned severely and Beowulf is bitten in the neck, but Wiglaf gets close enough to plunge his sword into the dragon and kill it. Beowulf dies of his wounds there in the cave while Wiglaf lives on to give Beowulf a great hero's funeral [3].

Grendel and his mother are described as:

(1) being able to stand on two legs like a man (or woman);
(2) having claws;
(3) being big and powerful, as they could knock out the door of the great hall easily;
(4) having a head with a mouth and gullet large enough to eat and swallow a couple of full grown men in a few gulps;
(5) having a hide so thick a sword or spear could not penetrate;
(6) having arms susceptible to being twisted off by a powerful human being;
(7) coming out at night, alluding to them being nocturnal, which befits a large predator to hunt under the cloak of darkness;
(8) having tracks easily followed (clearly visible) probably due its distinct shape, large size, and deep imprint; and

(9) making their abode in a cave in the midst of a swamp.

This story was told at a time when, according to the theory of evolution, there were no dinosaurs, therefore, these people should not have a clue as to any of the distinct characteristics of dinosaurs. On the contrary, all these descriptive narratives can easily be used to describe a certain dinosaur commonly known as *T.rex*, whose arms are depicted, in most every graphic artist rendition of the beast, as puny and almost comical in form. This can easily be recognized as his "Achilles' heel", if you will, an obvious weakness for the great beast and is very distinctive to a *T.rex*. These beasts have at least nine general characteristics that coincidently mirror an extinct creature. *T.rex* has supposedly been extinct for 65 million years according to evolutionary chronologies. For the author to describe his features, having no knowledge of a *T.rex*, is outstanding, but to have the identical "Achilles' heel" is incredibly remarkable.

Figure 5.1 Beowulf battles Grendel

Additionally, the second beast was easily recognized as an older female of the species (the mother of Grendel). She was probably smaller in size, as most female creatures are in comparison to their male counterparts. The story alludes to her lesser mass and weaker constitution: "the terror was less by just so much as is the strength of a woman, the war-horror of a woman is less than the horror of a sword forged with hammer". She was intimidated by the band of sword–bearing warriors, again alluding to her smaller and more susceptible frame. This fear caused her to react, fleeing immediately, unlike the larger and more ferocious Grendel who paid them no mind.

The author alluded many times to human qualities such as: these beasts being the offspring of Cain that was cursed of God for killing his brother Abel, "The evil creature, grim and hungry, grabbed thirty warriors and went home laughing", "Grendel killed more—blinded by sin, he felt no remorse", "Quickly the foe moved across the well-made floor in an angry mood", "Grendel felt sorry that he made the trip to Heorot", "The criminal knew he had not met in this middle earth another with such a grip. Grendel's heart was afraid and his heart was eager to get away, to flee to his hiding place, flee to the devils he kept for company", "Grendel, the foe of God, who had long troubled the spirit of men with his crimes" "So his mother, greedy and gloomy as the gallows went on a sorrowful journey to avenge her son's death", "she took her son's hand". These human attributes are conventional in epic story telling when the foe is a monstrous beast. The author took poetic liberties, as authors quite often do, to give the creature a more personable human quality in order for the reader to relate to his point of view. I remember reading a book my father gave me as young kid called *The Biography of a Grizzly* by Ernest Thompson-Seton (1899), featuring a bear named Meeteetse Wahb [4]. I must have read it a hundred times and have referred to it as many times throughout my life, especially in regard to one sneaky little black bear. It was a story from the late nineteenth century about a monstrously giant grizzly bear (a composite of real bear stories of the time) that had a large roaming territory in Wyoming on the edge of Yellowstone National Park. Even though this monster was a terror to other bears, animals, Indians, and especially the neighboring ranchers, mostly their livestock, the author helped us relate to him. The author often let us know how he felt, such as, "till the mother said in grizzly, let me show you how" or he came to distrust his human neighbors, or how he thought to himself *"I have dreadful pains; I feel better when I am in this stinking pool."* Note that the *T.rex* doesn't laugh (I wouldn't think), and bears don't lay in hot springs to relieve arthritis) according to Johnston & Preston winners the National Outdoor Book award][5]). The author could not have any knowledge of how Meeteetse Wahb felt but uses personification to show us how he might have felt. The author of Beowulf does not identify the creature as a dinosaur, probably because they never saw such a creature and could only associate it with Cain, as he and it were both a dreadful curse in the land; as a dragon, as dragons normally flew and breathed fire, which this creature did not do; or as a humanoid. Hollywood portrays Grendel and his mother as large ravaging humanoids either because of the human qualities the author gives them or because they would avoid any suggestion that man and dinosaurs lived as contemporaries and interacted in such an epic way.

The dragon is described as having a body able to recoil itself or tuck its wings tight to its body (the dragon coiled together, went forth burning). He breathed fire (he threw death–fire —widely sprayed battle flashes), was able to fly (that terrible sky-flier wished to leave nothing alive), he attacked under the cloak of darkness, and was a nocturnal creature (anxiously he awaited the fall of night; enraged, the cave-keeper would with fire avenge the loss of his cup). This fits the description of possibly several species of pterodactyl dinosaur, an extinct flying reptile also described as a thunderbird in Native American lore and cave drawing (petroglyphs).

Figure 5.2 Flying Pterosaurs

Although the ability to spew fire has not normally been associated with dinosaurs in modern science books, it is possible that this characteristic is an unknown trait in some of the beasts. There is precedence in nature for such features and there are cavities in many of the dinosaurs' skulls that science cannot explain the use of to date [6]. It is also possible that these beasts spewed acid that burned flesh and bone on contact, causing much smoke to be emitted from the burning, causing it to be associated with fire.

We can easily compare Beowulf fighting a *T.rex* to Steve Erwin fighting 15-foot-long monster crocodiles, in the end both our heroes being overcome by some beast. Were you or I to encounter a 15-foot crocodile, we would be lunch if he got close enough. Steve would have him wrapped up in a matter of minutes. Beowulf was further up the entropy scale – larger, stronger, quicker, and even more cunning and skilled than what we know from our time. Every generation of plant and animal degrades due to copying errors on a genetic level. (An average of 100 copying errors pass from the father to the child, plus whatever is passed on from the mother in humans). It would be safe to assume that because they were less degraded that they had greater capacity for use of their brains and muscles. The food would have been healthier with more potential energy, proteins, carbohydrates, and so on.

Lastly, the story is based on real historical characters, giving the story a solid foundation that suggests the events have some basis in truth, and the monsters were actual creatures of some sort, even if exaggerated to some extent to intensify the story. There are several references in the text to the Danes and Geats trusting in the one True God, references to God's creation, Cain and Abel, and other references of their history that align with biblical history at a time when they were not exposed to Christian influences. The Christianization of Scandinavia took place between the 8th and the 12th centuries.

Famous persons of history document encounters with extraordinary beasts (pterosaurs and dragons [dinosaurs]) in ancient Europe [7].

Aristotle wrote the following in 384 BC:

"The eagle and the dragon are enemies, for the eagle feeds on serpents"; and again, *"the Glanis in shallow water is often destroyed by the dragon serpent."*

"But there are others which, though they live and feed in the water, do not take in water but air, and produce their young out of the water; many of these animals are furnished with feet, as the otter and crocodile, and others are without feet, as the water-serpent."

Geoffrey of Monmouth records the story of Morvidus, king of the Britons from 341 to 336 B.C., who fought with a menacing dragon that apparently came up from the Irish Sea and began killing and eating the inhabitants of the western shores. Morvidus went out to kill the dragon using all types of weapons, but in the end, was consumed by the beast also. Geoffrey referred to the dragon as a Belua, which *"gulped down the body of Morvidus as a big fish swallows a little one"*.

The Wawel dragon, also known as the Dragon of Kraków in writings by Wincenty Kadłubek from the twelfth century, lived in a cave under Wawel Hill in the early eighth century. Many attempts to kill the dragon were made because it would prey on the nearby livestock, but they were to no avail. Finally, a man named Krakus, who later became the monarch and namesake for the city, was able to poison him with sulfur.

From the Jacobus de Voragine's *Legenda Aurea* (or *The Golden Legend*), a collection of saints' lives from 1260 and later translated into English by William Caxton in 1483, comes the story of Saint George and the dragon. A modern version of the legend says:

> At the town of Silene, in Libya, there was a dragon, who was appeased by being fed two sheep a day; when these failed, the townsfolk offered by lot one of their young people. One day the lot fell on the King's daughter, who was led out to the sacrifice, dressed in her wedding gown. George appeared and transfixed the dragon with his spear and then using the Princess's girdle led the bemused dragon into the town, where it was beheaded. This occurred under the rule of the Roman Diocletian, in the fourth century A.D. St. George was reported to have slain his first dragon in Africa. Later, in 1098 A.D., he was said to have slain dragons at Mansfeld in the center of Germany. He was also reported to have killed a dragon in Berkshire, England, and the specific location was later named "Dragon Hill." Dragon Hill is, apparently, an artificial mound with a flat-top, not unlike Silbury Hill, to which clings the legend that it was on its summit that St. George slew the dragon. A bare patch of chalk upon which no grass will grow, is purported to be where the dragon's blood spilled.

In 1614 this report was published about a large reptile menacing St. Leonard's Forest in Sussex, near the village known as Dragon's Green.

> *"This serpent (or dragon as some call it) is reputed to be nine feete, or rather more, in length, and shaped almost in the form of an axletree of a cart: a quantitie of thickness in the middest, and somewhat smaller at both endes. The former part, which he shootes forth as a necke, is supposed to be an elle [3 ft 9 ins or 1 l4 cms] long; with a white ring, as it were, of scales about it. The scales along his back seem to be blackish, and so much as is discovered under his belie, appeareth to be red... it is likewise discovered to have large feete, but the eye may there be deceived, for some suppose that serpents have no feete ... [The dragon] rids away (as we call it) as fast as a man can run. His food [rabbits] is thought to be; for the most part, in a conie-warren, which he much frequents ...There are likewise upon either side of him discovered two great bunches so big as a large foote-ball, and (as some thinke) will in time grow to wings, but God, I hope, will (to defend the poor people in the neighbourhood) that he shall be destroyed before he grows to fledge."*

Saxo Grammaticus writes about the Danish King Frotho in his publication the *Gesta Danorum (Deeds of the Danes)* in which he describes his fight with Fafnir, a giant reptile. A man that knew the ways of the beast and wanting to aid the king in his endeavor, describes the serpent to the king:

> *"wreathed in coils, doubled in many a fold, and with a tail drawn out in whorls, shaking his manifold spirals and shedding venom . . . his slaver (salvia) burns up what it bespatters . . . remember to keep the dauntless temper of the mind; nor let the point of the jagged tooth trouble thee, nor the starkness of the beast, nor the venom . . . there is a place under his lowest belly whither thou mayst plunge the blade."*

Armed with this knowledge, the dragon slayer Sigurd digs a pit in the pathway he was known to take to drink water from the lake. He then lays in it under cover until the beast passes over top. At just the right time, Sigurd sprang in to action and dispatches it with his spear.

Ulysses Aldrovandrus, an Italian doctor and naturalist, wrote a book titled *Historia Animalium (History of Animals)* in which he wrote about a man named Baptista that had encountered a small dragon near Bologna, Italy on May 13, 1572. Having hissed at his oxen while passing by, he hit the dragon over the head with his walking stick and killed it. Ulysses' description matches that of a *Tanystropheus* dinosaur. He also provides two wooden engravings of a bipedal Ethiopian winged dragon carved from a specimen he received in 1551 AD. Androvandi thoroughly described the Ethiopian dragon as:

having two feet armed with claws, and two ears, with five prominent and conspicuous tubercles on the back. The whole was ornamented with green and dusky scales. Above, it bore wings fit for flight, and had a long, flexible tail, colored with yellowish scales, such as shone on the belly and throat. The mouth was provided with sharp teeth, the inferior part of the head, towards the ears, was even, the pupil of the eye black, with a tawny surrounding, and the nostrils were two in number, and open.

He elaborates on many other encounters and sightings as well in his book. He described the winged dragon seen in Pistorian territory called Cotone with claws like an eagle, covered in scales, gaping mouth with big teeth, and wings interwoven with sinews a cubit in length, and of considerable width. He tells of a dragon that came to Styria, Germany with feet like lizards and wings after the fashion of a bat, with an incurable bite. He also wrote of a winged dragon brought to King Francis of the Gauls who killed it with a mattock near Sanctones.

Stories have come out of Glamorgan, Whales as early as the 1900s of a colony of winged serpents that lived in the woods around Penllin Castle. An elderly man that lived there all the while talked of their manner of coiling when in repose and how their beautiful appearance *"looked as if they were covered with jewels of all sorts. Some of them had crests sparkling with all the colours of the rainbow"*. When disturbed they glided swiftly, *"sparkling all over,"* to their hiding places. When angry, they *"flew over people's heads, with outspread wings, bright, and sometimes with eyes too, like the feathers in a peacock's tail"*. He said it was *"no old story invented to frighten children"*, but a real fact. He remembered that his father and uncle had killed a couple of them for devastating his poultry. He attributed their extinction to the fact that they were *"terrors in the farmyards and coverts"*. Then there is the account of bright flying serpents described by Marie Trevelyan: "The woods around Penllin Castle, Glamorgan, had the reputation of being frequented by winged serpents, and these were the terror of old and young alike." It was said that they abode in a four-mile radius about the town. Some of the folks that saw these creatures had their names printed in the pamphlet such as John Steele, Christopher Holder, and a certain *"widow dwelling near Faygate."* A man a woman were killed when one spit its poisonous venom on them. One man walking his dogs along the road was attacked and got away as the dogs fought with the creatures and were also killed.

In the 1800s an author named Athanasius Kircher tells how Christopher Schorerum, a noble man wrote,

"a true history summarizing there all, for by that way, he was able to confirm the truth of the things experienced, and indeed the things truly seen by the eye, written in his own words: On a warm night in 1619, while contemplating the serenity of the heavens, I saw a shining dragon of great size in front of Mt. Pilatus, coming from the opposite side of the lake [or 'hollow'], a cave that is named Flue [Hogarth-near Lucerne] moving rapidly in an agitated way, seen flying across; It was of a large size, with a long tail, a long neck, a reptile's head, and ferocious gaping jaws. As it flew it was like iron struck in a forge when pressed together that scatters sparks. At first I thought it was a meteor from what I saw. But after I diligently observed it alone, I understood it was indeed a dragon from the motion of the limbs of the entire body. From the writings of a respected clergyman, in fact a dragon truly exists in nature it is amply established."

The book ***History of the Kings of Britain*** (c. 1136 A.D.) chronicles much historical information about the ancient region of Britain. It was written by a Welsh cleric, Goeffrey of Monmouth, who lived from approximately 1100-1155 A.D. If you proceed to chapter 15, you will find the following quote:

"Morvidus, a most cruel tyrant, after the conquest of the king of Morini, is devoured by a monster. For he commanded them to be brought to him one after another, that he might satisfy his cruelty in seeing them killed; and when he grew tired of this, he gave orders that they should be flayed alive and burned.

In his time a certain king of the Morini arrived with a great force in Northumberland, and began to destroy the country. But Morvidus, with all the strength of the kingdom, marched out against him, and fought him. In this battle he alone did more than the greatest part of this army, and after the victory, suffered none of the enemy to escape alive.

During these and other monstrous acts of cruelty, an accident happened which put a period to his wickedness. There came from the coasts of the Irish sea, a most cruel monster, that was continually devouring the people upon the sea-coasts. As soon as he heard of it, he ventured to go and encounter it alone; when he had in vain spent all his darts upon it, the monster rushed upon him, and with open jaws swallowed him up like a small fish."

Descendants of Javan [8,9,10]

From Javan origins came the Indo-European subcultures of the Greeks, Franks, Latins, Albans, British, Bavarians, Vandals, Saxons, Thuringians, Goths (Germans), Walagoths, Gepids, Burgundians, Langobards, and Armenians that came to rule in their territories.

Greece

Although Prof. Waddell has shown that Menes (Mins) had established the Minoan kingdom in Crete. It was done so usurping authority over the Javan colonies that were being settled at that time. The Greeks and Romans referred to ancient Greece as "Hellas". The Hebrews referred to Greece as Javan. The Greeks were the first to develop city-states along with democracy and political civilization, the Mycenaean civilization. The Greeks grew into a powerful and organized culture and so expanded and started conquering the lands about them and "Hellenizing" them, that is assimilating them into Greek culture and ideas under the command of Alexander the Great. The Greek language soon became the "lingua franca" throughout the world. The Greek alphabet is the basis for all these languages.

The Oracle of Delphi [1]

The Greek city of Delphi became important in about 800 BC for, amongst other things, it's "oracle", a priestess (or Pythia) of Apollo that the Greeks believed could give prophetic advice to those seeking direction for future campaigns or engagements. The most famous prophetic utterance the oracle gave was to Croesus, king of Lydia, who was about to go to war with Persia. She predicted the outcome would be in his favor. The Lydia Empire fell to the Persians quickly, and it was attributed to a misinterpretation by King Croesus due to his pride.

Homer [12]

In the eighth century BC, epic stories *The Iliad* and *The Odyssey* were written, historians believe, by a poet named Homer. They are cited as some of the oldest extant works of Western literature. The following is a summary of *The Iliad* and *The Odyssey*.

The Iliad

The Iliad tells the story of the conquests of King Agamemnon (king of Mycenae [or Argos]) and the conflicts with one of his greatest battalion leaders, Achilles. It begins when Paris, one of the sons of the King of Troy, takes Helen the wife of Menelaus, the brother of the King. King Agamemnon uses it as an excuse to come against Troy, a war that lasted for 10 years. Helen of Troy, as she is now referred to in history, is known as "he face that launched a thousand ships". An epic duel between Achilles and Hector, the renowned older brother of Paris, ensues when Hector kills Patroclus, Achilles' nephew, in a scrimmage outside Troy's fortress walls. Achilles kills Hector after an intense fight. After several lost battles, King Agamemnon sends a gift to the Trojans, a great wooden construct of a horse, as if conceding the conflict, which is taken into the city walls by the Trojans. That night, several men who were hiding in the horse sneak out and open the gates to the Greeks ready in waiting. Troy puts up a noble resistance but is defeated and the city burned. In the battle, Achilles is shot with an arrow in the tendon of his heel, which rendered him immobile and vulnerable. He was then easily killed. This event has led to the expression "that's his Achilles' heel", meaning someone's area of weakness or most vulnerable spot.

The Odyssey

The Odyssey tells the story of a Greek Hero, Odysseus, who is on a journey home after the 10 years of fighting in the Trojan War. He played a key role in the plot of the gift horse used to trick the Trojans and was famous for his quarrels with Achilles. The journey takes him over 10 years to reach Ithaca where he left his wife, Penelope, and son, Telemachus, before the war. Before Odysseus returns, Telemachus, who is 20 years old now, goes in search to discover the whereabouts of his father in Sparta. He learns from Helen of Troy (who has returned to Menelaus) the fate of his father, who has been captured and held prisoner on the Island of Ogygia by the nymph Calypso. Calypso, who has fallen in love with Odysseus, finally allows him to leave in a raft by sea after seven years. Odysseus ends up shipwrecked on a Phaeacian island called Scherie where he hears the songs and tales of the Trojan War. Hearing about himself in the songs they sang, he is prompted to reveal himself and tell the tales of his ventures to the inland residents. He begins to regale the audience with the piratical raid of Ismaaros as a captain aboard one of 12 ships in his party returning from Troy. He continued with the tale of his encounter with the Lotus-eaters who made two of his men to forget their homes, leading to their capture by the cyclops Polyphemus. Odysseus aided their escape by blinding Polyphemus with a wooden stake after which Odysseus was virtually lost at sea and unable to find his way back for 10 years due to unrelenting storms. His tales included the cannibalistic Laestrygonians, who destroyed all the ships in his fleet but his as he entered their harbor and the witch-goddess Circe who turned half of his men into swine after eating the cheese and wine she offered them. Odysseus was able to resist, having taken the potion given him by Hermes. Circe changed the men back when Odysseus agreed to stay with her, which he did for one year. Leaving that place, he sailed on to the world's end where he made sacrifices to the dead. His offerings earned him an audience with the spirits of the legendary figures of the past including Agamemnon, Achilles, and his own mother, who had died in the time he was gone for grief. She told him of the suitors vying for his presumed widow. He then sails to Ithaca encountering several beastly entities along the way including sirens, whom they bested with beeswax in their ears (Odysseus was tied to a mast to hear the songs, the six-headed monster Scylla, who killed six of his men, and the whirlpool Charybdis, where all that remained of his crew were drowned, leaving him the sole survivor. After landing on Ithaca he meets up with his son, Telemachus, who has just returned from Sparta. Together, they plot the death of the suitors. Odysseus at first pretends to be a beggar and is abused by the suitors, especially one Antinous. His dog, who was just a puppy when he left, recognizes him and gets so excited that he has a heart attack and falls down dead. Penelope decides to test the suitors by challenging them to string Odysseus's bow and shoot it through a dozen axe heads, saying that whomever can do so can have her hand, confident that all will fail. After all try and fail as expected, the beggar (Odysseus) steps up amongst the laughing and ridicule and succeeds! He then takes an arrow and shoots Antinous. Odysseus, his son, and other conspiring cohorts then annihilate the remaining suitors. Odysseus, Penelope, and Telemachus are united after all.

Homer credits the cause of the events in both these epic tales to the interventions and manipulations of the gods observing from **Mount Olympus**. Predominant in theses manipulations were **Zeus** (king of the gods), **Hera** (sister/wife of Zeus), **Athena** (goddess of wisdom), **Aphrodite** (goddess of love), **Hermes** (son of Zeus, the emissary or trickster who favors the mortals), **Apollo** (son of Zeus and an oracle god), **Thetis** (goddess of water and Achilles mother), and **Poseidon** (god of the sea). Much of Odysseus' hardships were caused by Poseidon, who kept him from returning home those 10 years by creating the storms that threw him off course.

In the paper "Was There a Trojan War" written by Archaeologist Manfred Korfmann, he states the following: [13]

The Setting of the *Iliad*

Homer took for granted that his audience knew a war had been fought for what was alternately called Ilios or Troy. The bard was mainly concerned with describing the wrath of Achilles and its consequences. He used Troy and the war as a poetic setting for a conflict between men and gods. From the archaeologist's point of view, however, the *Iliad* can be interpreted as a "setting" in an entirely different sense. One may see Homer or his informants as eyewitnesses to Troy and the landscape of Troy at the close of the eighth century B.C., the period when scholars generally agree Homer composed his epic.

There is nothing in the archaeological record to contradict the assertion that Troy and the surrounding countryside formed the setting for Homer's *Iliad* in 700 B.C.

Famous Greek Philosophers who still influence modern western culture [14]

Pythagoras of Samos (570-495 BC) – Mathematician. Developed the trigonometry Pythagorean Theorem ($C^2 = A^2 + B^2$).

Zeno of Elea (c. 490-430 BC) – Referred to as the father of debate.

Herodotus (c. 484-425 BC) – Greek Historian. Known as the "Father of History" Born in Halicarnassus in the Persian Empire (modern-day Bodrum, Turkey). He wrote *The Histories*. *The Histories* serves as a record of the ancient traditions, politics, geography, and clashes of various cultures that were known in Western Asia, Northern Africa, and Greece at that time. His writings included epic conflicts with dinosaurs.

Socrates (c. 469-399 BC) – Was a student of Zeno. Famous for the Socratic Method, which aims to critically discuss, argue, and dialogue to discover the truth. It is a dialectic method that consists of asking and answering question to stimulate critical thinking. This method is still used in legal arbitration by lawyers to this day. He was Plato's teacher.

Democritus (c. 460-370 BC) – Advocate for the principles of democracy, equality and liberty. Formulated the first hypotheses of atoms making up the physical universe. He promoted the idea that people should take up arms against tyrants.

Plato (428-327 BC) – The father of political science. Founded the Academy in Athens (first known higher education institute). He taught subjects in philosophy, ethics, religion, and mathematics. He instituted the Socratic Method in law. He was the author of *The Republic*, which described a Utopian society.

Aristotle (c. 384-322 BC) – Adhered to Socrates' and Plato's philosophies. He was the teacher of Alexander the Great. Studied and wrote extensively on subjects matters of science, ethics, government, physics, and politics. He was the first to classify animals.

India

Archeological evidence seems to indicate that before the Flood India had been a place of planned cities spread throughout the Indus valley. The culture was highly advanced with a sophisticated water supply and sanitation system that would not be matched in ingenuity again until the Roman Empire some 2,000 years later. This culture came to a sudden end with no clue as to what happened (archeologically) in 2500 BC, around the time of the Flood [15].

The roots of India, Aryan peoples coming out of Sumer, is also supported by overwhelming evidence. Dr. Waddell very clearly shows how all the king lists, pictographs, monument carvings, and artifacts are of Sumerian origins. Dr. Waddell also explains how many of the first listed kings of the Sumerian, Egyptian, Indus (Vedas), Minoan King Lists are actually the same persons [16].

In about 2300 BC the Aryans, a people group of Sumerian origin (children of Madai), settled in the Punjab region in Northern India, establishing the caste system based on social hierarchy. The highest castes are the Brahmans (priests), next are the Kshatriya (nobles and warriors), the Vaisya (craftsman and merchants), and last the Sudra (servants and laborers). They spoke a language known as Sanskrit. They developed a set of sacred poems called *The Vedas*, which are the roots of the Hindu religion. These poems are the most ancient scripts we have from the Indus Valley containing knowledge of the Aryan people, so this period is referred to as the Vedas Period. They continued to populate and expand southward reaching the River Ganges in about 800 BC. The Janes (clans) of India were ruled by a raja (king). By 500 BC the Mahajanapada (ruling city or capital) was Magadha ruled by the powerful Raja Bimbisara [15].

The Hindu religion is based on the Vedas and other Purana scripts. It was the prominent religion until about 500 BC, when a religious teacher named Siddhartha Guatama (who became known as

Buddha, the enlightened one) founded the Buddhist religion. Soon afterwards, another teacher, Mahavira, founded Jainism. Both religions rejected the Vedas as sacred script [15].

The Hindu *Matsya Purana* and Vedic *Satapatha Brahmana* dating from about 600 BC tells the story of the Antediluvian period, worship of the gods, Adam and Eve, long lives, and the great Flood, with the only survivors being Noah, his sons and their families. The slaying of dragons is also acclaimed in these ancient historical documents [17].

Famous persons of history document encounters with extraordinary beasts, dinosaurs in ancient India (pterosaurs and dragons) [7].

Alexander the Great – When Alexander threw some parts of India into a commotion and took possession of others, he encountered among many other animals a serpent that lived in a cavern and was regarded as sacred by the Indians who paid it great and superstitious reverence. Accordingly, Indians went to all lengths imploring Alexander to permit nobody to attack the serpent, and he assented to their wish. Now as the army passed by the cavern and caused a noise, the serpent was aware of it. (It has, you know, the sharpest hearing and the keenest sight of all animals.) And it hissed and snorted so violently that all were terrified and confounded. It was reported to measure 70 cubits, although it was not visible in all its length, for it only put its head out. At any rate, its eyes are said to have been the size of a large, round Macedonian shield. Aelianus, Claudius, On Animals, Book #XV, Chapter 19-23, c.210-230.

Philostratus was a Greek scholar that lived from AD 170-245. He wrote a book called *The Life of Apollonius of Tyana*. In the book, he mentions dragons quite a bit. In one section, he wrote:

> *"The whole of India is girt with dragons of enormous size; for not only the marshes are full of them, but the mountains as well, and there is not a single ridge without one. now the marsh kind are sluggish in their habits and are thirty cubits long, and they have no crest standing up on their heads, but in this respect resemble the she-dragons. their backs however are very black, with fewer scales on them than the other kinds".*

He also wrote, *"And the dragons along the foothills and the mountain crests make their way into the plains after their quarry, and get the better all round of those in the marshes; for indeed they reach a greater length, and move faster than the swiftest rivers, so that nothing escapes them. These actually have a crest, of moderate extent and height when they are young; but as they reach their full size, it grows with them and extends to a considerable height, at which time also they turn red and get serrated backs. This kind also have beards, and lift their necks on high, while their scales glitter like silver; and the pupils of their eyes consist of a fiery stone".*

Gaius Plinius Secundus (Pliny the Elder) (23 - 79 AD) was an army/navy commander in the Roman Empire. He was also known for being a naturalist, an author, and close friends with Vespasian, the emperor. After his travels though Africa and India he wrote this:

> *"Africa produces elephants, but it is India that produces the largest, as well as the dragon, who is perpetually at war with the elephant, and is itself of so enormous a size, as easily to envelop the elephants with its folds, and encircle them in its coils. The contest is equally fatal to both; the*

elephant, vanquished, falls to the earth, and by its weight crushes the dragon which is entwined around it.

The sagacity which every animal exhibits in its own behalf is wonderful, but in these it is remarkably so. The dragon has much difficulty in climbing up to so great a height, and therefore, watching the road, which bears marks of their footsteps, when going to feed, it darts down upon them from a lofty tree. The elephant knows that it is quite unable to struggle against the folds of the serpent, and so seeks for trees or rocks against which to rub itself.

The dragon is on its guard against this, and tries to prevent it, by first of all confining the legs of the elephant with the folds of its tail; while the elephant, on the other hand, tries to disengage itself with its trunk. The dragon, however, thrusts its head into its nostrils, and thus, at the same moment, stops the breath, and wounds the most tender parts. When it is met unexpectedly, the dragon raises itself up, faces its opponent, and flies more especially at the eyes; this is the reason why elephants are so often found blind, and worn to a skeleton with hunger and misery."

"The blood of the elephant, it is said, is remarkably cold; for which reason, in the parching heats of summer, it is sought by the dragon with remarkable avidity. It lies, therefore, coiled up and concealed in the river, in wait for the elephants when they come to drink; upon which it darts out, fastens itself around the trunk, and then fixes its teeth behind the ear, that being the only place which the elephant cannot protect with the trunk. The dragons, it is said, are of such vast size that they can swallow the whole of the blood; consequently the elephant, being drained of its blood, falls to the earth exhausted; while the dragon, intoxicated with the draught, is crushed beneath it, and so shares its fate."

Pliny was also author of the thirty-seven volume *Natural History*. It tells of a dragon killed on Vatican Hill during the reign of Emperor Claudius who died in 54 AD. The body of a child was found in the beast. Pliny the Elder also recorded uses for dragons' teeth and the fat of dragons' heart. He describes ointments made from dried dragons' eyes and honey, and other such remedies.

REFERENCES

Biblical References from: The Holy Bible (1913). King James Version. Chicago, Ill. John A. Dickson Publishing Co.

1   J.A. Guile (2000). History of the Britons. Cambridge, ON. In Parentheses Publications. Retrieved from http://www.yorku.ca/inpar/nennius_giles.pdf

2   Cooper, Bill. The table of nations. Retrieved from http://www.biblebelievers.org.au/natindx.htm#Index

3   Breeden, D. Ph.D, (2011). *The adventures of Beowulf.* Seattle, WA: CreateSpace Independent Publishing Platform.

4   Thompson-Seton, Ernest, (1899). *The biography of a grizzly.* New York, NY: D. Appleton Century Company.

5   Freedman, L. (2015). Associated Press. Duo revisits Wahb the grizzly bear. Retrieved from http://www.washingtontimes.com/news/2015/nov/26/duo-revisits-wahb-the-grizzly-bear/?page=all

6   Creation Wiki. Fire breathing dragon. Retrieved from http://creationwiki.org/Fire_breathing_dragon#cite_note-Gish-24

7   History's Evidence of Dinosaurs and Men. Retrieved from http://historysevidenceofdinosaursandmen.weebly.com/written.html

8   Bible History. Greece and biblical archeology. Retrieved from http://www.bible-history.com/archaeology/greece/

9   Ancient Greece. History. Retrieved from http://www.ancientgreece.com/s/History/

10 C. Zimmer (2015). The New York Times. DNA deciphers roots of modern Europeans. Retrieved From http://www.nytimes.com/2015/06/16/science/dna-deciphers-roots-of-modern-europeans.html?_r=0

11 Ancient History Encyclopedia. Delphi. Retrieved from http://www.ancient.eu/delphi/

12 Homer, Samuel Butler (Translator), Michael Dirda (Introduction) (2008). Iliad and the Odyssey. Barnes and Noble Collectible Edition.

13 Korfmann, M. (2004). Was there a Trojan war? Retrieved from http://archive.archaeology.org/0405/etc/troy.html

14 Enkivillage. Famous Greek philosophers. Retrieved from http://www.enkivillage.com/famous-greek-philosophers.html

15 Wolf, A. (2008). *A short history of the world: The story of mankind from prehistory to the modern day.* New York, NY: Metro Books by arrangement with Arcturus Publishing Limited.

16 Waddell, L.A. (1930). Egyptian civilization: Its Sumer origins & real chronology. Retrieved from http://www.thechristianidentityforum.net/downloads/Egyptian-Chronology.pdf

17 Ancient Origins. Reconstructing the story of humanity's past. Retrieved from http://www.ancient-origins.net/human-origins-religions/startling-similarity-between-hindu-flood-legend-manu-and-biblical-020318

PART 6

Descendants of Shem

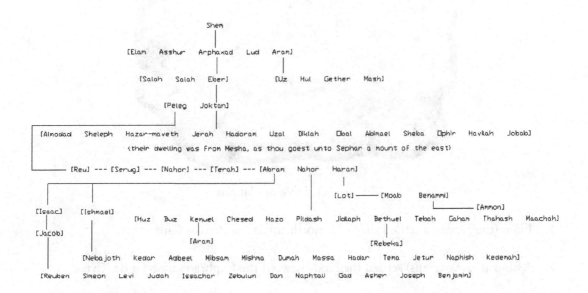

The Five Semitic Nations [1]:

Figure 6.1 Table of Nations

1. Elam (the Persians) settled the lands northeast of the Persian Gulf.

2. Asshur (the Assyrians) settled the land between the Euphrates and Tigris Rivers.

3. Arphaxad (the Babylonians) settled the land in Chaldea.

4. Lud (the Lydians) settled in Asia Minor and northern Africa.

5. Aram (the Syrians) settled the land north and east of Israel.

From the beginning, God chose to keep close relations with the generations of a particular line of people that would ultimately become known as the "chosen people". These were the Hebrews, who became the Israelites (or Jews) after the campaign to conquer the people of Canaan (their promised land). The Hebrew culture gets its name from Abram (whose name God changed to Abraham) of whom God promised would become the "father of many nations" and would have a seed of his offspring be the promised Messiah. The language spoken by the Israelite linage from the time of Babel to this day is the Hebrew language. God chose these people and spoke directly to them so they would be aware of their responsibility to the truth and accuracy of their writings and communications to the world. The Hebrews were used as a vehicle to maintain a connection (life line) to humanity within the most unique and prominent display of miracles that no other culture can lay claim to, as confirmation of His Word at every eventful moment in His Story. The congruency of God's character, physical acts and miracles, doctrinal statutes, and prophecies within the word of God over a span of 6,000 years is a sure witness of the maintenance wrought by the ever-watchful eye of the Lord of all the earth [2].

The Old Testament in today's Christian Bible is the written account and history (His Story) of that relationship and the physical and spiritual interfacing of God's activity within his creation cared for by a people who were keenly aware of its value to humanity. The Hebrew scribes were known for their meticulous scripting efforts, knowing that their predecessors captured the truth and word of God in those inherited parchments. They were cognizant of the fact that God had a plan for their lives and therefore gave the Israelites laws to live by to keep them aware of these cultural guide posts and pillars of the faith. These transcribing efforts were always under the watchful eye of God and their peers for accuracy [3]. Within this framework of understanding they were maintaining the accuracy of their scribal efforts and so hoping for the very eminent manifestation of the Messiah or savior that was promised from the beginning of time by the spoken testimony of God. These promises and prophecies are unique to the Hebrew lineage and as such are defended with the utmost passion as it sets them apart from all other cultures in the world. Just as God was able to create the world for his purposes and plans, he is well able to preserve his word as one of many vehicles he uses to accomplish those plans. The Word of God is much like the personification of God in Christ Jesus, he was a man and yet he was God. You can see both the efforts of man and the grace and sovereignty of God in the Word of God. It was the hand of man that wrote the text, but it was the spirit of God that inspired the man. The accuracy of the word of God in the physical aspect is self-evident at this point in our review of science and history, which in turn validates the spiritual and prophetic nature of God's word as well (e.g., the foresight of Noah to build a boat before the Flood came, the physically unexplainable Babel event, the genome complexity, the Exodus events, and not to mention the prophesies foretelling of the coming of Christ thousands of years before, the miracles of giving sight to the blind and raising of the dead, and resurrection of Jesus that was seen by hundreds and attested to in the New Testament by firsthand witnesses that changed the world). All the books of the Bible are congruent in their theology, continuity, and truths. In every translation of the word of God to every known language, God is not slack to watch over and preserve his word and ensure that the word is delivered to us in the current vernacular (e.g., plain everyday use of English, Arabic, Chinese, etc.). The essence of what he wants us to know about himself, ourselves, and his plans for us and the world today and to come are in his word. If you are a born-again believer and the spirit of God lives in you, then you can know his word. Read it, simply believe it and obey it, and he will manifest himself to you as he promised. There is no doubt copying errors are found in the word of God (thus it testifies to the human characteristics of the word); however, there is no divine communication errors to be found in the word, and so it is inerrant in that respect. When the Dead Sea scrolls were discovered and translated from a period (300 BC) and culture (a Hebrew sect known as the Essenes) with notable morphological differences, the translations matched congruently with insignificant copying errors when comparing it to the King James Version we have today. God preserves his word to all generations and people as he promised [4].

Psalms 19:7: The law of the LORD is perfect, converting the soul: the testimony of the LORD is sure, making wise the simple.

Mark 10:15: Verily I say unto you, whosoever shall not receive the kingdom of God as a little child, he shall not enter therein.

John 14:21: He that hath my commandments, and keepeth them, he it is that loveth me: and he that loveth me shall be loved of my Father, and I will love him, and **will manifest myself to him**.

1 Cor 2:13: Which things also we speak, not in the words which man's wisdom teacheth, but which **the Holy Ghost teacheth**; comparing spiritual things with spiritual.

Col 3:16: Let the word of Christ dwell in you richly in all wisdom; teaching and admonishing one another in psalms and hymns and spiritual songs, singing with grace in your hearts to the Lord.

Heb 8:11: And they shall not teach every man his neighbour, and every man his brother, saying, know the Lord: for **all shall know me**, from the least to the greatest.

1 John 2:27: But the anointing which ye have received of him abideth in you, and **ye need not that any man teach you**: but as **the same anointing teacheth you of all things, and is truth, and is no lie,** and even as it hath taught you, ye shall abide in him.

Biblical chronology with parallel patterns of evidence matching archeological chronology

Secular humanists are not going to accept the straightforward evidence supporting the biblical chronology at any point of issue. They will vigorously fight for every inch out of their prejudice, regardless of how many points of unique paralleling patterns of evidence or artifacts are discovered.

Biblical chronology mismatching archeological chronology has been the basis for secular humanistic arguments regarding the authenticity of biblical history since the dawn of the archeological sciences. In their ignorance, they initially concluded that all of the Old Testament (OT) history and much of the New Testament (NT) was just a fairytale with no archeological backing either way. Time has proven that assumption wrong in multiple instances. Some examples include NT cities of Capernaum, Chorazin, and Bethsaida being called a myth but yet are now well-established realities, the previous mythical empires of Assyria and Nineveh being discovered in 1840 by Henry Layard, and of course the mysterious elusive reality of the Hittite empire that was eventually discovered in 1905. It is only reasonable to assume all of it is true and accurate. They still ardently argue against most of the evidence while ignoring the overt clues and pattern of evidence of existing archeological sites and claim that it yet is still a myth. They do not acknowledge the overall precedent setting patterns of time and discovery, such as the fact that 95% of all discoveries fit well within biblical history. As in all other sciences, you must base your conclusions on the weight of the evidence. The humanist is quick to discount the majority (the 95%) for the exception (the <5%) without true critical evaluation. I continue to hear the same old adage repeated time after time — the Bible is just a myth, there has never been any archeological discoveries that align with its stories — pointing archeologist claims of incongruent dating and missing evidence, ignoring the numerous events that have a pattern of evidence in the archeological discoveries. Just because evidence of an event does not yet exist doesn't mean the event never happened. Hundreds of supporting bits of evidence of events formally classified as myths have been discovered in paralleling sequence and patterns for most of the heavier weighted matters in the biblical chronology. These include events such as the Global Flood, Noah and sons (and by association the Ark), Babel, Sodom and Gomorrah, the Exodus, and much of the lineage of King David. These discoveries lend credence to the less weighty and yet undiscovered matters.

Archeologists have initially established collaborating dating methods based on artifact grouping, C^4 dating, tree ring dating, and astronomy. Artifact grouping takes artifacts of similar typology and identifies a general period they are associated with within a particular culture and key historical figures or known events along a common order of morphology. C^4 dating and tree ring dating (which uses C^4 dating within its science), as previously reviewed, have been found to be in gross error when used as a quantitative tool before 1000 BC. Therefore, they have to be considered useless in dating ancient artifacts and strata eras quantifiably, as is commonly done with archeologists these days, based on unknown environmental conditions and the strength of magnetosphere as seen from the combined empirical data for the past 150 years and archaeomagnetic data for the past 6,000 years. A perfect example of this was reviewed previously with the discovery of Ötzi the Ice man where the initial artifact dating placed the man in about 2000 BC. After later testing with C^4, they adjusted the date to between 3300-3000BC (1,000 to 1,300 years difference). The Mungo Woman and Mungo Man debacle are two more classic examples of these unreliable dating methods. Testing laboratories readily admit that if the results of C^4 testing do not agree with their presuppositions that they are rejected (about 50% of the results). Rejecting test results without knowing the cause is tantamount to operating in the blind, just a guessing game. On that basis alone, C^4 testing must be viewed as an unreliable testing method. It is certainly not an absolute science as it is being propagated by the humanistic vanguard. The following is a disclaimer from the BETA Testing Laboratory [5]:

> Labs ask clients on the expected age of the radiocarbon dating samples submitted to make sure that cross-contamination is avoided during sample processing and that no sample of substantial age (more than 10,000 years) must follow modern ones.

> Interpretation of radiocarbon dating results is not straightforward, and there are times when archaeologists deem the carbon 14 dating results "archaeologically unacceptable." In this case, the archaeologist rejected the radiocarbon dating results upon evaluation of the chronology of the excavation site.

The errors and flaws within this system are becoming more and more apparent from the more we study the dating methods. Egyptology ideally tries to date the sequence of strata based on the Egyptian King Lists and the periods the pharaohs reigned, as much as can be determined from ancient scripts and artifact grouping, C^4 dating, tree ring dating, and astrological phenomena [6]. Egyptology has its own set of issues as the pharaohs sometimes had parallel reigns due to warring factions, only recognizing certain persons as heirs, and so on. There are discrepancies between the many King's lists concerning length of reigns, sequences, and nonconformities; therefore the further back in time, the greater the margin of error — to several hundred years in some cases [7].

The use of Egyptological dating outside of the Egyptian chronicles is now contrasting the archeological evidence that is being discovered every year. With the many active archeological dig sites in Egypt and Palestine, discoveries are being made showing patterns of evidence that match biblical chronologies in unique ways. The artifacts and relics are being found in parallel patterns with biblical accounts but in conflict with the established eras of geographical strata (which appear to be based on Egyptological dating but are consistently off by 200 to 350 years with biblical chronology). This has shed light on the significant errors of these dating methods. We will be reviewing evidence and dig sites that echo the biblical accounts in its many unique aspects but found to be out of sync with the Egyptological time periods. The site archeologists will attest to the findings, but in most cases, refuse to associate them with biblical chronology solely on the basis of their Egyptological dating methods, as they are bound to their humanistic prejudice. When confronted with the obvious and asked if they would consider reviewing and adjusting the dates they all unanimously reply, "I will not have anything to do with this matter". These highly reputable archeologists are willing to accept that these patterns of evidence, that perfectly match and parallel the biblical accounts, are not related to the biblical chronologies simply because of their commitment to discredit the Bible based on their Humanistic theology. Hence, every argument in science and public debate is based on that point of reference, the "expert's opinion" [8]. This whole matter has now moved into the realm of the ridiculous, especially when the truth cannot be any more obvious.

There is one bright spot in the midst of this debacle, an archeologist and Egyptologist by the name of David Rohl. Although an Agnostic, Rohl has not been blinded by humanistic theology and very early in his career began to see the parallel patterns in historic evidence and biblical chronology. Looking into the Egyptological dating methods that were set upon over 200 years ago, he has found what appears to be multiple errors in the identification of key figures and events that were associated with known periods upon which much of the sequential periods were compiled.

An article in the Lions and Lambs Ministries summarizes it thusly [7]:

> Rohl concludes that the Third Intermediate Period is "artificially over extended." He argues that it should be shortened by 141 years because of parallel dynasties. He then presents a convincing case for lengthening the Second Intermediate Period by 219 years.

> These and other adjustments result in a shift of 345 years for the beginning of the 19th Dynasty, from 1295 BC in the traditional chronology to 950 BC in the New Chronology. (See the "Close-up Chart" below.) This is a very significant shift because the third pharaoh of the 19th Dynasty was Ramesses II. This means Ramesses ceases to be the pharaoh of the Exodus and becomes, instead, the pharaoh who sacked the Jerusalem Temple in 925 BC.

> But how can this be when the Bible specifically states that the pharaoh who plundered the Temple was named Shishak (1 Kings 14:25-26 and 2 Chronicles 12:2-9)? Traditionally, this name has been identified with Pharaoh Shoshenk I, the founder of the 22nd Dynasty. But in one of the most fascinating chapters of the book, Rohl shows that pharaoh's had both regional names and nicknames (called hypocoristicons). The royal name of Ramesses II was Usermaatre-Setepenre Ramessu-Meryamnn. But his hypocoristicon was Sisah, which transliterated into Hebrew, becomes Shishak. Further, Rohl proves that Shoshenk's military campaign into Israel never touched Jerusalem whereas the records of Ramesses' campaign specifically states that he plundered Shalem the ancient name of Jerusalem.

One adjustment that Rohl makes affects the time of the Exodus, moving it from the 1250 BC period to the 1450 BC period. Additionally, he concluded that Israel's time in Egypt was only 215 years based on earlier versions of the Torah and references from Josephus and not the 430 years it was thought to have been.

We shall now look at the history of Israel starting with the Abrahamic lineage and the collaborating patterns of evidence considering these relatively new Egyptological dates from David Rohl and other indicators.

The Call of Abraham

God inspired Abram's father to move from Shinar (Mesopotamia) to Canaan in about 1960 BC where he revealed his plan for his life and descendants. God changed his name from Abram to Abraham meaning the "father of many nations".

Gen 11:28: And Haran died before his father Terah in the land of his nativity, in Ur of the Chaldees (Mesopotamia).

Gen 11:31: And Terah took Abram his son, and Lot the son of Haran his son's son, and Sarai his daughter in law, his son Abram's wife; and they went forth with them from Ur of the Chaldees, to go into the land of Canaan; and they came unto Haran, and dwelt there.

Gen 15:7: And he said unto him, I am the LORD that brought thee out of Ur of the Chaldees, to give thee this land to inherit it.

Gen 17:7: And I will establish my covenant between me and thee and thy seed after thee in their generations for an everlasting covenant, to be a God unto thee, and to thy seed after thee.

Gen 17:5: Neither shall thy name any more be called Abram, but thy name shall be Abraham; for a father of many nations have I made thee.

Gen 22:18: And in thy seed shall all the nations of the earth be blessed; because thou hast obeyed my voice.

Abraham was 75 years old when he came into Canaan and became the tribal leader of his people group or clan. He became very wealthy and commanded a large area with hundreds of peoples; however, he continue to live a nomadic life style, living in tents and moving about as he was led by God and never made any effort to build a city or permanent structures. Abraham had a very unique relationship with God in that God would talk to him audibly and even face-to-face, slowly revealing to him his destiny and that of his offspring. These destinies included places he would live during his life time, the eventual slavery in Egypt, and ultimately inheriting the land of Palestine, along with the promise of the coming Messiah from his seed. Abraham being cognizant of these things, and surely directed by the Lord, would have naturally started journaling these events in order to capture them and to pass these revelations, hopes, traditions, and promises onto his children to whom these promises belonged. It would have been natural for Abraham to appoint a scribe to begin to record his dictations and significant historical events, as writing on stone tablets in those days took a skilled artisan. The scribe would have naturally written them in the third person as a neutral observer.

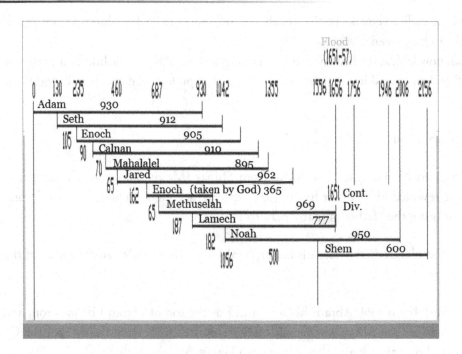

Figure 6.2 Patriarch lineage from Adam to Shem

Abraham was privy to the antediluvian stories as well as the events since then, such as the acts of Nimrod, the Tower of Babel, and the birth of the nations. He started out as a young boy living near Shinar, and whether from orators reading from tablets or stories told to him by his relatives, he would be intimately familiar with these stories as they were a part of the lives of all the people of those times. He may have even sat at the feet of Shem or Noah, who was still alive and living in Shinar at the time of his youth. These stories would have been the first to be captured in his journals and certainly every spoken word of God thereafter. Communication between cities and families in those days commonly depended on emissaries, runners, or travelers that ventured about the lands, communities, and cities. A person of Abraham's stature would have maintained diplomatic relationships with his neighbors, having emissaries coming and going to supply him with intelligence. He was especially keen to know what was going on in Sodom and Gomorrah out of concern for his nephew Lot. In the case where the runner came to him to inform him of the fate of the cities of the plain and Lot along with them, he immediately chased after them, over taking them and subduing them with only 300 men, obviously a very skilled commander who knew he had God's favor. There is no doubt that he would have gleaned as much information from them as possible. For self–preservation alone, he would have wanted to know where they came from, what cities they destroyed, who their kings were, and so on to know what to expect in response from their countrymen over these circumstances. It is obvious that Abraham was the central figure and recipient of the knowledge of these events and therefore the author of these first of biblical records. Again, Abraham (as any human being would after having met God face to face) was cognizant of the importance of these records and the teachings that he received from his ancestors and God, and so he passed them onto Isaac, who would have passed them on to Jacob (whom God called Israel). It would be a fair assumption that by the time Joseph received all the children of Israel in Egypt, who had all the scribes of Egypt at his disposal, that he would have them transcribed onto the latest and highest quality papyrus medium available at the time. Joseph, being the highest official in Egypt under the pharaoh, had a great estate where he was very well guarded. The elders of Israel would have maintained the parchments after Joseph's death to eventually come into Moses's possession when he came to deliver them from Egypt, recognizing the hand of God that was on him.

Sodom and Gomorrah

Abraham was about 99 years old and living in Canaan (about 1936 BC) when the Lord and two angels appeared to Abraham for a face–to–face meeting. The Lord revealed to Abraham that Sarah would be having a child after having been barren for so long. The Lord affirmed that this child would inherit the promises of God and that his lineage would inherit the land of Canaan. Also, the Lord informed Abraham of the coming doom he planned for the cities of the plain. The Lord then sent his angels on to Sodom to rescue Lot, Abraham's nephew, from the judgment brought on by the depravity of the people he lived amongst.

Gen 10:19: And the border of the Canaanites was from Sidon, as thou comest to Gerar, unto Gaza; as thou goest, unto Sodom, and Gomorrah, and Admah, and Zeboim, even unto Lasha.

Gen 13:10: And Lot lifted up his eyes, and beheld all the plain of Jordan, that it was well watered everywhere, before the LORD destroyed Sodom and Gomorrah, even as the garden of the LORD, like the land of Egypt, as thou comest unto Zoar.

Gen 13:11: Then Lot chose him all the plain of Jordan; and Lot journeyed east: and they separated themselves the one from the other.

Gen 13:12: Abram dwelled in the land of Canaan, and Lot dwelled in the cities of the plain, and pitched his tent toward Sodom.

Gen 13:13: But the men of Sodom were wicked and sinners before the LORD exceedingly.

Gen 13:18: Then Abram removed his tent, and came and dwelt in the plain of Mamre, which is in Hebron, and built there an altar unto the LORD.

Gen 18:1: And the LORD appeared unto him in the plains of Mamre: and he sat in the tent door in the heat of the day;

Gen 18:2: And he lift up his eyes and looked, and, lo, three men stood by him: and when he saw them, he ran to meet them from the tent door, and bowed himself toward the ground,

Gen 18:3: And said, My Lord, if now I have found favour in thy sight, pass not away, I pray thee, from thy servant:

Gen 18:20: And the LORD said, because the cry of Sodom and Gomorrah is great, and because their sin is very grievous;

Gen 18:22: And the men turned their faces from thence, and went toward Sodom: but Abraham stood yet before the LORD.

Gen 18:26: And the LORD said, if I find in Sodom fifty righteous within the city, then I will spare all the place for their sakes.

Gen 19:1: And there came two angels to Sodom at even; and Lot sat in the gate of Sodom: and Lot seeing them rose up to meet them; and he bowed himself with his face toward the ground;

Gen 19:4: But before they lay down, the men of the city, even the men of Sodom, compassed the house round, both old and young, all the people from every quarter:

Gen 19:13: For we will destroy this place, because the cry of them is waxen great before the face of the LORD; and the LORD hath sent us to destroy it.

Gen 19:15: And when the morning arose, then the angels hastened Lot, saying, arise, take thy wife, and thy two daughters, which are here; lest thou be consumed in the iniquity of the city.

Gen 19:17: And it came to pass, when they had brought them forth abroad, that he said, escape for thy life; look not behind thee, neither stay thou in all the plain; escape to the mountain, lest thou be consumed.

Gen 19:18: And Lot said unto them, Oh, not so, my Lord:

Gen 19:19: Behold now, thy servant hath found grace in thy sight, and thou hast magnified thy mercy, which thou hast shewed unto me in saving my life; and I cannot escape to the mountain, lest some evil take me, and I die:

Gen 19:20: Behold now, this city is near to flee unto, and it is a little one: Oh, let me escape thither, (is it not a little one?) and my soul shall live.

Gen 19:21: And he said unto him, See, I have accepted thee concerning this thing also, that I will not overthrow this city, for the which thou hast spoken.

Gen 19:22: Haste thee, escape thither; for I cannot do any thing till thou be come thither. Therefore the name of the city was called Zoar.

Gen 19:23: The sun was risen upon the earth when Lot entered into Zoar.

Gen 19:24: Then the LORD rained upon Sodom and upon Gomorrah brimstone and fire from the LORD out of heaven;

Gen 19:25: And he overthrew those cities, and all the plain, and all the inhabitants of the cities, and that which grew upon the ground.

Gen 19:26: But his wife looked back from behind him, and she became a pillar of salt.

Gen 19:28: And he (Abraham) looked toward Sodom and Gomorrah, and toward all the land of the plain, and beheld, and, lo, the smoke of the country went up as the smoke of a furnace.

Gen 19:29: And it came to pass, when God destroyed the cities of the plain, that God remembered Abraham, and sent Lot out of the midst of the overthrow, when he overthrew the cities in which Lot dwelt.

The key points in these scriptures that should have parallel patterns of evidence in any archeological discoveries are as follows: "all the plain of Jordan...was well watered everywhere", "Lot sat in the gate of Sodom", "escape to the mountain", "Lot entered into Zoar", "Then the LORD rained upon Sodom and upon Gomorrah brimstone and fire", "overthrew those cities, and all the plain", and "he (Abraham) looked toward Sodom and Gomorrah, and toward all the land of the plain, and beheld, and, lo, the smoke of the country went up as the smoke of a furnace".

There are two major sites that lay claim to the location of this event that have similar archeological signage [9,10]. One is to the north of the Dead Sea where the river Jordan divides the Jordan Valley, and the other to the south of the Dead Sea known for its slime pits. Both sites make a good argument having parallel patterns of evidence, they both were fertile valleys, both had similar gated fortified cities, and both came to a fiery destructive end; however, the destruction of these sites date to different times based on secular dating methods (C^4/Egyptological). The southern site was dated to about 2350 BC whilst the northern site to the end of the MB age, a 500-year difference.

Before the discovery of the ancient city of Alba with its archival library and the sixth century Madaba Map, the story of Sodom and Gomorrah was said to be pure myth.

The five cities of the plain that included Sodom and Gomorrah were located where they could be viewed by Abraham from the mountains on the west side of the Dead Sea. With the aid of a sixth century map of the Holy Land discovered on the floor of a church in Madaba (which identified the ancient city of Zoar where Lot fled to for a safe haven before the event started) the cities of both of these sites to the north and south of the Dead Sea were rediscovered and excavated. The south site also referenced the aid of an Alba geographic map dating from about 2300 BC. The patterns of evidence within these excavations echoed the events of the Bible in concise detail. The north site's secular date falls within the date range for the estimated time determined from the biblical clues. The South site's secular date falls in the Antediluvian period and therefore would have been destroyed in the Flood. All the cities in both sites appeared to be destroyed by fire as they laid under a layer of ash. The city of Zoar continued to be mentioned elsewhere in the Bible and external references from Hellenistic sources to the middle ages. Sodom is in close proximity to the mountains where the angels told him to flee at the first. Both plains were found to be very fertile valleys in those days, according to paleobotany studies. "Most common were barley, wheat, grapes, figs, lentils and flax. Less common were chickpeas, peas, broad beans, dates and olives". Tall el-Hammam in the north and Bab edh-Dhra in the south jockey for the claim to be the historical Sodom as they were the largest of the cities in their perspective valleys and well-fortified with impressive main gates where Lot first received the angels [9,10].

Arguments for the North Site [11].

Gen 13:3: And he went on his journeys from the south even to Bethel, unto the place where his tent had been at the beginning, between Bethel and Hai;

Gen 13:7: And there was a strife between the herdmen of Abram's cattle and the herdmen of Lot's cattle: and the Canaanite and the Perizzite dwelled then in the land.

Gen 13:11: Then Lot chose him all the plain of Jordan; and Lot journeyed east: and they separated themselves the one from the other.

The Bible tells us that Abraham initially dwelt in Bethel near the Canaanites and Perizzites in the plain of Jordan. The Perizzites' dwellings were further identified as being relatively close to Judah and Ephraim (Joshua 11:3 17:14-18) where the children of Joseph (Manasseh and Ephraim) initially abode west of the "Mountain Country of Ephraim" and needed to confront the Canaanites and Perizzites in the valley beyond the mountains to the east (the Jordan Valley by proxy) to expand their territory. The north, west, and south were already occupied about the hill country of Ephraim by Manasseh (N), Ephraim (W), and Benjamin (S). That places the initial site north of the Dead Sea. Lot chose to go east from that place, which would have led him to the east of the Jordan Valley, north of the Dead Sea, and just west of the Tall el-Hammam site. Steven Collins, the leading archeologist at the Tall el-Hammam (his city of Sodom) dig site, places the strata at about the middle of the MBA II (~ 1700 BC) period. This appears to be based on Egyptological dating, which is consistently off by 200 years compared to biblical chronology. Adjusting his date by 200 years would put the approximate time within the margins of our biblical timeline (which is within the 5% margin of error range [BTR]) for the 99-year-old Abraham (1936 BC) [BTR = 2033 - 1839].

Collins has hypothesized that the fiery destructive end could have resulted from an ancient 'airburst', a mid-air explosion caused by an object in the air above the 'target' area, such as that of an incoming meteor.

Ge:13:18: Then Abram removed his tent (from where He and Lot departed company), and came and dwelt in the plain of Mamre, which is in Hebron, and built there an altar unto the LORD.

Hebron is on the west side of the Dead Sea about midway of the north and south sites, while Mamre is just north of Hebron. Prior to the "fire and brimstone" end of the cities of the plain, Babylonian armies from Mesopotamia (Amraphel, king of Shinar; Arioch, king of Ellasar; Chedorlaomer, king of Elam and Tidal king of nations) came to recover the nations throughout Palestine from rebelling against their rule. They came upon the city of Ham from the northeast and then continued westward. After many successful campaigns against major cities throughout the region as far north as Kiriathaim, above the Sea of Galilee and then making their way as far south as Mount Seir, they turned back north. They eventually arrived in the country of the Amorites on the south end of the Dead Sea and defeated them. The five kings of the cities of the plain (Bera, king of Sodom; and with Birsha, king of Gomorrah, Shinab, king of Admah; and Shemeber, king of Zeboiim; and the king of Bela, which is Zoar) chose to go on the offense rather than hold up in their fortified city walls subjecting their cities to the ills of war. This was a reasonable tactical move, as they would have had more strength in numbers. They would have marched down the eastern seaboard by the way of Zoar, using the mountains as cover in an attempt to come upon them unawares where they joined the battle in the Vale of Siddim on the south end of the Dead Sea. The Palestinian kings were defeated. Some turned to flee, some were trapped in the slime pits, and others fled to the mountains.

Gen 14:10: And the vale of Siddim was full of slime pits and the kings of Sodom and Gomorrah fled, and fell there; and they that remained fled to the mountain.

That these kings would flee and be trapped by slime pits (a natural petroleum product similar to asphalt) rather than fleeing to their own walled cities gives one the impression that they were some distance from their homes in unfamiliar territory. That the rest of the men fled to the mountains rather than their own cities reinforces that notion as well.

Location of Zoar

The Madaba Map shows Zoar at what appears to be south of the Dead Sea; however, Steve Collins argues that the map of the Dead Sea is only showing the north deep basin of the sea (evidence of a historical low level at that time) and that would place Zoar closer to the north site, just south of the Arnon River, about 27 miles from Sodom. This is a reasonable deduction because Zoar was listed with the five cities of the plain of Jordan.

Additionally, there is no reason to believe that the Vale of Siddim has any connection with the Jordan Valley. The fact that the Vale of Siddim has slime pits (Ge:14:10) positively identifies it as the southern plain of the Dead Sea. The Bible clearly distinguishes the two valleys and positively states that five cities of the plain were in the Jordan Valley (Ge:13:11, 12), and that the battle took place in the Vale of Siddim (Ge:14:3, 8). Nowhere does the biblical account give any hint or clue that we should assume that the locations of the slime pits and the location of the cities were in the same valley, but that seems to be where many proponents for the southern site make the connection, using the slime pits as a clue to which valley the cities were located. There is nothing in the scripture to prohibit the movement of their armies to do battle away from their cities, but quite the contrary, they "**went out**" of their cities. Sodom was about 30 miles from Zoar (less than one day's march) where they could rest, regroup, and launch from that base camp to their tactical advantage. The Vale of Siddim was only 20 miles from Zoar (half a day's march), which is well within range for a battle of this magnitude and circumstance.

Furthermore, the Babylonians' last campaign was with the Amorites on the south end of the Dead Sea just west of the Vale of Siddim. For the Palestinians to meet them in the Vale of Siddim on the south end of the Dead Sea to do battle makes perfect sense.

Figure 6.3 Madaba Map showing the city of Zoar and possibly Sodom and Gomorrah

Furthermore, the tribes of Moab and Ammon, the sons of Lot from his daughters, appear to have expanded outward (north and south) from the mountainous region and central location of the Arnon River where the City of Zoar is believed to have been. This is precisely where the Bible tells us Lot fled to after leaving Zoar.

The Bab edh-Dhra excavation is an Early Bronze age site on the southern site, which places it in the Antediluvian period. This site would have been a ruin in the Vale of Siddim at the time of the Siddim Battle.

Despite the fact that no evidence making a direct link between the archeological evidence and the biblical account (names of the cities, the names of the kings, etc.) has been discovered, and despite the critics' negative reviews that ignore the overt clues, the events of the Sodom and Gomorrah story in the Bible have significant unique parallels with the discoveries made at the north site, e.g., the time (about 1936 to 1839 BC considering errors now obvious with the dating methods) and place of the event (Jordon Valley), the fortified cities with gated entrants, the fertile valleys, and the fiery end to all the cities in the valley at the same time except Zoar. Supporting evidence from the artifacts found in the city of Alba include the naming of two of the major cities of the plain, (Sodom and Admah) and the sixth century Madaba Map showing the location of Zoar (and possibly Sodom and Gomorrah). These give significant credence to the story [9]. There are just too many congruent facts and parallel patterns of evidence to be a made-up story. Someone from the time of these events knew these points of fact and recorded them, most likely Abraham.

The Birth of the Nation of Israel [8]

Genesis records the events that led to Israel's migration into Egypt, their time there as slaves to the Egyptians as was foretold by God to Abraham, their exodus from Egypt, and their conquest of the lands that God promised to Abraham and his descendants in Palestine.

Archeological discoveries in Avaris in the city of Ramses (formally known as Goshen) in Egypt has turned up some of the most amazing findings and unique points of fact that perfectly parallel the chronological events and descriptions of the Israelites in Egypt.

The Bible tells of how Joseph, son of Jacob (Israel) was sold as a slave into Egypt by his brothers and through the providence of God (being able to interpret the dreams of the Pharaoh of a coming drought) became the highest official in Egypt just under the Pharaoh. Approximately 70 peoples of Israel migrated into Egypt in about 1745 (BTR 1832-1657) according to Exodus 1:5. After Joseph's death, a new Pharaoh arose that did not know Joseph and forced Israel into slavery for 215 years. Four generations later, God raised up Moses as a deliverer to lead Israel out of Egypt into the promised lands in about 1535 (BTR 1612-1458). Through many incredible miracles including the 10 plagues of Egypt, the parting of the Red Sea, being sustained on manna in the wilderness for 40 years, being healed from the bites of fiery serpents, and many others, Moses brought them to the Promised Land. Moses first camped at Mount Sinai where God gave him the Ten Commandments, the blueprints for the Ark of the Covenant, and the tabernacle, and the laws that the Israelites were to live by as his chosen people.

The archeological excavation site at Avaris has discovered a community laid out on virgin soil in the area that was formally known in antiquity as Goshen. This community contained a high official's estate, sporting a mansion with 12 pillars and about 70 to 100 other houses similar in build as those of Haran in Mesopotamian where Abraham was originally from. In the back of the mansion was found 12 tombs, 11 of which had skeletons laid on their side as a Palestinian would be buried, as opposed to an Egyptian who would be buried on his back facing up. The twelfth tomb was in a style that is normally reserved for Egyptian royalty, except that this person was not Egyptian, suggesting that he was regarded with the highest esteem by the pharaoh. This particular tomb was empty; however, it was found with a great statue of the person of whom the tomb was built for. He is described as a Palestinian due to his hair style and throw stick across his shoulder. Additionally, he is wearing a coat of many colors.

These patterns of evidence parallel the biblical account in all respects, from the 70 original souls that came into Egypt, the 12 sons of Israel matching the 12 pillars and the 12 tombs about the mansion, the description of the exceptional royal tomb built for a Palestinian with the statue of what appears most ardently to be Joseph with his coat of many colors that was given to him by Jacob before he was sold into slavery, to the tomb being empty at the request of Joseph when they left Israel to be buried with his father in the field of Machpelah.

Figure 6.4 Statute of Joseph

Furthermore, patterns of evidence discovered at the site in Avaris that parallel the biblical account of the children of Israel living in Goshen, especially the slaughter of the babies at the time of the birth of Moses, include:

A. the period of residence in Egypt from the 1600s to 1400s BC;

B. Kahun, homes of the Egyptian slaves, where wooden boxes were found under the floors of many of the houses containing the skeletons of sometimes several babies only months old;

C. homes abandoned quickly, apparent as tools and other belongings dropped on the floor and left behind;

D. the mortality rate of the children - the 3/2 ratio of the women to men at the time;

E. the Brooklyn Papyrus, a list of names of slaves (mostly names of Hebrews or women);

F. remains of sheep and goats that are not of Egyptian culture but certainly Palestinian culture;

G. pottery and tools, especially brass tools from the region of Palestine; and

H. the Channel of Joseph dating to the time period of the occupation of the Semites in Goshen (Avaris) and still in use today.

From an article in reference to David Rohl's new dates [7]

> For example, according to the New Chronology, the pharaoh of the Exodus becomes Dudimose at the end of the 13th Dynasty. The history of Egypt written by the High Priest Manetho in the Third Century BC contains this remarkable observation: "In his reign [Dudimose], for what cause I know not, a blast of God smote us…"

> Could this be a reference to the plagues of Moses? Excavations dated to the revised time of Dudimose (mid-1400's BC) reveal "plague pits" where hundreds of bodies were thrown one on top of the other.

The 10 Plagues of Egypt [8]

For Moses to deliver the children of Israel from under the hand of Pharaoh, God had to persuade the Pharaoh by bringing ten plagues upon the land of Egypt. This event was a judgment for their cruelty toward Israel and the decadence of the Egyptians, and was a foreshadowing of things to come to the kingdoms of the regions around Palestine. These fantastic events were heard of by all in the ancient world and proceeded the Israelites, striking fear in the hearts of their enemies as they began the conquest of the lands of Canaan. The last plague that finally convinced the Pharaoh to let the people go was the death of all the first born throughout the land of Egypt. God sent a destroying angel to execute this final judgment but established an exception for the children of Israel if they were to smear lamb's blood over the doorposts, in which case the destroying angel would "pass over" the house and all inside the house would be safe. The Passover from then on was to be an annual ceremony to remind the children of Israel of the mercy of God and ingrain it in their minds so they would recognize and understand the salvation of God through the shed blood of the coming Christ. The blood of Christ cleanses us of our sins and God's judgment passes over us if we accept the work of the cross.

Evidence of these plagues and great events leading up to the Exodus of the children of Israel are confirmed by the following external sources:

A. the Ipuwer Papyrus (dated to 1400s BC) - The writings of an Egyptian official to the Pharaoh describing many of the plagues of Egypt congruent with the plagues described in the Bible;

B. the mass graves of the Egyptians at this time; and

C. the writings of Manetho (third century BC Egyptian historian/ pagan high priest) regarding King Thutmose II, also known as Djhutmose (reign 1493-1479bc/18th dynasty), the devastation of Egypt, and the invading hoards that filled the vacuum left behind by the Exodus.

Evidence of the Conquests of Israel.

The biblical account of the conquests of Israel

Jos 12:1: Now these are the kings of the land, which the children of Israel smote, and possessed their land on the other side Jordan toward the rising of the sun, from the river Arnon unto mount Hermon, and all the plain on the east:

Jos 12:2: Sihon king of the Amorites, who dwelt in Heshbon, and ruled from Aroer, which is upon the bank of the river Arnon, and from the middle of the river, and from half Gilead, even unto the river Jabbok, which is the border of the children of Ammon;

Jos 12:3: And from the plain to the sea of Chinneroth on the east, and unto the sea of the plain, even the salt sea on the east, the way to Beth-jeshimoth; and from the south, under Ashdoth-pisgah:

Jos 12:4: And the coast of Og king of Bashan, which was of the remnant of the giants, that dwelt at Ashtaroth and at Edrei,

Jos 12:5: And reigned in mount Hermon, and in Salcah, and in all Bashan, unto the border of the Geshurites and the Maachathites, and half Gilead, the border of Sihon king of Heshbon.

Jos 12:6: Them did Moses the servant of the LORD and the children of Israel smite: and Moses the servant of the LORD gave it for a possession unto the Reubenites, and the Gadites, and the half tribe of Manasseh.

Jos 12:7: And these are the kings of the country which Joshua and the children of Israel smote on this side Jordan on the west, from Baal-gad in the valley of Lebanon even unto the mount Halak, that goeth up to Seir; which Joshua gave unto the tribes of Israel for a possession according to their divisions;

Jos 12:8: In the mountains, and in the valleys, and in the plains, and in the springs, and in the wilderness, and in the south country; the Hittites, the Amorites, and the Canaanites, the Perizzites, the Hivites, and the Jebusites:

Jos 12:9: The king of Jericho, one; the king of Ai, which is beside Bethel, one;

Jos 12:10: The king of Jerusalem, one; the king of Hebron, one;

Jos 12:11: The king of Jarmuth, one; the king of Lachish, one;

Jos 12:12: The king of Eglon, one; the king of Gezer, one;

Jos 12:13: The king of Debir, one; the king of Geder, one;

Jos 12:14: The king of Hormah, one; the king of Arad, one;

Jos: 12:15: The king of Libnah, one; the king of Adullam, one;

Jos 12:16: The king of Makkedah, one; the king of Bethel, one;

Jos 12:17: The king of Tappuah, one; the king of Hepher, one;

Jos 12:18: The king of Aphek, one; the king of Lasharon, one;

Jos 12:19: The king of Madon, one; the king of Hazor, one;

Jos 12:20: The king of Shimron-meron, one; the king of Achshaph, one;

Jos 12:21: The king of Taanach, one; the king of Megiddo, one;

Jos 12:22: The king of Kedesh, one; the king of Jokneam of Carmel, one;

Jos 12:23: The king of Dor in the coast of Dor, one; the king of the nations of Gilgal, one;

Jos 12:24: The king of Tirzah, one: all the kings thirty and one.

Moses hands off the leadership to Joshua and dies before Israel crosses the Jordan to conquer the inhabitants, God's instrument of choice to execute judgment on the people living in decadence and defiance of God's lordship.

The ruins of Jericho, the first city that Joshua defeated entering the Promised Land, echo the biblical account very accurately with the destruction of the walls and the burning of the city in about 1400BC. One unique fact that stays congruent with the biblical account are the walls of the city. The walls of Jericho were rubble about the entire city except one portion of the wall believed to have been the abode of Rahab, who is in the genealogy of Christ and who helped the Israelites, as her home was on the wall. According the biblical account, the two spies escaped through her window and were lowered down outside of the city walls. She was protected by God and the people of God during the siege. Additionally, the ruins were under a layer of ash as expected with Joshua burning the city to the ground [2].

Figure 6.5 Ruins of Jericho

The ruins of Hazor, the third city that Joshua defeated entering into the Promised Land, echo the Bible's account very accurately with the destruction of the walls and the burning of the cities around the same time as Jericho. The king of Hazor (Jabin) was killed by Joshua. There were writings found in the ruins of Hazor where the text clearly stated that the name of the king of Hazor was Jabin [3].

Initially, Jericho and Hazor were considered to not have been destroyed by the Israelites due to the dates of their demise being about 200 years earlier than the Exodus event (their estimated time of 1250 BC). David Rohl's adjustment to the Egyptological dating now places the destruction of Jericho and Hazor right in the time range of that period of Israel's history (BTR 1565 - 1416). Refusing to align these cities and events with the biblical account, with all its many overt and direct clues and its congruent points of fact is outright biased and is only held to for the sake of the humanist religion. Truth, fact, scientific deduction and pure common sense are right out the window.

There are two lists that mention Israel as a political entity, the "Merenptah Stela" (1210 BC) and an Egyptian text of Ramesses II, pharaoh of Egypt (reign 1279-1213BC). The Merenptah Stela lists Israel as a defeated foe, which testifies to the fact that they were a well-established political entity at the time of his reign in 1200s BC. Israel's name on the Ramesses II text establishes the fact that they could not have just come out of Egypt in the Exodus event at that time, and also reinforces the fifteenth century date ranges [4].

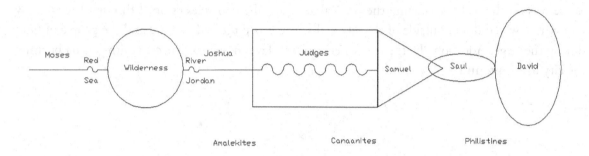

Figure 6.6 Israel's Early Years

The author of the Exodus writings had to have had firsthand knowledge of the events, given the intimate and numerous details of these events as collaborated by archeological finds at numerous digs. Anyone living before the fall and destruction of these cities may have been acquainted with these places and kings but would not have been able to predict the manner, sequence, specific details, or time of their fall with such accuracy as given in the biblical account and collaborated in the archeological discoveries. Anyone living after the fall and destruction of these cities (especially 1,000 years after as many opponents of the Bible would like to claim) would not have access to details recorded in the biblical account, such as the specific names of the cities, the kings of those cities, or the manner, sequence, or time of their fall, as they were but rubble and ruins with no plaques posted to explain what had happened at those places. There are just too many congruent facts to be a made-up story. Someone from the time of these events knew these details and recorded them. Up to 200 years ago, the humanists proclaimed that these places and events were just made up stories, myths. After 200 years of archeological discovery, many of the places and events have been verified; however, the periods or timelines of these events are in dispute based on the chronologies and dating methods used to determine the periods and times as set forth by renowned archeologists resting heavily on Egyptian chronology. On one hand, you have a perfect match in the archeological record with the names, sequence, and magnitude of events as set forth in the Bible. On the other hand, you have the time periods established by scientists leaning heavily on Egyptian calendars and C^4 testing not matching up. Common sense would obviously place the error with the dating methodology. Again, only someone with firsthand knowledge could have recorded the minutia of these events; there is just too many congruent facts! What an amazing coincidence it would be for events specified in the Bible to have happened in a different age, by a different people, to the exact details. And not just one incident, but dozens, over and over, with their overt clues congruent with their biblical accounts (e.g., the Sodom and Gomorrah judgment, the Hebrew/Egyptian occupation, the Exodus, and the fall of Jericho and Hazor), especially when all these events are chronologically out of sync by about the same time (200 years). Additionally, the mathematical odds (*conditional probability*) of so many events with numerous details matching so closely overwhelmingly places these matchups in the >1/2 plausible category, as assessed by the principles of statistics. With little doubt, the first five books of the Bible were authored by Abraham, Moses and Joshua!

The writings of Genesis were very likely recorded and available to Moses in order for Moses to have such accurate genealogy and account of extraordinary events up to his own time, as he was called of God to communicate God's Word to the world. He was a prophet, a man of integrity and reputation, and certainly would not have taken liberties to just make up these stories, nor did he need to. Moses was in a face–to–face relationship with God as Abraham was. Indeed, the patterns of evidence in all the sciences, geology, and archeology align in an astounding manner (95 percentile) for these stories to have been fabricated. Looking at the timeline, Noah was only one generation from Adam and was alive during Abraham's life time. Abraham abode in Haran before he moved on to Canaan at God's direction and could have had contact with Noah (and/or his sons and their wives), who most definitely had firsthand knowledge of the times and conditions before the Flood and the stories of creation, that again, would have only been one generation removed from Noah, whose fathers would have known Adam directly as well as having firsthand knowledge of Adam's stories. Nevertheless, the overwhelming evidence leans to the distinct possibility that Abraham had these written chronicles and had them passed down to eventually come into Moses's possession. The first accounts of creation would have been conveyed to Adam by God to explain where he and his world came from, his purpose, and God's plan for his creation. The lack of extant writings does not conclude that there were no written records (as some opponents are quick to conclude). The Hebrew were meticulous about their scripts (recording, copying, and preserving). With all the wars and destruction of antiquity, much has been lost along with the sands of time. It can only have been the hand of God that preserved what we do have in the Bible to this day to such accuracy, copies of the originals preserving the original writings as a natural course of literary history. To point to some less than five percent coping errors (CE) is absurd in the face of the >95% accuracy of God's word. The human body incurs CE with every generation, but it is fully functional. We do not discard the body because of these CE's, and for the most part do not even detect them until you get into the minute details of the DNA. To portray the Bible as untrustworthy because of <5% CE does so in defiance of all sociological and scientific protocol. Court judgments are made based on the congruency of the testimonies with disregard to the minor incongruences; engineering material stresses are established based on the consistent test results with the major highs and lows discarded due to flaws in the material; prescription medicines are sold on the market as safe, even though in some cases patients have experienced harmful reactions and even death; car wrecks due to mechanical defects are the cause of thousands of deaths every year, but we still drive without a thought of it. The Bible tells us in 2Tm2:15, "Study to shew thyself approved unto God, a workman that needeth not to be ashamed, rightly dividing the word of truth" and to proceed on the basic principle of letting every word be established by two or three witnesses (Mt:18:16, 2Co:13:1, 1Tm:5:19, Heb:10:28). We have at our disposal several translations (KJV, NIV, NAS) with several Hebrew, Greek, and Latin sources as well (Hebrew Scripture, Septuagint, Samarian, Codex Vaticanus, Vulgate) to use when studying and working out the minor conflicting issues in the word, which are all available on the internet these days. For the most part, the Word of God is in the vernacular of the language one speaks and is straightforward so that you only need your common sense and the Holy Spirit to understand the "milk" of the Word. There are several levels or depths to the meanings and understanding of the Word that God can reveal to us through study and teachers of the Word; what is referred to as the "meat" of the Word. The deeper revelations will never contradict the initial simple meaning of the precept; it will never end up meaning just the opposite or inverse of the basic concept as many cultic leaders tend to teach. God says in his word he will teach us line upon line, precept upon precept. There is the "milk" of the Word, which are the "first principles of the oracles of God"; and then comes "meat" of the Word, the deeper theological understandings (Heb 5:12, 13).

Keys to Determining Biblical Generations, Events, and Time of Creation

The Bible gives specific times, generations, and landmark events from the creation of Adam down to the birth of Christ. Developing a timeline can be worked out if diligent in your research. The key to determining the time of major events in the Bible is to find a key event that can be reasonably verified somewhere along that timeline to start with, and then work up or down the timeline based on the definitive ages found throughout certain passages given in the Bible. This author has chosen to start with the reign of King David. This event is close enough in time to have a good amount of supporting archeological evidence and is just within the period where C^4 dating can be used as a quantitative method with some reasonable bit of confidence. As previously discussed in Part 1, historical dates yielded by the C^4 dating method earlier than 1000 BC include an ever-increasing margin of error due to unknown environmental conditions. Use of C^4 dating should only be used as a qualitative dating method for artifacts dated earlier than 2000 BC (artifacts less than 60,000 years old). Dates determined before 1000 BC should be adjusted based on the chart given in Part 1.

Archaeologist David Rohl has just recently discovered that artifacts known as The Amarna Letters are directly linked to the person of King David. Collaboration between the biblical account, which was the first known mention of King David, the Amarna Letters, the archaeology finds of Philistia, and the references to the "House of David" within several texts discovered in ancient Inscriptions from the mid 800 BC has well established King David as a historical figure in Israeli history [15].

Most historians place the start of King David's reign at about 1000 BC. (Both secular historians and Bible scholars appear to agree on this). The archaeological evidence backed by C^4 dating that collaborates this period and the person of King David include:

A) A stone tablet from Jordan discovered in 1868 that references "The House of David". The stone was dated to 840 BC, 160 years after David's reign. It was written by a Moabite king named Mesha [16].

B) The "Khorbit Doub", as referred to by the local Bedouin, which means the "ruins of David". It has been confirmed to be of Hebrew habitants at about the time of David (1020 -980 BC based on C^4 dating). The Hebrew name for it is "Khirbet Qeiyafa", which is translated as "Fortress of Elah". This is found on the frontlines of the Philistia ruins where the Valley of Elah separates them. This is the valley where David fought with Goliath. Buildings, cultural artifacts, and historical geography are being found constantly that collaborate the biblical account. The Fortress of Elah is referred to in the Bible as Sha'Araym, "the city of two gates", in Samuel 17. This is the place where the Philistines fled after David killed Goliath [16].

C) The Tel Dan inscription on a stone found in northern Israel discovered in 1993 that references "the house of David". The stone was dated to 800 BC, 200 years after David's reign. It was written in Aramaic and speaks of a king that boasted of the defeat of two kings of Israel. The script does not reveal who the kings of this story were, but based on the time and description of events it is believed the Aramaic king was Hazael of Damascus that killed several thousand Israelites under Jehoram, king of Israel, and Ahaziah, king of Judah (1Kings 19:15, 2Kings:8 - 9) [17].

David Rohl has made some recent discoveries in the body of the "The Amarna Letters"[5]. Ancient documents, cuneiform tablets written primarily in Akkadian, written as correspondence between the pharaoh and other surrounding kingdoms originally dating from 1350 - 1380 were discovered in a building in the ruins of the city of Amarna. There are about 380 of these "Amarna Letters" believed to have been written under the reign of Pharaoh Akhenaten.

There were no connections made to Israel, originally due to the conventional dating of the period in which Pharaoh Akhenaten reigned; however, the new period reassign after David Rohl's adjustments places them in the period of Saul, David, and Solomon. Searches made in these letters have turned up numerous references that parallel the biblical texts. One such reference is the mention of the Habiru (Hebrew) that went around pillaging the country side, paralleling the activity, places, and times that David's band of discontents were living in the caves and touring around the country side hiring themselves out as mercenaries. The site also relates the following [7]:

> Rohl's second discovery was a series of letters written by a King Labayu of the hill country north of Jerusalem. His name means "Great Lion of Yaweh." Rohl believes this was the true name of King Saul and that Saul was his hypocoristic name (nickname). Rohl reviews the letters in detail to show that they describe events that parallel incidents during the reign of Saul.

> These remarkable letters some by Saul and some by his son, Ish-bosheth (2 Samuel 2:8), contain references to Ayab (Joab, commander of David's forces) and also to Benenima, Dadua, and Yishuya. Rohl concludes from what is said in the letters that Benenima is Baanah, one of Israel's tribal chieftains who later assassinates Ish-bosheth (2 Samuel 4). He concludes that Dadua is David and that Yishuya is David's father, Jesse (Yishay in Hebrew). The evidence he presents in behalf of these conclusions is fascinating and convincing.

David Rohl explains the shift in the Egyptological dating, and at one point sets forward a 1350 date to 1012, which in turn re-dates the Amarna letters from the 1350 date to 1012. This is exactly around the time of King Saul and David. There are excerpts in the Amarna letters that exactly parallel the stories in 1st Samuel in regard to Saul and David, Saul's son Jonathan, and how Jonathan would often conspire with David, much to Saul's dismay, as David was Saul's adversary at that time. The story goes on to relate how Saul and Jonathan both died together the same day on Mount Gilboa. Additionally, it talks about how the inhabitants of Palestine were beseeching the king of Egypt to help them fight against the Habiru (the Hebrew) when Saul was made King and began to do battle with the enemies of Israel.

The following references from the Bible give an approximate account of the years between key events. Starting from 1000 BC with the key event of King David's inauguration, we can work backwards to the times of the preceding events, adding up the years to determine the approximate time of creation.

A 5% margin of error may be accepted as the ages did not include months or days, the use of "about" by Paul when referring to the period of the Judges, some time of Joshua not accounted for, and best guess for David's inauguration. These unknowns force us to assess time periods in ranges rather than exact dates.

Gen 21:5: Abraham was **100** years old when Isaac was born.

Gen 25:26: Isaac was **60** years old when Jacob was born.

Gen 47:28: Jacob was **130** years old when he went into Egypt.

Total = 290 years

Determining the time of the children of Israel in Egypt. There are several verses that seem to conflict as to the exact length of time from when Jacob and the children of Israel went into Egypt to when the Exodus occurred. Following the principles of God's word that says to "let every word be established by 2 or 3 witnesses" (Mt 18:16, 2Co 13:1, 1Tm 5:19, Heb 10:28), this author has concluded that there is a copying error that must be addressed first. In **Ex 12:40:** "Now the sojourning of the children of Israel, who dwelt in Egypt, was four hundred and thirty **(430)** years" given in the King James Bible derived from the Hebrew Bible. Both the Septuagint and the Samaritan OT text infer that instead it should read "from the time Abraham came into Canaan to the Exodus was 430 years".

Ex 12:40: The Septuagint scripture reads, and the sojourning of the children of Israel, while they sojourned in the land of Mizraim{gr.Egypt} and the land of Canaan{gr.Chanaan}, [was] four hundred and thirty years.

Ex 12:40: The Samaritan scripture reads, 'Now the sojourning of the children of Israel, and of their fathers in the land of Canaan and in the land of Egypt, was four hundred and thirty years.

Gen 12:4: So Abram departed, as the LORD had spoken unto him; and Lot went with him: and Abram was seventy and five years old when he departed out of Haran.

Paul, Josephus, and David Rohl appear to agree with this interpretation.

Paul in Gal 3:16: Now to Abraham and his seed were the promises made. He saith not, and to seeds, as of many; but as of one, and to thy seed, which is Christ.

Gal 3:17: And this I say, that the covenant, that was confirmed before of God in Christ, the law, which was four hundred and thirty years after, cannot disannul, that it should make the promise of none effect.

Josephus, in his *Antiquities of the Jews* (Chapter XV:2) puts it this way: "They left Egypt in the month of Xanthiens, on the fifteenth day of the lunar month; four hundred and thirty years after our forefather Abraham came into Canaan, but two hundred and fifteen years only after Jacob removed into Egypt."

So, it is well established by *five* witnesses (versus the *one*) that the time should better be accepted as Abraham's coming into Canaan at 75 years old. If you subtract the 290 years previously determined from the 430, you come up with 140 years, then add Abraham's age of 75 years, and it comes to 215 years they were in Egypt. Furthermore, in **Gen 15:16**, the Lord states that they would be in Egypt for (4) generations. In **Exod 6:14-25** you can deduce exactly four generations from Levi to Moses (Levi/Kohath/Amram/Moses). The average generation from Selah to Abraham is roughly 36 years (36 yrs. x 4 Gen. = 140 yrs.); Taking Moses generation out as he was 80 when they came out of Egypt and dividing the three remaining generations you come up with 45 years/Gen ([215-80/3). This is far more reasonable than 116yrs/Gen ([430-80]/3).

And finally, in **Acts 13:18-22:** 18 And about the time of forty **(40)** years suffered he (Moses) their manners in the wilderness. 19 And when he had destroyed seven nations in the land of Canaan, he divided their land to them by lot **(5? years)**. 20 And after that he gave unto them judges about the space of four hundred and fifty **(450)** years, until Samuel the prophet. 21 And afterward they desired a king: and God gave unto them Saul the son of Cis, a man of the tribe of Benjamin, by the space of forty **(40)** years. 22 And when he had removed him, he raised up unto them David to be their king; to whom also he gave testimony, and said, I have found David the son of Jesse, a man after mine own heart, which shall fulfill all my will.

Judges of Israel				Total Years	451					
Mesapot.	Othniel	Moab	Ehud	Shamgar	Deborah	Midian	Gideon	Abimelech	Tola	Jair
8	40	18	80	1	40	7	40	3	23	22
1490	1482	1442	1424	1344	1343	1303	1296	1256	1253	1230
Philistines	Jephthah	Ibzan	Elon	Abdon	Philistines	Samson	Eli	Samuel	Saul	David
18	6	7	10	8	?40?	20	40	60	40	40
1208	1190	1184	1177	1167	1159	1159	1139	1099	1039	999

Figure 6.7 Judges of Israel

Of note is the period of the Philistines' rule in Israel and Samson and Eli's ministries under that rule.

Judg 13:1: And the children of Israel did evil again in the sight of the LORD; and the LORD delivered them into the hand of the Philistines forty years.

Judg 13:5: For, lo, thou shalt conceive, and bear a son; and no razor shall come on his head: for the child shall be a Nazarite unto God from the womb: and he shall begin to deliver Israel out of the hand of the Philistines.

Judg 15:20: And he (Samson) judged Israel in the days of the Philistines twenty years.

The account does not tell when Samson was born, whether before or after the rule of the

Philistines began, or where during the forty-year rule of the Philistines Samson's 20 years as judge fits in. We only know he was going to "begin the battle", that his full term was under their rule, and that they were still ruling when he died. Eli was a priest and may have been in office during some period of Samson's term as well. The Bible does not say "after Samson God raised up Eli to Judge Israel" as it did for many of the other judges. During some point in Eli's term, Israel came out from under the Philistines' rule, because at the time that they went to war against the Philistines at the end of Eli's term, Israel had a standing army. Eli and the story of Samuel's birth were introduced in the chronology at the same time. Samuel was with Eli through his childhood, approximately 17-20 years. The length of time for Samuel's judging Israel is not given in the Bible; however, it infers that it was for a significant period. Given that he was subordinate to Eli for about 17-20 years and that he was still alive for the start of Saul's term, approximately 10-12 years, that would be 27 years accounted for, leaving a maximum of approximately 60 years in the interim, as Samuel was 98 when he died. If that is right, then the period for the judges would be somewhere in the neighborhood of 451 years. Paul used the term "about" 450 years".

The timeline beginning with David's reign and accounting for all the time back to Abraham is 1035 years total and places the birth of Abraham at about 2040 BC (w/ ± 5% margin of error - Biblical Time Range (BTR) within 2142 to 1938 BC).

Biblical Time line	Abraham	Isaac	Jacob	Egypt	Desert	Joshua	Judges	Saul	David
Age at Birth	100	60	130	215	40	5	450	40	0
Time BC	2040	1940	1880	1750	1535	1495	1490	1040	1000

Figure 6.8 Patriarch lineage from Abraham to David

Manetho, a priest to Pharaoh Ptolemy in the third century BC, and Josephus, a Jewish historian from the first century AD, both place the Exodus at 1552 BC, which falls within an acceptable margin of error (1%) with the literal chronology this author used from the King James Bible. Historians of antiquity had access to records and documents extant in their day that we do not have for references.

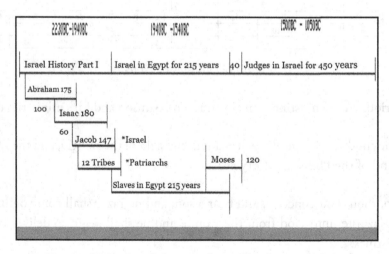

Figure 6.9 Patriarch lineage from Abraham to Moses

The fathers' age at which each of the patriarchs were born in the lineage of Christ, from Shem to Abram, are given in Genesis 5:32 and Genesis 11:10-26. From the time of Abraham to Shem was 390 years. Shem was born in 2430 BC (BTR 2552 - 2309). The biblical author of these passages noted that in the time of Peleg the earth was divided. Scholars believe that this is a reference to Babel. Peleg was probably the family matriarch at the time and so was the one named in association with the event, as opposed to Selah, Eber, Reu, or Serug, who also would have been alive then. As people were living close to 200 years in those days, he would have been in his prime at the age of 76.

Biblical Patriarch	Shem	Arphaxad	Selah	Eber	Peleg	Reu	Serug	Babel	Nahor	Terah	Abram
Ages at Birth	0	100	35	30	34	30	32	Peleg's Age	30	29	70
Years in Time	0	100	135	165	199	229	261	76	291	320	390
Year BC	2430	2330	2295	2265	2231	2201	2169	2155	2139	2110	2040

Figure 6.10 Patriarch lineage from Shem to Abraham

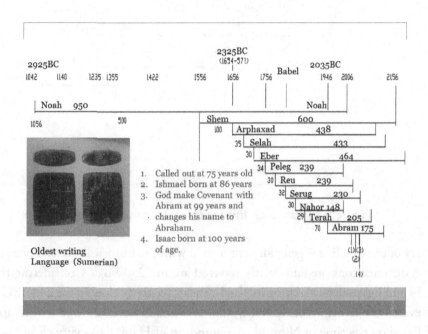

Figure 6.11 Patriarch lineage from Noah to Abraham

The fathers' ages at which each of the patriarchs were born in the lineage of Christ from Adam to Shem are given in Genesis 5. From the time of Adam to Shem was 1,556 years. Adam was created along with all creation in approximately 3989 BC (BTR 4188 - 3790). The Flood occurred 100 years after the birth of Shem in 2330 BC (BTR 2447 - 2214).

Biblical Patriarch	Adam	Seth	Enoch	Cainan	Mahalalel	Jared	Enoch	Methuselah	Lamech	Noah	Shem	Flood
Ages at Birth	0	130	105	90	70	65	162	65	187	182	500	100
Years in Time	0	130	235	325	395	460	622	687	874	1056	1556	1656
Year BC	3986	3856	3751	3661	3591	3526	3364	3299	3112	2930	2430	2330

Figure 6.12 Patriarch lineage from Adam to the flood

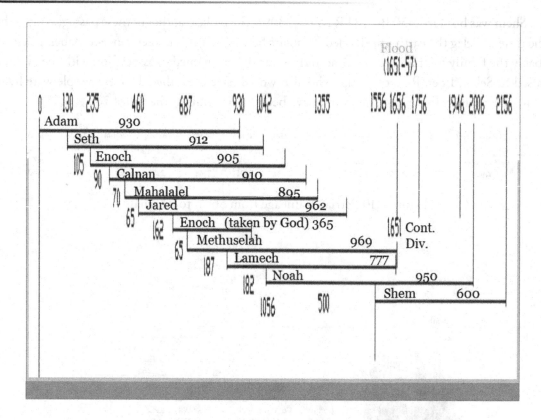

Figure 6.13 Patriarch lineage from Adam to the Shem

The accuracy of the timeline is generally confirmed with the historical events reviewed up to this part. The Flood demarcations predominantly wavered around 2500 BC. Considering the margin of errors in the C14 and Egyptological dating methods, that is relatively close to the 2447 BC upper target range for this event. The Babel event, which would have had to have followed within approximately 3 generations based on the time of Nimrod, the grandson of Ham, has a very close margin of error with the archeological discoveries and historical records of the start of the main cultures of the world at between 2350 and 2047 BC. The exodus of the Israelites from Egypt in 1535 BC, as collaborated by Josephus and Manetho, are well within the 5% margin. Given the ambiguous dating methods we have today, any margin of error being within 10% after 1000BC should be considered an acceptable level of congruency. Most of the major events appear to be within ±5% margin of error based on the body of evidence, such as the Flood date between 2500 and 2209, the Babel event between 2350 and 2047, and the Exodus between 1612 and 1458.

Israeli and Judean Kingdoms

After the period of the Judges, Israel and Judah were united as one nation under King Saul (the people's choice), King David (the man after God's own heart), and King Solomon (the wisest of all men). After Solomon's reign, Israel chose to separate from Judah and Benjamin and from then on existed as two separate kingdoms. Judah retained the kings in the lineage of David and had more Godly leadership, whilst Israel separated from Judah and experienced a more chaotic and violent leadership.

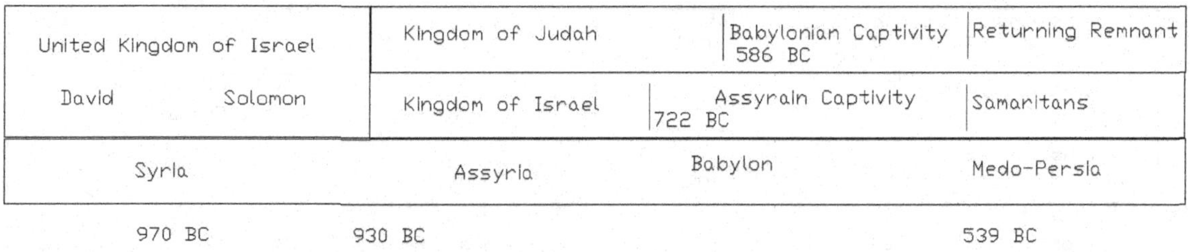

United Kingdom of Israel		Kingdom of Judah	Babylonian Captivity 586 BC	Returning Remnant
David	Solomon	Kingdom of Israel	722 BC Assyrain Captivity	Samaritans
Syria		Assyria	Babylon	Medo-Persia

970 BC	930 BC		539 BC

Figure 6.14 The divided kingdom

Figure 6.15 Kings of Judah

David	Solomon	Rehoboam	Abijah	Asa	Jehoshaphat	Jehoram	Ahaziah	Athaliah	Jehoash	Amaziah	Uzziah
40	40	17	3	41	25	8	1	6	40	29	52
1010	970	930	913	910	872	853	841	841	835	796	792

	Jotham	Ahaz	Hezekiah	Manasseh	Amon	Josiah	Jehoahaz	Jehoiakim	Jehoiachin	Zedekiah	Zedekiah
	16	16	29	55	2	31	<1	11	<1	11	End Rule
	750	735	715	696	642	640	609	598	598	597	586

First line: Length of reign (years), Second line: Start of reign (year BC)

Figure 6.16 Kings of Israel

David	Solomon	Jeroboam I	Nadab	Baasha	Elah	Zimri	Tibni	Omri	Ahab	Ahaziah
40	40	22	2	24	2	<1	5	12	22	2
1010	970	930	909	908	886	885	885	885	874	853

Joram	Jehu	Jehoahaz	Jehoash	Jeroboam II	Zechariah	Shallum	Menahem	Pekah	Pekahiah	Hoshea
12	28	17	16	41	<1	<1	10	20	2	9
852	841	814	798	793	753	640	752	752	742	732

From the Bible Study site [8]

> After the death of Zimri in 885 B.C. Tibni ruled half the nation and Omri ruled the other half (1Kings 16:21 - 22). Except for this brief mention in Scripture nothing else is known about Tibni. After his death Omri became sole king of the Northern kingdom in 880 B.C. Pekah began as a ruling rival of Menahem in 752 B.C. This rivalry lasted ten years (2Kings 15:17) until Menahem's death in 742. From 742 to 740 Pekah and Pekahiah maintained rival thrones (2Kings 15:23), with Pekah beginning his sole rule of the Northern kingdom in 740 B.C. with his assassination of Pekahiah. Pekah's reign ended when he was assassinated by Hoshea in 732 (2Kings 15:30).

The kings frequently heard from the prophets of God but often rejected their words. God tolerated this for a time, but then having had enough of their idolatry and rebellion, put an end to their kingdoms. The kings of Israel and Judah reigned for about 414 years before they were overtaken and subjected to the rule of the Assyrians, the Babylonians, the Medo-Persians, the Greeks, and eventually the Romans.

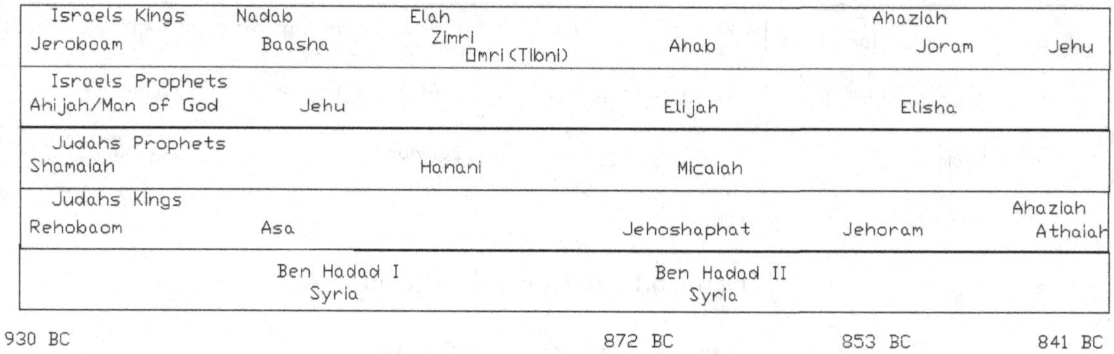

Israels Kings	Nadab	Elah		Ahaziah	
Jeroboam	Baasha	Zimri Omri (Tibni)	Ahab	Joram	Jehu
Israels Prophets					
Ahijah/Man of God	Jehu		Elijah	Elisha	
Judahs Prophets					
Shamalah		Hanani	Micaiah		
Judahs Kings					Ahaziah
Rehoboam	Asa		Jehoshaphat	Jehoram	Athaiah
	Ben Hadad I Syria		Ben Hadad II Syria		
930 BC			872 BC	853 BC	841 BC

Figure 6.17 Kings and Prophets of Israel and Judah

Kings Omri, Ahab and Jehoram [19]

The Moabite Stone is an ancient monument dated to the mid-800s BC and often referred to as the Mesha stele that was discovered in 1868 near the Dead Sea. This monument tells of the rebellion of King Mesha from under the Israelite King Jehoram and mentions the tribute that he paid to Kings Omri and Ahab up to that point. It also mentions Israel, Yahweh, and the "House of David". This is only 150 years after David's reign.

An excerpt from the text:

> "I am Mesha, son of Kemosh[it], king of Mesha, the Dibonite. My father ruled over Moab for 30 years, and I ruled after my father … Omri (was) king of Israel, and he oppressed Moab many days … And his son succeeded him, and he too said: 'I will oppress Moab.'… And Omri had taken possession of the land … and he dwelt in it in his days and the sum of the days of his sons: 40 years; but [the god] Kamosh restored it in my days" (translated by Andre Lemaire, *Biblical Archaeology Review*, May-June 1994, p. 33).

This precisely parallels the biblical text "Mesha, king of Moab rebelled against the king of Israel…" (2 Kings 3:5).

King Ahab is also mentioned in the Kurkh Monolith's inscription of Shalmaneser III (858-824) and some Samarian scripts of that period as well.

King Jehu and Hazael King of Syria [19]

An Assyrian monument from the ninth century BC called the "Black Obelisk", honoring the achievements of King Shalmaneser III, was discovered in 1846. It depicts the Israeli King Jehu keeling down while offering tribute to the Assyrian king. The top inscription reads, "Tribute of Iaua [Jehu], son of Omri. Silver, gold, a golden bowl, a golden beaker, golden goblets, pitchers of gold, tin, staves for the hand of the king, [and] javelins, I [Shalmaneser] received from him."

Figure 6.18 Israeli King Jehu kneeling down while offering tribute to the Assyrian king.

The Black Obelisk also mentioned Hazael, "I (King Shalmaneser III) fought against Benhadad and take credit for his downfall. Hazael, the son of a worthless man, then ascended to the throne."

The prophets of Israel showed miraculous signs and wonders and were often martyred for their stand against the king or heathen priests. Many of them prophesied of the coming Messiah. The chronicles of the kings and prophets were carefully recorded by the Jewish Levitical priests and scribes.

Israels Kings	Zechariah Shallum Menahem	Pekahiah Pekah		Hoshea	Fall of Sameria	
Israels Prophets			Obadiah (Edom)			
Judahs Prophets		Michah Isaiah				
Judahs Kings	Azariah (Uzziah)	Jotham		Ahaz	Hezekiah	Manasseh
		Tiglath-Pileser (Assyria) Rezin (Syria)		Shalmeneser Assyria	Sennacherib Assyria	

792 BC   750 BC   752 BC   715 BC   642 BC

Figure 6.19 Fall of Israel

Kings Pekah & Hoshea [20]

In 2Kings 15:29 we read, "In the days of Pekah king of Israel, Tiglath-pileser king of Assyria came and captured Ijon and Abel-beth-maacah and Janoah and Kedesh and Hazor and Gilead and Galilee, all the land of Naphtali; and he carried them captive to Assyria."

2Kings 15:30 "And Hoshea the son of Elah made a conspiracy against Pekah the son of Remaliah, and struck him and put him to death and became king in his place, in the twentieth year of Jotham the son of Uzziah."

This event is confirmed in the annals of Tiglath-Pileser III, the king of Assyria (733 BC), who wrote the following:

> "They had overthrown their king Pekah, Hoshea I placed as ruler over them. From him I received a tribute of 10 talents of gold and 1,000 talents of silver."

The event of the fall of Sameria in 2Kings 17:6 reads, "In the ninth year of Hoshea the king of Assyria took Samaria, and carried Israel away into Assyria, and placed them in Halah and in Habor by the river of Gozan, and in the cities of the Medes."

An inscription from the Asserian King Sargon II states the following:

> "In the first year of my reign I captured Samaria along with 27,290 captives. The foreigners of lands who had never paid me tribute, I settled in Samaria."

King Hezekiah [21]

The Siloam inscription written in Hebrew in about 701 BC describes the construction of the Siloam Tunnel (aka Hezekiah's Tunnel) that Hezekiah built in preparation for the Assyrian siege against Jerusalem, as mentioned in 2Kings 20:20 and 2Chron 32.

The Lachish relief is a portion of the Sennacherib relief written in Assyrian cuneiform, depicting Judean captives being taken away after the Siege of Lachish in 701 BC.

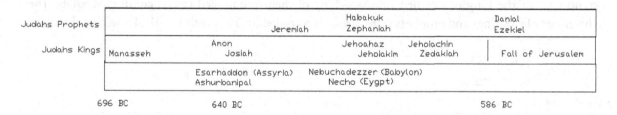

Figure 6.20 Fall of Juda

Babylonian King Belshazzar, Persian King Cyrus, and Darius the Mede [22]

The fall of Israel and Judah, followed by the relocation of the Jews to Babylon and the eventual fall of Babylon to Persia and the Medes, has been confirmed by inscriptions on tablets found in the city of Ur in 1853. Evidence of Belshazzar of the Babylonian Empire and Darius the Mede found in the book of Daniel have been confirmed along with many parallel events found in these inscriptions.

That Belshazzar was the second ruler under his father Nabonidus in Akkad, as inferred in the book of Daniel, is established by the following inscriptions:

> "May it be that I, Nabonidus, king of Babylon, never fail you. And may my firstborn, Belshazzar, worship you with all his heart."

"Putting the camp under the rule of his oldest son, the firstborn. The army of the empire he placed under his command. His hands were now free; He entrusted the authority of the royal throne to him."

"In regards to the bright star which has appeared, I will undertake to interpret its meaning for the glory of my lord Nabonidus, Babylon's king, and also for the crown prince, Belshazzar."

"Nabonidus, the king stayed in Tema; the crown prince, his officials and the troops were in Akkad."

This aligns perfectly with Daniel 5:16 which says, "Now if you can read the writing and make known to me its interpretation, you shall be clothed with purple and have a chain of gold around your neck, and shall be the third ruler in the kingdom." This implies that Daniel would be the third ruler under Belshazzar, who was indeed the second ruler of the kingdom.

In Daniel Chapter 5, we find that Belshazzar was holding a feast, where he saw a hand writing on the wall, the night that King Cyrus of Persia and Darius the Mede overran the city, took Akkad, and killed Belshazzar. This event is found in the writings of historians Herodotus, Berosus, and Xenophon, verifying the accuracy of the biblical record.

"Cyrus then dug a trench and diverted the flow of the Euphrates River into the new channel which led to an existing swamp. The level of the river then dropped to such a level that it became like a stream. His army was then able to take the city by marching through the shallow waters . . . The Babylonians at the time were celebrating intensely at a feast to one of their gods and they were taken totally by surprise."

Darius the Mede (Gubaru) was born in 601 BC, which would have made him 62 years old when he invaded Babylon, exactly the age found in Daniel 5:31. From the Babylonian Chronicles we read:

"In the month of Tashritu, at the time when Cyrus battled the forces of Akkad in Opis on the Tigris River, the citizens of Akkad revolted against him, but Nabonidus scattered his opposition with a great slaughter. On the 14th day, Sippar was taken without a fight. Nabonidus then fled for his life. On the 16th day, Gubaru (Darius the Mede) the leader of Gutium along with the army of Cyrus entered Babylon without any opposition."

Gubaru was given the title of "Darius" as a ruler in Babylon meaning "holder of the scepter." In other words, "the scepter holder (king) of the Medes". Josephus wrote about Darius, saying, "Darius the Mede, who along with his relative, Cyrus the King of Persia, brought an end to the Babylonian empire. Darius was the son of Astyages."

Excerpts from the book of Daniel:

Dan 5:1: Belshazzar the king made a great feast to a thousand of his lords, and drank wine before the thousand.

Dan 5:2: Belshazzar, whiles he tasted the wine, commanded to bring the golden and silver vessels which his father Nebuchadnezzar had taken out of the temple which was in Jerusalem; that the king, and his princes, his wives, and his concubines, might drink therein.

Dan 5:5: In the same hour came forth fingers of a man's hand, and wrote over against the candlestick upon the plaster of the wall of the king's palace: and the king saw the part of the hand that wrote.

Dan 5:24: Then was the part of the hand sent from him; and this writing was written.

Dan 5:25: And this is the writing that was written, MENE, MENE, TEKEL, UPHARSIN.

Dan 5:26: This is the interpretation of the thing: MENE; God hath numbered thy kingdom, and finished it.

Dan 5:27: TEKEL; Thou art weighed in the balances, and art found wanting.

Dan 5:28: PERES; Thy kingdom is divided, and given to the Medes and Persians.

Dan 5:29: Then commanded Belshazzar, and they clothed Daniel with scarlet, and put a chain of gold about his neck, and made a proclamation concerning him, that he should be the third ruler in the kingdom.

Dan 5:30: In that night was Belshazzar the king of the Chaldeans slain.

Dan 5:31: And Darius the Median took the kingdom, being about threescore and two years old.

These inscriptions also recount how Darius the Mede set up sub-governors throughout Babylon, which the prophet Daniel was one of. This account parallels the biblical account in every respect:

> "It pleased Darius to set over the kingdom one hundred and twenty satraps, to be
> over the whole kingdom; and over these, three governors, of whom Daniel was one,
> that the satraps might give account to them, so that the king would suffer no loss.
> (Da:6:1)"

	536 BC				445 BC	438 BC	
Event	Fall of Jerusalem	Gedaliah Exile	1st Return	Temple Completed (516 BC)	2nd Return	3rd Return City wall rebuilt	
Prophets			Joel	Haggai Zechariah			Malachi
Leaders		Zerubbabel Joshua		Esther	Ezra	Nehemiah	
		Cyrus (Persia)	Darius	Xarxes	Artaxerxes		

Figure 6.21 Restoration of the temple

Figure 6.22 Second Temple

These archeological inscriptions, patterns of evidence, and artifacts form a consensus to validate the accuracy and truth of the historical biblical records. If every extra biblical piece of the puzzle found aligns perfectly with the biblical text, there is no reason to be critical of the missing pieces unless you're a humanist that is blinded by your religion. The Bible, having been found true in the physical aspects, lends itself to validate the spiritual and prophetic aspects as well. The prophecies of the coming Messiah have been recorded through the ages alongside of these events. When you think about that, the Bible is the only source that you can go to and read about prophets foretelling future events, knowing they were spoken up to 4,000 years before the event by many different peoples in many different eras, that came true as record. Only God can foresee the future with such accuracy, so then only God can be credited for inspiring the prophets and the writers of his word.

Prophesies of the Profits of Israel.

The prophecies of both the contemporary warnings and those regarding the Messiah were captured in text and survived the many attempts of Israel's enemies to destroy them.

There were 44 prophecies of the Messiah fulfilled in Jesus Christ, some examples:

Would come from the tribe of Judah, Genesis 49:10, sixteenth century BC
Soldiers would gamble for Messiah's garments, Psalm 22:18, eleventh century BC
Messiah's bones would not be broken, Exodus 12:46 Psalm 34:20, eleventh century BC
Messiah would resurrect from the dead, Psalm 16:10 Psalm 49:15, eleventh century .C

211

Born in Bethlehem, Micah 5:2, eighth century BC

Born of a virgin, Isaiah 7:14, eighth century BC

A messenger (John the Baptist) would prepare the way for Messiah, Is. 40:3-5, eighth century BC

Messiah would be called a Nazarene, Isaiah 11:1, eighth century BC

Messiah would be spat upon and struck, Isaiah 50:6, eighth century BC

Messiah would be crucified with criminals, Isaiah 53:12, eighth century BC

Would spend a season in Egypt, Hosea 11:1, eighth century BC

Messiah would be betrayed, Psalm 41:9 Zechariah 11:12-13, sixth century BC

Messiah's price would be used to buy a potter's field, Zech 11:12-13, sixth century BC

Messiah's hands and feet would be pierced, Psalm 22:16 Zechariah 12:10, sixth century BC

Soldiers would pierce Messiah's side, Zechariah 12:10, sixth century BC

Israelites, the chosen ones, were showcased by God as an example of the relationship between God and man, having the laws but not the Spirit. This period in history was meant to communicate to the nations what to expect from God as a nation under God and as an individual unto God. God's Law and the scriptures bring us to Christ and teach us about the sacrifice of the lamb. The 450 years of Judges revealed how the people with godly leaders would prosper, and those with no godly leadership would fall into depravity and bondage with no deliverance from their enemies. The 400 years of the kings in Israel and Judah established the need for the leaders of the nations to honor God in their laws and government. The fall of Israel and consequent banishment to Babylon shows this. The return of Israel to the Promised Land echoed a prophecy Paul talked about: the time of the Gentiles fulfilled and salvation returning to Israel. Four hundred years of silence preceding the coming of the Christ in which there would be no prophets, signifying a change and heightening of the expectation of the coming Messiah.

The Hellenistic World begins [23]

With the conquest of Alexander the Great came the Hellenization of the known world. At this time, the Greek culture was being adopted by all the nations that were conquered by the Greeks in about 323 BC. The Greek language soon became the "lingua franca" throughout the world. When Alexander destroyed Tyre, most of the towns on the route to Egypt quickly capitulated. A later tradition recorded his entry into Jerusalem: according to Josephus, Alexander was shown the Book of Daniel's prophecy, presumably chapter 8, which described a mighty Greek king who would conquer the Persian Empire. He spared Jerusalem and pushed south into Egypt. However, Alexander met with resistance at Gaza. The stronghold was heavily fortified and built on a hill, requiring a siege. When "his engineers pointed out to him that because of the height of the mound it would be impossible… this encouraged Alexander all the more to make the attempt". After three unsuccessful assaults, the stronghold fell, but not before Alexander had received a serious shoulder wound. As in Tyre, men of military age were put to the sword and the women and children were sold into slavery.

The Roman World Conquest begins [23]

In 31 BC the Romans began their march on the world, starting with the Battle of Actium and the takeover of Egypt.

The Genealogies of Christ

The two genealogies of Christ recorded in the Bible have two possible explanations. Eusebius believed that there was one genealogy belonging to Jacob, Joseph's biological father. Jacob's half-brother, Heli, died without having any sons. As it was tradition for a man to marry his brother's widow and have a son to carry on the deceased man's name, Jacob would have fathered Joseph after marrying Heli's widow. The other genealogy follows the first husband, Heli, to honor him based on the Jewish tradition of "Levirate marriage". Jacob and Heli were half-brothers because their mother was married to two different men in her lifetime, Melchi and Matthan. The other theory is that one genealogy is Joseph's lineage and the other is Mary's. Although Jesus was not fathered by Joseph, Mary being wed to Joseph made him the head of the house and so the son–in–law of Mary's father, which by Jewish tradition is credited as his son[4].

Davidic line for Joseph (Matthew)

Gen.	1	2	3	4	5	6	7	8	9	10	11	12	13	14
Ave lngth	78	78	78	78	78	78	78	78	78	78	78	78	78	78
Lineage	Abraham	Isaac	Jacob	Judas	Phares	Esrom;	Esrom	Aram	Aminadab	Naasson	Salmon	Booz	Obed	Jesse
Year BC	2035	1957	1879	1801	1723	1645	1567	1489	1411	1333	1255	1177	1099	1021
				Into Egypt			Exodus						Ruth	Samual

Gen.	1	2	3	4	5	6	7	8	9	10	11	12	13	14
Ave lngth	32	32	32	32	32	32	32	32	32	32	32	32	32	32
Lineage	David	Solomon	Roboam	Abia	Asa	Josaphat	Joram	Ozias	Joatham	Achaz	Ezekias;	Manasses	Amon;	Josias
Year BC	989	957	925	893	861	829	797	765	733	701	669	637	605	573
	Bathsheba													

Gen.	1	2	3	4	5	6	7	8	9	10	11	12	13	14
Ave lngth	41	41	41	41	41	41	41	41	41	41	41	41	41	41
Lineage	Jechonias	Salathiel	Zorobabel;	Abiud	Eliakim	Azor	Sadoc	Achim;	Eliud	Eleazar;	Matthan	Jacob	Mary	Jesus
Year BC	532	491	450	409	368	327	286	245	204	163	122	81	40	-1
	Babylon		2nd Temp										Joseph	

Davidic line for Mary (Luke)

Gen.	1	2	3	4	5	6	7	8	9	10	11	12	13	14
Ave lngth	78	78	78	78	78	78	78	78	78	78	78	78	78	78
Lineage	Abraham	Isaac	Jacob	Judas	Phares	Esrom;	Esrom	Aram	Aminadab	Naasson	Salmon	Booz	Obed	Jesse
Year BC	2035	1957	1879	1801	1723	1645	1567	1489	1411	1333	1255	1177	1099	1021
				Into Egypt			Exodus						Ruth	Samual

Gen.	1	2	3	4	5	6	7	8	9	10	11	12	13	14
Ave lngth	24	24	24	24	24	24	24	24	24	24	24	24	24	24
Lineage	David	Nathan	Mattatha,	Menan	Melea	Eliakim	Jonan	Joseph	Juda	Simeon	Levi,	Matthat	Jorim	Eliezer
Year BC	997	973	949	925	901	877	853	829	805	781	757	733	709	685
	Bathsheba													

Gen.	1	2	3	4	5	6	7	8	9	10	11	12	13	14
Ave lngth	24	24	24	24	24	24	24	24	24	24	24	24	24	24
Lineage	Jose	Er	Elmodam	Cosam	Addi	Melchi	Neri	Salathiel	Zorobabel	Rhesa	Joanna	Juda	Joseph	Semei
Year BC	661	637	613	589	565	541	517	493	469	445	421	397	373	349
						Babylon								

Gen.	1	2	3	4	5	6	7	8	9	10	11	12	13	14
Ave lngth	24	24	24	24	24	24	24	24	24	24	24	24	24	24
Lineage	Mattathias	Maath	Nagge	Esli	Naum	Amos	Mattathias	Joseph	Janna	Melchi	Levi	Matthat	Heli	Joseph
Year BC	325	301	277	253	229	205	181	157	133	109	85	61	37	13
			2nd Temp										Mary	

24	
Jesus	
-11	

Figure 6.23 Lineages of Christ

The Canon and Hellenization of the Old Testament Books

The Aleppo Codex is the oldest compete Hebrew Bible in existence, copied in 930 AD. The Dead Sea Scrolls are the oldest partial parchments of the Hebrew Bible. There is a portion of Hebrew scripture found (Numbers 6:24-26) that dates from 600 BC [25].

The oldest surviving translation of Hebrew scripture to the Greek is the **Greek Septuagint** [26], a translation undertaken by 70 Jewish scholars in Alexandria in the third century before Christ (BC) into Koine Greek language. **Septuagint** is from the Latin word **Septuagint**, meaning *seventy*. The Greek codices arranged the books in a *fourfold* division, in a different way than Hebrew Scripture, by placing the Law of Moses first, then the Historical books, then the Wisdom books, and then the Prophets. The earliest writer who gives an account of the Septuagint version is Aristobulus, a Jew

214

who lived at the commencement of the second century B.C. The Greek Septuagint Old Testament was in circulation at the time of Christ and was widely read. In fact, the majority of Old Testament quotations in the Greek New Testament were from the Greek Septuagint Old Testament, primarily from Psalms, Isaiah, Genesis, Exodus, Leviticus, Deuteronomy, and the Book of the Twelve. For example, when Jesus read Isaiah (61:1-2) in the synagogue at Nazareth (Luke 4:16-19), he followed the language of the Greek Septuagint. The early Christian Churches referred to the Septuagint as their source of scripture. The Orthodox Churches have retained the Septuagint for their canon of the Old Testament to the present day!

The Codex Vaticanus, so called because it is the most famous manuscript in the possession of the Vatican library, is generally believed to be from the fourth century, and is thought to be the oldest (nearly) complete copy of the Greek Bible in existence. Lacking from it are most of the book of Genesis, Hebrews 9:14 to the end, the pastoral Epistles, and the book of Revelation; these parts were lost by damage to the front and back of the volume, which is common in ancient manuscripts.

The Greek Septuagint canonized 10 books more than the Hebrew canonized books, referred to as the "Apocrypha" books. The Apocrypha books from the Greek Septuagint were canonized into the Catholic and Eastern Orthodox Bibles as well but were removed from the Protestant Bible when Martin Luther produced the first Protestant Bible canon.

REFERENCES

Biblical References from: The Holy Bible (1913). King James Version. Chicago, Ill. John A. Dickson Publishing Co.

1 Bible History Online. Retrieved From http://www.bible-history.com/maps/2-table-of-nations.html

2 Rendsburg, G. Ancient Hebrew morphology. Retrieved From http://jewishstudies.rutgers.edu/docman/rendsburg/121-ancient-hebrew-morphology/file

3 Thompson B. & Lyons E. The reality of copyists' errors. Retrieved From http://helpmewithbiblestudy.org/5system_moses/dh13_copyistError.aspx

4 Evans, C.A. (2010). *Holman QuickSource*^{TM} *guide to the Dead Sea scrolls*. North Nashville, TN: B&H Publishing Group.

5 BETA. Beta analytical radiocarbon dating. Retrieved From http://www.radiocarbon.com/archaeology.htm

6 Bible History Online. Siloam Inscription. Retrieved From http://www.bible-history.com/archaeology/israel/siloam-inscription.html

7 Lamb & Lion Ministries. The new Egyptian chronologies. Retrieved From http://christinprophecy.org/articles/the-new-egyptian-chronology/

8 Mahoney, T. P. Pattern of evidence: The exodus. Retrieved from http://patternsofevidence.com/

9 Associate for Biblical Research. The discovery of the sin cities of Sodom and Gomorrah (2008). Retrieved from http://www.biblearchaeology.org/post/2008/04/The-Discovery-of-the-Sin-Cities-of-Sodom-and-Gomorrah.aspx

10 Gerson, I. (2007). Popular Archeology. Making a case for Sodom. Retrieved from http://popular-archaeology.com/issue/06052014/article/making-the-case-for-sodom

11 Bible History Daily (2013). Retrieved from http://www.biblicalarchaeology.org/daily/archaeology-today/biblical-archaeology-topics/locating-zoar/

12 Bible Archaeology. The Walls of Jericho. Retrieved from http://www.biblearchaeology.org/post/2008/06/The-Walls-of- jericho.aspx?gclid=CMnEkZunrNICFdOIswody8ICNg

13 Christian Answers. Hazor. Retrieved from http://christiananswers.net/dictionary/hazor.html

14 Bible Archaeology. Great discoveries in biblical archeology: The Merenptah stela. Retrieved from http://www.biblearchaeology.org/post/2006/03/15/The-Merenptah-Stela.aspx

15 Domain of Man. David Rohl's "new chronology". Retrieved from http://www.domainofman.com/ankhemmaat/rohl.html

16 CBN News. Inside Israel (2013). Did David, Solomon exist? Dig refutes naysayers. Retrieved from http://www.cbn.com/cbnnews/insideisrael/2013/june/did-david-solomon-exist-dig-refutes-naysayers/?mobile=false

17 The Bible History Daily (2015). The Tel Dan inscription: The first historical evidence of king David from the Bible. Retrieved from http://www.biblicalarchaeology.org/daily/biblical-artifacts/artifacts-and-the-bible/the-tel-dan-inscription-the-first-historical-evidence-of-the-king-david-bible-story/

18 The Bible Study Site. Kings of Israel and Judah. Retrieved from http://www.biblestudy.org/prophecy/israel-kings.html

19 Beyond Today. The Bible and archeology. Retrieved from https://www.ucg.org/the-good-news/the-bible-and-archaeology-the-early-kings-of-israel-a-kingdom-divided

20 Historical Evidence for King Hoshea. Retrieved from http://www.biblehistory.net/newsletter/hoshea.htm

21 Wikipedia. List of artifacts in biblical archaeology. Retrieved from https://en.wikipedia.org/wiki/List_of_artifacts_in_biblical_archaeology

22 Bible Believers Archeology. Historical evidence Belshazzar and Darius the Mede. Retrieved from http://www.biblehistory.net/newsletter/belshazzar_darius_mede.htm

23 Wolf, A. (2008). *A short history of the world: The story of mankind from prehistory to the modern day*. New York, NY: Metro Books by arrangement with Arcturus Publishing Limited.

24 Got Questions?.org. Why are Jesus' genealogies in Matthew and Luke so different? Retrieved from https://www.gotquestions.org/Jesus-genealogy.html

25 Ancient Hebrew Research Center. Extant manuscripts of Hebrew Bible. Retrieved from http://ancient-hebrew.org/bible_manuscripts.html

26 Scripture and Bibles. The Septuagint (LXX). Retrieved from https://www.ecclesia.org/truth/septuagint.html.

THE CONCLUSION

If the Bible is a true and accurate historical record, then biblical chronology should align with discoveries in archeology, literary works, artifacts, cave art, etc. regarding those subject matters in time and place. As with all critical analysis, the more facts or patterns of evidence in an area of interest, such as science or archeology, that match the chronologies of events or story lines in the Bible, the more confidence we can have in pointing to the Bible as a true and accurate historical record. Common sense must prevail, if there is a conflict between the evidence and the time period, the weight of the evidence should put the time period in question. If it can be said that it is possible that this condition could be the result of this action or circumstance then it must be accepted as a competing theory. The serious scientist should seek the truth and not just seek for evidence that supports one belief or theory. You cannot take empirical evidence and add theory to it to make it fit your belief and then call it fact if there are competing theories it fits as well and it fits those competing theories without adding extraneous theories to the empirical evidence to "make it fit".

1) If the Bible is a true and accurate historical record regarding the time of creation and the cradle of civilization, then you would expect to find evidence of early civilization (buildings, art, literary works, government, infrastructure, etc.) originating in and around Mesopotamia in about 4000 BC.
    This is exactly what you find, as a matter of fact!

2) If the Bible is a true and accurate historical record regarding the fallen angels manifesting themselves as gods for men to worship during the Antediluvian period, then you would expect to find ancient literature making reference to such and remains of worship centers from before 2500 BC around the world with little to no idols.
    This is exactly what you find in all the king lists and other literature of all the major cultures before 1800 BC, and ancient worship centers such as Stonehenge and the Sechin Bajo Peru, as a matter of fact!

3) If the Bible is a true and accurate historical record regarding people living extremely long lives for the first 1,800 years of creation, then you would expect to find ancient literature making reference to such, skeletal remains of people with accentuated facial and body features, and animals many times larger than in today's world.
    This is exactly what you find in the king lists of all the major cultures before 1800 BC, the remains of Neanderthal man, and many of the animals dating from before 2500 BC, as a matter of fact!

4) If the Bible is a true and accurate historical record regarding Noah's World Wide Flood, then you would expect to find massive fossiliferous strata laid down with multiple layers due to continental drifting and catastrophic events of that magnitude. You should find oceanic sea creatures in every place in the world, including the top of mountains.

   This is exactly what you find throughout the world and exemplified in North America, as can be seen in the Grand Canyon where oceanic fossiliferous sandstone makeup 95% of the strata, e.g., the Morrison formation spread out from Texas to Canada covering 580,000 square miles and an average of 328 feet thick, the source for the Navajo Sandstone layer in southern Utah coming from the Appalachian Mountains over 1,200 miles away, and sea creatures such as trilobites at the top of Mount Everest, as a matter of fact!

5) If the Bible is a true and accurate historical record regarding Noah's World Wide Flood, then you would expect to find a demarcation in the cultures and civilizations around the world at about the same time interval (BTR 2500-2209 BC).

   This is exactly what you find in the archeological discoveries attested to by many credible archeologists and the DNA scientific discoveries, as a matter of fact!

6) If the Bible is a true and accurate historical record regarding Noah's World Wide Flood, then you would expect to find ancient literature making reference to the Great Flood, Noah, the Ark, and his sons and their families being the only survivors.

   This is exactly what you find in many epic tales such as *The Epic of Gilgamesh*, chronologies of the nations such as China and Sumer, and poems such as the Indian Verdas from before 1800 BC, as a matter of fact!

7) If the Bible is a true and accurate historical record regarding Noah's Ark, then you would expect to discover evidence of dinosaurs such as *T.rex*, Stegosaurs, and Pterosaurs.

   This is exactly what you find in many epic tales such as *The Epic of Gilgamesh*, and *Beowulf*, in Chinese chronicles and writings of Marco Polo, Herodotus, Alexander the Great, in cave drawings and pottery decor, referred to in history as dragons and flying fiery serpents in the bible and cultures from every part of the globe, as a matter of fact!

8) If the Bible is a true and accurate historical record regarding the Babel event, then you would expect major cultures to appear suddenly in history all about the same time, with complete unique language and scripts, and with the earmarks of civilization. You would also expect to find ancient literature and artifacts dating no further back than BTR 2350-2042 BC from the major cultures of the world such as Sumer, Egypt, China, India, etc. with roots from Mesopotamia, all claiming antediluvian ancestry as an integral period in their history.

   This is exactly what you find in the chronologies and artifacts of ancient cultures such as India, China, and Sumer. Artifacts discovered include Chinese bronze tools and geographic descriptions via Egypt, the Narmer Pallets of Egypt, the Sumerian steles out of Mesopotamia, and the India Verdas established from before 1800 BC, as a matter of fact!

9) If the Bible is a true and accurate historical record regarding the age of the universe and the Earth, then you would expect to find such reflected in various scientific discoveries.
This is exactly what you find in the empirical evidence regarding the decay rate of the earth's magnetic field, Dr. Humphreys' planetary magnetosphere model, Dr. Humphreys' theory of the creation of the universe fitting known physics, the life of comets, the moon's recession rate, and the rapid rock and fossiliferous strata formations, as a matter of fact!

10) If the Bible is a true and accurate historical record regarding the creation of the universe and the Earth, then you would expect to find the sudden appearance of creatures as well–marked species in the fossil record with no traces of transitional.
This is exactly what you find in every fossiliferous stratum discovery starting with the Cambrian explosion, with the complexity of the genome beyond known physics and scientific explanation, as a matter of fact!

11) If the Bible is a true and accurate historical record regarding Sodom and Gomorrah, then you would expect to find the remains of walled cities in the Jordan valley, in strata from about that time period, close enough to Mamre to see smoke ascending, not far from a valley that has slime pits, with four of the five cities of the plain buried under ash from a fiery end.
This is exactly what you find in the archeological discoveries, as a matter of fact!

12) If the Bible is a true and accurate historical record regarding Israel's stay in Egypt for 215 years, then you would expect to find traces of a Palestinian culture and possible unique artifacts in remains from the area of Avaris (Goshen) at about that time period.
This is exactly what you find with the Hebrew names on Egyptian servants' lists, the High official's house with 12 pillars and 12 tombs, one empty with a statue of a Palestinian in a multicolored coat as Joseph had, and the number of houses equal to the number of people in the Bible of the people that came to Egypt with Jacob, as a matter of fact!

13) If the Bible is a true and accurate historical record regarding the events surrounding Moses' appearance and the Exodus of Israel from Egypt, then you would expect to find unique artifacts and Egyptian records reflecting that in remains from the area of Avaris (Goshen) at about that time period.
This is exactly what you find with the skeletal remains of infants buried in boxes under many of the Hebrew houses, the census with 3/2 Hebrew women, the plague pits full of skeletal remains of Egyptians, houses abandoned suddenly, the Ipuwer Papyrus describing the same plagues of Egypt, and Manetho's comments on the "blast from God" under Pharaoh Dudimose, as a matter of fact!

14) If the Bible is a true and accurate historical record regarding the events surrounding the Israeli Kings Saul, David, and Solomon, then remains or records from the surrounding nations should have paralleling points of facts in any evidence of discovery from that period in history from extra biblical sources.

This is exactly what you find in the Amarna Letters describing the unique relationship Saul had with his son and David, Jonathan's conspiring with David, and also the many references to the "house of David" in other extra biblical inscriptions, as a matter of fact!

15) If the Bible is a true and accurate historical record regarding the events surrounding any of the Judean and Israeli kings and prophets from the time of Rehoboam to the fall of Judah, then you would expect to find evidence from that period in history from extra biblical sources.
This is exactly what you find in inscriptions found in the "Black Obelisk" regarding King Shalmaneser III of Assyria, and his relationships with King Jehu and Hazael King of Syria, matching the biblical story in all points, as a matter of fact!

16) If the Bible is a true and accurate historical record regarding the events surrounding the fall of Samaria and the end of the Israeli kingdom, then you would expect to find evidence of these events from that period in history from extra biblical sources.
This is exactly what you find in inscriptions found in the annals of Tiglath-Pileser III, the king of Assyria, regarding Israeli Kings Pekah and Hoshea and Assyrian King Sargon II who took captives from Samaria back to Assyria, matching the biblical story in all points, as a matter of fact!

17) If the Bible is a true and accurate historical record regarding the events surrounding the fall of the Babylonian kingdom to the Persians and Medes in Daniel's time, then you would expect to find evidence of these events from that period in history from extra biblical sources.
This is exactly what you find in inscriptions on tablets found in the city of Ur in 1853 regarding the Babylonian King Belshazzar being taken by the Persian King Cyrus and Darius the Mede during a raging banquet, matching the biblical story in all points, as a matter of fact!

18) If the Bible is a true and accurate historical record regarding the prophesies of the coming Christ down through 4,000 years, then you would expect the one who would claim to be the Christ to fulfill them as foretold.
This is exactly what you find from the birth of Jesus, the son of God, to the sacrifice of the Lamb of God that was slain before the foundations of the world, and then afterwards the resurrection and ascension of the Lord almighty, as a matter of fact!

19) If the Bible is a true and accurate historical record regarding the process of creation, then you would expect to find the density of the galaxies approximately the same in any direction, all objects in the universe expanding out from our location, and to see the light of the stars millions of light years away due to the GR time delineation.
This is exactly what you find, as a matter of fact!

Many critics of the Bible have taken issue with the accuracy of the translations given the time and numerous copies that it would have been through to make it to us today. This particular issue has been satisfactorily debunked with the discovery of the Dead Sea scrolls along with the following historical and scientific reflections. Prior to the discovery of the Dead Sea scrolls, which date back to the third century BC, we only had extant copies from the seventh century AD. Now with these, 1,000 years earlier, all the scriptures have been adequately compared and found congruent with today's translation. The entire book of Isaiah was discovered amongst the Dead Sea scrolls and was found to be completely identical to our present-day translations! One thing that the non-Christian fails to comprehend is that God, from the beginning, created all things with foreknowledge of all future events. He anticipated the fall of man and his need for redemption. In his plans to redeem mankind was the sacrifice of his son, the Lamb of God, slain before the foundations of the world, whose blood would cleanse us of all sin as we put our faith in him. Through the ages, God told us of his forthcoming, as his word was being recorded and preserved though the prophets and men of God. There is no possibility that any action taken by man, either in error or on purpose, could keep the knowledge of his love and salvation from mankind. Could God have created all of the universe as grand as it is with such a plan and purpose in mind and not have the ability to preserve his word? Anyone that thinks that man could have lost the essence of God's word due to copying errors does not have a grip on reality. God's plans and ability to get that word and knowledge to all people in every place throughout all generations cannot be hampered by man! God has preserved his word to all generations.

Jesus was God's word made flesh...Jesus was perfect as God's word is perfect!

Rom 8:38: For I am persuaded, that neither death, nor life, nor angels, nor principalities, nor powers, nor things present, nor things to come,

Rom 8:39: Nor height, nor depth, nor any other creature, shall be able to separate us from the love of God, which is in Christ Jesus our Lord.

An article titled "In Search of Historical Adam" ran on the Christianity Today website written by Richard N. Ostling on June 3, 2011. The article tells of some Christian sects that are changing their belief in the Genesis story from a literal chronology to an analogical story. These disciples of the Christian faith are yielding to the supposed solid scientific facts that the Genome Project espouses, along with the eons of time that geologists assert the rocks testify to. These assertions supposedly settle the argument that the earth is billions of years old and that the DNA construct absolutely confirms hundreds of thousands of years of human ancestry. These Church leaders believe that the sciences are infallible, and that belief requires a reconciliation of the biblical model with the evolutionary model. In doing so, they have compromised their beliefs to reshape the Genesis story to reflect the supposed realities of the sciences. How do they reconcile the two? They concede that God created a society of homo sapiens from our ape–like ancestors via an evolutionary process some 100,000 years ago and that Adam and Eve are just representatives of those acts and not real individuals as portrayed in the Bible[1]. These folks really need to consider the following before they cross that line into a pseudo-scientific based faith:

1) The source of these scientific publications by and large comes from a sect of society that are hell–bent on extinguishing religious theology, especially Christianity. The secular humanist (atheists and agnostics that make up the majority of the scientific community), with their mandate to conform the "sciences to destroy religion" as Sam Harris puts it, are far from a reliable source to put your trust in when their intentions override true scientific inquiry and their approach to science is based on a close–minded agenda! (Reference the Introduction of this publication.)

God's word says in 2Cor 6:14: Be you not unequally yoked together with unbelievers: for what fellowship has righteousness with unrighteousness? and what partnership has light with darkness?

And in Eph 5:11: Have no fellowship with the fruitless deeds of darkness, but rather expose them.

And then in 1John 1:6: If we say we have fellowship with Him yet walk in the darkness, we lie and do not practice the truth.

And finally in Col 2:8: Beware lest any man spoil you through philosophy and vain deceit, after the tradition of men, after the rudiments of the world, and not after Christ.

2) These scientific publications never have the vera causa as the basis for their assumptions, thus leaving their publications in the arena of theory and not fact. They have no consensus of empirical data, lab results, or observable findings that support these theories – just some very technical jargon aimed at dazzling and deceiving the public. Most people would not understand the material in these publications because of the highly technical verbiage and so depend on the vanguard of evolutionists to interpret the meanings for them. (Reference the introduction of this publication.)

3) The base assumption for these genomic evaluations is based on an evolutionary timeline and therefore looks to identify patterns and relationships that confirm the evolutionary theory while neglecting to see how well these patterns and relationships fit the Adamic timeline. (Reference Steve Meyers' book *Darwin's Doubt* and part 2 of this publication.)

4) When interrogating the genome from a biblical perspective, the DNA relationship agrees more with the biblical model than the evolutionary model and puts it within the 6K to10K years of earth history. An article from *Science* looking at demographics of diverse cultures over time and location shows a marked bottleneck in the history of humankind about 5,000 years ago and confirmed in the genome. Excerpts from an ICR article states the following [2]:

The authors wrote, "The maximum likelihood time for accelerated growth was 5,115 years ago." Old-earth proponents now have a new challenge: to explain why—after millions of years of hardly any genetic variation among modern humans—human genomic diversity exploded only within the last five thousand years?

5) All the radiological and Egyptological dating methods that evolutionists base their conclusions on are flawed. Only about < ½ of the radiological test results are accepted of the overall results and therefore cannot be relied upon to validate their claims. (Reference part 3 of this publication.)

6) The geological record aligns perfectly with the Global Flood event just as it is described in the Bible and as reviewed in this publication based on the known processes of rock and fossil formations and examples we have seen in nature. (Reference parts 1 & 2 of this publication.)

7) All the naked scientific facts fit the biblical model "as is", whereas the evolutionist has to add theory to the facts to force fit it into the evolutionary model (e.g., the decay of the magnetosphere, the moon's recession rate, the Oort cloud, punctuated equilibrium, etc.) [Reference part 3 of this publication.]

8) More than 95% of the archeological discoveries fit the biblical chronologies that were once called myth (e.g., time of creation, the Antediluvian inhabitants, Noah's Flood, the Babel event, the genealogies of the nations, the Exodus, the Israeli conquest, the lineage of King David, etc.) [Reference the volume of this publication.]

Degreed scientists whose research have come to agree with the biblical model.

Dr. J.Y. Chen
Excerpts from an Article by Arthur V. Chadwick *Sat, 20 Feb 1999* [3]

> Prof. Chen is one of the world's top experts on Cambrian animal fossils. His main point was that the major animal phyla arose suddenly and fully formed in the early Cambrian. Since the early Cambrian fauna from Chengjiang, China, includes soft-bodied animals, the absence of precursors presents a serious challenge to Darwinian evolution (the usual excuse being that the precursors were soft-bodied and thus did not fossilize well). Prof. Chen made his point forcefully and repeatedly, and compared the seriousness of his challenge to Darwinism with the irreducible complexity argument of Mike Behe.
> The correspondent pointed out to Prof. Chen that criticizing Darwinism in the U.S. can be quite controversial — even risky. Prof. Chen laughed, and said he wasn't afraid. He remarked that in the U.S. it's OK to criticize the government, but not Darwinism, while in China it's OK to criticize Darwinism, but not the government.

Stephen Meyer

Stephen **Meyer** is an advocate for intelligent design (ID). Meyer was a professor at Whitworth College and is currently a Senior Fellow of the DI and Director of its Center for Science and Culture (CSC). **Meyer** holds a B.S. degree in physics and earth science from Christian Whitworth College and has worked as a geophysicist for the Atlantic Richfield Company. **Meyer** earned his Ph.D. in history and philosophy of science from the University of Cambridge [4].

Meyer's book *Darwin's Doubt* has overwhelmingly shown that all theories of DNA variations at the macro level, when put to the test based on evolutionary assumptions, have come back negative. There is no consensus within the scientific community for **the divergence hypothesis** or **the phylogenetic reconstruction (molecular sequences)** such as molecule vs. molecule, molecule vs. anatomy, and the anatomy vs. anatomy to validate the evolutionary theology [5]. (A summary of his findings is found in part 2 of this publication.)

David Berlinski

Berlinski identifies himself as a secular Jew. David **Berlinski** holds a Ph.D. in philosophy from Princeton University. He was a research assistant in molecular biology at Columbia University as well as a research fellow at IIASA in Austria and at IHES in France. **Berlinski** authored many publications such as system analysis, differential topology, analytic philosophy, the philosophy and history of mathematics, and many other types of books. **Berlinski** is a Senior Fellow of the Discovery Institute's Center for Science and Culture based in Seattle, WA[6].

Excerpts from his video interview with the producers of "Icons of Evolution" [7, 8]

David says he is neither Christian nor a fundamentalist. He knows of dozens of mathematicians that "scratch their heads and say, 'you think this is how life originated'". He states, "One of the greatest mathematicians of the 20th century, John von Neumann, just laughed, he hooted at the theory of evolution". He goes on to say there is a consistent group of secular scientists (mathematicians, physicists, and speculative biologists) that do not even consider evolution to be a legitimate scientific theory. After reading about the Wistar Symposium held in 1966, Berlinski read several essays about Darwinian theory (articles by Murray Eden and Marcel-Paul Schützenberger). He tried talking about it with other post—doctorate biologists that he worked with at the time. To his surprise, they did not have an answer to the critical points made in these publications, which started his doubts about Darwinian theory. David often refers to the evolutionary sciences as pseudo-science. He shares the three most outstanding points against Darwinian theory:

First, he states that the fossil record "is simply mystifying, we cannot make sense of [it]". He also asserts that "it does not sustain any kind of Darwinian prediction that can be intelligently derived at".

Second, no one has been able to examine the central Darwinian theoretical claims that natural selection can account for the wide variations of complexity. There is no canonical demonstration that can be made in Darwinian biology as can be made in physics, for example, such as Newton's theory of the inverse square forces in play in the orbit of the planets about the sun. There is nothing like that in Darwinian biology. From the viewpoint of the serious scientist, one is completely adrift without being able make those demonstrations.

Third, when you turn to the serious sciences such as general relativity and quantum mechanics, you can program a computer that follows logical algorithms that produce logical consequences. You cannot do any of this in Darwinian biology. Berlinski has looked into these Darwinian biological algorithms and even tried to write some. He found that without a tremendous amount of manipulation, you cannot get any reasonable results.

Additionally, the 1966 convention held at The Wistar Institute in Philadelphia, which brought together leading scientists to discuss the "mathematical challenges to the Neo-Darwinian interpretation of evolution", concluded that the odds of an evolutionary process working are 1 in 10^77! Many mathematicians today agree with this assessment according to David Berlinski.

David Rohl

David Rohl is an archeologist and Egyptologist, having earned a B.A. in ancient history and Egyptology from the University of London. He became the director of the Institute for the Study of Interdisciplinary Sciences (ISIS) in 1985 where he was the editor of its *Journal of the Ancient Chronology Forum*. He was the president of the Sussex Egyptology Society (SES) where he edited the *The Followers of Horus: Eastern Desert Survey Report*. He has published many books on ancient Egypt and Palestine such as *Test of Time*. Rohl was involved in the making of several TV documentaries such as "Pharaohs and Kings: A Biblical Quest" and "Patterns of Evidence: Exodus" [9]. Although an agnostic, Rohl has not been blinded by humanistic theology and very early in his career began to see the parallel patterns in historical evidence and biblical chronology. Looking into the Egyptological dating methods that were set upon over 200 years ago, he has found what appears to be multiple errors in the identification of key figures and events that were associated with known periods upon which much of the sequential periods were compiled. The adjustments that Rohl makes to the Egyptological timeline affects the time of the Exodus, moving it from the 1250 BC period to the 1450 BC period. Additionally, he concluded that Israel's time in Egypt was only 215 years based on earlier versions of the Torah and references from Josephus, and not the 430 years it was thought to have been. These changes effectively adjusted much of the Egyptological timeline, so that now the patterns of evidence in many of the different eras that had been deemed unrelated to the biblical chronologies due to the time periods now align perfectly with the biblical accounts including the time of the children of Israel in Egypt, the Exodus, the Israelite campaigns in Palestine, and many others. The archeologists of these sites could plainly see patterns related to the biblical accounts and in all cases congruent with the misalignment (200 years in most all cases), yet they chose to disregard the evidence in favor of a flawed dating method to satisfy the humanistic culture that dominates the sciences [10,11,12]. With these archeologists exposed, we now have a clear example of how much of the scientific community operates. They will ignore or deny evidence that fits the biblical model and defend their stance based on flawed dating methods or extraneous theoretical jargon that lacks supporting empirical evidence.

References

Biblical References from: The Holy Bible (1913). King James Version. Chicago, Ill. John A. Dickson Publishing Co.

1   Ostling, R. N. (2011). In search of historical Adam. *Christianity Today*. Retrieved from http://www.christianitytoday.com/ct/2011/june/historicaladam.html
2   Tomkins, J.P. Ph.D. ICR. Human dna variation linked to biblical event timeline. Retrieved from http://www.icr.org/article/human-dna-variation-linked-biblical
3   Chadwick, A.V. (1999). RE: Cambrian explosion in Berkeley. Retrieved from http://www2.asa3.org/archive/evolution/199902/0212.html
4   Wikipedia. Stephen Meyers. Retrieved from https://en.wikipedia.org/wiki/Stephen_C._Meyer
5   Meyers, S.C. (2013). *Darwin's doubt*. New York, NY: HarperCollins Publishers.
6   Wikipedia. David Berlinski. Retrieved from https://en.wikipedia.org/wiki/David_Berlinski
7   Dr. David Berlinski (2008): Youtube.com. Introduction (Part 1). Retrieved from https://www.youtube.com/watch?v=Ec8lpcA5hls
8   Dr. David Berlinski (2013): Youtube.com. Rebellious intellectual defies darwinism. Retrieved from https://www.youtube.com/watch?v=S89IskZI740
9   Wikipedia. David Rohl. Retrieved from https://en.wikipedia.org/wiki/David_Rohl
10 David Rohl (2015). Egyptology Chronologist. Retrieved from https://www.youtube.com/watch?v=GtmYTRg-2X4
11 David Rohl (2015). The mystery of the missing exodus: The David Rohl lectures - Part 1. Retrieved from https://www.youtube.com/watch?v=q2He5ZyIP8k
12 David Rohl (2015). Finding the Israelites in Goshen: The David Rohl lectures - Part 2. Retrieved from https://www.youtube.com/watch?v=xhHV2scE0-k

CREDITS AND PERMISSIONS

The inclusion of any figures, illustrations, photographs, diagrams, charts, or other types of images in this book should not be construed as an endorsement of the ideas and arguments contained in this book on the part of any copyright holder or creators of those images, other than the author of the book himself.

Cover Page Image. Allosaurus bone fossil, photo taken by the author in the Dinosaur National Monument in Jensen UT managed by the National Park Services.

Figure I.1 Ernst Haeckel's image that faked the resemblance in these embryonic stages. Retrieved from http://www.wikiwand.com/en/Ernst_Haeckel. Image was produced earlier than 1923 (1874) and therefore in the Public Domain.

Figure I.2 Hylonomus, Thinkstock Image 75489342

Figure I.3 Elginia, (Wikipedia). Nobu Tamura (http://spinops.blogspot.com) - Own work, made available under the Creative Commons Attribution-ShareAlike License; Retrieved from https://en.wikipedia.org/wiki/Elginia#/media/File:Elginia_BW.jpg Public Domain

Figure I.4 Ctenophores, (Wikipedia). Kevin Raskoff - Mertensia on oceanexplorer.noaa.gov, This image is in the public domain because it contains materials that originally came from the U.S. National Oceanic and Atmospheric Administration, taken or made as part of an employee's official duties. Retrieved from https://commons.wikimedia.org/wiki/File:LightRefractsOf_comb-rows_of_ctenophore_Mertensia_ovum.jpg and permitted under https://www.usa.gov/government-works. Public Domain

Figure I.5 Nautilus, Thinkstock Image 75489352

Figure I.6 Horseshoe Crab, Thinkstock Image 516849576

Figure I.7 Coelacanths (Wikipedia). Alberto Fernandez Fernandez - Own work, made available under the Creative Commons Attribution-ShareAlike License; Retrieved from https://en.wikipedia.org/wiki/Coelacanth#/media/File:Latimeria_Chalumnae_-_Coelacanth_-_NHMW.jpg . Public Domain

Figure I.8 Ginkgo Thinkstock Image 831167286

Figure I.9 Dawn Redwood. Authors Photo's

Figure 1.1 Picture of the Cosmic Gases and Galaxies. Thinkstock Image 524554638.

Figure 1.2 Sumerian god with wings. Thinkstock Image 616247562

Figure 1.3 Sandstone table with the Sumerian Kings list. Thinkstock Image 616247562

Figure 1.4 Cave drawing of dinosaurs in the hunting parting. Sketch by Author.

Figure 1.5 Petroglyph of an Apatosaurus found at the Natural Bridge Monument in SE Utah. Retrieved From GenPack website http://www.genesispark.com/exhibits/evidence/historical/ancient/dinosaur Copied by permission.

Figure 1.6 Carvings of a dinosaur in head to head combat with a mammoth in Bemifal Cave in S. France. . Retrieved From http://jackcuozzo.com/bernifal.html. IUniverse to reproduce graphic image

Figure 1.7a,b,c,d Baby dragon carvings. Retrieved From GenPack website http://www.genesispark.com/exhibits/evidence/historical/ancient/dinosaur Copied by permission.

Figure 1.8 Petroglyph of a Pterosaur. History's Evidence of Dinosaurs and Men. Reference From http://historysevidenceofdinosaursandmen.weebly.com/visual.html Thinkstock Image 821666222

Figure 1.9 Picture of the Skara Brae in Scotland. Thinkstock Image 491813884.

Figure 1.10 Picture of the Skara Brae in Scotland. Thinkstock Image 491813732.

Figure 1.11 Stonehinge in England. Thinkstock image 100170070.

Figure 1.12 The Grand Canyon. Thinkstock Image 485927656.

Figure 1.13 The Mini Grand Canyon. NJ Bible Science. Reference From

http://www.icr.org/research/index/researchp_sa_r04/ IUniverse to reproduce graphic image.

Figure 1.14 Rock Strata in the Grand Canyon Thinkstock Image 532006091.

Figure 1.15 Evolution era's next to Grand Canyon Strata and Elevations (National Park Service [NPS]). Retrieved From https://www.nature.nps.gov/geology/parks/grca/age/ Work of the United States Department of the Interior, taken or made as part of that person's official duties. As a work of the U.S. federal government, the image is in the public domain. Reference https://www.nps.gov/aboutus/disclaimer.htm

Figure 2.1 Model of the DNA molecule Author's rendition and Wikipedia. Madeleine Price Ball - Own work, made available under the Creative Commons Attribution-ShareAlike License; With written Permission. Retrieved From https://en.wikipedia.org/wiki/DNA#/media/File:DNA_chemical_structure.svg Public Domain

Figure 2.2 The Kish Tablet. Scanned from Sacred Books of the East *Babylonia & Assyria* editorship by Prof. Charles F. Horne (copyright 1907 has expired). Retrieved From http://www.billheidrick.com/Orpd/Sacr1917/Sacred_Books_1.pdf Public Domain

Figure 2.3 The Narmer Palette. This is a photographic copy from the Manual of Egyptian archæology and guide to the study of antiquities in Egypt. Year: 1914. Authors: Maspero, G. (Gaston), 1846-1916 Johns, Agnes Sophia Griffith, 1859- public domain

Figure 2.4 Generations from Noah to Abram. Combined authors work with The Kish Tablet The Kish Tablet. Scanned from Sacred Books of the East *Babylonia & Assyria* editorship by Prof. Charles F. Horne (copyright 1907 has expired). Retrieved From http://www.billheidrick.com/Orpd/Sacr1917/Sacred_Books_1.pdf. Public Domain

Figure 3.1 The Oort Cloud (NASA). Retrieved from https://herschel.jpl.nasa.gov/solarSystem.shtml Work of the United States Department of the Interior, taken or made as part of that person's official duties. As a work of the U.S. federal government, the image is in the public domain. Reference https://www.jsc.nasa.gov/policies.html#Guidelines

Figure 3.2 Full-Sky Image of the Oldest Light (NASA). Retrieved from https://www.nasa.gov/pdf/55393main_10%20SEU.pdf Work of the United States Department of the Interior, taken or made as part of that person's official duties. As a work of the U.S. federal government, the image is in the public domain. Reference https://www.jsc.nasa.gov/policies.html#Guidelines

Figure 3.2 Illustration by the author us Thinkstock images 511478884, 518275339, & 526599449

Figure 4.1 Table of Nations Map . Reference From http://www.bible-history.com/maps/2-table-of-nations.html . IUniverse to reproduce graphic image

Figure 4.2 Picture of an Allosaurus taken by the author in the Dinosaur National Monument in Jensen, Utah.

Figure 4.3 Flying Pterosaurs Thinkstock Image 683674452

Figure 4.4 Chinese dragons Thinkstock Image 672988478

Figure 4.5 Stegosaurus carving at Ta Prohm, Cambodia Thinkstock Image 523378336

Figure 4.6 Mayan man that appears to be carrying a pterodactyloid pterosaur on his shoulders. Sketch by the Author Reference Genesis Park website http://www.genesispark.com/exhibits/evidence/historical/ancient/pterosaur/ .

Figure 4.7 Indian vs Dinosaur. From Genesis Park website. Copied by permission.

http://www.genesispark.com/exhibits/evidence/historical/ancient/dinosaur

Figure 4.8 Petroglyph of an *Apatosaurus* found at the Natural Bridge Monument in SE Utah Retrieved From http://www.genesispark.com/exhibits/evidence/historical/ancient/dinosaur Copied by permission.

Figure 5.1 **Beowulf battles Grendel** IUniverse rendered graphic.

Figure 5.2 Flying Pterosaurs Thinkstock Image 683674452

Figure 6.1 Map of Ancient Mesopotamia. Thinkstock Image 529272887

Figure 6.2 Patriarch lineage from Adam to Shem. Work of the author.

Figure 6.3 Madaba Map P-1090131 Thinkstock Image 509586889

Figure 6.4 Joseph's Statue. Used by permission from Patterns of Evidence. Reference http://press.patternsofevidence.com/the-film/resources/

Figure 6.5 Ruins of Jericho. Thinkstock Image 475543690

Figure 6.6 Israel's Early Years. Authors work

Figure 6.7 Judges of Israel's Early Years. Authors work.

Figure 6.8 Patriarch lineage from Abraham to David. Authors work.

Figure 6.9 Patriarch lineage from Abraham to Moses. Authors work.

Figure 6.10 Patriarch lineage from Shem to Abraham. Authors work.

Figure 6.11 Patriarch lineage from Noah to Abraham. Authors work

Figure 6.12 Patriarch lineage from Adam to the Flood. Authors work

Figure 6.13 Patriarch lineage from Adam to Shem. Authors work

Figure 6.14 The divided Kingdom. Authors work

Figure 6.15 Kings of Judah. Authors work

Figure 6.16 Kings of Israel. Authors work

Figure 6.17 Kings and prophets of Israel and Juda. Authors work

Figure 6.18 Israeli King Jehu keeling down while offering tribute to the Assyrian king. Steven G. Johnson own work; Retrieved From https://en.wikipedia.org/wiki/British_Israelism#/media/File:Jehu-Obelisk-cropped.jpg. Written Permission. Public Domain

Figure 6.19 Fall of Israel. Authors work.

Figure 6.20 Fall of Juda. Authors work.

Figure 6.21 Restoration of the temple. Authors work.

Figure 6.22 Second Temple Thinkstock Image 178527354

Figure 6.23 Lineage of Christ. Authors work

ABOUT THE AUTHOR

Jeff Walling, the sole author of this book, was born in Chicago, IL in May of 1958. He grew up predominantly in Manassas, VA. He went through his teens in the 70s, the time of the hippies, of which his mom and dad were a part of. There was a period when the home of his upbringing (along with teepees about the place) served as a sort of hippy commune with about 10 to 15 residents coming and going at the time. Jeff also spent much time growing up in Clay County, WV with his grandmother, aunts, and uncles from his mother's side of the family. Jeff joined the Navy out of Beckley, WV in 1978 where he attended Boiler Technician "A" School for propulsion engineering in Chicago, IL and served on the guided missile cruiser "Harry E. Yarnell, CG 17" for four years based out of Norfolk, VA. It was during his time in the Navy he had gotten "saved" and started attending church regularly. Jeff remained in Virginia Beach, VA after he was honorably discharged from the Navy, married, had two children, and attended the Rock Church for the next eight years. During this time, he attended Bible College (the Rock Bible Institute) and earned his certification in Ministerial Training. Over the next thirty years, Jeff attended colleges off and on (TCC, Rice Aviation, Penn Foster College, Kaplan University). Jeff has developed a passion for reading over the past 20 years and is an avid student of biblical studies, science, technology, physics, and history. Today Jeff holds several state and industrial certifications from API, STI, NDE organizations and owns and operates a small engineering business in Chesapeake, VA. Jeff is the author of API Toolbox, a cloud–based engineering software that's on the market for evaluating the mechanical integrity of industrial assets such as pressure vessels, storage tanks, and piping. Jeff is the Inventor of many items such as the Quantum Sleeper, a thermal powered generator, and other miscellaneous tools (resilient mount mics, tot-a-ray retrieval components, boiler tube puller, pneumatic fiberfax gun, UT ROV, lemon squeezers, etc.). Jeff earned a degree in Mechanical Engineering Technology from Penn Foster College 2012 and is presently attending Kaplan University working on his BA in Professional Studies.

Jeff's Testimony

I was in the Navy at the time. We were stationed in Charleston, SC where the ship was in a yearlong overhaul. We originally had orders to go Guantanamo Bay, Cuba for sea trials and then to the Mediterranean (the Med) when the Iranian hostage crisis broke out. I remember the day they announced that our orders had changed, that we were no longer going to the Med but would instead be heading to the Indian Ocean to be on station for the Iranian hostage crisis. I remember thinking how easily the ships in the Falkland Island scrimmage went down with just one torpedo, and that it now looked like we could run into the same circumstances. I remember thinking "I did not join the Navy to fight, I joined for the adventure". I guess it was the spirit of God pressing on me, because

I began to have such anxiety about the prospect of dying in the middle of the ocean that I could not contain it. I thought "I'm 19 years old and could die…what for, what was this life all about?" I was on a midnight cold iron watch one time down in the aft boiler room when the watch from the forward hole came to pass the time. I was so buggered that he said he could not take it and left back to his station. I was so filled with anxiety that I wanted to just run, but could not, because I was bound to my duty station. I finally picked up an iron wrench and started beating on the deck plates as hard as I could. This did nothing for my anxiety, so I threw the tool across the boiler room. I sat down on the edge my chair and cried out, "Somebody help me!" When I did not receive an answer, I then cried out, "God help me!" At that moment, I felt what I can only describe as an invisible cloud (the presence of God) starting to descend upon on me. I could feel what I can only describe as a thermocline between any points at which this "cloud" was descending, the bottom part filled with extreme anxiety and the top with the most incredible peace I had ever known. As it descended and finally engulfed me completely, I sat back in the chair in total peace. I heard Jesus audibly say to me, over my right shoulder, in a whisper "Be at peace, everything is going to be all right". I intuitively knew it was Jesus. I can't explain how, I just knew. That was an experience that was forever impressed into my heart and mind. From this time the ship left Charleston, SC to Norfolk where a real revival started on the ship. About ten percent of the ship's company was converted in a matter of about six months (40ish souls), of which I was one. I was witnessed to by a fellow snipe (boiler tech) that I looked up to. He too had just recently got saved and eventually invited me to Rock Church in Virginia Beach, VA. I remember the feeling I had when I walked in the building– a refreshing, happy feeling. We sat in the upper balcony that April 1979. As I sat there, I prayed to God saying, "God if this right, if this is where I should be and what I should do, please let me know somehow." At that time, everyone got up to sing, so I stood up. As the singing went along, I just closed my eyes and listened. By and by, that same cloud of peace, the presence of God, came upon me. I seemed to naturally lift my hands up over my head and remained entranced, standing there listening and enjoying the singing and God's presence, when someone tapped me on the shoulder. I opened my eyes and nobody was standing, much less singing, but I heard the signing all the way up to the moment I opened my eyes. He then said, "Do you want to come with me", to which I replied, "YES". He led me to the altar, led me in the sinner's prayer, and then told me to stay after the service to get baptized. When I got baptized, that same incredible peace came upon me when I came up out of the water. I felt like I was going to keep rising up through the ceiling, I felt so light. Since that time, I have had many similar incredible encounters with Christ as I have ventured to do his will. Between specific prayers being answered to seeing incredible events take place in his name, I no longer believe in God by faith. I know, as a Matter of Fact, that he exists, and he is the God of the Bible, and that every knee shall bow and every tongue confess that Jesus Christ is Lord!

Printed in the United States
By Bookmasters